International Civil Aviation Organization (ICAO)

International Civil Aviation Organization (ICAO)

Fifth Edition

Ludwig Weber

This book was originally published as a monograph in the International Encyclopaedia of Laws/Intergovernmental Organizations.

Founding Editor: Roger Blanpain
General Editor: Frank Hendrickx
Volume Editor: Jan Wouters

Wolters Kluwer

Published by:
Kluwer Law International B.V.
PO Box 316
2400 AH Alphen aan den Rijn
The Netherlands
E-mail: lrs-sales@wolterskluwer.com
Website: www.wolterskluwer.com/en/solutions/kluwerlawinternational

Sold and distributed by:
Wolters Kluwer Legal & Regulatory U.S.
920 Links Avenue
Landisville, PA 17538
United States of America
E-mail: customer.service@wolterskluwer.com

ISBN 978-94-035-1527-4

e-Book: ISBN 978-94-035-1537-3
web-PDF: ISBN 978-94-035-1547-2

This title is available on www.kluwerlawonline.com

The Author

Ludwig Weber studied Law at the Universities of Tübingen, Lausanne and Heidelberg. He obtained an LL.M. degree in Air and Space Law from McGill University, Montreal, and a Doctor of Laws degree in Air Law and European Law from the University of Heidelberg in 1980. He also obtained German bar qualifications.

From 1982 to 1995 he was Legal Counsel of the International Air Transport Association (IATA), Geneva and Montreal. He was responsible for air carrier liability issues, IATA BSP and Clearing House matters as well as competition law, and represented IATA at numerous international meetings.

From 1995 to 2004 he was Director of the Legal Bureau of International Civil Aviation Organization (ICAO) responsible *inter alia* for the Warsaw Convention modernization process on air carrier liability leading to the adoption of the 1999 Montreal Convention. He also had responsibility for the Cape Town process resulting in the adoption of the 2001 Cape Town Convention and Protocol on asset-based financing of aircraft equipment.

From 2004 to 2011 he was a Consultant to ICAO responsible for the setting up of the new International Registry under the Cape Town instruments and for other multilateral and bilateral civil aviation projects. From 2011 he served as Senior Adviser in various capacities and continues to serve as a Senior Certified Instructor to ICAO.

Since 1991 he has been an Adjunct Professor at the Faculty of Law, McGill University, Montreal, teaching Aviation Law at the Institute of Air and Space Law and at other universities for many years. He has also given numerous guest lectures and presentations at universities, international institutions and conferences and has published widely, particularly in the field of aviation law and the law of international organizations.

The Author

Table of Contents

Table of Contents

List of Abbreviations

ACAC	Arab Civil Aviation Commission
ADREP	Accident/Incident Data Reporting System
AFCAC	African Civil Aviation Commission
AFDI	*Annuaire Français de Droit International*
AFS	Aeronautical Fixed Services
AIP	Aeronautical Information Publication
AIS	Aeronautical Information Services
AMS	Aeronautical Mobile Services
AN	Air Navigation
ANC	Air Navigation Commission
AnnASL	Annals of Air and Space Law (McGill, Montreal)
AOSC	Administrative and Operational Services Cost
AT	Air Transport
ATC	Air Traffic Control
ATM	Air Traffic Management
CAEP	Committee on Aviation Environmental Protection
CAPS	Civil Aviation Purchase
C-DEC	ICAO Council Decision
CFIT	Controlled flight into terrain
C-MIN	ICAO Council Minutes
CNS	Communications, Navigation, Surveillance
C-WP	ICAO Council Working Paper
DCW	Diplomatic Conference on the Modernization of the Warsaw System
DGCA	Directorate General of Civil Aviation
EC	European Community
ECAC	European Civil Aviation Conference
EGR	Equitable Geographical Representation
ETOPS	Extended Range Operations
EU	European Union

List of Abbreviations

FIR	Flight Information Region
FRY	Federal Republic of Yugoslavia (Serbia and Montenegro)
GASP	Global Aviation Safety Plan
GNSS	Global Navigation Satellite System
IAEA	International Atomic Energy Agency
IATA	International Air Transport Association
ICAO	International Civil Aviation Organization
ICJ	International Court of Justice
IFR	Instrument Flight Rules
ILM	International Legal Materials
IMO	International Maritime Organization
IMSO	International Mobile Satellite Organization
IPCC	Intergovernmental Panel on Climate Change
ITU	International Telecommunication Union
KAL	Korean Air Lines
LACAC	Latin American Aviation Commission
LC	ICAO Legal Committee
MET	Meteorology
MOU	Memorandum of Understanding
MRTD	Machine Readable Travel Document
NOTAM	Notice for Airmen
PANS	Procedures for Air Navigation Services
PANS-ATM	Procedures for Air Navigation Services – ATM
PICAO	Provisional International Civil Aviation Organization
PIO	Public Information Office
PKI	Public Key Infrastructure
RCC	Rescue Coordination Centre
REIO	Regional Economic Integration Organization
SAR	Search and Rescue
SARPs	Standards and Recommended Practices
STP	Standard Training Package
TCB	Technical Cooperation Bureau
US	United States of America
UN	United Nations
UNDP	United Nations Development Programme
UNFCCC	United Nations Framework Convention on Climate Change
UNTS	United Nations Treaty Series
UPU	Universal Postal Union
USAP	Universal Security Oversight Audit Programme

USOAP	Universal Safety Oversight Audit Programme
VFR	Visual Flight Rules
WAFSOPSG	World Area Forecast System Operations Study Group
WCO	World Customs Organization
WHO	World Health Organization
WMO	World Meteorological Organization
WTO	World Tourism Organization
ZLW	*Zeitschrift für Luft – und Weltraumrecht*

List of Abbreviations

Chapter 1. Historical and Constitutional Background

§1. CHICAGO CONFERENCE, 1944

1. The International Civil Aviation Organization (ICAO) came into being on 4 April 1947 upon entry into force of the Convention on International Civil Aviation.[1] Part II of the Convention sets forth the constitutive provisions regarding ICAO, including its objectives, organs and institutional structure and status as an international intergovernmental organization.

2. The Convention on International Civil Aviation was adopted and signed on 7 December 1944, the final day of the **International Civil Aviation Conference** which was held from 1 November to 7 December 1944 in Chicago, Illinois.[2] The Conference, which was attended by fifty-two States, was called by the United States Government with the objective of establishing a legal framework for the development of international civil aviation after the Second World War.[3] This action was taken even prior to the Conference of San Francisco in the spring of 1945, which adopted the United Nations (UN) Charter.[4]

3. During the Chicago Conference, four main proposals were submitted. Australia and New Zealand advocated the internationalization of all civil aviation (save on domestic routes), including the setting up of a single international global airline and an international air authority to regulate and supervise it.[5] The United Kingdom proposal provided for the establishment of an 'International Air Authority' with extensive regulatory powers in economic as well as technical matters.[6] The proposal of

1. ICAO Doc. 7300. The current edition of the Convention as of March 2021 is Doc. 7300/9.
2. *Proceedings of the International Civil Aviation Conference, Chicago, Illinois, 1 Nov.–7 Dec. 1944* (Washington, US Department of State Printing Office, 1948), 2 Vols.
3. *See*: Invitation of the United States of America to the Conference, in: *Proceedings*, *supra* n. 2, at p. 11.
4. *Guide to the Charter of the United Nations* (New York, United Nations Publication Office, 1962).
5. Conference Doc. 49: International Ownership and Operation of Air Services on Prescribed International Trunk Routes, Resolution to be moved by Hon. D.G. Sullivan, Chairman, New Zealand Delegation, in: *Proceedings*, *supra* n. 2, at p. 549; *see also* Verbatim Minutes of Plenary Session, 8 Nov. 1994, in: *Proceedings*, *supra* n. 2, at pp. 539–543.
6. Conference Doc. 48: United Kingdom Proposal on International Air Transport, in *Proceedings*, *supra* n. 2, at p. 566.

the United States emphasized freedom of the air and a pro-competitive environment, where free enterprise airlines would operate in a competitive international market, with a free exchange of landing rights between States.[7] It envisaged the creation of an 'International Aviation Assembly', with functions in the field of setting technical standards. Finally, the Canadian proposal envisaged an 'International Air Authority' with powers in the field of economic regulation, where regional councils would issue certificates for, and would regulate international air services.[8]

4. As a result of its deliberations, the Conference adopted a compromise under which a new international body called ICAO would be set up with mainly technical standard-setting responsibilities and general overall supervisory functions.[9] Economic regulation was to be left to bilateral regulation between States, except regulation of fares, rates and tariffs, which was left to multilateral self-regulation by industry conferences subject to governmental approval. This compromise was embodied, first, in the **Convention on International Civil Aviation**, which was the main instrument adopted by the Conference and which also sets forth the constitution of ICAO; second, in the **International Air Services Transit Agreement**,[10] which provides for the mutual exchange of transit rights; third, the Five Freedoms Agreement',[11] which provides for the mutual exchange of traffic rights, but which has remained a dead letter; and fourth, the **Interim Agreement on International Civil Aviation,**[12] which provided for the setting up of the Provisional International Civil Aviation Organization (PICAO), pending the entry into force of the main Convention, which occurred on 4 April 1947.

§2. PICAO and Early Developments

5. The Interim Agreement on International Civil Aviation entered into force only six months after its adoption, on the day of the twenty-sixth acceptance, 6 June 1945.[13] Pursuant to its Articles I to VII, the **Provisional International Civil Aviation Organization (PICAO)** was established, with an interim Assembly, an interim

7. Conference Doc. 16: United States Proposal of a Convention on Air Navigation, in *Proceedings*, *supra* n. 2, at p. 554.
8. Conference Doc. 50: Canadian Revised Preliminary Draft of an International Air Convention in: *Proceedings*, *supra* n. 2, at Vol. I, pp. 570 et seq.
9. *See* L. Weber, *Chicago Convention,* in R. Bernhardt (ed.), *Encyclopedia of Public International Law* (Amsterdam/London/New York/Tokyo, North Holland/Elsevier), Vol. I, (1992) pp. 571 et seq., with further references.
10. 84 *UNTS* 389.
11. 171 *UNTS* 387. The UK refrained from adhering. The United States signed the Agreement, but withdrew on 25 Jul. 1947, after it became sufficiently clear that the Agreement would not receive the necessary international support. For the notice of withdrawal, *see* 22 Avi 728.
12. 171 *UNTS* 345.
13. Article XVII of the Interim Agreement provided for entry into force upon acceptance by twenty-six States, specifying that acceptance may be expressed by informing the United States Government as depositary 'whether signature on its behalf shall constitute an acceptance of the Agreement by that Government and an obligation binding upon it', *ibid.*, n. 12.

Council, a Secretary General and a headquarters in Montreal, Canada.[14] Three Committees were created, namely a Committee on Air Transport, a Committee on Air Navigation (AN) (which was later transformed to become the ICAO Air Navigation Commission (ANC)) and a Committee on International Convention on Civil Aviation.[15] Article VII provided that at the time of the coming into force of the Convention on International Civil Aviation, the records and property of PICAO shall be transferred to the permanent organization ICAO, and all PICAO functions shall cease. Hence, after twenty months of operation of PICAO, ICAO came into being on 4 April 1947 and succeeded PICAO.[16]

6. Parallel to these developments and in accordance with the compromise agreed upon at the Chicago Conference, the **International Air Transport Association (IATA)** was set up on 19 April 1945 during the International Air Transport Conference of international airlines held in Havana, Cuba.[17]

7. The main objective was to re-establish an industry body which would provide the machinery for setting fares and rates on international routes, subject to governmental approval. Another objective was to re-establish a global trade association body of international airlines.[18] Therefore, the new IATA was set up with a two-tier structure, comprising the IATA conference machinery for the setting of fares, rates and conditions, subject to government approval, and the IATA trade association machinery.[19] Both tiers become part of the 'new IATA', which was incorporated in

---

14. Pursuant to Art. III s. 3 of the Interim Agreement, Edward Warner (United States), member of the US Civil Aeronautics Board, was elected President of the PICAO Interim Council. Pursuant to Art. III s. 5 para. 4, of the Interim Agreement, Albert Roper (France), who had been Secretary General of the International Commission for Air Navigation (ICAN) since 1922, was appointed Secretary General of PICAO on 17 Aug. 1945.
15. *See* Art. III, ss 5 and 6 of the Interim Agreement, *ibid.*, n. 12.
16. *See* B. Cheng, *The Law of International Air Transport* 64 (Stevens 1962); J.C. Cooper, *Air Transport and World Organization*, 55 Yale L. J. 1191 et seq., 1205 (1946); M. Le Goff, *The Present State of Air Law* 8 (Nijhoff 1956). In accordance with Art. 91(b) of the *Convention on International Civil Aviation,* the Convention came into force thirty days after deposit of the twenty-sixth instrument of ratification.
17. R.Y. Chuang, *The International Air Transport Association* 26 et seq. (Sijthoff 1972).; K. Hailbronner, *International Air Transport Association*, in *Encyclopedia* (R. Bernhardt ed.); *supra* n. 9, at Vol. II 1995, pp. 1047 et seq. *see also* A.D. Groenewege, *Compendium of International Civil Aviation* 224 et seq. (3d ed., IADC 2003); L. Weber, 'Internationaler Luftverkehrsverband' (International Air Transport Association/IATA), in: U. Andersen & W. Woyke (eds), *Handwörterbuch Internationale Organisationen*, 2nd ed. (Opladen, Leske und Budrich, 1995), pp. 219 et seq.
18. The 'International Air Traffic Association' (also called 'old IATA') had operated from 1919 to 1945, with headquarters at The Hague, the Netherlands. It had pioneered trade association work for the emerging international airlines which were members, namely twenty-nine airlines from twenty-four countries in 1939, in particular in such matters as interlining, standardization of tickets and forms, traffic matters and revenue accounting. *See* in particular Groenewege, *supra* n. 17, at pp. 220 et seq.
19. On the IATA structure, *see*: IATA Act of Incorporation; IATA Articles of Association, as amended by the 76th Annual General Meeting held virtually in Amsterdam on 24 Nov. 2020, https://www.iata.org/en/about/corporate-structure/.

late 1945 as a non-profit association under Canadian law by the Special Act of Parliament of Canada,[20] with headquarters in Montreal.

8. In a further application of the compromise reached at the Chicago Conference, the United Kingdom (UK) and the United States (US) met at Bermuda in the spring of 1946 to negotiate the first post-war bilateral Air Services Agreement.[21] The purpose of this agreement, which came to be known as the **'Bermuda Agreement'**, was to settle the terms of traffic rights for transatlantic scheduled air services between the two countries, including routes, frequency, capacity, and the setting of fares and rates, thus regulating the economic terms of these services on an essentially bilateral basis.[22] The only multilateral element was contained in the tariff clause, which provided that the setting of fares and rates would be entrusted to the airlines operating under the Agreement, thus referring to the conference machinery of IATA. The Bermuda Agreement became a model for a large number of bilateral air services agreements which were subsequently concluded by many countries during the post-war period.[23]

9. Thus, the setting up of PICAO/ICAO, the setting up of IATA and the conclusion of the Bermuda Agreement of 1946 constituted the three main, interrelated elements for the **implementation of the compromise** which had been negotiated at the Chicago Conference.[24]

§3. Objectives of the Organization

10. The objectives of the Organization are set out in **Article 44 of the Convention on International Civil Aviation,** which provides as follows:

> *Objectives*
>
> *The aims and objectives of the Organization are to develop the principles and techniques of international air navigation and to foster the planning and development of international air transport so as to:*

---

20. An Act to Incorporate International Air Transport Association, Statutes of Canada, 1945, Ch. 51 (Assented to 18 Dec. 1945), as amended by Statutes of Canada, 1974-75-76, Chap. III (Assented to 27 Feb. 1975).
21. UK-US Agreement dated 11 Dec. 1946, *UKTS* No. 3 (1946); *See* J.C. Cooper, *Air Transport and World Organization*, in *Explorations in Aerospace Law* 357 et seq. (I.A. Vlasic ed., McGill University Press, 1968); G. Cribbett, *The Influence of Bilateral Agreements, Tariffs and Subsidies in International Air Transport*, 3 J. Aeronautical Sci. India 1 et seq. (1951); M. Gillilland, *Bilateral Agreements*, in: *The Freedom of the Air* 159 et seq. (McWhinney and M.A. Bradley eds, 1968).
22. B. Cheng, *The Law of International Air Transport, supra* n. 16, at pp. 422 et seq.; B. Cheng, *Beyond Bermuda*, in *International Air Transport: Law, Organization and Policies for the Future* 81 et seq. (N.M.Matte ed., 1976); N.M. Matte, *Treatise on Air-Aeronautical Law* 144 et seq. (McGill/Carswell 1981).
23. P.P.C. Haanappel, *Bilateral Air Transport Agreements: 1913-1980*, 5 Intl. Trade L. J. 241 et seq., 245 (1979); *see also* A.F. Lowenfeld, *A New Takeoff for International Air Transport*, 54 For. Affairs 36 et seq. (1975).
24. *See supra* Ch. 1 §1, para. 4.

(a) *Insure the safe and orderly growth of international civil aviation throughout the world;*
(b) *Encourage the arts of aircraft design and operation for peaceful purposes;*
(c) *Encourage the development of airways, airports, and air navigation facilities for international civil aviation;*
(d) *Meet the needs of the peoples of the world for safe, regular, efficient and economical air transport;*
(e) *Prevent economic waste caused by unreasonable competition;*
(f) *Insure that the rights of contracting States are fully respected and that every contracting State has a fair opportunity to operate international airlines;*
(g) *Avoid discrimination between contracting States;*
(h) *Promote safety of flight in international air navigation;*
(i) *Promote generally the development of all aspects of international civil aeronautics.*

11. These aims and objectives are to be seen in the context of the preamble of the Convention, which in its essential parts reads as follows:

– *Whereas the future development of international civil aviation can greatly help to create and preserve friendship and understanding among the nations and peoples of the world, yet its abuse can become a threat to the general security; and*
– *Whereas it is desirable to avoid friction and to promote that cooperation between nations and peoples upon which the peace of the world depends;*
– *Therefore, the undersigned governments having agreed on certain principles and arrangements in order that international civil aviation may be developed in a safe and orderly manner and that international air transport services may be established on the basis of equality of opportunity and operated soundly and economically.*

12. The reference in the chapeau clause of Article 44 to the development of '**the principles and techniques of international air navigation**' and to the fostering of '**the planning and development of international air transport**' emphasizes the predominantly technical nature of the mandate of the Organization,[25] while planning and development functions in relation to air transport are also part of the broad overall mandate of ICAO. The term 'air navigation' relates principally to the technical and operational aspects of aircraft movement, whereas 'air transport' relates to the transportation by air of passengers, baggage, cargo and mail.

25. *See* K. Hailbronner, *International Civil Aviation Organization* in: R. Bernhardt (ed.), *Encyclopedia* (R. Bernhardt ed.), *supra* n. 9, at Vol. II (1995), pp. 1070 et seq.; W. Binaghi, *The Role of ICAO*, in *The Freedom of the Air*, *supra* n. 21, pp. 17 et seq.

13. The overall mandate of ICAO comprised, from a historical perspective, first and foremost the rebuilding of international civil aviation, since the Second World War had brought it largely to a standstill.[26] In so doing, the promotion of aviation safety and later the promotion of aviation security became a central element. While the term '**aviation safety**' relates to technical and operational safety of flight, the term '**aviation security**' relates to safeguarding civil aviation against acts of unlawful interference. The objective of safety is mentioned in paragraphs (a), (d) and (h) of Article 44 as well as in the preamble, third paragraph, and thus figures prominently among the specifically enumerated objectives. In the course of the more than seventy-five years of operation of the Organization, the objective of safety has clearly been recognized as the objective with the highest overall priority.[27] Safety of flight is the basis, the *conditio sine qua non*, for all aviation activities, be they commercial, non-commercial, general aviation or other flying activities.[28]

14. The promotion of safety has mainly been carried out through development and continuous updating of a comprehensive set of technical **standards and recommended practices (so-called SARPS)** set out in the Annexes to the Convention. In recent years, the standard-setting activities of the Organization have been supplemented by a comprehensive audit system to monitor implementation of the technical safety standards by ICAO Member States (Universal Safety Oversight Audit Programme (USOAP)),[29] as well as by an integrated Global Aviation Safety Plan (GASP).[30]

15. Due to the increasing number of hijackings, acts of sabotage and terrorist attacks on civil aircraft since the 1960s,[31] the objective of ensuring and promoting **aviation security** has similarly gained high priority. Although prevention of unlawful interference is not expressly mentioned in Article 44 of the Convention, since

---

26. A.D. Groenewege, *Compendium of International Civil Aviation* 18 et seq. (2d ed., IADC 1998/99).
27. *See* Assembly Resolution A40-13: The Universal Safety Oversight Audit Programme (USOAP) continuous monitoring approach, first Whereas clause; A32-11: *Establishment of an ICAO universal safety oversight audit programme,* first Whereas clause, ICAO Doc. 9790 (Assembly Resolutions in Force), I-53; *see also* Assembly Resolution A38-2: ICAO Global Planning for safety; and previous resolutions A37-4, A36-7, A32-15 and A33-16:*ICAO Global Aviation Safety Plan (GASP),* first Whereas clause.
28. Assembly Resolutions A40-2 and A40-3, first whereas clause; Resolution A33-16, *ibid.* (n. 27); *see also*: ICAO Global Aviation Safety Plan (GASP), 2020-2022 ed., Doc. 10004; D. Olson, 'Striving for Aviation Safety', in: ICAO (ed.), *100 Years of Civil Aviation* Montreal and London, ICAO and ICS Ltd., 2003), pp. 114 et seq.
29. ICAO Assembly Resolution A40-13: *The Universal Safety Oversight Audit Programme (USOAP) Continuous Monitoring Approach (CMA)*; and previous Resolutions A37-5; A36-4; A35-6; A32-11; A33-8; and A33-9; *see also* the *Report of the DGCA Conference on a Global Strategy for Safety Oversight*, ICAO Doc. 9707; *ICAO Oversight Audit Manual*, ICAO Doc. 9735; *ICAO Safety Oversight Manual*, Doc. 9734.
30. *See* Assembly Resolution A40-1: *ICAO global planning for safety and air navigation;* for more detail *see* below Ch. 3 §2 II: GASP and GANP.
31. B. Cheng, *Crimes on Board Aircraft*, 12 Current Leg. Probs. 177 et seq. (1959); E. McWhinney, *The Illegal Diversion of Aircraft and International Law* (1987); D.D. Joyner, *A Contemporary Concept of Piracy in International Law: The Status of Aerial Highjacking as an International Crime* (Dobbs Ferry/Leiden, Oceana/Sijthoff, 1974).

this phenomenon did not exist at the time of its adoption, Article 4 prohibits misuse of civil aviation, namely the 'use [of] civil aviation for any purpose inconsistent with the aims of this Convention'. Aviation safety and aviation security have in practice come to be regarded as two sides of the same coin.[32] Therefore, the objective of promoting and ensuring aviation security has been recognized as being of equal priority as that of promoting aviation safety. As a consequence, standard-setting activities in this area have been supplemented by a system to monitor implementation of the aviation security standards by ICAO Member States (Universal Security Audit Programme)[33] as well as a Civil Aviation Security Action Plan.[34]

16. Among the other numerous objectives of the Organization, the development and implementation of a satellite-based system to improve communications, air navigation, surveillance and air traffic management should be mentioned.[35] The use of satellite technology and advanced communications systems have been combined to support Communications, Navigation, Surveillance (CNS), and Air Traffic Management (ATM) for the needs of commercial and non-commercial aviation **CNS/ATM System**.[36] This system is in a stage of advanced implementation and is further discussed in Chapter 3, §2.V.D. below.

§4. Amendments to the Convention

17. At the time of the adoption of the Convention on 7 December 1944, the Second World War was still ongoing. While the Convention makes reference to the situation in several respects (preamble, Article 4 and Articles 92 and 93), the Convention was drafted and adopted with a view to rebuilding international civil aviation after the end of the war.[37]

18. The subsequent record of **amendments to the Convention** shows that, broadly speaking, its provisions were well-suited for the purpose for which they had been drafted.[38] Amendments were made over the years in nineteen instances to

32. G.D. Kyriakopoulos, *La sécurité de l'aviation civile en droit international public* (Athens/Brussels, A.N. Sakkoulas/Bruylant, 1999).
33. The ICAO Universal Security Audit Programme (USAP) was launched in November 2002 as part of the Aviation Security Action Plan. *See* the Report in ICAO Doc. 9826–Supplement, pp. 18 et seq.; for more detail *see* below Ch. 3 § 10: Universal Aviation Security Audit Programme (USAP).
34. The ICAO Aviation Security Action Plan was adopted by the Council of ICAO during its 166th Session (June. 2002), ICAO Doc. 9826 – Supplement. *See* Assembly Resolution A35-9, Appendix E; A37-17, Appendix A; A38-15, Appendix E; Resolution A39-18, Appendix E; Resolution A40-11, Appendix D; ICAO Doc. 10140.
35. *See infra*, Ch. 3 §2. V. D. For the Strategic Objectives of ICAO, *see* Appendix C. below; for the ICAO Business Plan, *see* Appendix D. below.
36. *Report of the World-wide CNS/ATM Systems Implementation Conference*, ICAO Doc. 9719; Global Air Navigation Plan for CNS/TM Systems, ICAO Doc. 9750.
37. *See Proceedings*, *supra* n. 2; Weber, *supra* n. 9.
38. L. Weber, *Convention on International Civil Aviation – 60 Years*, 53 ZLW 289–311, at 311 (2004) with further references.

bring institutional or procedural provisions up to date, in line with current requirements; only in two instances were amendments required in relation to substantive provisions of the Convention (Articles 3bis and 83bis).[39]

I. Institutional and Procedural Amendments

19. The first amendment, made on 27 May 1947, introduced a provision for the disbarment and expulsion of members of ICAO by the action of the General Assembly of the UN.[40] The new provision of Article 93bis thus adapted the Convention's membership provisions to those of the **Charter of the United Nations** which had not yet existed at the time of adoption of the Convention, but which had meanwhile come into force on 24 October 1945.[41]

20. In 1954, further amendments were made to provide for decision-making of the ICAO Assembly regarding the permanent seat of the Organization by a three-fifth vote (Article 5),[42] to permit triennial Assemblies instead of annual ones (Article 48 subparagraph (a)),[43] and to permit adoption of triennial budgets instead of annual ones (Article 49 subparagraph (e) and Article 61).[44]

21. From 1961, several amendments were made to **increase the membership in the ICAO Council,** first from twenty-one to twenty-seven members (Article 50(a));[45] then in 1971 to thirty members,[46] in 1974 to thirty-three members,[47] in 1990 to thirty-six members,[48] and in 2016 to forty members. These amendments were designed to align the representation of States in the Council with the increase in membership of ICAO from 26 States in April 1947 to 162 States in 1990 and to

39. ICAO Doc. 9318 and Doc. 9436. *See infra*, Ch. 1 §4.
40. *Protocol Relating to an Amendment to the Convention on International Civil Aviation (Article 93 bis)*, incorporated into ICAO Doc. 7300; it entered into force on 20 Mar. 1961.
41. *See* the membership provisions of Ch. II of the UN Charter. The Charter came into force upon ratification by all five permanent members of the UN Security Council and by the majority of the other Signatory States. *See* H. Kelsen, *The Law of the United Nations* (London, Stevens, 1950).
42. Assembly Resolution A8-4: *Amendment to Article 45 (Permanent Seat of the Organization); Protocol Relating to an Amendment to the Convention on International Civil Aviation (Article 45),* incorporated into ICAO Doc. 7300.
43. *See* Assembly Resolution A14-5: *Protocol Relating to an Amendment of Article 48 (a) of the Convention on International Civil Aviation.* This Amendment was adopted together with consequential amendments to Arts 49€ and 61, all of which entered into force on 12 Dec. 1956. *See also* Assembly Resolution A21-15.
44. Article 49(e) and Art. 61, in their amended form, were adopted by the 8th Session of the Assembly, along with amended Art. 48 (a), on 14 Jun. 1954; *see* Assembly Resolution A8-1.
45. Assembly Resolution A13-1: *Amendment to Article 50 (a) of the Convention Increasing the Membership of the Council to Twenty-seven.* This amendment entered into force on 17 Jul. 1962.
46. *Protocol relating to an Amendment to the Convention on International Civil Aviation (Article 50 (a)),* signed on 12 Mar. 1971, ICAO Doc. 8970.
47. *Protocol relating to an Amendment to the Convention on International Civil Aviation (Article 50 (a))*, signed on 16 Oct. 1974, ICAO Doc. 9123.
48. *Protocol relating to an Amendment to the Convention on International Civil Aviation (Article 50 (a)),* signed on 26 Oct. 1990, ICAO Doc. 9561. *Protocol relating to an Amendment to the Convention on International Civil Aviation (Article 50 (a))*, signed on 6 Oct. 2016, ICAO Doc. 10077.

191 States in 2016 (193 States in 2021) and came respectively into force in 1962, 1973, 1980 and 2002. The most recent amendment of 2016, an increase to forty members, has not yet entered into force as it will require 128 ratifications. As for the expected time required for entry into force, *see* paragraph 26 below.

22. Similar amendments were made in 1971, 1989, and 2016 to **increase the number of members of the ICAO Air Navigation Commission** (Article 56).[49] The 1971 amendment provided for an increase from twelve to fifteen members, the 1989 amendment to nineteen members, and the 2016 amendment to twenty-one members. The 1971 amendment entered into force in 1974 and the 1989 amendment in April 2005 upon reaching 108 ratifications.[50] The 2016 amendment will enter into force upon ratification by 128 States.

23. A further amendment made in 1962 to Article 48 (a) increased the minimum number of members required to request an extraordinary meeting of the Assembly from ten members to one-fifth of the total membership.[51] This amendment was also an adjustment to the growing number of members.

24. The final clause of the Convention, which mentions that the authentic text of the Convention shall exist in the English, French and Spanish languages, was amended in 1977, 1995 and 1998.[52] The purpose of these amendments was to provide **additional authentic texts** of the Convention in the Russian, Arabic and Chinese languages. The texts in these languages were adopted separately by respective Protocols. The 1977 amendment entered into force in 1999; the 1995 and 1998 amendments are not yet in force.

II. Substantive Amendments

25. The first substantive amendment to the Convention was made in 1980 in order to insert a new provision on the **lease, charter and interchange of aircraft**

---

49. *Protocol relating to an Amendment to Article 56 of the Convention on International Civil Aviation,* signed at Vienna on 7 Jul. 1971, ICAO Doc. 8971; *Protocol relating to an Amendment to the Convention on International Civil Aviation (Article 56),* signed on 6 Oct. 1989, ICAO Doc. 9544. *Protocol relating to an Amendment to the Convention on International Civil Aviation (Article 56),* signed on 6 Oct. 2016, ICAO Doc. 10076.
50. The instrument, signed on 6 Oct. 1989, reached 108 ratifications on 18 Apr. 2005 and entered into force on that day, almost 16 years after its adoption.
51. *Protocol relating to an Amendment to the Convention on International Civil Aviation (Article 48 (a)),* signed on 15 Sep. 1962, incorporated into ICAO Doc. 7300.
52. *Protocol relating to an Amendment to the Convention on International Civil Aviation (Final Clause, Russian Text),* ICAO Doc. 9208; (Final Clause, Arabic Text), Doc. 9664; (Final Clause, Chinese Text), Doc. 9722.

(Article 83bis).[53] The purpose of the provision was to allow a transfer of responsibilities under Articles 12, 30, 31 and 32 (a) of the Convention from the State of the registry to the State of the operator with effect *erga omnes*.[54] The amendment entered into force in 1997.

26. The second substantive amendment was made in 1984, in the wake of the shoot-down of Korean Airlines flight KE 007 by Soviet fighter aircraft (Article 3bis).[55] It inserted a new provision, **prohibiting the use of weapons against civil aircraft in flight** except in cases of self-defence under Article 51 UN Charter.[56] This amendment, which was designed to end a long series of shoot-down incidents involving in most cases civil airliners inadvertently straying from their scheduled flight path,[57] entered into force in October 1998.

27. Under Article 94 subparagraph (a) of the Convention, amendments require a two-thirds vote of the ICAO Assembly and the **subsequent ratification of at least two-thirds of all ICAO Member States**. In view of the fact that total membership in ICAO stands presently (2023) at 193 States, new amendments now require the support of at least 129 States and as many ratifications. This will render future amendments more difficult to adopt, as based on experience it may take – fifteen to twenty years or more to obtain 129 ratifications.[58] When the European Proposal for the increase in Council membership from 36 to 40 States was submitted to the Council in 2015, the option to provide for early implementation by making use of Article 25 (Provisional Application) of the Vienna Convention on the Law of Treaties was considered. This option would have rendered the decision to increase the seats on the Council effective immediately from its adoption by the Assembly, so as

53. *Protocol Relating to an Amendment to the Convention on International Civil Aviation (Article 83 bis),* signed on 6 Oct. 1980, ICAO Doc. 9318.
54. B. Verhaegen, 'Air Law Instrument Facilitates Transfer of Safety Responsibilities between States', 52 *ICAO Journal*, No. 8, 1997, 15 et seq.; L. Weber & B. Verhaegen, 'Entrée en vigueur de l'Article 83*bis* de la Convention de Chicago: un plus pour la sécurité aérienne', XLIII *Annuaire français de droit international*, 1997, 551 et seq. *See also* ICAO Circular 295*: Guidelines on the Implementation of Article 83bis*, and Doc. 10059: Manual on the Implementation of Art. 83bis of the Convention on International Civil Aviation. 1st ed., 2017.
55. *Protocol Relating to an Amendment to the Convention on International Civil Aviation (Article 3 bis),* signed on 10 May 1984, ICAO Doc. 9436; on the shoot-down, *see* Report of ICAO Fact Finding Investigation, 23 *ILM* 1984, 864–923; B. Cheng, 'The Destruction of KAL Flight KE 007 and Art. 3*bis* of the Chicago Convention', in: J.W.E Storm van's Gravesande/A. van der Veen Vronk (eds), *Liber Amicorum Diederiks-Verschoor* (Deventer et al., Kluwer, 1985), pp. 47–74; J.H.H. Weiler, *Korean Air Lines Incident*, in *Encyclopaedia* (R. Bernhardt ed.) *supra* n. 9, at Vol. III (1997), pp. 93 et seq.
56. *See* the wording of Art. 3*bis*. On this subject B. Cheng, *ibid.*, n. 55 at pp. 47 et seq.; Kyriakopoulos, *supra* n. 32, at 334 et seq., 342 et seq.; M. Milde, Interception of Civil Aircraft vs. Misuse of Civil Aviation, 11 Annals Air & Space L. 105 et seq. (1986).
57. Kyriakopoulos, *supra* n. 32, at pp. 307 et seq.; K. Hailbronner, *Der Schutz der Luftgrenzen im Frieden* (Köln/Bonn, C. Heymanns Verlag, 1972); G. Guillaume, *Les grandes crises internationales et le droit* (Paris, Editions du Seuil, 1994), pp. 63 et seq.; K. G. Park, *La protection de la souveraineté arienne* (Paris, Pedone, 1991), pp. 403 et seq.
58. E.g. the Protocol on the Final Clause (Russian Text), of 1977 (Doc. 9208), which entered into force on 17 Aug. 1999, and the Protocol on the Authentic Quadrilingual Text of the Convention (Doc. 9217) of 1977, which entered into force on 16 Sep. 1999.

to avoid a long waiting time of more than ten years. However, the Council decided to forward the proposal to the Assembly without proposing early implementation, on the ground that provisional application was not in line with past practice of ICAO when dealing with constitutional amendments.

§5. Other Constitutional Issues

28. ICAO has the **status of a specialized agency of the United Nations** in the sense of Article 7 of the UN Charter, by virtue of the Agreement between the UN and ICAO of 1947 which came into force on 13 May 1947,[59] and by virtue of the Convention on the Privileges and Immunities of the Specialized Agencies of 21 November 1947.[60] It possesses a legal personality, both at the level of international law (Article II of the 1947 Convention) as well as at the level of national law (Article 47 of the Convention on International Civil Aviation). Under the latter provision, ICAO shall enjoy full juridical personality wherever compatible with the constitution and laws of the State concerned.

29. In accordance with the terms of the 1947 Convention, including its Annex III,[61] ICAO enjoys the diplomatic privileges and immunities spelt out therein. In addition, as regards the headquarters of the Organization in Montreal, Canada, ICAO enjoys the privileges and immunities set out in the **Headquarters Agreement between ICAO and Canada** signed on 4 and 9 October 1990,[62] and the Agreements supplementary thereto dated 28 May 1999 and 29 May 2013, respectively.[63] The privileges and immunities under the Headquarters Agreement are in line with those enjoyed by other UN specialized agencies and include in particular the immunity of the Organization's property and assets, the inviolability of its headquarters premises, and recognition of the Organization's juridical personality.

30. **ICAO's constitution** is set out in **Part II of the Convention on International Civil Aviation**. When the Convention was adopted in 1944, its drafters may have envisaged ICAO as a global, all-encompassing international intergovernmental agency for civil aviation, as can be concluded from Article 44 subparagraphs (d)

59. *Agreement between the United Nations and the International Civil Aviation Organization*, dated 13 May 1947, ICAO Doc. 7970; *UNTS* Vol. 8 (1947), pp. 324 et seq.
60. 33 *UNTS* 242-261 (1948). *See* C.W. Jenks, International Immunities (London, Stevens and Sons, 1961); D.B. Michaels, International Privileges and Immunities, A case for a Universal Statute (The Hague, Nijhoff, 1971). The final text of the Annexes to the 1947 Convention, which includes 'Annex III: International Civil Aviation Organization' was approved on 29 Dec. 1951.
61. Annex III was approved by the ICAO Assembly in Assembly Resolution A2-26 and transmitted to the UN Secretary General on 11 Aug. 1948. For the text of Annex III, *see ibid.* (n. 60).
62. ICAO Doc. 9541.
63. *Supplementary Agreement between the International Civil Aviation Organization and the Government of Canada Regarding the Headquarters of the International Civil Aviation Organization*, ICAO Doc. 9591 – Supplementary Agreement. A new Supplementary Agreement was signed between ICAO and Canada on 29 May 2013, in force since December 2016 until November 2036, *see* http://www.icao.int/Newsroom/Pages/ICAO-and-Canada-sign-new-supplementary-agreement.aspx.

and (i) and Article 55 subparagraph (a). Under the latter provision, ICAO may set up subordinate air transport commissions on a regional basis, in order to respond to regional needs.[64]

31. However, Article 55 subparagraph (a) has never been used. Instead, several **regional intergovernmental bodies for civil aviation** have been set up outside of Article 55(a), namely the European Civil Aviation Conference (ECAC), the African Civil Aviation Commission (AFCAC), the Latin American Civil Aviation Commission (LACAC) and the Arab Civil Aviation Commission (ACAC).[65] Three of these, namely ECAC, AFCAC and LACAC, are neither part of ICAO nor completely independent from it but enjoy an intermediate status.[66] They operate their headquarters from the premises of the respective Regional Office of ICAO, coordinate their work as appropriate with ICAO[67] and have important political coordination functions in preparation for ICAO elections, in particular the triennial elections of the Council at the ICAO Assembly. Since 2000, AFCAC and ECAC have set up their own legal bodies for greater autonomy in administrative and financial matters. ACAC operates its headquarters from Rabat and does not have a formal institutional link to ICAO, but de facto cooperates with ICAO as required.[68]

32. The setting up of such bodies with 'intermediate' status has to some extent been controversial, in view of Article 55(a) of the Convention.[69] However, these bodies should be seen as in line with the Convention as long as their activities do not overlap, duplicate or impede the work carried out by ICAO. In fact, Article 83, the first sentence of the Convention provides that subject to Article 82, any contracting State may make arrangements not inconsistent with the provisions of the Convention.[70]

---

64. *See* on Art. 55(a): *Repertory-Guide to the Convention on International Civil Aviation*, 2nd ed., 1977, ICAO Doc. 8900/2, Art. 55.
65. *See* for more details *infra*, Ch. 6. §2. and Assembly Resolutions A10-5: *Relationship of ICAO with the European Civil Aviation Conference,* superseded by A27-17 and A18-21: *Air Transport Work in the Regions – General Policy*, also superseded by A27-17. For the latter Resolution, *see* ICAO Doc. 9790. *See also* Assembly Resolution A37-21 Cooperation with regional organizations and regional civil aviation bodies, in: Assembly Resolutions in Force (as of 4 Oct. 2013), ICAO Doc. 10022.
66. L. Weber, '*European Civil Aviation Conference*' in *Encyclopaedia* (R. Bernhardt ed.), *supra* n. 9, at Vol. II (1995), pp. 137 et seq., with further references; Assembly Resolution A27-17: *Relationship Between ICAO and Regional Civil Aviation Bodies*, ICAO Doc. 9790 and Assembly Resolution A37-21, *ibid.* (n. 65).
67. Assembly Resolution A27-17, Resolving clause 2.a), *ibid.* (n. 66).
68. ACAC participated in the recent ICAO Assemblies and invited, in turn, ICAO representatives to certain of its meetings; ACAC also receives certain documentation from ICAO relating to ACAC's activities.
69. L. Weber, 'Les éléments de la coopération dans le cadre de la Commission européenne de l'aviation civile (CEAC)', 31 *RFDA* 388 et seq., at 408–409 (1977), with further references.
70. Weber, *supra* n. 66, pp. 137 et seq., at 138.

Chapter 2. Institutional Framework

§1. Membership

33. As of March 2023, the membership of ICAO stands at 193 States. The list of Member States is set out in Appendix B below.

I. Acceding to Membership

A. Adherence

34. States that are members of the UN may accede to membership in ICAO by **adherence to the Convention on International Civil Aviation**, Article 92(a) of the Convention. Adherence shall be effected by a notification addressed to the Government of the United States, the depository of the Convention, which shall take effect thirty days thereafter. The depositary then notifies ICAO and all contracting States of the adherence. The same rules also apply, in line with Article 92(a), to States associated with States that are members of the UN, and States that remained neutral during the Second World War. The original fifty-two signatories to the Convention became members upon ratification in accordance with Article 91 of the Convention[71] (*see* section C *infra*).

B. Admission

35. States not falling within the categories of the preceding paragraph (the former 'enemy States' of the Second World War) may, subject to the approval of the UN, be admitted to membership by a four-fifth vote of the Assembly and on such conditions as the Assembly may prescribe, provided that in each case the assent of any State invaded or attacked by the State seeking admission shall be necessary (Article 93 of the Convention). In practical terms, this provision has now virtually lost its significance, as all the former enemy States are now members of the UN and of ICAO and ICAO membership covers virtually all States around the globe.[72]

C. Signature and Ratification

36. In theory, Article 91 and the Final Clause of the Convention could be interpreted to the effect that a State may also accede to membership of ICAO by signing and ratifying the Convention, since the Final Clause of the Convention kept the

71. *See* Art. 91(a) of the Convention. *See* on this matter T. Buergenthal, *Law-Making in the International Civil Aviation Organization* 14 et seq. (Syracuse U. Press 1969).
72. Since 2019, when ICAO membership reached 193 States, all members of the UN are also members of ICAO. Of the former 'enemy States', Italy was admitted to 'participation' in the Chicago Convention in 1947 (Resolution A1-5), Austria in 1948 (Resolution A2-3), Finland in 1948 (Resolution A2-4), Japan in 1953 (Resolution A7-2) and the Federal Republic of Germany in 1955 (Resolution A9-1).

Convention open for signature indefinitely, and under Article 91 ratification is open to any signatory State.[73] However, in State practice, **Article 91** has been generally **interpreted to apply to the original twenty-six signatory States only**. Therefore all States having joined ICAO subsequent to the entry into force of the Convention on 4 April 1947 have done so by formal adherence under Article 92.

II. Suspension and Termination of Membership

37. Suspension and termination of membership[74] are regulated in Articles 93bis to 95 of the Convention. A special suspension provision is also found in Chapter XVIII (disputes and default), namely in Article 88.

38. In accordance with Article 49 (k) of the Convention, it is for the **ICAO Assembly to decide on suspension or termination of membership** in ICAO.

39. Suspension of membership of a State is foreseen in the case of Article 93bis subparagraph (c), where a State has been suspended from membership in the UN and a request is made by the UN that the State be also suspended from membership in ICAO. In this case, the State shall be suspended from membership accordingly. However, this clause has never been used.

40. **Termination of membership** of a State may be the result of any of the following actions:[75]

(a) recommendation of the UN General Assembly that the State be debarred from membership in UN agencies (Article 93*bis* paragraph (1), automatic termination); or
(b) expulsion of the State from membership in the UN (Article 93*bis* paragraph (2), automatic termination); or
(c) failure of the State to ratify an amendment to the Convention which the Assembly has resolved requires ratification within a specified period (Article 94(b)); or
(d) denunciation of the Convention by a State by giving notice to the depositary, the Government of the United States, under Article 95 of the Convention, which shall take effect one year after notification.

41. **Suspension of membership** is different from termination of membership in that the State remains formally a member of the Organization and continues to have

73. *See* Buergenthal, *supra* n. 71, at pp. 14 et seq.
74. *See* on this subject L. B. Sohn, Expulsion or Forced Withdrawal from an International Organization, Harvard Law Review Vol. 77 (1963–1964), 1381–1425.
75. On this subject Buergenthal, *supra* n. 71, at pp. 35 et seq.

membership obligations, including the obligation to pay yearly contributions, but is suspended from the rights and privileges of membership.[76]

42. A case *sui generis* arose in 1992 when the Assembly decided in Assembly Resolution A29-2 that the Federal Republic of Yugoslavia (Serbia and Montenegro) (FRY) could not automatically continue the membership of the former Yugoslavia and that it should apply for membership *de novo*. The FRY later formally adhered to the Convention and thereby acquired membership in ICAO. However, when Montenegro became an independent State, both Montenegro and Serbia became members separately and the membership of the FRY ended.

43. Suspension of membership should also be distinguished from the suspension of voting rights.

44. **Suspension of voting rights** of a State has narrower effects than suspension of membership: it has the effect of suspending only the right of the State to vote in the Assembly and in the Council (if it is a member of this body). All other rights, privileges and obligations connected with membership remain unaffected.

45. Suspension of voting rights may be the result of the following situations:[77]

(a) **failure of a State to discharge its financial obligations** to the Organization for more than three consecutive years, and failure to conclude an agreement with the Council for the settlement of its indebtedness[78] (Assembly Resolution A31-26, first adopted in 1995 under Article 62 of the Convention, now superseded by A39-31); or
(b) **default** of a State under the provisions of Chapter XVIII (disputes and default) of the Convention and a finding of the Assembly to that effect (Article 88).

46. While cases of termination of membership have occurred only in exceptional circumstances,[79] cases of suspension of voting rights due to failure to discharge financial obligations have been numerous.[80]

47. Since 1995, when Resolution A31-26 was first adopted, a **list of Member States whose voting rights were suspended** has been published at every triennial Assembly. For example, in June 2004, the voting rights of twenty-eight Member

---

76. Under Assembly Resolution A39-31, Resolving Clause 10(a)-(e), certain additional measures shall be applied to Contracting States whose voting rights have been suspended. *See infra,* Ch. 4. §5.
77. *See* on this subject: Repertory-Guide to the Convention on International Civil Aviation, 2d ed. ICAO Doc. 8900/2, Art. 62, Introductory Comments. *See also* Assembly Resolution A35-26, and previously Assembly Resolution A31-26.
78. Previously Assembly Resolution A31-26. *See* on this subject *infra,* Ch. 4 §5.
79. *See* Assembly Resolution A29-2 on the termination of membership of the former Yugoslavia.
80. Since 1995, at every triennial Assembly a number of Member States had their voting rights suspended. *See* for example A39-WP/61 Rev.1 Addendum No. 2, and A40 WP/46 EX/15 AD/16.

States had been suspended in accordance with Assembly Resolution A31-26 clause 3[81] for non-payment of annual contributions of more than three years.

48. Since then, the situation has gradually improved. At the 41st Assembly in September/October 2022, only six Member States had their voting rights suspended.[82] Moreover, while the outstanding contributions totalled US Dollars (USD) 8.9 million in 2004,[83] the balance of Member States' contributions in arrears as of 20 September 2022 stood at CAD 10.2 million, of which CAD 8.5 million was for arrears in respect of 2020 and prior years, and CAD 1.7 million was related to arrears for 2021.[84]

III. Special Problems Relating to Membership

A. Membership Open to Sovereign States Only

49. Although the Convention does not contain a specific membership clause, Articles 91–93bis are predicated on the principle that **only sovereign States may adhere** to or be admitted, and thereby become members of the Organization.

50. Therefore, territorial units of sovereign States, even if they enjoy a large degree of autonomy, cannot become members of ICAO in their own right. This question came up as early as 1948 in the case of the application of Trieste, which could not be entertained, as Trieste was not a sovereign State.[85] The practice of the Organization in relation to the question of whether a candidate State is to be regarded as a sovereign State has relied largely on the practice of the UN.[86]

51. This also applies in relation to Taiwan, or as it is also referred to, Taipei-China.[87] As the People's Republic of China maintains the one-China theory under which this territory is part of one China, along with Hong Kong and Macao, the UN and hence ICAO do not recognize separate statehood for Taiwan. Consequently, Taiwan is not a member of the UN nor of ICAO.[88] While this situation is politically

81. *See* ICAO Doc. 9826 Supplement (July 2004).
82. *See*, A41-WP/30 Revision No. 1 Addendum No. 3 EX/18, AD/2.
83. *See* 9826 Supplement (July 2004); in comparison, *see* A41-WP/30 EX/18, AD/2 11/7/22 Revision No. 1 21/9/22.
84. *See,* A41-WP/30 EX/18, AD/2 11/7/22 Revision No. 1 21/9/22.
85. *See* the discussion in the Council regarding the application of Trieste, ICAO Council, 3rd Session (1948), Doc. 5302 (C/657).
86. This practice is based on Arts 92 a), 93 and 93*bis* of the Convention, which establish in each case a link between membership in ICAO and membership in the UN or decision-making in the UN, although they do not, strictly speaking, address the sovereign State issue. *See also* Art. II of the Agreement between the UN and ICAO dated 13 May 1947, ICAO Doc. 7970.
87. The name Taipei-China, as well as China(Taipei), has been used with the agreement of the Government of China (People's Republic of China) in certain international organizations, such as the World Trade Organization (WTO),where both entities have membership or associate membership status.
88. *See* on the Taiwan issue: R. Heuser, Taiwan in R. Bernhardt (ed.) *Encyclopedia supra* Ch. 1, n. 9, Vol. IV (2000), pp. 753 et seq. with further references.

predicated, it is not entirely satisfactory from an aviation safety and aviation security viewpoint, since the implementation of globally applicable aviation safety and security standards in Taiwan/Taipei-China cannot be ensured, cannot be audited and is at risk. It would therefore be preferable to find a way to associate Taiwan/Taipei-China in one way or another with relevant safety and security programmes in ICAO in the absence of formal membership status.

B. Organizations Not Eligible for Membership

52. Due to the principle that only sovereign States may become members of ICAO, **international organizations are excluded from membership.** The question came up as a result of the desire of the European Community (EC), now commonly referred to as the European Union (EU), to become a member of ICAO in 2003. As the EU Member States have transferred part of their sovereign functions and powers in civil aviation matters to the EU,[89] the question arose whether the EU may become a member alongside the EU Member States and participate in the work and decision-making of ICAO with respect to those subject matters for which the EU has authority. In view of Articles 91 to 93bis and the structure of the Convention, this is *de lege lata* not possible.[90] An amendment to the Convention to permit such membership of 'Regional Economic Integration Organizations' (REIOs)[91] would be theoretically possible under Article 94 of the Convention; however, as such an amendment could not enter into force unless ratified by two-thirds of all members (Article 94 paragraph (a)), i.e., now 129 out of 193 States, such amendment and ratification process would likely take fifteen to twenty years. As a result, it has been regarded as preferable on the part of the EU not to seek membership in ICAO, for the time being, but to participate in ICAO's work through a resident observer.[92]

C. Adherence to the Convention as Amended

53. As indicated in Chapter 1 above, nineteen amendments to the Convention have been adopted since 1944, some of which have not yet entered into force.[93] When a State wishing to become a member of ICAO deposits a notification of

89. L. Weber, Convention on International Civil Aviation – 60 years, ZLW Vol. 53 (2004), 289 et seq., at 308; W. Schwenk & E. Giemulla, *Handbuch des Luftverkehrsrechts*, 3d ed. (Köln, Heymanns Verlag 2005), p. 100.
90. Weber, *supra* n. 89, at p. 308, with further references.
91. The term 'Regional Economic Integration Organization' (REIO) was used in the Montreal Convention of 1999 (ICAO Doc. 9740), Art. 53 para. 2 and in the Cape Town Convention of 2001 (Convention on International Interests in Mobile Equipment), ICAO Doc. 9793, Art. 48, in order to allow the EC (now EU) to sign and ratify these international instruments.
92. Weber, *supra* n. 89, at p. 309.
93. *See*, e.g., the amending protocols relating to the Final Clause (Arabic Text, 1995) and (Chinese Text, 1998), relating to the Authentic Quinquelingual and Six-Language Texts of the Convention (1995 and 1998); the amending Protocol relating to an Amendment to Art. 56 (increase of the ANC from fifteen to nineteen members, 1989) entered into force in April 2005.

adherence to the Convention without specifying adherence to any of the amendments, the question arises whether the State will be bound to the 1944 original unamended Convention only or to the Convention as amended. From a practical viewpoint, the question for States wishing to become a member of ICAO is whether ratification or accession to the nineteen Protocols of the amendment, in addition to the adherence to the Convention, is necessary in order to be bound by the latest version of the Convention as amended.[94]

54. While in practice notifications of adherence to the 1944 Convention have in many cases encompassed instruments of ratification or accession to prior amendment protocols, additional ratification of all the individual amendment protocols is considered legally not necessary. Under Article 40, paragraph 5, of the **Vienna Convention on the Law of Treaties,**[95] accession or adherence to an amended multilateral treaty will be deemed to be accession or adherence to the treaty as amended, unless there is an express stipulation to the contrary. Therefore, notification of adherence to the 1944 Convention on International Civil Aviation will be **deemed adherence to the Convention as amended** at the time of the adherence. Certain protocols of amendment provide expressly that this principle shall apply.[96] However, any amendments adopted, but not yet in force, at the time of adherence are not encompassed.[97] For these, a separate instrument of accession or ratification will be required if the adhering State wishes to be bound by them.

D. Membership and UN Sanctions

55. **UN sanctions** have in certain cases included a ban on all commercial flights to and from the State under sanction, including commercial and financial activities related thereto.[98] The question arises in these cases whether this affects the respective State's membership in ICAO.

---

94. The traditional treaty practice of the Organization has been to suggest to States wishing to adhere to the Convention to include an express mention of all amending protocols to the Convention in their instrument of adherence, including those already in force. As a result of Art. 40 para. 5 of the *Vienna Convention on the Law of Treaties* (1969), such mention may be useful as clarification, but is legally not necessary.
95. Signed at Vienna on 23 May 1969, ILM Vol. 8 (1969), 679–735. The Vienna Convention is in force since 1980, and is generally regarded as a codification of customary international law.
96. *See,* e.g., Art. V of the *Protocol on the Authentic Trilingual Text of the Convention on International Civil Aviation (Chicago, 1944)*, signed at Buenos Aires on 24 Sep. 1968, ICAO Doc. 7300/8.
97. Article 40 para. 5. of the Vienna Convention refers to 'Any State which becomes a party to the treaty after the entry into force of the amending agreement … ', *ibid.* (n. 94).
98. *See*, e.g., UN Security Council Resolution 1267 (15 Oct. 1999): Sanctions against Afghanistan; UN Security Council Resolutions 748 (31 Mar. 1992); 883 (11 Nov. 1993); 1192 (27 Aug. 1998): Sanctions against Libya; UN Security Council Resolutions 661 (6 Aug. 1990), 986 (14 Apr. 1995), 1051 (27 Mar. 1996), 1111 (4 Jun. 1997), 1137 (12 Nov. 1997) and 1284 (17 Dec. 1999): Sanctions against Iraq. All UN Security Council Resolutions are available at http://www.un.org/documents/scres.htm. The UN Sanctions List is available at https://www.un.org/sc/suborg/en/sanctions/un-sc-consolidated-list.

56. This type of sanction[99] will normally result in the **suspension** of bilateral air transport agreements regarding international scheduled or non-scheduled operations as well as the suspension of related permits regarding international non-scheduled operations to and from the State concerned. However, the **membership status of the State concerned in ICAO will remain legally unaffected.**[100] The State retains not only its membership rights and privileges but also its obligations, in particular in relation to its annual contributions. As a practical matter, the participation of representatives from the State under sanction in ICAO activities will normally be reduced or will cease; however, this is due to political, financial and practical reasons and not due to the State's membership status, unless the sanctions include drastic action under Article 93 or 93bis of the Convention (suspension or termination) which has not occurred so far.[101]

§2. ORGANS

I. The Assembly

57. The Assembly is the **main policy-setting body** of ICAO. Each of the 193 members of ICAO has a seat in the Assembly and one vote.[102] It meets in ordinary session once every three years and may meet in extraordinary session at any time upon the call of the Council, or at the request of at least one-fifth of the membership.[103]

58. A majority of the contracting States constitute a **quorum** for the meetings of the Assembly. Decisions require a **simple majority** of votes cast;[104] in practice, however, most decisions of the Assembly are taken by **consensus** and the taking of formal votes is fairly rare. Most decisions on substantive matters are taken in the form of a resolution.

59. Many Assembly resolutions are **detailed policy-setting documents** not only for the Council, the Secretariat, and other organs of the Organization but also for

99. *See* the Resolutions cited in *supra* n. 98.

100. *See* certain budget resolutions of ICAO, in particular A31-21, A32-26, and A33-26, which list Afghanistan, Iraq, Libya and other States under UN sanctions as members of ICAO subject to assessment of contributions.

101. Assembly Resolution A35-26, even though broadening the effects of action under Art. 62 of the Convention, nevertheless makes it clear that membership status as such of States affected remains in effect: *See* A35-26, operating clauses 4 to 9.

102. Article 48 b) of the Convention; Rule 3 of the *Standing Rules of Procedure of the Assembly of the International Civil Aviation Organization*, 8th ed. (2014), Doc. 7600/8.

103. Article 48 a) of the Convention; Rules 1 and 2 of the *Standing Rules of Procedure of the Assembly*, *ibid.* (n. 101).

104. Article 48 c) of the Convention; Rule 28 of the *Standing Rules of Procedure of the Assembly*, *ibid.* (n. 101).

the Member States.[105] While they may contain instructions to the Council, the Secretariat or other ICAO bodies, they may also contain principles, policies or guidance to be followed by the Member States.[106]

60. Whether or not ICAO Assembly resolutions have **legally binding effects** on Member States is controversial; reference is made in this regard to the notion of **'soft law'**.[107] However, regardless of this controversy, the persuasive nature of the material used in such resolutions based on expertise, and the general acceptance by States at the time of adoption usually have the effect of ensuring their implementation.[108] In recent years, several ICAO Assembly Resolutions in particular those relating to climate change and the reduction of greenhouse gas emissions have been the subject of express reservations by States at the time of adoption.[109] In these cases, it is understood by all Member States that the respective resolutions do not bind the States having made the reservations to the extent specified therein.[110]

61. The **Assembly's powers and duties** are laid down in Article 49 of the Convention and include in particular powers to:[111]

- elect the States' members of the Council for three years;[112]
- vote annual budgets and determine the financial arrangements of the Organization (in practice, a package of three annual budgets, referred to as triennial budget, is voted upon);[113]
- review expenditures and approve the accounts of the Organization;[114]

---

105. *See,* e.g., Assembly Resolution A40-17: *Consolidated statement of continuing ICAO policies and practices related to environmental protection – general provisions, noise and local air quality, in: 40th Assembly, Resolutions adopted by the Assembly, Provisional edition, (October 2019);* Assembly Resolution A40-11: *Consolidated statement of continuing ICAO policies related to aviation security*, ICAO Doc. 10140.
106. *See,* e.g., A38-17, Appendices C to F; A38-15, Appendices C to G, *ibid.*
107. The term 'soft law' has been coined with particular reference to the declarations and resolutions of the UN General Assembly, as well as with regard to similar acts of the Assemblies of Parties of the UN Specialized Agencies. *See* on this matter D. Thürer, Soft Law, in R. Bernhardt (ed.). *Encyclopedia, supra* Ch. 1, n. 9, Vol. IV (2000), pp. 452 et seq., with further references.
108. *See* Buergenthal, *supra* Ch. 2, n. 71, pp. 226 et seq., 229–230.
109. Resolutions A40-18: *Consolidated statement of continuing ICAO policies and practices related to environmental protection – Climate change,* and A40-19: *Consolidated statement of continuing ICAO policies and practices related to environmental protection – Carbon Offsetting and Reduction Scheme for International Aviation (CORSIA),* Doc. 10140 Appendix A: Appendix A Reservations to Resolutions Adopted by the ICAO Assembly.
110. While some reservations relate to individual clauses of a Resolution (e.g. the reservations of China and India to Resolution A40-18), other reservations relate to a Resolution as a whole (e.g. the reservation of the Russian Federation to Resolution A40-19): Doc. 10140 Appendix A: Appendix A: Reservations to Resolutions Adopted by the ICAO Assembly.
111. On decision-making of the Assembly under Art. 49 of the Convention, *see*: *Repertory-Guide to the Convention on International Civil Aviation,* 2d ed. (1977), ICAO Doc. 8900/2, Art. 49.
112. Article 49 b) Convention; Rules 54-62 *Standing Rules of Procedure of the Assembly*, *supra* n. 104.
113. Article 49 e) Convention; Rules 24 et seq. *Rule 42A* Standing Rules of Procedure, *ibid.*
114. Article 49 f) Convention; Rules 24 et seq. *Rule 42A,* Rules 43 et seq. Standing Rules of Procedure, *ibid.*

- delegate to the Council the powers and authority necessary or desirable;[115]
- consider proposals for amendments to the Convention;[116]
- deal with any matter within the sphere of action of the Organization not specifically assigned to the Council.[117]

62. For the discharge of these responsibilities, the Assembly usually establishes subsidiary bodies for the duration of its ordinary triennial session, in accordance with Rules 14–22 of the **Standing Rules of Procedure of the Assembly of ICAO,**[118] in particular:

- the Executive Committee,[119] which has the task of coordinating the work of all other subsidiary bodies of the Assembly and of preparing the main policy decisions in the Plenary (Article 15 of the Standing Rules of Procedure);
- the Technical Commission, which has responsibility for air navigation matters and related subjects;[120]
- the Economic Commission, which has responsibility for air transport matters;
- the Legal Commission, which has responsibility for legal matters;[121]
- the Administrative Commission,[122] which has responsibility for budgetary, financial and related matters. As regards the triennial budget, the Administrative Commission is usually assisted by a Budget Working Group,[123] which reports to the Administrative Commission.

63. The four Commissions report to the Plenary of the Assembly, directly or if coordination is required through the Executive Committee;[124] in some cases, a Co-ordination Committee may also be established.[125]

64. Assembly Resolutions adopted by the plenary are **published immediately** after their adoption on the ICAO website, and after the Assembly also as hardcopy publication, first in provisional format; sometime later a definitive document is

115. Article 49 h) Convention; Rules 24 et seq. Standing Rules of Procedure, *ibid.*
116. Article 49 j) Convention; Rules 10 (d), 24 et seq. Standing Rules of Procedure, *ibid.*
117. Article 49 k) Convention; Arts 24 et seq. *Standing Rules of Procedure, ibid.* Art. 49 k) of the Convention thus provides for the principle of residual powers of the Assembly.
118. *Standing Rules of Procedure of the Assembly of ICAO*, Doc. 7600/8, 8th ed. (2014).
119. Rules 14 a) and 15 of the *Standing Rules of Procedure*, *ibid.*, n. 117.
120. This Commission, which is not specifically mentioned in the *Standing Rules of Procedure for the Assembly*, is established under Rules 14 c) and 18, and has the composition as set out in Rules 17 and 21.
121. For the Legal Commission, the same as for the Technical Commission applies, *see* previous n. 122. For details regarding the Legal Commission, *see* Ch. 3. §5, I, below.
122. This Commission is foreseen in Rule 14 c) of the *Standing Rules of Procedure,* n. 117. It has the composition as set out in Rules 17 and 21.
123. Under Rule 19 of the *Standing Rules of Procedure*, any Commission may create Working Groups. A Working Group shall consist of a limited number of members appointed by the Chairman of the Commission, not more than one member being appointed from any one delegation; *see* Rule 21.
124. *See* Rules 14 (a) and 15 of *the Standing Rules of Procedure, ibid.* (n. 117).
125. *See* Rules 14 b) and 16 of the *Standing Rules of Procedure*, *ibid.* (n. 117).

issued in both hardcopy and softcopy which sets out all new Resolutions adopted along with all previous Resolutions continuing to be in force.[126]

II. The Council and Its Committees

65. The Council is a **'permanent body responsible to the Assembly'**, Article 50(a) of the Convention. It is presently composed of thirty-six contracting States elected by the Assembly,[127] which have each one seat and one vote. The Council is the executive governing body of the Organization.

66. In electing the members of the Council, the Assembly shall, in accordance with Article 50(b) of the Convention, give adequate representation to:[128]

(1) the States of chief importance in air transport (so-called Part 1, eleven States);[129]
(2) the States which make the largest contribution to the provision of international air navigation facilities (so-called Part 2, twelve States);[130]
(3) the States whose designation will ensure that all the major geographic areas of the world are represented on the Council (so-called Part 3, thirteen States).[131]

67. Decisions of the Council require approval by a **majority of all its members (absolute majority)** in accordance with Article 52 Convention. However, when adopting Annexes to the Convention or amendments to such Annexes,[132] decisions of the Council require a **two-thirds majority** (twenty-five votes) in accordance with Articles 90 and 54 paragraph (l) of the Convention. Under its Rules of Procedure, the Council may also take certain decisions of procedural nature by a simple majority of votes cast in accordance with Articles 37, second sentence, and 42 paragraph b) of the Rules of Procedure for the Council.[133]

---

126. *See Resolutions adopted at the 40th session of the Assembly (Provisional Edition)*, October 2019; Assembly Resolutions in Force (as of 4 Oct. 2019), Doc. 10140; for the Assembly Resolutions in Force as of October 2016, *see* ICAO Doc. 10022.
127. The most recent enlargement of 2016 to 40 States is not yet in force, *see supra* para. 21. The Council had previously been enlarged in 2003 from 33 to 36 States, 34th Session (Extraordinary) of the Assembly, 31 Mar.–1st Apr. 2003.
128. *See* Rule 55 of the Standing Rules of Procedure of the Assembly.
129. Rule 55 a) i) of the Standing Rules of Procedure; the number of States elected in Part 1 is subject to the decision of the Assembly.
130. Rule 55 a) ii) of the Standing Rules of Procedure; the number of States elected in Part 2 is subject to the decision of the Assembly.
131. Rule 55 a) iii) of the Standing Rules of Procedure; the number of States elected in Part 3 is subject to the decision of the Assembly.
132. Articles 54 e) and m) and 90 of the Convention.
133. Article 52 of the Convention provides that 'decisions of the Council shall require approval by a majority of its members'. In light of this provision, the question may arise whether the *Rules of Procedure for the Council*, which are permitting simple majority voting (*see* Rule 63 of the *Rules of Procedure for the Council*, Doc. 7559/10), are 'constitutional'. It has been argued in this respect that the Council, when adopting its Rules of Procedure, decided with absolute majority under Art. 52, and that the requirement of Art. 52 was therefore satisfied. It has also been pointed out that the

68. In accordance with Articles 54 and 55 of the Convention, the Council has **legislative, administrative and judicial functions**. These are divided into mandatory functions (Article 54) and permissive functions (Article 55).

Among the **legislative functions** are in particular:[134]

- the adoption of international SARPs in the form of Annexes to the Convention and amendments thereto (Articles 90, 54(l)); the Council has up to now adopted nineteen Annexes and one of its major functions in practice is to keep these nineteen Annexes up-to-date by adopting appropriate amendments.[135]

Among the **administrative functions** of the Council are:[136]

- administration of the finances of the Organization in accordance with Chapters XII and XV;
- appointment of the Secretary General and making provision for other personnel of the Secretariat, as required (Article 55(h));
- collection and dissemination of information on air navigation and air transport services;
- reporting of infractions of the Convention (Article 54(j) and (k));
- submission of annual reports to the Assembly and the carrying out of directions of the Assembly (Article 54(a)and (b)).

69. Regarding the last point, the Council fulfils the important function of administering and supervising the **Universal Safety Oversight Audit Programme (USOAP)**[137] as well as the **Universal Security Audit Programme (USAP).**[138] The gradual implementation of these programmes from 1998 and 2002, respectively, and the use of audit results for enhancing aviation safety and security has been a key activity of the Council and the Secretariat and can be regarded as highly successful.[139]

---

decisions of the Council falling under the simple majority rule in the *Rules of Procedure* are mainly of procedural nature and not substantive. In practice, the Council applies the consensus principle on virtually all issues (except adoption of Annexes and amendments thereto). Therefore, this issue has more theoretical than practical significance.

134. *See* on this matter Buergenthal, *supra*. Ch. 2, (n. 71).

135. Articles 54 m) and 90 of the Convention; *see infra*, Ch. 2, §2, III; Ch. 3, §2, III and Ch. 5, §3.

136. *Repertory-Guide to the Convention on International Civil Aviation*, 2d ed., ICAO Doc. 8900/2, Arts 54 a), b), f), h)-k).

137. H. Belai, *Expanding Programme to Adopt Systems Approach to Future Audits*, 58 ICAO J. 4 et seq. (2003); Weber, *supra* Ch. 2, n. 9, at pp. 301 et seq. with further references. *See infra* Ch. 3 § 8.

138. ICAO Secretariat, *Historic Conference Agrees on Strategy for Strengthening Aviation Security*, 57 ICAO J. 5 et seq. (2002); A. Kotaite, *Civil Aviation Security is an Integral Part of Our Global Security*, 57 ICAO J. 4 et seq. (2002).; D. Antonini, *Annex 17 Standards Will Be Primary Focus of Forthcoming Security System Audits*, 57 ICAO J. 11 et seq. (2002). On the USAP programme as it evolved since 2002, *see* Weber, *supra* Ch. 2, n. 9, at pp. 307 et seq.; A38-WP/15: USAP: Transition to a Continuous Monitoring Approach (31/05/2013); A38-16 (12/07/2013); A37-WP/32 EX/12: Implementation and Evolution of the ICAO Universal Security Audit Programme (26/07/10); Assembly Resolution A37-5, Whereas clauses; *see also infra* Ch. 3.§7.

139. *See Report on the Evolution of the Universal Safety Oversight Audit Programme (USOAP) Continuous Monitoring Approach* (CMA) (A40-WP/11); *Report on the Implementation of the ICAO*

70. Among the **judicial functions** of the Council are:[140]

- adjudication of disputes between contracting States relating to the interpretation or application of the Convention or its Annexes (Articles 84 and 54(b) of the Convention);
- adjudication of disputes between contracting States relating to the interpretation or application of the International Air Services Transit Agreement (Article 66 of the Convention, Article II Transit Agreement).

71. In practice, and in accordance with the ICAO **Rules for the Settlement of Differences,**[141] the Council has, to the extent possible, acted as a mediator between the parties when they brought complaints before the Council.[142] Therefore, in virtually all cases brought before the Council, it was possible to arrive at a settlement agreed between the parties.[143] Where necessary, the Council has not hesitated to take clear procedural decisions in adversarial situations.[144] However, the Council's policy of favouring negotiated settlements has been predicated on the consideration that disputes between contracting States, even if brought before as a result of a legal disagreement, are usually predominantly political in nature and should therefore be settled by political means, i.e., negotiation whenever possible instead of adjudication.[145]

72. Under **Article 54(n)**, the Council 'shall consider any matter relating to the Convention which any contracting State refers to it'. In practice, the majority of

Continuous Monitoring Approach (CMA) Audit Programmes (A40-WP/23); *Report on the Review of the Scope and Methodology of the Universal Security Audit Programme – Continuous Monitoring Approach (USAP-CMA)* (A40-WP/32); *Report of The Executive Committee On Agenda Item 13,* A40-WP/623; and Assembly Resolution A37-5, 8th Whereas clause; A35-6, operating clause 1; and Assembly Resolution A35-9, Appendix E, 9th Whereas clause, ICAO Doc. 9848.

140. On the judicial functions of the Council, *see*: J. Erler, *Rechtsfragen der ICAO: Die Internationale Zivilluftfahrtorganisation und ihre Mitgliedstaaten* (Berlin, Heymanns Verlag 1967), p. 185–196; B. Cheng, *The Law of International Air Transport* (London, Stevens and Sons, 1962), p. 100–105; R. Mankiewicz, 'Organisation internationale de l'aviation civile', III *Annuaire Français de droit international* (1957), pp. 383 et seq.; Buergenthal, *supra* (n. 71), pp. 123 et seq.; *Repertory-Guide to the Convention on International Civil Aviation, supra* (n. 136), Arts 84 et seq.
141. ICAO Doc. 7782/2.
142. For the cases submitted to the Council, *see infra* Ch. 2. §3, III A (para. 127).
143. *Infra*, Ch. 2. §3, III. A, para. 127.
144. *See,* e.g., the decisions of the Council to reject the Preliminary Objections raised by Respondents in the following three cases: *United States and 15 European States (2000)* ('Hushkits'), C-DEC 161/6; *Brazil v. United States (2016),* C-DEC 211/10; and *Qatar v. Bahrain, Egypt, Saudi Arabia and the UAE (Application A); and Qatar v. Bahrain, Egypt, and the UAE (Application B) (2017)* C-DEC 214/11, Appendices A and B. Regarding the Hushkit dispute, *see also* C-WP 11380, Memorandum SG 1670/00 and SG 1674/00, and C-DEC 161/4 and 5.
145. Buergenthal, *supra* n. 71, at p. 161 remarks with regard to the complaint procedure under the Transit and Transport Agreements that it 'is designed primarily to provide machinery for the adjustment of frictions of an economic or political type that might otherwise disrupt the orderly operation of the system established by the Transit and Transport Agreements'. A similar remark could also be made with regard to the complaint procedures under Ch. XVIII (Arts 84 et seq.) of the Convention.

cases brought before the Council under this provision involved complaints about other contracting States allegedly not complying with the provisions of the Convention.[146]

73. As a matter of standing practice, these **cases under Article 54(n)** have not been treated as cases of formal adjudication, so the Rules for the Settlement of Differences do not apply.[147] Instead, the parties complaining and complained of are invited by the Council to attend as invited observers under Article 53 of the Convention[148] (unless they are members of the Council) and are given an opportunity to state their case before the Council. The **Rules of Procedure for the Council** apply in these cases.[149] The Council will usually favour negotiations between the parties and, if necessary, will make recommendations or suggestions to the parties. If appropriate, the Council may proceed to take a decision on the matter.[150] The proceedings under Article 54(n) can be regarded as quasi-judiciary.

74. Meetings of the Council are presided over by its **President.** In accordance with Article 51, the President of the Council is an official elected for a term of three years, subject to re-election.[151] He shall serve as a representative of the Council and carry out the functions which the Council assigns to him. In practice, a large number of functions are delegated to the President of the Council, in particular during those periods when the Council is not in session.[152] In accordance with Articles 59 and 60, the President of the Council has the status of an international civil servant of ICAO who receives emoluments from ICAO and who must not be under employment with any contracting state.[153]

75. In accordance with Article 54(d), the Council has established the **Air Transport Committee.**[154] Similarly, under Article 54(c) and its Rules of Procedure, the Council has established a number of **other Committees,** namely:

---

146. *See infra*, paras 128–130, Ch. 2 §3, III. B.
147. This fact renders the procedure under Art. 54 (n) more flexible in relation to the needs of the particular dispute. From a formal viewpoint, Art. 54 (n) is an entirely open-ended provision as regards the subject-matter which a contracting State may refer to the Council, and does not presuppose an adversarial procedure. In all cases of Art. 54(n), the *Rules of Procedure for the Council*, Doc. 7559/10, apply.
148. Article 53 of the Convention requires that the party invited to participate, without a vote, in the discussions of the Council be especially affected in its interests by the question to be considered by the Council.
149. ICAO Doc. 7559/10, 10th ed. (2014).
150. *See*, e.g., C-DEC 164/5 regarding the item 'Amendment to the Common Nadi/Auckland Oceanic FIR boundary'.
151. Since 2007, re-election of the President is limited to one additional term of three years, *see* A36-28: *Term limits for the Offices of Secretary General and the President of the Council*, Doc. 9902.
152. Delegation of functions is done on the basis of Art. 51 c) of the Convention and Arts 18–21, 63, of the Rules of Procedure for the Council, ICAO Doc. 7559/10.
153. Both Arts 59 and 60 of the Convention mention the President of the Council expressly for the avoidance of doubt about his status. *See Repertory-Guide to the Convention of International Civil Aviation*, 2d ed., ICAO Doc. 8900/2, Arts 59 and 60.
154. The Air Transport Committee is the only Committee of the Council expressly mentioned in the Convention, and under Art. 54 d) it is a mandatory Committee; the other Committees have been set

- the Finance Committee;[155]
- the Technical Cooperation Committee;[156]
- the Joint Support Committee;[157]
- the Committee on Unlawful Interference;[158]
- the Human Resources Committee.

76. These committees are composed of representatives on the Council or their Alternates, and they have between eleven and fifteen members. The Committees usually meet during the first phase of each Council session (so-called **Committee Phase**) in order to prepare the discussion in full Council during the second phase (so-called **Council Phase**).[159] Their work is subject to the **Rules of Procedure for the Standing Committees of the Council.**[160] All Committees report to the Council through the respective Committee Chairman, who is elected by the Council and is usually an experienced representative on the Council.

77. In order to prepare the Council's decisions on the **Edward Warner Award**, the Council has established the Edward Warner Committee, whose work is governed by the Rules of Procedure of the Edward Warner Fund. It is the object of the Fund to award every three years the Edward Warner Award, the highest distinction in international civil aviation consisting of a gold medal and an Award Certificate, to a person having made an outstanding contribution to the advancement of international civil aviation. The Committee is responsible for receiving nominations, making a shortlist, and submitting the shortlist to the Council for decision.

III. The Air Navigation Commission

78. The ANC, established by the Council under Article 54(e) and Chapter X of the Convention, is the **main technical body of the Organization**.[161] In accordance with Article 57(a) of the Convention, its principal function is to consider and prepare amendments to the Annexes to the Convention, or to PANS,[162] and to recommend them for adoption to the Council. It shall also advise the Council on the

---

up under the Council's Rules of Procedure, Rule 17. *See also* the Special Provisions applicable to the Air Transport Committee, ICAO Doc. 8146 C930/6, p. 17.

155. *See* Rule 17 of the *Rules of Procedure for the Council*, ICAO Doc. 7559/10; Rule 1(a) of the *Rules of Procedure for Standing Committees of the Council*, ICAO Doc. 8146 C930/6 – (6th ed. 2011).
156. *Rules of Procedure for Standing Committees of the Council*, *ibid.* (n. 154), Rule 1 a).
157. *Rules of Procedure ibid.* (n. 154).
158. *Ibid.*, and the *Special Provisions applicable to the Joint Support, Finance, Human Resources, Unlawful Interference and Technical Co-operation Committees* ICAO Doc. 8146 C930/6, p. 18.
159. Rule 20 of the *Rules of Procedure for the Council*, Doc. 7559/10.
160. ICAO Doc. 8146 C930/6.
161. *See* the *Rules of Procedure for the Air Navigation Commission*, Doc. 8229-AN/876/2, 2nd ed. 17 Mar. 1975, Arts 1–3; Buergenthal, *supra* (Ch. 2, n. 71), pp. 9 et seq.
162. *Procedures for Air Navigation Services*, *see* on this matter Assembly Resolution A39-22: *Formulation and implementation of Standards and Recommended Practices (SARPs) and Procedures for Air Navigation Services (PANS) and notification of differences*, Doc. 10140; on PANS, *see also* Buergenthal, *ibid.* (n. 71), pp. 115 et seq.

collection and dissemination of information it considers necessary and useful for the advancement of air navigation in line with Article 57(c) of the Convention.[163]

79. The ANC is composed of nineteen members appointed by the Council **in their personal capacity as experts,** and not as representatives of States, from among persons nominated by contracting States.[164] An amendment to Article 56 providing for an increase of the members of the Commission from nineteen to twenty-one members has been adopted at the 39th Assembly in 2016 but has not yet come into force as 128 ratifications will be required.[165]

80. The **President of the Air Navigation Commission** is appointed by the Council, usually for a term of office of one year, subject to re-appointment.[166] The **members** are appointed by the Council from among persons nominated by contracting States; their term of office extends from the time of their appointment until their nomination is withdrawn by the State having nominated them.

81. It is the practice of the ANC to develop and prepare **recommendations for amendments to the Annexes to the Convention or to PANS** through a detailed and elaborate procedure, which is designed to ensure consensus and support among contracting States for the amendment.[167] This procedure facilitates the implementation by contracting States of amendments setting forth new or revised SARPs or PANS once the amendment is formally adopted by the Council.

82. The ANC reports on all matters to the Council.[168] The Council may, under Article 55(b), delegate to the ANC duties additional to those set out in the Convention; however, it has made use of this option only sparingly.

IV. The Legal Committee

83. The **Legal Committee** was set up by the Assembly during its first session in 1947 (Assembly Resolution A1-46).[169] It has the task of advising the Council and

163. *See* the *Rules of Procedure for the Air Navigation Commission, ibid.* (n. 160).
164. Article 56, first sentence, of the Convention; Rule 16 a) of the Rules of Procedure for the Council, *supra* (n. 159).
165. *Protocol Relating to an Amendment to the Convention on International Civil Aviation (Article 56)*, signed at Montreal on 5 Oct. 2016, which will enter into force upon reaching 128 ratifications. Doc. 10075.
166. Rule 15 (a) of the *Rules of Procedure for the Council*, Doc. 7559/10.
167. For the procedure, *see* Assembly Resolutions A39-22 *ibid.* (n. 164), and A38-11: *Formulation and implementation of Standards and Recommended Practices (SARPs) and Procedures for Air Navigation Services (PANS) and notification of differences*, superseding A37-15: *Consolidated statement of ICAO continuing policies and associated practices related specifically to air navigation*, Appendix A.
168. Article 57(a) of the Convention; *Rules of Procedure for the Air Navigation Commission*, Doc. 8229-AN/876/2, 2nd ed. 17 Mar. 1975.
169. No longer in force (*see* Doc. 10140 – Assembly Resolutions in force as of 4 Oct. 2019), Appendix A; superseded by A40-28: *Consolidated statement of continuing ICAO policies in the legal field*, Appendices A–G.

the Assembly on legal questions and the important function of preparing drafts for international conventions or protocols in the field of air law.[170] Its membership comprises all 193 ICAO Member States and each member has one vote.[171] Decisions require a simple majority of votes cast, including decisions in the preparation of drafts for instruments of international air law when adopting a draft for submission to the Council.[172] In practice, however, most decisions in the Legal Committee are taken by consensus. The procedure which the Committee applies in the preparation of draft instruments of international air law is laid down in the '**Procedure for approval of draft conventions on international air law**' (Assembly Resolution A31-15,[173] Appendix B) and additionally in the Appendix to the **Rules of Procedure for the Legal Committee** (ICAO Doc. 7669-LC/139/5), entitled 'Organization and Working Methods of the Legal Committee'.

84. The **elaboration of a draft text** for an international instrument is first entrusted to a Sub-Committee of the Legal Committee or to the Secretariat. More recently, this task has been entrusted in several cases to the Secretariat assisted by a Study Group.[174] When the Sub-Committee or the Secretariat assisted by a Study Group, has completed its work in drafting a first draft text it will be submitted to the Legal Committee. The Committee will usually revise the draft, in light of the views of its membership. Once the Legal Committee has completed its work on the text, it is adopted by the Committee and submitted to the Council for consideration, together with a report thereon. The Council may take such action as it deems appropriate, including the circulation of the draft to contracting States and international organizations for comment.[175] The comment period shall not be less than four months. If it considers the text is not yet sufficiently mature, it may refer the text back to the Committee, or to a special Group, for further consideration; if it considers that the text is sufficiently mature, it will convene a Diplomatic Conference for the purpose of formal adoption and signature of the new instrument.[176] For further detail, *see also* below Chapter 2, §3, II, paragraphs 114–118.

170. *See Legal Committee – Constitution – Procedure for Approval of Draft Conventions – Rules of Procedure*, Doc. 7669 – LC/139/6 (2018). The Rules of Procedure of the Legal Committee were last amended at the 36th Session of the Committee, Doc. 10061, Report on the 36TH SESSION of the Legal Committee, Montréal, 30 Nov. to 3 Dec. 2015, Agenda Item 5 (Amendment of Rules 6 and 44).

171. Legal Committee, Rules of Procedure, Doc. 7669, 6th ed. 2018, (*see* n. 169).

172. Legal Committee, Rules of Procedure, Rule 38, Doc. 7669–LC/139/6. However, a two-thirds majority is required for decisions on adoption of a text at international conferences on air law (Diplomatic Conferences) convened under the auspices of ICAO; the same applies in case the Legal Committee does not accept the text prepared by a subcommittee as a basis of discussion.

173. Assembly Resolution A31-15, Appendix B, which superseded Resolutions A7-6 and A27-3.

174. This was the case in the Warsaw Convention modernization process, which led to the adoption of the Montreal Convention of 1999, *see* ICAO Doc. 9775, Vol. III: Preparatory Material; similarly, in the Rome Convention modernization process, a text was elaborated by the Secretariat with the assistance of a Secretariat Study Group.

175. *See* Assembly Resolution A40-28, Appendix B.

176. *Ibid.* (nn. 171 and 172).

85. This elaborate procedure has resulted in the widespread acceptance and ratification of virtually all international air law instruments which the ICAO Legal Committee (LC) developed over the years.

V. Air Navigation Conferences and Divisional Meetings

86. **Air Navigation Conferences** may be convened by the Council from time to time, as circumstances require.[177] An Air Navigation Conference will usually be called when its task encompasses a substantial number of interrelated subjects of worldwide scope falling within several air navigation fields, so as to discuss and recommend new techniques, new technology or new procedures for the advancement of air navigation.[178]

87. All ICAO Member States are entitled to attend an Air Navigation Conference. While according to the Rules of Procedure,[179] each State has one vote, recommendations and conclusions are usually adopted by consensus. An Air Navigation Conference may set up Committees and Sub-Committees, as required. Its work will usually result in recommendations and conclusions taking into account the **advancement of aeronautical science and technology** resulting in **improvement of techniques, technology or procedures**, which it will address to the Council for decision.[180] For example, the Tenth Air Navigation Conference in 1992 recommended the introduction of the satellite-based CNS/ATM concept for international civil aviation, and the eventual phasing out of terrestrial air navigation services.[181] The Eleventh Air Navigation Conference held in 2003 reviewed the implementation of the CNS/ATM system and endorsed the development of the Global Air Traffic Management (ATM) Operational Concept encompassing CNS/ATM. The 12th Air Navigation Conference in 2012 adopted the Global Air Navigation Plan (GANP), 4th edition, which developed the Global ATM Operational Concept further. The conclusions and recommendations of an Air Navigation Conference may have a far-reaching impact on the advancement of air navigation.

88. **Divisional Meetings** are meetings of worldwide scope dealing with one or a few specific subject matters in the air navigation or air transport fields, e.g., aircraft accident investigation, aviation meteorology or facilitation.[182] Such meetings are convened by the Council for the purpose of progressing problems of worldwide

177. *See Directives to Divisional-type Air Navigation Meetings and Rules of Procedure for their Conduct*, ICAO Doc. 8143 – AN/873/3, Part I, s. 4.
178. *See ibid.* (n. 176), Part I s. 2.2.
179. *See ibid.*, Part III, s. 2 and s. 16.
180. *See* Directives to Divisional-type Air Navigation Meetings, *ibid.* (n. 176), Part I.
181. *Report of the 10th Air Navigation Conference*, 5-20 Sep. 1991, ICAO Doc. 9583. For the Report on the most recent 12th Air Navigation Conference, *see* Doc. 10007, AN-Conf/12.
182. *See*, e.g., *Report of the 10th Air Navigation Conference*, 5-20 Sep. 1991, ICAO Doc. 9583; Report of the 12th Air Navigation Conference, 19-30 Nov. 2012, ICAO Doc. 10007; *Report of the Aeronautical Information Services Aeronautical Charts (AIS/MAP) Divisional Meeting (1998)*, Doc. 9733; *Report of the Meteorology (MET) Divisional Meeting (2002)*, Doc. 9812.

importance, including the development of amendments to the Annexes, to PANS, and to other documents in the air navigation field.[183]

89. All Member States may participate in such meetings on an equal basis. They shall be convened only when justified by the number and importance of the problems to be dealt with, and when there is the likelihood of constructive action on them.[184] Meetings convened on this basis may be requested to conduct exploratory discussions on matters not yet mature for definitive action.

90. Any recommendations or conclusions of a Divisional Meeting will be addressed to the Council, which may decide to have them reviewed by the ANC or other relevant bodies, in particular where amendments to Annexes are being considered.

VI. Panels and Working Groups

91. **Air Navigation Panels** are groups of experts of limited size which may be set up by the ANC[185] or by the Council. Such panels shall be established when it is necessary to advance the solution of special problems requiring expert advice, including technical problems which cannot be solved adequately or expeditiously by the ANC through other established facilities.[186] The experts who are members of a Panel sit on the Panel **in their personal capacity as experts**, not as a representative of their State.

92. In practice, Panels have been an important element in the **advancement of the work of the Air Navigation Commission or of the Council** as regards the various Annexes, e.g., in recent years the Operations Panel, the Obstacle Clearance Panel, the Airworthiness Panel, the Aviation Security Panel, and the RPAS Panel.[187]

93. The advice which Panels provide is expert advice. Therefore, their reports are presented as the advice of a group of experts to the ANC or to the body having set up the Panel; consequently, they cannot be considered as representing the view of contracting States.[188]

---

183. Assembly Resolution A40-4, Appendix A: *Air navigation meetings of worldwide scope*, operating clause 1.
184. Appendix A, para. 2 to Assembly Resolution A40-4: *Consolidated statement of continuing ICAO policies and associated practices related specifically to air navigation*, ICAO Doc. 10140.
185. *See* the *Directives for Panels of the Air Navigation Commission*, ICAO Doc. 7984/4, ss 1–3. *See also* the *Directives for Panels of the Air Transport Committee and the Committee on Unlawful Interference, ICAO* Doc. 9482.
186. *See* Assembly Resolution A41-10: *Consolidated statement of continuing ICAO policies and associated practices related specifically to air navigation*, Appendix B: *Panels of the Air Navigation Commission (ANC)*, para. 1, Doc. 10184.
187. *See*, e.g., Doc. 9826 – Supplement, pp. 3, 5.
188. *See* Appendix B to Assembly Resolution A40-4 *supra*, n. 186, Associated Practice.

94. Panels, as well as many other ICAO subsidiary bodies, may set up **Working Groups** in accordance with their Rules of Procedure in order to advance their work. These Working Groups will usually have a specific task set out in their terms of reference, and limited membership. It is general practice that States' members of the parent body not represented in a Working Group may participate as an observer if they so wish. Working Groups should be distinguished from **Secretariat Study Groups**, which are set up by the Secretariat and are composed of experts from contracting States. They are moderated by an officer of the Secretariat. Their task is usually to advance the work of the Secretariat in developing proposals or draft texts, such as draft international air law instruments for the consideration of the Legal Committee or a Legal Sub-Committee.

VII. The Secretariat

95. The Secretariat of the Organization is headed by the **Secretary General**, who is the **chief executive officer of ICAO,** in accordance with Article 54(h) of the Convention. The Secretary General is appointed by the Council, which shall also make provision for 'the appointment of such other personnel as may be necessary, in accordance with the provisions of Chapter XI'.[189] Chapter XI of the Convention leaves it to the Council to determine 'the method of appointment and termination of appointment, the training, and the salaries, allowances, and conditions of service of the Secretary General and other personnel of the Organization ... '[190] In particular, Article 59 provides for the **international character of the personnel** of the Organization, and Article 60 sets out the basis for the privileges and immunities of such personnel.[191] The Organization's staff enjoys privileges and immunities in accordance with the 1947 Convention on the Privileges and Immunities of the Specialized Agencies,[192] including its Annex III.

96. On the basis of Articles 58 and 59, the Council has adopted Staff Regulations (the **ICAO Service Code**, including the Ethics Framework in Appendix I), which govern the conditions of service of all ICAO staff.[193] These are modelled upon the UN Service Code since ICAO is part of the UN Common System. In practice, most aspects of the ICAO Service Code, in particular as regards appointments, salaries and conditions of service, are therefore governed by the rules and practices of the UN Common System.[194]

189. Article 54(h) of the Convention, second half-sentence.
190. Article 58 of the Convention.
191. Article 60 of the Convention should be read in conjunction with the 1947 *Convention on the Privileges and Immunities of the Specialized Agencies,* adopted by the UN General Assembly on 21 Nov. 1947, 33 *UNTS* (1948), p. 242, including its Annex III (International Civil Aviation Organization), approved 29 Dec. 1951.
192. *Ibid.* (n. 190).
193. *ICAO Service Code*, Doc. 7350.
194. *See* Art. XII of the Agreement between the UN and ICAO, Doc. 7970, which recognizes that the eventual development of a single unified international civil service is desirable from the standpoint of effective administrative coordination. *See also* Assembly Resolution A21-12: *International Civil Service Commission*, ICAO Doc. 9848.

97. The **Secretariat** consists of approximately 700 staff, of which approximately 550 are located at headquarters in Montreal and around 150 are located at the seven Regional Offices,[195] namely Bangkok, Cairo, Dakar, Lima, Mexico City, Nairobi and Paris. A Sub-regional Office was established in 2013 in Beijing, China.

98. Organizationally, the Secretariat is divided into **five Bureaux**, namely the Air Navigation Bureau, the Air Transport Bureau, the Legal Affairs and External Relations Bureau, the Administration and Services Bureau, and the Technical Cooperation Bureau (TCB).[196] Each of these Bureaux is headed by a Director who reports to the Secretary General. The seven Regional Offices report to the Office of the Secretary General (OSG). In recent years, the Secretariat structure has been subject to a number of reorganization decisions.

§3. Competence

99. Part II of the Convention on International Civil Aviation sets out the **institutional framework** of the Organization, including the objectives of the Organization (Article 44),[197] the powers and duties of the Assembly (Article 49), the mandatory and permissive functions of the Council (Articles 54 and 55), the duties of the ANC (Article 57) and other provisions relating to the competence of the Organization and of its bodies.[198] Certain provisions in Parts III (International Air Transport) and IV (Final Provisions) of the Convention also contain rules giving specific tasks and powers to the Council, in particular on improving and financing air navigation facilities (Chapter XV) and on the judicial and quasi-judicial functions of the Council (Chapter XVIII).

100. Bearing in mind the broad objectives of the Organization set out in Article 44, the **powers and duties of its organs** are accordingly wide. In particular, Articles 54 and 55 of the Convention spell out broad powers and duties for the Council; additional powers are set out in Chapters XV and XVIII. As regards the Assembly, specific powers and duties are spelt out in detail in Article 49(a)–(j). In accordance with Article 49(k), the Assembly is mandated to 'deal with any matter within the sphere of action of the Organization not specifically assigned to the Council'.

195. These figures relate to 2020. They obviously fluctuate with the triennial budget. From 2005 onwards, a slight decrease of permanent staff took place due to the 'zero nominal growth' triennial budgets 2005–2007 and onwards.
196. This structure is reflected in the Programme Budget of ICAO; *see* Assembly Resolution A40-34, Part C Regular Programme, Clause 1; *see* ICAO Doc. 10140, Assembly Resolutions in force (as of 4 Oct. 2019).
197. Article 44 of the Convention should be read in conjunction with the preamble of the Convention, which provides guidance for its interpretation, in particular the institutional provisions in Part II of the Convention.
198. In particular Ch. XI (Personnel), Ch. XII (Finance), Ch. XIII (Other international arrangements), Ch. XIV (Information and reports), Ch. XV (Airports and other air navigation facilities). Ch. XVI (Joint operating organizations and pooled services), and Ch. XVIII (Disputes and default).

101. Due to these wide powers, the Organization so far never had to resort to the 'implied powers' theory[199] but has been in a position to function on the basis of the express powers set out in the Convention.

I. Standard-Setting: Adoption of International Standards and Recommended Practices

102. Under Article 54 subparagraph (l), the Council is vested with the competence to adopt, in accordance with the provision of Chapter VI of the Convention, **international standards and recommended practices**; to designate them, for convenience, as **Annexes** to the Convention; and to notify in each such case all contracting States of the action taken.[200] Under Article 54 subparagraph (m), the Council is empowered to consider recommendations of the ANC for amendment of the Annexes and to take action in accordance with Chapter XX of the Convention.[201]

103. In accordance with Article 54 subparagraph (l) and Chapter VI of the Convention, the Council has since 1947 adopted nineteen Annexes to the Convention, which are discussed in more detail in Chapter 3 §2 and Chapter 5 §3 below.

104. In accordance with Article 54 subparagraph (m), the Council has **kept the Annexes and the PANS up to date** by adopting from time to time **amendments** in accordance with the procedure set out in Chapter XX of the Convention.[202] Chapter XX consists of Article 90 paragraphs (a) and (b), which provide that the adoption by the Council of the Annexes described in Article 54, subparagraph (l), shall require the vote of two-thirds of the Council at a meeting called for that purpose and shall then be submitted by the Council to each contracting State. Any such Annex or any amendment of an Annex shall become effective within three months after its submission to the contracting States or at the end of a longer period of time as the Council may prescribe unless in the meantime a majority of the contracting

---

199. On the implied powers theory, *see* M. Zuleeg, *International Organisations – Implied Powers*, in: R. Bernhardt (ed.), *Encyclopedia, supra* Ch. 1, n. 9, Vol. II (1995), pp. 1312 et seq.; on the implied powers of the UN, *see* the Advisory Opinion of the ICJ in the Reparations Case: *Reparation for Injuries Suffered in the Service of the United Nations*, Advisory Opinion, *ICJ Reports* (1949), pp. 174–220.

200. Article 54(l) should be read in conjunction with Arts 37 and 38 of the Convention; it has been supplemented by Assembly Resolution A-39-22: *Formulation and implementation of Standards and Recommended Practices (SARPs) and Procedures for Air Navigation Services (PANS) and notification of differences*, ICAO Doc. 10075; previously A38-11 and A37-15 (Consolidated Statement of continuing ICAO policies).

201. Chapter XX (Annexes) of the Convention contains only one provision, namely Art. 90 – *Adoption and Amendment of Annexes.*

202. Article 90 of the Convention and Assembly Resolution A39-22: *Formulation and implementation of Standards and Recommended Practices (SARPs) and Procedures for Air Navigation Services (PANS) and notification of differences,* ICAO Doc. 10075; previously Resolution A38-11, ICAO Doc. 10022; and Resolution A37-15, Appendix A.

States registers its disapproval with the Council. Furthermore, the Council shall immediately notify all contracting States of the coming into force of any Annex or amendment thereto.[203]

105. The **status of the Annexes** to the Convention is governed by Articles 37 and 38 of the Convention. These provisions clarify that the Annexes do not have the same legally binding force as the articles of the main body of the Convention.[204] One reason is that they are not subject to ratification and that they are a form of 'technical international legislation'.[205] Article 37 provides that each 'Contracting State undertakes to collaborate in securing the highest practicable degree of uniformity in regulations, standards, procedures, and organization in relation to aircraft, personnel, airways and auxiliary services in all matters in which such uniformity will facilitate and improve air navigation'. For this purpose, ICAO shall adopt and amend from time to time, as may be necessary, international SARPs and procedures dealing with matters concerned with the safety, regularity, and efficiency of air navigation as may from time to time appear appropriate.[206]

106. Article 38 deals with **departures from international standards and procedures** and provides that any State which finds it impracticable to comply in all respects with any such international standard or procedure **shall give immediate notification to ICAO.**[207] The same applies if any State finds it impracticable to bring its own regulations or practices into full accord with any international standard or procedure after the amendment of the latter, or where it deems it necessary to adopt regulations or practices differing in any particular respect from those established by an international standard. Any notification to ICAO under Article 38 shall set out the differences between the State's own practice and that established by the international standard.[208] Detailed guidance regarding such notifications is set out in the ICAO **Manual on Notification and Publication of Differences,**[209] and the notified differences are accessible through the Electronic Filing of Differences (EFOD) system.[210]

---

203. Article 90 para. b) of the Convention.
204. This is clear from the wording 'undertakes to collaborate in securing the highest practicable degree of uniformity' in Art. 37, as well as the term 'impracticable' in Art. 38.
205. *See* on this matter Buergenthal, *supra* Ch. 2, n. 71, pp. 57 et seq. *See also* Cheng, *supra* n. 16, at pp. 63 et seq.; Le Geoff, 'Les Annexes techniques à la Convention de Chicago', 19 *Revue Générale de l'Air* (1956), pp. 146 et seq.; R. Mankiewicz, 'L'adoption des annexes à la Convention de Chicago par le Conseil de l'Organisation internationale de l'aviation civile', in: L. Brandt (ed.), *Beiträge zum Internationalen Luftrecht.* Festschrift zu Ehren von Alex Meyer, (Düsseldorf, Droste Verlag 1954) pp. 82 et seq.
206. Article 37, second sentence, of the Convention.
207. This rule is to be regarded as a legally binding obligation on contracting States ('shall give immediate notification'). This interpretation has played an important role during the DGCA Conference in 1997, which recommended the establishment of a universal and mandatory safety oversight audit programme. *See*: *Report of the DGCA Conference on a Global Strategy for Safety Oversight*, ICAO Doc. 9707.
208. Article 38, first sentence, of the Convention. *See also* A39-22, operating clauses and Associated Practices, Doc. 10075.
209. Doc. 10055 AN/518.
210. www.icao.int/usoap.

107. In the case of amendments to international standards, any State which does not make the appropriate amendments to its own regulations or practices shall give **notice** to the Council **within sixty days of the adoption of the amendment** to the international standard or indicate the action it proposes to take.[211] In any such case, the Council shall make immediate notification to all other States of the difference which exists between one or more features of an international standard and the corresponding national practice of that State.[212]

108. Under Article 38, obligations to notify relate only to departures from international standards or procedures, but strictly speaking not to **departures from recommended practices.** Such recommended practices are only 'recommended' and therefore their non-observance will have no legal effects.[213] Nevertheless, due to the important safety implications of recommended practices, States were urged for the first time, in Assembly Resolution A39-22 adopted in 2016, to either comply with recommended practices or file a difference with ICAO. Although this Resolution clearly goes beyond Article 38 of the Convention, it should be regarded as **policy guidance for States**. International standards and procedures, on the other hand, shall be followed unless a given State has notified a departure by 'filing a difference'.[214] Therefore, Articles 37 and 38 leave only two alternatives to States, either to follow an international standard or procedure or to immediately file a difference once the standard or procedure has become effective. Under the policy guidance of Assembly Resolution A39-22, the same applies with respect to recommended practices.

109. In the Annexes to the Convention international standards are **visually distinguished** from recommended practices.[215] While the main body of each of the Annexes will typically consist of international standards, recommended practices will be clearly marked as such and printed in italics.[216] Furthermore, international Procedures for Air Navigation Services – (PANS)[217] are published separately from SARPs but are legally and in practice treated on a similar footing as standards.

110. An **'international standard'** in the sense of Articles 37, 38 and 54 is defined as 'any specification for physical characteristics, configuration, material, performance, personnel or procedure, the uniform application of which is recognized as necessary for the safety or regularity of international air navigation and to

---

211. Article 38, second sentence, of the Convention.
212. Article 38, last sentence, of the Convention.
213. *See* the definition of 'recommended practice', *infra* (para. 110); Art. 38 mentions only international standards and procedures, but not recommended practices in relation to the obligation to immediately file a difference.
214. *See* Assembly Resolution A39-22, Associated Practices, paras 7 and 8; previously A38-11, A37-15, A36-13 and A35-14, Appendix D, Associated Practice 3.
215. *See* the Foreword to the Annexes, where this difference is highlighted, e.g., Doc. AN 1, Foreword.
216. While standards are shown as consecutive paragraphs in normal print, recommended practices are usually designated as such and are printed in italics. *See* Doc. AN 1.
217. *See* in particular the PANS-OPS, Doc. 8168; PANS/ATM, Doc. 4444; PANS/ABC, Doc. 8400; and the SUPPS, Doc. 7030.

which contracting States will conform in accordance with the Convention; in the event of impossibility of compliance, notification to the Council is compulsory under Article 38 of the Convention'.[218]

111. A **'recommended practice'** in the sense of Articles 37 and 54 is defined as 'any specification for physical characteristics, configuration, material, performance, personnel or procedure, the uniform application of which is recognized as desirable in the interest of safety, regularity or efficiency of international air navigation and to which contracting States will endeavour to conform in accordance with the Convention'.[219]

112. SARPs and PANS have become **essential tools for the planning processes** of ICAO, both at the global and regional levels, as well as for the planning and implementation processes of Member States. They are amended as necessary to reflect changing requirements and techniques and thus, *inter alia*, to provide a sound basis for regional planning and the provision of facilities and services.[220] Nevertheless, a high degree of stability shall be maintained to enable the Member States to maintain stability in their national regulations. According to the respective provisions of ICAO Assembly Resolution A38-11 paragraph 9, 'no Annex or PANS document shall be amended more frequently than once per calendar year' and under paragraph 3 of the Resolution, 'amendments shall be limited to those significant to safety, regularity and efficiency and editorial amendments shall be made only if essential'.[221]

113. As regards the substance of SARPs and PANS, reference is made to Chapter 3, §2 III and IV, §3, and Chapter 5, §3 below.

II. Law-Making: Preparation of International Conventions and Protocols

114. **Law-making** is one of the important functions of the Organization. The Convention on International Civil Aviation does not specifically mention any competences of the Organization for the **development and adoption of international conventions or protocols in the field of air law**. From a strictly legal viewpoint, the adoption of such conventions or protocols is an act of the participating Member States, not of organs of the Organization, since the Diplomatic conferences which adopt them, though convened under the auspices of the Organization, are sovereign bodies not forming part of the Organization itself.[222] The conventions and protocols

218. ICAO Assembly Resolution A36-13: *Consolidated statement of continuing ICAO polices and associated practices relating specifically to air navigation*, Appendix A. In Assembly Resolutions A41-10, A40-4, A39-22, A38-11 and A37-15, Appendix A no longer contains this definition.
219. *Ibid.* (n. 218).
220. Assembly Resolutions A38-11 and A38-12, Resolutions adopted at the 38th session of the Assembly, Doc. 10022.
221. *Ibid.* (n. 219), *see* ICAO Doc. 10022.
222. *See* on this matter generally S. Rosenne, Conferences and Congresses, International, in R. Bernhardt (ed.) *Encyclopedia supra* (Ch. 1, n. 9), Vol. I (1992), pp. 739 et seq.

adopted are subsequently signed and ratified by the participating Member States; once ratified, the role of the Organization is usually limited to the function of a depositary of the respective legal instrument as a result of the final clauses of the instrument specifically entrusting the Organization with this function.[223]

115. Nevertheless, it has been the long-standing practice of the Organization to initiate, develop and prepare new international air law instruments whenever a need for such instruments is felt among its Member States.

116. Assembly Resolution A1-46, which was adopted at the first ICAO Assembly in 1947, provided for the creation of the **ICAO Legal Committee** as a 'permanent body of the Organization constituted by the Assembly'. The constitution of the Legal Committee was set out in the Annex to Resolution A1-46.[224] The Legal Committee was tasked with giving legal advice to the Organization and its bodies, as well as with the **development of international air law**. For the purposes of this latter function Assembly Resolution A1-48, also adopted at the First Session of the Assembly,[225] set out the procedure for the development and approval of draft conventions in the field of air law.[226] Essentially, the **procedure for the approval of draft conventions** involves the following steps[227] (*see also* above, Chapter 2, §2, IV):

(1) study of the problems involved by the Secretariat, assisted if necessary by a Secretariat Study Group;
(2) submission of the Secretariat's Report, including if possible a draft text, to the Legal Committee or a Rapporteur, or both;
(3) discussion of the Report of the Secretariat by the Legal Committee, which may appoint a Sub-Committee, and if it considers the draft text mature enough, approval and submission of its report to the Council;
(4) discussion of the Report of the Legal Committee by the Council which may take such action as it deems fit, including circulating the draft text to contracting States and international organizations for comment within a period of not less than four months;
(5) convening, if appropriate, of a Diplomatic Conference by the Council, the opening of which shall not be less than six months from the date of transmission of the draft text to the Contracting States.

---

223. *See*: *Legal Committee – Constitution – Procedure for Approval of Draft Conventions – Rules of Procedure*, Doc. 7669 – LC/139/6 (2018).
224. This constitution was later revised by Resolution A7-5, and subsequent amendments, ICAO Doc. 10140, part I. *See also ibid.* (n. 222).
225. Assembly Resolution A1-46; *see also* Assembly Resolution A7-5, operating clause 2. Resolution A1-46 was later revised in 1953 by Resolution A7-5, and Resolution A1-48 was replaced by Resolution A7-6 and later superseded by Resolution A31–15.
226. Resolution A7-6 was consolidated at the 31st Session of the Assembly into Resolution A31-15: *Consolidated statement of continuing ICAO policies in the legal field*, Doc. 9848, part V and became Appendix B of Resolution A31-15.
227. *See* Resolution A31-15, Appendix 3.

117. It should be noted that for the **adoption of a text by the Diplomatic Conference**, at least a two-thirds majority is required in line with the Rules of Procedure for Diplomatic Conferences.[228]

118. On the basis of the procedure for the development and approval of draft conventions (Resolutions A1-48, A7-6 and A 31-15), the Organization has developed a large number of **international air law instruments,** which were subsequently adopted by a Diplomatic Conference, in particular, the following:

(1) Convention on the International Recognition of Rights in Aircraft, signed in Geneva on 19 June 1948.
(2) Convention on Damage Caused by Foreign Aircraft to Third Parties on the Surface, signed in Rome on 7 October 1952.
(3) Protocol to Amend the Convention for the Unification of Certain Rules Relating to International Carriage by Air, Signed in Warsaw on 12 October 1929 and done in The Hague on 28 September 1955.
(4) Convention, Supplementary to the Warsaw Convention, for the Unification of Certain Rules Relating to International Carriage by Air Performed by a Person Other than the Contracting Carrier, signed in Guadalajara on 18 September 1961.
(5) Convention on Offences and Certain Other Acts Committed on Board Aircraft, signed in Tokyo on 14 September 1963.
(6) Convention for the Suppression of Unlawful Seizure of Aircraft, signed in The Hague on 16 December 1970.
(7) Protocol to Amend the Convention for the Unification of Certain Rules Relating to International Carriage by Air signed in Warsaw on 12 October 1929 as Amended by the Protocol done in The Hague on 28 September 1955 and signed in Guatemala City on 8 March 1971.
(8) Convention for the Suppression of Unlawful Acts Against the Safety of Civil Aviation, signed in Montreal on 23 September 1971.
(9) Additional Protocol No. 1 to Amend the Convention for the Unification of Certain Rules Relating to International Carriage by Air signed in Warsaw on 12 October 1929 and signed in Montreal on 15 September 1975.
(10) Additional Protocol No. 2 to Amend the Convention for the Unification of Certain Rules relating to International Carriage by Air signed in Warsaw on 12 October 1929 as Amended by the Protocol done in The Hague on 28 September 1955 and signed in Montreal on 25 September 1975.
(11) Additional Protocol No. 3 to Amend the Convention for the Unification of Certain Rules relating to International Carriage by Air signed in Warsaw on 12

228. *See,* e.g., Rule 20(1) of the Rules of Procedure for the International Conference on Air Law, Montreal, 10–28 May 1999, in: *Proceedings of the Conference*, Doc. 9775, Vol II-*Documents*, DCW Doc. No. 2, dated 9/11/98. These 'Provisional Rules of Procedure' were adopted without change as the definitive Rules of Procedure of the Conference at its first meeting. They follow a model draft text, called 'Provisional Rules of Procedure', which is used for all Diplomatic Conferences convened under the auspices of ICAO. *See* Doc. 9775, Vol. II, DCW Doc. No. 2.

October 1929 as Amended by the Protocols done in The Hague on 28 September 1955 and in Guatemalan City on 8 March 1971 and signed in Montreal on 25 September 1975.

(12) Montreal Protocol No. 4 to Amend the Convention for the Unification of Certain Rules Relating to International Carriage by Air signed in Warsaw on 12 October 1929 as Amended by the Protocol done in The Hague on 28 September 1955 and signed in Montreal on 25 September 1975.

(13) Protocol to Amend the Convention on Damage Caused by Foreign Aircraft to Third Parties on the Surface signed in Rome on 7 October 1952 and in Montreal on 23 September 1978.

(14) Protocol for the Suppression of Unlawful Acts of Violence at Airports Serving International Civil Aviation, Supplementary to the Convention for the Suppression of Unlawful Acts against the Safety of Civil Aviation done in Montreal on 23 September 1971 and signed in Montreal on 24 February 1988.

(15) Convention on the Marking of Plastic Explosives for the Purpose of Detection, done in Montreal on 1 March 1991.

(16) Convention for the Unification of Certain Rules for International Carriage by Air, done in Montreal on 28 May 1999.

(17) Convention on International Interests in Mobile Equipment, signed in Cape Town on 16 November 2001.

(18) Protocol to the Convention on International Interests in Mobile Equipment on Matters Specific to Aircraft Equipment, signed in Cape Town on 16 November 2001.

(19) Convention on Compensation for Damage to Third Parties, Resulting from Acts of Unlawful Interference Involving Aircraft, done in Montreal on 2 May 2009.

(20) Convention on Compensation for Damage Caused by Aircraft to Third Parties, done in Montreal on 2 May 2009.

(21) Convention on the Suppression of Unlawful Acts Relating to International Civil Aviation, done in Beijing on 10 September 2010.

(22) Protocol Supplementary to the Convention for the Suppression of Unlawful Seizure of Aircraft, done in Beijing on 10 September 2010.

(23) Protocol to Amend the Convention on Offences and Certain Other Acts Committed on Board Aircraft, signed in Montreal on 4 April 2014.

For nearly all of these international air law instruments, the Organization serves as a depositary.

119. Depositary functions should be distinguished from registration functions. Under Article 83 of the Convention, the Organization, and more specifically the Council, is entrusted with the task to **register all aeronautical agreements and arrangements** submitted to it by contracting States and to render them public as soon as possible. In accordance with Articles 81 and 83 of the Convention, contracting States shall submit all aeronautical agreements or arrangements they conclude, whether bilateral or multilateral, to the Organization for registration. It is also a requirement that any such agreements or arrangements be 'not inconsistent' with the Convention.[229]

120. Furthermore, under Article 83bis of the Convention, **agreements or arrangements for the transfer of certain functions and duties** in connection with the lease, charter or interchange of aircraft shall not become effective until they are registered and rendered public by the Organization.[230]

121. On the basis of Articles 83 and 83bis, the Organization has registered close to 6,000 aeronautical agreements and arrangements.[231] It publishes them electronically on its public website[232] which also permits Member States to register their aeronautical agreements or arrangements.

III. Judicial and Quasi-judicial Functions

122. Under Chapter XVIII of the Convention, the Council is entrusted with certain **judicial functions** regarding disputes between contracting States; such judicial functions of the Council are also foreseen in certain other multilateral and bilateral agreements, in particular in the International Air Services Transit Agreement and the International Air Transport Agreement.[233]

123. These judicial functions should be distinguished from quasi-judicial functions under Article 54 (n), 54 (j) and 54 (k) of the Convention,[234] *see* below, Chapter 2 §3 III. B. (paragraphs 128–130).

229. *See* the wording of Art. 83, first sentence, of the Convention: 'Subject to the provisions of the preceding Article, any contracting State may make arrangements not inconsistent with the provisions of this Convention.'

230. *See* Art. 83*bis*, para. b) of the Convention. On this matter, *see Guidance on the Implementation of Article 83bis of the Convention on International Civil Aviation*, ICAO Circular 295 (2003); and the *Manual on the Implementation of Article 83 bis of the Convention on International Civil Aviation,* Doc. 10059 (1st ed. 2017).

231. As of February 2021.

232. *See* https://dna.icao.int/WAGMAR; preexisting registrations may also be accessed through http://cfapp.icao.int/dagmar/main.cfm?UserLang=_e Treaty Collection, Aeronautical Agreements ('DAGMAR'). The former hardcopy publication ICAO Doc. 9511: *Database of the World's Air Services Agreements* has been discontinued.

233. *See* Art. II s. 1 of the *International Air Services Transit Agreement*, Doc. 7500, and a similar dispute settlement clause is also contained in the *International Air Transport Agreement*, 171 *UNTS* 387, Art. 4 s. 2. Other international instruments which entrust the Council with judicial functions are: *Convention on Damage Caused by Foreign Aircraft to Third Parties on the Surface, (Rome, 1952), Multilateral Agreement on Commercial Rights of Non-Scheduled Air Services in Europe (Paris, 1956), Agreement on the Joint Financing of Certain Air Navigation Services in Greenland (1956) as amended in 1982 and 2008*, and the *Agreement on the Joint Financing of Certain Air Navigation Services in Iceland (1956) as amended in 1982 and 2008.*

234. *See also* Buergenthal, *supra* Ch. 2, n. 71, at pp. 123 et seq.

A. *Judicial Functions under Chapter XVIII: Disputes and Default*

124. Article 84 of the Convention provides:

> Settlement of disputes
>
> *If any disagreement between two or more contracting States relating to the interpretation or application of this Convention and its Annexes cannot be settled by negotiation, it shall, on the application of any State concerned in the disagreement, be decided by the Council.*

125. The procedure to be applied by the Council in hearing the dispute is laid down in the **Rules of Procedure for the Settlement of Differences.**[235] Under these Rules, the Council functions as a judicial body on the basis of formal written submissions of the parties which must be in conformity with the requirements of the Rules (memorials and counter-memorials)[236] and on the basis of formal oral hearings of the parties which are also governed by the Rules.[237] It shall, before proceeding to reach a decision, **attempt to bring about a settlement** between the parties through inducing direct negotiations or through conciliation.[238] For this purpose, the Council may appoint a **Conciliator.** Only if these attempts to bring about a settlement between the parties fail, shall the Council proceed to give judgment.

126. In accordance with Article 84 of the Convention, any such **decision of the Council may be appealed**, either to an ad-hoc arbitral tribunal[239] or to the **International Court of Justice (ICJ).**[240] In case of a lack of agreement on an ad-hoc tribunal and non-acceptance of the jurisdiction of the ICJ, a special arbitral tribunal set up under Article 85 will hear the appeal. The decision of an ad-hoc arbitral tribunal, of the ICJ, or of a special arbitral tribunal under Article 85 shall be final and binding.[241]

127. In application of these provisions, the Council has dealt with the following **disputes under Chapter XVIII:**

---

235. ICAO Doc. 7782/2. These Rules of Procedure were adopted in 1957 and revised in 1975. As a result of a decision of the Legal Committee taken at its 37th session in 2017, work to update the Rules is currently ongoing (since 2018) by the *Working Group for the Review of the ICAO Rules for the Settlement of Differences*, which reports to the Legal Committee.
236. Articles 2 (c)–(g) and 4 of the *Rules of Procedure for the Settlement of Differences*, *ibid.* (n. 234).
237. *See* Art. 11 of the Rules of Procedure, *ibid.*
238. Articles 6 and 14 of the Rules of Procedure, *ibid.*
239. This option has so far not been applied in practice.
240. In the case *Pakistan v. India* (1971), India appealed to the ICJ against the decision of the Council to reject the Preliminary Objections of India, in which India had challenged the jurisdiction of the Council. *See*: *Appeal relating to the Jurisdiction of the ICAO Council*, Judgment, ICJ Reports (1972), 46–179; ICJ Pleadings, *Appeal Relating to the Jurisdiction of the ICAO Council; see also infra.*
241. *See* Art. 86, third sentence, of the Convention. *See also* Art. 19 of the *Rules of Procedure for the Settlement of Differences*, Doc. 7782/2.

(1) ***India v. Pakistan (1952)***[242] regarding the legality of a prohibited zone established by Pakistan, under Articles 5, 6 and 9 of the Convention. The dispute was settled through direct negotiations between the parties induced by the Council.
(2) ***UK v. Spain (1967)***[243] regarding the legality of a prohibited zone established by Spain in the vicinity of Gibraltar airport under Article 9 (a) of the Convention. The dispute was deferred *sine die* and subsequently settled by direct negotiation.
(3) ***Pakistan v. India (1971)***[244] regarding the suspension of flights of Pakistani aircraft over Indian territory, based on Article 5 of the Convention. India submitted preliminary objections against the jurisdiction of the Council, which were rejected by the Council. India appealed to the ICJ, which confirmed the Council's decision. The parties thereafter jointly suspended the proceedings before the Council and settled the dispute through direct negotiations.
(4) ***Cuba v. United States (1996)***[245] regarding the denial by the US of rights of overflight for Cuban aircraft engaged in scheduled flights between Cuba and Canada. The Council, after hearing the parties' submissions, appointed its President as Conciliator.[246] As a result of the conciliation, the parties reached a settlement which was registered with the Council, and which provided for overflight rights for Cuban aircraft subject to certain restrictions.
(5) ***United States v. Fifteen Member States of the European Union (2000)***[247] regarding the legality of the so-called hushkit Regulation of the EU[248] under the Convention and related provisions. The fifteen EU Member States submitted preliminary objections to the jurisdiction of the Council, which were rejected by the Council. After hearing the parties on the substance, the Council appointed its President as Conciliator.[249] As a result of the conciliation, the 'hushkit' Regulation was repealed and replaced by an EC Council Directive acceptable to the parties.[250] The case was thereupon settled and the settlement was registered with the Council.[251]

---

242. *Report of the Council* 1952, ICAO Doc. 7367, A7-P/1, p. 74–76 (1953); ICAO Doc. C-WP/1169 (1952); ICAO Council, 16th Session, Doc. 7291, C/845, p. 11 (1952); Doc. 7328 (C/853), 129; C-WP/1341 (1952). For the settlement between the parties, *see* Council, 18th Session, Doc. 7361 (C/858), 15 et seq.
243. *See Annual Report of the Council – 1967*, ICAO Doc. 8724 (1968), pp. 116 et seq.; A16-P/3.
244. *See* on this matter *ICJ Reports* (1972), *supra* n. 240; K. Hailbronner, *Jurisdiction of the ICAO Council Case*, in: R. Bernhardt (ed.), *Encyclopedia, supra* Ch. 1, n. 9 Vol. III (1997) pp. 62 et seq. with further references.
245. *See* Decision of the Council, C-DEC 154/16; C-WP 10864 (Restricted); C/DEC 149/7; C-DEC 150/17; C-DEC 152/14 and C-DEC 153/14.
246. C-DEC 149/7 and Art. 14, paras 2 and 3 of the *Rules for the Settlement of Differences,* Doc. 7782/2; *see also* C-DEC 150/17, C-DEC 152/14 and C-DEC 153/14.
247. *See* C-DEC 170/16; C-WP/12075, C-DEC 169/11, C-DEC 166/12 and C-DEC 161/6.
248. Regulation (EC) No. 925/1999, OJ L 115, pp. 1–4 (4 May 1999).
249. *See* C-DEC 161/6; PRES AK/823, dated 11 Jun. 2002; *see* the progress reports on the conciliation C-DEC 163/17; 164/11; 168/5 and 169/11.
250. EC Council Directive DIR (EC) 2002/30/EC, OJ L 85, pp. 40–46 (28 Mar. 2002).
251. *See* C-MIN 170/16; C-WP/12075; C-DEC 170/16. For the revised EC Council Directive, *see* DIR (EC) 2002/30/EC.

(6) ***Brazil v. United States (2016)*** arising from a 2006 mid-air collision near Matupá, Brazil, between a B 737-8EH operated by Brazilian airline Gol on its domestic flight 1907 and a US-registered Embraer Legacy 600 business jet on a privately operated flight. All Embraer occupants survived, while all 154 passengers and crew of the Gol B 737-8EH perished. The complaint by Brazil brought before the Council in December 2016 alleged failure by the US authorities to assist Brazilian authorities in criminal proceedings against the two US pilots of the Embraer business jet, who had been convicted *in absentia* in October 2012 by a Brazilian criminal court.[252] The United States raised a preliminary objection against the jurisdiction of the Council, which was dismissed by the Council on 23 June 2017.[253] The Council also initiated negotiations between Brazil and the United States by inviting its President to provide good offices as Conciliator, and in early 2021 such negotiations were still ongoing.

(7) ***Qatar v. Bahrain, Egypt, Saudi Arabia and the UAE (Application A); Qatar v. Bahrain, Egypt, and the UAE (Application B) (2017)*** arising from the June 2017 closure of airspace of the four respondent States for aircraft registered in Qatar as part of a larger political and diplomatic dispute.[254] Application A alleged breach of the Convention on International Civil Aviation, while Application B alleged breach of the International Air Services Transit Agreement. The respondent States raised Preliminary Objections to the jurisdiction of the Council in relation to both applications, which the Council dismissed on 29 June 2018.[255] In July 2018, the respondent States appealed against this decision to the ICJ which on 14 July 2020 rendered two judgments dismissing the appeal.[256] Since that time, negotiations between the parties have been held

252. It had been found that the Embraer jet's transponder and collision avoidance system (TCAS) had been turned off at the time of the accident: Aide-Memoire of Brazil in the Dispute *Brazil v. United States* dated 30 May 2017. *See also* ICAO Doc.SG2364/17 dated 24 May 2017 transmitting the comments of Brazil in response to the Statement of preliminary objection of the United States.
253. Decision of the Council dated 23 Jun. 2017, ICAO Doc. C 211/10.
254. The respondent States alleged that Qatar had failed to abide by its commitments in the Riyadh-Agreement to cease to actively support and finance terrorism in the region. As a result, they severed diplomatic relations, closed their land borders with Qatar, closed their airspace to Qatari aircraft, and expelled many Qatari citizens from their territory. *See Statement of the Kingdom of Bahrain on the Severance of Diplomatic Relations with the State of Qatar* (5 Jun. 2017), http://www.mofa.gov.bh/Default.aspx?tabid=7824&language=en-US&ItemId=7474.; KINGDOM OF SAUDI ARABIA, MINISTRY OF FOREIGN AFFAIRS, *Kingdom of Saudi Arabia Severs Diplomatic and Consular Relations with Qatar* (5 Jun. 2017), http://www.mofa.gov.sa/sites/mofaen/ServicesAndInformation/news/MinistryNews/Pages/ ArticleID201765134958689.aspx.; UAE, Ministry of Foreign Affairs & Int'l Cooperation, UAE Supports *Statements of Kingdom of Bahrain and Kingdom of Saudi Arabia on Qatar* (5 Jun. 2017), https://www.mofa.gov.ae/EN/MediaCenter/News/Pages/05-06-2017-UAE-Qatar.aspx; EGYPT, MINISTRY OF FOREIGN AFFAIRS, Declaration of the Arab Republic of Egypt (5 Jun. 2017), https://www.facebook.com/MFAEgypt/posts/1521555834583024.
255. Decisions of the Council, C-DEC 214/11, Appendices A and B.
256. ICJ Judgments of 14 Jul. 2020, *Appeal Relating To the Jurisdiction of the ICAO Council Under Article 84 of The Convention on International Civil Aviation (Bahrain, Egypt, Saudi Arabia and United Arab Emirates v. Qatar*); and *Appeal Relating to the Jurisdiction of the ICAO Council Under Article II, Section 2, of the 1944 International Air Services Transit Agreement (Bahrain, Egypt And United Arab Emirates v. Qatar)*, https://www.icj-cij.org/public/files/case-related/174/174-20200714-JUD-01-00-EN.pdf.

with the support of the Council and assisted by the mediation by the Emir of Kuwait, which resulted in a settlement between the parties in January 2021 lifting the airspace closure, and in a decision in March 2021 to discontinue the proceedings before the Council.

(8) ***Australia and the Netherlands v. Russian Federation (2022)*** arising from the shoot down of Malaysia Airlines Flight MH17 in 2014. The flight crashed in eastern Ukraine as a result of the shoot down by a missile while on its way from Amsterdam to Kuala Lumpur. All of the 283 passengers and 15 crew on board perished in the crash, of whom 196 were Dutch citizens and 38 were Australians. After a detailed investigation, both Australia and the Netherlands took the view that Russia bears international responsibility for the crash. It occurred in eastern Ukraine during the early days of the conflict between Ukraine and Russia in July 2014, and both applicants claimed that the crash occurred as a result of a Russian Buk missile being fired by two Russians and a Ukrainian separatist using Russian equipment in the rebel-held portion of eastern Ukraine. The case was filed with the Council in April 2022.

B. *Quasi-judicial Functions of the Council*

128. Under **Article 54 (n)**, the Council 'shall consider any matter relating to the Convention which any Contracting State refers to it'. From time to time, contracting States make written submissions to the Council in which they complain about other contracting States and **request the Council to settle the dispute or difference.** Unless such complaints are made expressly under Article 84 and follow the formalities of the 'Rules for the Settlement of Differences',[257] such complaints are usually handled as referrals under Article 54 (n). This means *inter alia* that the **Rules of Procedure for the Council**[258] apply instead of the Rules for the Settlement of Differences[259] which apply only to formal disputes. Consequently, the Council will hear such cases in a **quasi-judicial capacity**, but without the procedures and legal formalities foreseen in the 'Rules for the Settlement of Differences'. The Council will invite the parties to the complaint to be present in the Council, to make written and/or oral statements, and will then discuss the matter in the presence of the parties.[260] The Council may, as a result of the discussions, express views, make statements, issue recommendations, or take decisions in the form of a Council Resolution as may be appropriate under the Rules of Procedure for the Council.[261]

257. ICAO Doc. 7782/2.
258. ICAO Doc. 7559/10. It is submitted that the procedure under the *Rules of Procedure for the Council*, which allows for greater flexibility from a procedural viewpoint, is generally better tailored to such 'non-formal disputes' due to the political role which the Council plays in relation to the contracting States of ICAO.
259. ICAO Doc. 7782/2.
260. Article 53 of the Convention, Art. 32 of the *Rules of Procedure for the Council*, *ibid.* (n. 157).
261. Doc. 7559/10.

129. In this quasi-judicial capacity, the Council has dealt with **numerous complaints**, e.g., the *Republic of the Congo v. Rwanda and Uganda*[262] (State hijacking of civil aircraft and other matters); *PLO v. Israel*[263] (destruction of Gaza Airport); *Cuba v. U.S.*[264] (violation of Cuban airspace); *Samoa and Tonga v. Fiji* (amendment to the common Nadi/Auckland oceanic FIR boundary);[265] *UAE v. Qatar*[266] (serious 'airprox' incidents between Qatari military and UAE civil aircraft); and a number of other cases.

When a contracting State is alleged to have committed an **infraction to the Convention** or to have failed to carry out a recommendation or determination of the Council, complaints may be brought under Article 54(j) or (k) of the Convention. According to a related study of the Secretariat, 'infractions' in the sense of the Convention are limited to particularly grave breaches of the Convention.[267] At the 41st Assembly session in 2022, three resolutions were adopted which condemned certain actions of **Belarus**[268] the **Russian Federation**[269] **and North Korea**[270] and stated that they were infractions of the Chicago Convention. As against Belarus, **Resolution A41-1** condemned the actions of the State against Ryanair Flight FR4978 in 2021[271] as an infraction of Article 4 of the Chicago Convention.[272] The report of the ICAO Fact-Finding Investigation Team (FFIT) had found that the safety of Ryanair Flight FR4978 was endangered when a false bomb threat was communicated to the flight crew, on the instructions of senior government officials of Belarus.[273] **Resolution 41-2** condemned the actions of the Russian Federation in violating the sovereign airspace of Ukraine, wrongfully re-registering certain aircraft in its own registry[274] and using such aircraft without valid certificates of airworthiness,[275] constituting infractions of Articles 1, 18, 19, 29 and 31 of the Chicago Convention.[276] **Resolution 41-3** strongly condemned the actions of North

262. Council – 155th Session, C-DEC 155/1, para. 13; 156th Session, C-DEC 156/10; C-MIN 156/10; Memorandum AK/639; Council Declaration adopted on 10 Mar. 1999.
263. Council – 165th Session, C-MIN 165/9; C-WP/11790 and 11791 revised; *see also* AVSEC-Conf/02-IP/29.
264. Council – 159th Session, C-MIN 159/1; C-DEC 159/1; *see also* the Council Resolution adopted on 27 Jun. 1996, C-DEC 148/20; C-MIN 159/1, paras 28 et seq.
265. *See* C-WP/11723, C-WP/11427, C-DEC 161/11, C-DEC 163/2, C-DEC 163/6 and C-DEC 164/5.
266. *See* C-WP/14777 restricted (1/5/2018): *Request of the UAE for the consideration by the ICAO Council under Article 54 n) of the Chicago Convention.*
267. *See*: *Infractions of the Convention on International Civil Aviation*, C-WP/11186, Council Working Paper submitted by the Secretary General at the request of the Council (C-DEC 156/7, 158/1).
268. Resolution A41-1: *Infraction of the Convention on International Civil Aviation by the Republic of Belarus, ICAO Doc.10184.*
269. Resolution A41-2: *Infractions of the Convention on International Civil Aviation by the Russian Federation;* also *see* A41-WP/430.
270. Resolution A41-3: *Unannounced missile launches by the Democratic People's Republic of Korea.*
271. A41-1, clause 2.
272. A41-1, clauses 1 & 4.
273. A41-1, clause 2.
274. A41-2, clause 1.
275. A41-2, clause 3.
276. A41-2, clause 2.

Korea in continuing its unannounced ballistic missile launches, thereby seriously endangering international civil aviation and constituting an infraction of the Chicago Convention under Article 54 k).[277]

IV. Airports and Air Navigation Facilities (Chapter XV)

130. Under Chapter XV of the Convention, the Organization is vested with important functions for the **improvement of airports and other air navigation facilities**. These provisions allow in particular the joint financing of such facilities to remedy shortcomings.[278]

131. Article 69 provides for the power of the Council, if it finds that airports or air navigation facilities are not reasonably adequate, to **recommend means by which the situation may be remedied**. The Council may under Article 70 conclude an arrangement with the State concerned to remedy the situation, the cost of which may be borne by the State, or at the State's request, partly or wholly by the Council. Such financing arrangements are spelt out in more detail in Article 71, which provides that the Council may, at the contracting State's request, agree to provide, man, maintain and administer any or all of the airports and other air navigation facilities required in the respective State's territory and may specify just and reasonable charges for their use. Articles 72–76 deal with financial and administrative details of such involvement of the Council, and Article 74 deals specifically with technical assistance which the Council may provide under the arrangements with the respective contracting State.

132. In practice, the concept behind these provisions has been applied in the area of **'Joint Financing' of certain air navigation facilities** through a large number of technical cooperation projects. In one instance, namely the Somalia Project, the Council decided that the project would itself provide, man, maintain and administer the air navigation facilities in the country concerned[279] in line with the concept of Article 71, on a temporary basis.

133. In the case of the **'Joint Financing Agreements'**, concluded and administered under the auspices of the Council, the contracting States parties to the Agreements, finance jointly the air navigation facilities and services in Denmark and

277. A41-3, operating clauses 1 and 3. The title of the resolution does not mention the term infraction, however clause 1 does.

278. The joint financing activities of the Organization, in particular the Joint Financing Agreements, are based on Ch. XV of the Convention. *See* the Joint Financing Agreements, Doc. 9585 and 9586. For further details, *see infra*, Ch. 3, §4.

279. *See* ICAO Doc. 9732, Ch. 5, with reference to the 'Civil Aviation Caretaker Authority' in Somalia set up through a large-scale ICAO Technical Cooperation Project.

Iceland for the North Atlantic routes,[280] but these services are provided by the national administrations of Denmark and Iceland. Each contracting State party to the Agreement contributes financially in proportion to the number of flights of its airlines on the routes involved.[281] The Agreements operate on a special budget, administered by the Organization on behalf of the parties to the Agreements, separately from other budgets of the Organization.[282]

134. From 1998 onwards, the **ICAO Universal Safety Oversight Audit Programme (USOAP)**[283] has uncovered a large number of deficiencies in the safety of air navigation facilities and airports of contracting States. In many cases, the deficiencies are addressed by follow-up action by which Corrective Action Plans, agreed upon between the audited State and ICAO, play an important role. Technical Cooperation projects, financed by the respective State or by multilateral agencies, assist States in this regard; reference is made to Chapter 3 §6 (Technical Cooperation) below.

V. Other Competences

135. Under Chapter XIII of the Convention, the Organization is vested with certain **treaty-making powers.** In particular, Article 64 empowers it to enter into appropriate arrangements with the UN. A formal agreement on cooperation and assistance was concluded between the UN and ICAO dated 13 May 1947.

136. Article 65 of the Convention empowers the Organization to enter into **arrangements with other international bodies** and a large number of such arrangements have, in fact, been concluded.[284] Article 66 provides that the Organization shall also carry out the functions placed upon it by the International Air Services Transit Agreement[285] and by the International Air Transport Agreement.[286] These functions involve essentially oversight functions of the Council with regard to charges imposed on foreign aircraft for the use of airports and air navigation services, and related dispute settlement functions.[287]

137. Article 67 gives the Organization, and more specifically the Council, the **power to collect traffic reports, cost statistics and financial statements** from contracting States regarding their international airlines. The Organization consequently

280. *See Agreement on the Joint Financing of Certain Air Navigation Services in Greenland (1956)* ICAO Doc. 9585, *as amended in 1982 and 2008*, and the *Agreement on the Joint Financing of Certain Air Navigation Services in Iceland (1956)* ICAO Doc. 9586 *as amended in 1982 and 2008*; *infra.*, Ch. 3, §4.
281. Annex III, s. III of the Danish Joint Financing Agreement, Doc. 9585, 17th ed.; Annex III, s. III of the Icelandic Joint Financing agreement, Doc. 9586, 17th ed.
282. *See* Doc. 9585, Annex III, and Doc. 9586, Annex III.
283. *See infra*, Ch. 3 §9.
284. *See infra*, Ch. 6, §2 to §4.
285. ICAO Doc. 7500.
286. 171 *UNTS* 387 et seq.
287. *See supra*, Ch. 2 §3, III and IV.

collects, processes and publishes yearly a large amount of statistical data regarding the operation of international air services.[288] The collection, processing and publication of such data may also be carried out on the basis of Article 54(i) of the Convention for the advancement of air navigation and the operation of international air services.

138. In certain cases, the Organization is also vested with **powers of investigation**. Under Article 55(e), the Council may at the request of any contracting State investigate any situation which may appear to present avoidable obstacles to the development of international air navigation. In a number of cases, notably in cases of a shoot-down of civil aircraft, the Council decided at the request of one or more contracting States to carry out an investigation. Examples are the investigation by ICAO into the shoot-down of the Korean Airlines flight KAL 007 by Soviet military aircraft[289] and the investigation by ICAO into the shoot-down of two US civil aircraft by Cuban military aircraft.[290] Such investigations have international status and should be distinguished from national investigations carried out under Annex 13.

139. Finally, under Article 55(c) and (d), the Organization has powers to **'conduct research into all aspects of air transport and air navigation**, which are of international importance' and to communicate the results to contracting States, as well as to 'study any matters affecting the organization and operation of international air transport, including the international ownership and operation of international air services on trunk routes'.

288. *See*: ICAO *Civil Aviation Statistics*, available online at http://icaodata.com.

289. *Report of the ICAO fact-finding investigation into the shooting-down of Korean Airlines flight 007 by Soviet military aircraft on 1 Sep. 1983* (unpublished); Report of the President of the Council to the Assembly, Doc. A24-WP/49.

290. *Report of the ICAO fact-finding investigation regarding the shooting-down of two U.S.-registered private civil aircraft by Cuban military aircraft on 24 Feb. 1996*, C-WP/10412 Restricted (Interim Report); C-MIN 148/1 (Closed); C-WP/10441 Restricted (Final Report); Information Paper No.1; Corrigendum to C-WP/10441.

Chapter 3. Activities

§1. Constitutional and General Policy Matters

I. Constitutional Amendments

140. Since the inception of ICAO, seventeen **Protocols of Amendment to the Convention** on International Civil Aviation providing for nineteen amendments have been adopted:[291] Of these, two amendments were substantive ones (insertion of Article 3bis and Article 83bis),[292] the others were institutional or procedural in nature.

141. As regards the **appropriateness of amending the Convention**, the Assembly decided early on to take a restrictive approach. In Resolution A4-3, it decided that either one or both of the following conditions for an amendment to the Convention need to be satisfied:[293] (1) it is proved **necessary** by experience; (2) it is demonstrably **desirable or useful.** It also decided that the Council should not initiate any proposal for amendment to the Convention for submission to the Assembly unless, in the opinion of the Council, such amendment is urgent in character.[294] Rather, proposals for amendment of the Convention are basically a matter for the Assembly. Contracting States wishing to propose an amendment should submit such proposal to the Council[295] which shall transmit it to all contracting States for their consideration at least three months before the opening date of the next Assembly. Subsequent to Resolution A4-3, this procedure has been followed in practice with regard to all amendments to the Convention.

142. Amendments to the Convention need to satisfy the **procedural requirements of Article 94 of the Convention**: any proposed amendment must be approved by at least a two-thirds vote of the Assembly. It shall then come into force in States which have ratified such amendment when ratified by the number of contracting States specified by the Assembly, which shall not be less than two-thirds of the total number of contracting States.[296]

---

291. *See supra* Ch. 1, paras 19–24. One of the Protocols, adopted in 1954, provided for three amendments to the Convention.
292. *See supra* Ch. 1, nn. 53 and 55.
293. Assembly Resolution A4-3: *Policy and programme with respect to the amendment of the Convention*, Doc. 9790, p. I-1, operating clause 7.
294. *Ibid.* (n. 282).
295. Resolution A4-3, *ibid.* (n. 282), operating clause 8.
296. This rule raises the question of the legal situation of contracting States which have not ratified amendments of institutional nature, i.e., enlargement of the Council, or enlargement of the Air Navigation Commission vis-à-vis the amended institution. The question may arise whether these States have a right to be a candidate for election to the enlarged body and whether if elected, these States are entitled to be represented on the enlarged body. In the practice of the Organization, both questions are answered in the affirmative. *See* on these issues Buergenthal, *supra.* (Ch. 2, n. 71), pp. 38 et seq.; *Repertory-Guide to the Convention on International Civil Aviation,* 2d ed., Doc. 8900/2, Art. 94 b), Art. 50(a).

143. In most cases, the **Resolution** by which the Assembly approved the respective Amendment under Article 94 set forth the wording of the Protocol of Amendment itself, including its final clauses. The Resolution usually determined that the Protocol shall be signed by the **President of the Assembly and its Secretary General** on behalf of the Assembly and the number of ratifications required for its entry into force (two-thirds).[297] This procedure is unusual from the viewpoint of international treaty law, since the Protocol is not signed by Plenipotentiaries who have submitted their credentials in writing but by the two Principal Officers of the Assembly[298] on the basis of a delegation of authority given in Assembly Resolution A13-1.[299] Furthermore, the adoption of the text occurs not in a formal Diplomatic Conference, but in the Assembly without applying the formal rules on credentials applicable to Plenipotentiaries in a Diplomatic Conference.[300]

144. Nevertheless, the **success of the amendments** speaks for itself. All of the above amendments have entered into force,[301] or in the case of the more recent ones have a reasonable expectation to enter into force[302] despite the high hurdle of the two-thirds requirement.[303] The reduced formality in certain regards in the Assembly

---

297. *See,* e.g., Assembly Resolution A13-1: *Amendment to Article 50 (a) of the Convention increasing the membership of the Council to twenty-seven*; Assembly Resolution A17A-1 (sic): *Amendment to Article 50 (a) of the Convention increasing the membership of the Council to thirty,* Doc. 9790, pp. I-11 et seq.
298. *See,* e.g., Assembly Resolution A13-1, operating clause 3 (a): 'The Protocol shall be signed by the President of the Assembly and its Secretary General.'
299. *Ibid.* (n. 286).
300. Under Rule 6(a) of the Standing Rules of Procedure of the Assembly (ICAO Doc. 7600/5), 'Delegations shall be provided with credentials signed on behalf of the State or Organization concerned, by a person duly authorized thereto … .' Under Rule 6(b), a Credentials Committee shall be established at the beginning of the Session, with the task to examine the credentials and to report to the Assembly. The question who is 'a person duly authorized thereto' may in some cases be open to interpretation. While Art. 7 of the *Vienna Convention on the Law of Treaties* requires that either the Head of State, or the Head of Government, or the Minister of Foreign Affaires signs the credentials of a Plenipotentiary who signs a Treaty on behalf of his State (full powers), the Assembly normally does not involve signing of Treaties. In a number of cases, credentials signed by the Minister of Transport, or the Minister of Aviation, will therefore be accepted by the Credentials Committee of the Assembly. This is in line with Art. 10 of the *Vienna Convention on the Representation of States in their Relations with International Organizations of a Universal Character*, adopted on 14 Mar. 1975 (UN Conference, 4 Feb.–14–Mar. 1975, Official Records, 2 Volumes 1976, not yet entered into force), which permits signing of credentials 'by another competent authority of the sending State' (besides the Head of State, Head of Government or Minister of Foreign Affaires), 'if the rules of the organization so permit'. *See* in this context also Art. 7 para. 2.c) of the *Vienna Convention on the Law of Treaties* relating to adoption of texts of treaties by representatives of States accredited to an international conference or to an international organization.
301. *Supra*, Ch. 3 §1, I., first paragraph; the most recent amendment to enter into force was the *Protocol relating to an Amendment to Article 56 of the Convention on International Civil Aviation*, signed on 6 Oct. 1989, which entered into force on 18 Apr. 2005; ICAO Doc. 9544.
302. Protocol *Amending the Final Clause of the Convention (Arabic text)*, Doc. 9664; and *Protocol Amending the Final Clause of the Convention (Chinese text)*, 9722; *see also* the related Protocols providing for the Authentic Quinquelingual Text, Doc. 9663 and Authentic Six-language Text of the Convention, Doc. 9721.
303. With 193 Member States, the two-thirds requirement amounts now to 129 States.

will not reduce the commitment to subsequently ratify the respective Protocol which States' delegates feel after the adoption of an amendment to the Convention at the Assembly.

II. Relations with Contracting States, International Organizations and Other Bodies

145. Already at its first Assembly the Organization took steps to facilitate **relations with contracting States** which continue to be effective today. In particular, it recommended that contracting States formally designate, within their respective national administration, one or more officials with the specific responsibility of **liaison with ICAO**. Further,[304] it recommended that contracting States second staff of their national administration to ICAO for training and experience purposes.[305] Accordingly, most contracting States have designated national administration staff to ensure liaison with ICAO. They are the front-line recipients of information, reports, documents, invitations to meetings, and State Letters from the Organization by e-mail, through online transmission, or in hard copy. Furthermore, a number of contracting States have also put in place **policies or arrangements for the seconding of national staff to the Organization.**[306] However, while short-term secondment has been accepted fairly frequently by the Organization, medium-term or long-term secondment has been less readily approved in view of the exigencies of Article 59 of the Convention. It provides that the personnel of ICAO shall not seek or receive instructions with regard to the discharge of the responsibilities from any authority external to the Organization: 'Each contracting State undertakes fully to respect the international character of the responsibilities of the personnel and not to seek to influence any of its nationals in the discharge of their responsibilities'. Seconded personnel are more at risk as regards the required neutrality than non-seconded staff; therefore, the Organization has developed a **policy** under which secondment[307] is in principle only acceptable for short-term assignment of experts, subject to certain conditions. Other personnel from contracting States for long-term assignments need to take leave without pay, or sever their employment status, in order to be admissible for service with the Organization.

146. In its relations with contracting States, the Organization accepted, soon after its inception, the **General Convention on the Privileges and Immunities of the Specialized Agencies** adopted on 21 November 1947[308] and in particular its

304. Assembly Resolution A1-14: *Improvement of liaison with contracting States*, operating Clause 2, ICAO Doc. 9848.
305. Assembly Resolution A1-14, *ibid.*, operating Clause 5.
306. For example, by participating in the JPO (Junior Professional Officer) programme and AE (Associate Expert) programme of the UN Common System.
307. *See* Assembly Resolution A1-51: *Personnel policy*, operating clause 3; the personnel policy and procedures on secondment are based on the principles set out therein, ICAO Doc. 9848.
308. 33 *UNTS* (1948), p. 261.

Annex III thereto relating to ICAO.[309] Under the terms of the 1947 Convention, the Organization and the members of its staff are accorded privileges and immunities similar to those granted to the UN and its staff by the related 1946 Convention, including *inter alia* as regards recognizing the staff of ICAO for the use of the UN Laissez Passer for purposes of travel for duty.[310]

147. Consequently, the Organization was authorized in Assembly Resolution A2-25 to conclude a **Supplementary Agreement with the UN** covering the use of the **UN Laissez Passer** by ICAO officials.[311] As not all contracting States have acceded to the 1947 Convention (notably the United States, host state to the UN), the ICAO Assembly at its 26th Session urged all contracting States which have not done so to take steps to become parties to the 1947 Convention.[312]

148. As regards **relations with other public international organizations** (whose members are States or government authorities), the Assembly at its First Session in 1947 laid down a number of policy principles in Assembly Resolution A1-10,[313] which continue to be applicable. It authorized the Council to make appropriate arrangements with public international organizations whose activities affect international civil aviation, particularly with regard to technical collaboration, exchange of information and documents, etc., provided that such arrangements can be implemented without any increase in the approved budget. Further, it provided that such arrangements may preferably be established through informal working arrangements rather than formal agreements wherever practicable.[314] Finally, it requested the Council to report to the next Assembly on the nature and scope of each arrangement entered into.[315] These principles were supplemented by Assembly Resolution A27-17 which provides that the Organization supports the work and activities of any existing or future regional civil aviation body wherever such support is requested by the regional body concerned. They were further supplemented by Assembly Resolution A37-21 endorsing ICAO's Policy and Framework on Regional Cooperation and calling for synergy between ICAO and each regional civil aviation body in accordance with arrangements as reflected by the Memoranda of Cooperation concluded by them, thereby obviating duplication of work. Reference is made to Chapter 6, *infra.*

---

309. Assembly Resolution A2-26: *General Convention on the Privileges and Immunities of the Specialized Agencies and Annex III thereto relating to ICAO*, ICAO Doc. 9790, I-25.
310. Article VIII of the *General Convention on the Privileges and Immunities of the Specialized Agencies* of 1947, *ibid.* (n. 298).
311. Resolution A2-25: *Supplementary Agreement covering the use of the United Nations laissez-passer by ICAO officials,* ICAO Doc. 9790, p. I-32.
312. Resolution A26-3: *Convention on the Privileges and Immunities of the Specialized Agencies*, ICAO Doc. 9790, p. I-26.
313. Resolution A1-10: *Relations with public international organizations*, ICAO Doc. 9790, p. I-30.
314. *See ibid.*, operating clause 2.
315. *Ibid.*, operating clause 3. Regarding regional cooperation, *see also* A39-14, *Regional cooperation and assistance to resolve safety deficiencies, establishing priorities and setting measurable targets,* ICAO Doc. 10075.

149. As regards **relations with private international organizations** (whose members are non-governmental entities), the Assembly laid down policy principles in Resolution A1-11.[316] It authorized the Council to make appropriate arrangements with private international organizations whose activities affect international civil aviation and which have 'a wide and well-established international representation and possess a governing international body having a permanent character and authorized representatives'.[317] Their aims and objectives shall not be in conflict with the general principles laid down in the Convention. The extent of the cooperation provided for by such arrangements shall be governed by the degree to which 'specific matters within the respective responsibilities of the two organizations are of interest to both'.[318] The cooperation may be in the form of exchange of information and documentation, reciprocal representation and participation in the work of technical meetings, committees or working groups, and the participation of any private international organization must necessarily be on a non-voting basis, i.e., participation as an observer.[319] Certain other principles applicable to relations with public international organizations apply here as well, in particular, no increase in the approved budget as a result of the cooperation, informal working arrangements whenever practicable, and reports by the Council to the next Assembly on the nature and scope of any such arrangement.[320] These principles continue to guide the Organization with regard to its present relations with private international organizations. Reference is made to Chapter 6, *infra*.

III. General Policy on Special Programmes

150. In successive stages, the Assembly has also formulated general policy statements, guidelines and principles on **special programmes** of the Organization and specific aspects of the Organization's work. Such statements comprise *inter alia*, the following:

- Improvement of Safety Oversight.[321]
- Establishment of an ICAO USOAP.[322]
- Transition to a comprehensive systems approach for audits in the ICAO USOAP[323].

316. Assembly Resolution A1-11: *Relations with private international organizations*, ICAO Doc. 9790, I-31.
317. Assembly Resolution A1-11, *ibid.* (n. 305), clause 1(a).
318. A1-11, *ibid.* (n. 305), clause 2.
319. A1-11, *ibid.* (n. 305), clause 4.
320. A1-11, *ibid.* (n. 305), clause C.
321. Assembly Resolution A29-13, ICAO Doc. 9790: *Assembly Resolutions in force as of 5 Oct. 2001, at* I-52.
322. Assembly Resolution A32-11, ICAO Doc. 9790, I-53.
323. Assembly Resolution A35-6, ICAO Doc. 9848: Assembly *Resolutions in force as of 8 Oct. 2004*, at I-57 later superseded by A37-5).

- Universal Safety Oversight Audit Programme (USOAP) Continuous Monitoring Approach.[324]
- Resolving deficiencies identified by the USOAP and encouraging quality assurance for technical cooperation projects.[325]
- Regional cooperation and assistance to resolve safety deficiencies, establishing priorities and setting measureable targets.[326]
- The Safety Fund (SAFE).[327]
- Implementation of the ICAO Programme for the Prevention of Controlled Flight into Terrain (CFIT).[328]
- Improving accident prevention in civil aviation.[329]
- Non-disclosure of certain accident and incident records.[330]
- Support of the ICAO policy on radio frequency spectrum matters.[331]
- Consolidated Statement of continuing ICAO policies and practices related to communications, navigation and surveillance/air traffic management (CNS/ATM) systems.
- Global rule harmonization.[332]
- A global design code for aircraft.[333]
- Smoking restrictions on international passenger flights.[334]
- Role of ICAO in the suppression of illicit transport of narcotic drugs by air.[335]
- Consolidated statement of continuing ICAO policies and practices related to environmental protection – General provisions, noise and local air quality.[336]
- Assistance to victims of aviation accidents and their families.[337]
- Humanitarian flights.[338]

For further details on these statements of policy, reference is made to §2 and §3 below of the present Chapter 3.

---

324. Assembly Resolution A37-5, ICAO Doc. 10022, I-97.
325. Assembly Resolution A33-9, ICAO Doc. 9790, I-55.
326. Assembly Resolution A38-5, ICAO Doc. 10022, superseding A35-7, A36-2, A37-5 and A37-8.
327. Assembly Resolution A37-16, superseding A33-10, ICAO Doc. 9958: *Assembly Resolutions in force as of 8 Oct. 2010*, at I-96.
328. Assembly Resolution A31-9, ICAO Doc. 9790, I-58.
329. Assembly Resolution A31-10, ICAO Doc. 9790, superseded by A36-10.
330. Assembly Resolution A33-17, ICAO Doc. 9790, superseded by A38-3.
331. Assembly Resolution A36-25, ICAO Doc. 9902, superseding A32-13.
332. Assembly Resolutions A38-11 and A38-12, ICAO Doc. 10022, superseding A33-15.
333. Assembly Resolution A33-11, ICAO Doc. 9790, I-50.
334. Assembly Resolution A29-15, ICAO Doc. 9602, I-48.
335. Assembly Resolution A27-12, ICAO Doc. 9790, I-42.
336. Assembly Resolution A38-17, ICAO Doc. 10022, superseding A33-7, A35-5, A36-22, A37-18.
337. Assembly Resolution A39-27, ICAO Doc. 10075, superseding A38-1 and 32-7; *ICAO Policy on Assistance to Aircraft Accident Victims and their Families*, Doc. 9998.
338. Assembly Resolution A29-14, ICAO Doc. 9602, I-60.

§2. Air Navigation

I. Overview

151. The activities of the Organization in the field of air navigation basically serve the overall objective of ensuring and enhancing the **safety of international civil aviation**.[339]

152. They comprise a vast number of activities, including **updating of the standards and recommended practices (SARPS)** and the **procedures for air navigation services (PANS)**;[340] coordination of activities in the field of global planning and guidance on implementation of Global Plans (GASP) and (GANP); updating of Regional Supplementary Procedures (SUPPS); convening of regional air navigation meetings (RANS), development and adoption of regional air navigation plans (Regional Plans), including delineation of FIRs; administration and updation of the Universal Safety Oversight Audit Program (USOAP); development and publication of ICAO safety manuals and circulars; promotion of aviation training through an ICAO global aviation training programme; and coordination of research related to flight safety and human factors and other safety-related actions.[341]

II. Global Aviation Safety Plan and Global Air Navigation Plan (GANP)

153. Since 1997, the Organization has developed and updated a **Global Aviation Safety Plan (GASP)**,[342] which is a broad-based approach to improve aviation safety by 'concentrating the safety-related activities of ICAO on those safety initiatives, planned or currently under way, that offer the best safety dividend in terms of reducing the accident rate'.[343] It focuses, in particular, on improving the existing aviation safety database systems,[344] the exchange of safety-related information, and the development of a comprehensive data analysis and information dissemination

339. Assembly Resolutions A39-22 superseding 38-11: *Formulation and implementation of Standards and Recommended Practices (SARPs) and Procedures for Air Navigation Services (PANS) and notification of differences*; and A40-4: *Consolidated Statement of Continuing ICAO policies and associated practices related specifically to air navigation,* superseding A37-15 in: ICAO Doc. 10140 (Assembly Resolutions in force as of 4 Oct. 2019); *ICAO Global Aviation Safety Plan* (GASP) *see* below (n. 331); A40-4, *ibid.*, Appendices A and D: A39-22, Appendices A and D.

340. Assembly Resolution A39-22, superseding A38-11 and A37-15, Appendix A; A36-13 and A35-14, Appendices A and D, ICAO Doc. 10022, at II-2.

341. Assembly Resolution A38-12, superseding A37-15; A36-13 and A35-14, Appendices B – X., Doc. 10022.

342. ICAO Global Aviation Safety Plan, Third Updated edition 2020-2022, Doc. 10004, http://www.icao.int/safety/airnavigation /Pages/default.aspx; *see also* the Global Aviation Safety Roadmap, Parts 1 and 2, *ibid.*

343. Assembly Resolution A33-16, operating clause 6; *see* now A40-1: *ICAO global planning for safety and air navigation*, ICAO Doc. 10140 (Assembly Resolutions in force as of 4 Oct. 2019).

344. The development and improvement of voluntary reporting systems by the private industry, and the development of industry databanks regarding incidents, safety-related occurrences and related facts are important elements of the coordinated efforts under GASP. *See* in this context Assembly Resolution A40-2: *Protection of accident and incident investigation records*, and A40-3: *Protection of*

network. It further encourages the free communication of safety-related information amongst users of the aviation system, including the reporting of accident and incident data by States to the ICAO Accident/Incident Data Reporting System (ADREP).[345] Other elements of the Global Plan include the promotion of a regulatory environment in contracting States which encourages increased voluntary reporting of aviation safety-relevant events;[346] the development of a programme to implement approach procedures with vertical guidance (APV) utilizing such inputs as GNSS or Distance Measuring Equipment (DME), in accordance with ICAO provisions;[347] the setting up of regional safety groups and international advisory groups of experts so as to study safety issues; and develop an enhanced aviation safety management framework for improving safety and providing assistance.[348]

154. Furthermore, a **Global Air Navigation Plan (GANP)**[349] was developed, in addition to the GASP, designed to guide complementary and sector-wide progress over the period 2013–2028. The GANP represents a fifteen-year forward planning methodology which leverages existing air navigation service technologies and anticipates future developments based on State/industry-agreed operational objectives. The Block Upgrades are organized in five-year time increments starting in 2013 and continuing through 2028 and beyond. This structured approach provides a basis for sound investment strategies in order to generate commitment from States, equipment manufacturers, operators and service providers. Although the related ICAO work programme is endorsed by the ICAO Assembly on a triennial basis, the Global Plan offers a long-term vision that assists ICAO, States and industry to ensure continuity and harmonization among their air navigation equipment modernization programmes.

155. Both the GASP and the GANP have been well received and widely supported by the contracting States of ICAO. A number of voluntary safety-related **reporting systems and databases** have been developed, mainly at the level of private industry. The protection of the information collected in these systems and databases is, however, the subject of some debate and controversy.[350] 'Freedom of

---

safety data and safety information collected for maintaining or improving safety and of flight recorder recordings in normal operations, ICAO Doc. 10140.

345. On ADREP, *see* Accident/Incident Reporting (ADREP) Manual, ICAO Doc. 9156., ss 3.4 b) and c) of the GASP.
346. A33-16, Operating Clause 10; s. 3.4 of the Global Plan, 2004 version; *see* now the updated 2020-2022 version, *ibid.* (n. 331).
347. A33-16, Operating Clause 12; s. 3.6.2.b) of the Global Plan, 2004 version; *see* now the updated 2020-2022 version, *ibid.* (n. 331).
348. A33-16, Operating Clause. 14 c); s. 3.6.2 i) of the Global Plan, 2004 version; *see* now the updated 2020-2022 version, *ibid.* (n. 331).
349. Doc. 9750 – AN/963 6th ed. (2019): *2013–2028 Global Air Navigation Plan.*
350. *See* Assembly Resolution A40-3: *Protection of safety data and safety information collected for maintaining or improving safety and of flight recorder recordings in normal operations,* ICAO Doc. 10140; previously A38-4: *Protecting information from safety data collection and processing systems in order to maintain and improve aviation safety,* ICAO Doc. 10022, II-28, superseding A37-3, A36-9, ICAO Doc. 9902, and previously A35-17, ICAO Doc. 9848. *See also* A37-2, superseding A36-8, ICAO Doc. 9958.

information' legislation in many countries and the vested powers of judicial authorities to gain access to such information for purposes of criminal and civil proceedings are seen as potentially stifling the availability of accident-related and incident-related information.[351] Resolution A35-17 adopted in 2004 at the 35th Assembly called therefore for enhanced protection of such safety-related information, in particular that collected through voluntary reporting systems. The policies for such enhanced protection initially set out in A35-17 were further developed and are now reflected in Assembly Resolutions A40-2 and A40-3.[352]

156. In order to help ensure that the global aviation community has sufficient competent human resources to support a safe, secure and sustainable air transportation system, ICAO launched the **Next Generation Aviation Professionals** initiative (NGAP) in 2009. This was seen as highly important as a large section of the current generation of aviation professionals will retire, while access to affordable training and education for the next generation is increasingly problematic. In this regard, aviation competes with other industry sectors for highly skilled professionals. In order to promote and gain acceptance for NGAP among all stakeholders, including airlines, air navigation service providers, airports, manufacturers, training providers, universities and others, ICAO developed the initiative into a programme and adopted a data-driven approach that justifies the future investment of resources in NGAP action. The ICAO NGAP Programme has been incorporated into the ICAO Global Plans, GASP and GANP.

III. Standards and Recommend Practices (SARPs)

157. The Organization has developed, in accordance with Article 54 subparagraph (l) and Chapter VI of the Convention, **nineteen technical Annexes to the Convention**, setting forth SARPs[353] as well as PANS.[354] It updates the technical Annexes as required, in accordance with Article 54 (m) and Chapter XX of the Convention.

351. *See* in particular Assembly Resolution A37-2: *Non-disclosure of certain accident and incident records,* operating clauses 1 and 2, and A37-3, ICAO Doc. 9958. *See* previously A33-17, ICAO Doc. 9798.

352. Assembly Resolution A40-2, ICAO Doc. 10140, superseded Resolution A38-3, ICAO Doc. 10022; and Resolution A40-3 superseded Resolution A38-4. *See also* the *Manual on Protection of Safety Information*, Doc. 10053.

353. Annex 19 – *Safety Managemen*t was adopted by the ICAO Council during its 198th session in February 2013 and became applicable on 14 Nov. 2013; *see* A38-WP/82; ICAO Doc. AN 19. For the notions of 'standard' and 'recommended practice', *see supra*, paras 110 and 111

354. For the notion of PANS and their implementation, *see*: *Procedures for Air Navigation Services – Air Traffic Management (PANS-ATM)*, Doc. 4444 (14th ed.); *see also* Docs. 8400 (5th ed.) and 8168 (4th ed.).

A. *Annex 1: Personnel Licensing*[355]

158. This Annex contains **standards and recommended practices for the licensing** of flight crew members (pilots, flight engineers), air traffic controllers, and maintenance engineers/technicians. The SARPs describe the skills necessary to ensure proficiency, the medical standards required, periodic medical examinations, and other exigencies for the different types of personnel licences set out in the Annex. Licensing is the act of authorizing defined activities which are otherwise prohibited in the absence of such a license, due to the inherent risk of such activities being improperly performed without training, proficiency and fitness. Licensing is performed at the level of each contracting State under national legislation implementing the SARPs of Annex 1.[356]

159. Related training manuals provide guidance to States for the scope and depth of training curricula.[357] They also provide guidance for the training of other aviation personnel such as aerodrome emergency crews, flight operations officers, radio operators and others.

B. *Annex 2: Rules of the Air*[358]

160. This Annex contains a set of **'rules of the air' to ensure the safety of aircraft while in flight**. They consist of general rules, Visual Flight Rules (VFR), and instrument flight rules (IFR).[359] Flight under VFR is permitted if a flight crew is able to stay clear of clouds by at least 5,000 ft. (1,500 m) horizontally and 1,000 ft. (300 m) vertically and maintain forward visibility of at least 8 km.[360] Save for certain exceptions, flights must be performed under IFR in the absence of these conditions and by night. Most commercial aircraft fly by IFR at all times.

161. A **flight plan** must be filed with air navigation service units for all flights that will cross national borders and for most other flights that are engaged in commercial services. However, regardless of the flight plan, the pilot is responsible for avoiding collisions while the aircraft is in the air in accordance with the 'see-and-avoid' principle,[361] aided by collision avoidance systems, collision hazard

355. ICAO Doc. AN 1, 11th ed. (2011) incorporating Amendments 1-173, applicable as of 08/11/2018.
356. *See* Annex 1, 13th ed. (July. 2020), *ibid.*
357. *See* the ICAO *Training Manual*, Doc. 7192; *Manual of Procedures for Establishment and Management of a State's Personnel Licensing System,* Doc. 9379; *Human Factors Training Manual*, Doc. 9683.
358. ICAO Doc. AN 2, 10th ed. (2005), incl. Amendments 1-46, applicable from 8/11/2018.
359. *Ibid.*, Chs 4 and 5.
360. When flying below 10,000 ft, the flight visibility minimum is 5 km. *See* Annex 2, s. 4.1 and Table 3.1.
361. Doc. AN 2, 10th ed. (2005), incl. Amendments 1-46. *See* s. 3.2; *Pilot Skills to make 'Look-out' more effective in Visual Collision Avoidance*, ICAO Circular 213.

information and the advisories from Air Traffic Control (ATC) units. Flights operating under IFR are to be separated by ATC.[362]

162. Annex 2 also contains important rules and recommendations relating to the **interception of civil aircraft.**[363] Since interception of civil aircraft is carried out by military aircraft to which the Convention and its Annexes do not apply in line with Article 3(a) of the Convention, and since interception manoeuvres are potentially hazardous, difficult problems may arise. In most States, air navigation services for military aircraft are provided by military entities, separately from the civilian air navigation service provider, which raises the issue of civil-military coordination of air navigation services in such situations. The recommendations in Attachment A to Annex 2, setting out procedures which military aircraft of contracting States should apply when intercepting civil aircraft, are intended to mitigate the main risks arising from interception.[364] In some countries, interception manoeuvers occur on an almost regular basis.

C. Annex 3: Meteorological Service for International Air Navigation[365]

163. The Annex sets out **SARPS for meteorological (MET) services** which are an important factor for the safety, regularity and efficiency of air navigation, in particular for commercial aircraft operation.[366] The standards cover the weather information which should be supplied to aeronautical users at international airports, and the suitable telecommunications facilities which should be made available by States to supply MET information to air traffic services as well as to Search and Rescue (SAR) services. They also cover the types of MET data which should be made available, the intervals for updating such data, and the availability of information, including forecasts, to flight crews before take-off and landing.[367]

164. In the 1980s, the **ICAO World Area Forecast System (WAFS)**[368] was set up and implemented to assist States in providing standardized and reliable route forecasts for international civil aviation users. Supported by MET satellite

---

362. Doc. AN 2, ss 5.2 and 3.6.
363. Doc. AN 2, ss 5.2 and 3.6.
364. Doc. AN 2, s. 3.8 and Attachment A. On the coordination of civil and military aircraft operations, *see* Assembly Resolution A40-4 Appendix I; A37-15, Appendix O; *Manual on Civil-Military Cooperation in Air Traffic Management*, ICAO Doc. 10088.
365. Doc. AN 3, Parts I and II, 20th ed. (2018), incl. Amendments 1-79 (4/11/2021).
366. Doc. AN 3, *ibid.* (n. 359), Part I, s. 2.1.1; *Manual for Aeronautical Meteorological Practice*, Doc. 8896; *see also* the *Training Manual*, Doc. 7192, Part F-1.
367. Doc. AN 3 Chs 2, 4–6; *see also Manual for Aeronautical Meteorological Practice*, *ibid.* (n. 355).
368. Doc. AN 3, Ch. 3. Two World Area Forecast Centres (London and Washington D.C.) provide global upper air wind/temperature and significant weather forecasts (SIGWX) in digital code form directly to States and users worldwide through three ICAO satellite broadcasts. *See* AN 3, Chs 3 and 9; Appendices 1, 2 and 3.

technology and automated observation on the ground, it has been further developed to enhance forecasting and reporting services, including those for long-haul routes.[369]

D. Annex 4: Aeronautical Charts[370]

165. This Annex provides SARPs for three series of **aeronautical charts for flight planning and visual navigation**, each with a different scale. ICAO small-scale charts provide a general-purpose chart series for long-range flight planning. ICAO 1:1,000,000 charts provide complete world coverage with uniform presentation of data at a constant scale and are used, *inter alia*, for the production of other charts. The ICAO 1:500,000 chart series gives more details and is used by low-speed, short or medium-range aircraft operating at low or intermediate altitudes, as well as for pilot and navigation training.[371]

166. In recent years, electronic charting and mapping have progressed rapidly and **electronic versions of ICAO charts** have been produced. Annex 4, Chapter 5 sets out the SARPs for Aerodrome Terrain and Obstacle Charts in electronic format. Annex 4, Chapter 20 provides SARPs for Electronic Aeronautical Chart Display. The relevant ICAO SARPs and resultant maps are constantly updated so as to reflect changes in all aviation-relevant data.

167. Aeronautical charts may be distinguished by the purpose for which they are used. The ICAO series consists of seventeen different types, each intended to serve a special purpose.[372] For example, the en-route charts contain the air traffic service system, radio or other navigation aids and other aeronautical information essential to en-route navigation. The ICAO plotting charts are useful in complementing the more complex en-route charts over the extensive oceanic and sparsely settled area. Area charts are useful in the transition from the en-route phase to the final approach, and from take-off to the en-route phase. Instrument approach charts facilitate the graphic presentation of instrument approach procedures; visual approach charts fulfil a similar purpose for VFR approach procedures. Aerodrome charts and aerodrome obstacle charts provide illustrations of the layout and facilities of aerodromes and of the obstacles in their vicinity.[373]

---

369. Since 2002, WAFS operates under the guidance of the WAFSOPSG, *see* Recommendation 1/6 of the MET Divisional Meeting, Montreal 2002.

370. Doc. AN 4, 11th ed. 2009, incl. Amendments 1-61. Amendment 61, applicable as of 11 /4/2021, ICAO Doc. AN 4/E/12. *See also* the *Aeronautical Chart Manual*, Doc. 8697.

371. *Aeronautical Chart Manual*, *ibid.* (n. 365); *Aeronautical Chart Catalogue*, Doc. 7101; *Aeronautical Information Services Manual*, Doc. 8126.

372. *Aeronautical Chart Manual*, Doc. 8697; Doc. AN 4, 11th ed. *See also Aeronautical Information Services Manual*, Doc. 8126; *Aeronautical Information Services Provided by States*, Doc. 7383; *Location Indicators*, Doc. 7910.

373. *Aeronautical Chart Manual*, Doc. 8697; *Aircraft Characteristics Data Bank (ACDB)*, Vol. 1 to 6.

E. Annex 5: Units of Measurement to Be Used in Air and Ground Operations[374]

168. This Annex, which was first adopted in 1948, contains **tables of measurements based essentially on the metric system,** and also interim tables of units for use in those States using systems other than the metric system. Annex 5 was initially only applicable to units used in air-ground communications.

169. As from Amendment 13 adopted in 1979, the scope of Annex 5 was considerably broadened to cover all aspects of air and ground operations.[375] It also introduced the **International System of Units**, also known as SI (*'Système internationale d'unités'*) as a standardized system for civil aviation.[376] Certain non-metric units of measurement, such as the nautical mile, the knot and the foot, may still be used in parallel, the latter only for measurement of altitude, elevation or height.[377] The introduction of the SI represented a major step forward for the aviation, scientific and engineering communities.

F. Annex 6: Operation of Aircraft[378]

170. The Annex consists of Part I: International Commercial Air Transport – Aeroplanes; Part II: International General Aviation – Aeroplanes; and Part III: International Operations – Helicopters. It covers not only operations properly speaking, but also sets out aircraft performance criteria, requirements for communications and navigation equipment, maintenance, flight documents, responsibilities of flight personnel, responsibilities of States for oversight of operators, and responsibilities of operators in relation to the aircraft and flight crew. Of particular practical importance are the SARPs for the Aircraft Operating Certificate (AOC), which certifies that an airline is fit to operate commercial international services and is a legal prerequisite for operating any commercial international flight. Annex 6 keeps these SARPs current and in line with the evolving situation.

171. An example of evolving SARPs in Annex 6 is the **aircraft performance criteria for the operation of twin-engine aircraft** over extended land and ocean ranges (formerly Extended Range Operations (ETOPS)).[379] The performance criteria for such operations have been successively extended to increasingly larger ranges, and are now regulated in Chapter 4 of Annex 6 Part I as **Extended Diversion Time Operations (EDTO)**[380] in relation to the diversion time required to

374. Doc. AN 5, 5th ed. (July 2010), incl. Amendments 1-17.
375. Doc. AN 5, Foreword, Table A: Amendments to Annex 5.
376. Doc. AN 5, Ch. 3, s. 3.1.
377. Doc. AN 5. Ch. 3, Table 3-3, and Ch. 4.
378. Doc. AN 6, Parts I-III, Part I, 12th ed. (2022), Amendment No. 48 (18 /11 /2022); Part II, 11th ed.2022; Part III, 11th ed. (2022).
379. Formerly ETOPS: Additional Requirements for extended range operations by aeroplanes with two turbine power units (ETOPS).
380. *See* Annex 6, Part I, Ch. 4, s. 4.7: Additional requirements for operations by aeroplanes with turbine engines beyond 60 minutes to an en-route alternate aerodrome including Extended Diversion

safely reach the nearest airport in case of engine failure. Another example of evolving performance criteria was the operational rules adopted with the advent of large aircraft such as the A380.[381] In 2022, a proposal for a **new Part IV to Annex 6, on international remotely piloted aircraft systems (RPAS) operations** in controlled airspace/aerodromes, was considered by the ANC. It was based on a proposal by the RPAS Panel which also included consequential amendments to Annexes 1, 2, and 8. The proposal was sent to contracting States and international organizations for their comments.[382]

172. In the last twenty years, Annex 6 has also focussed on automated warning systems as important tools to enhance safety, including the **Ground Proximity Warning System (GPWS)**, the Airborne Collision Avoidance System (ACAS II), and forward-looking wind shear warning systems.[383] Advancing technology in the field of cockpit display has resulted in SARPs for head-up display (HUD) or equivalent displays, enhanced vision systems (EVS), synthetic vision systems (SVS) and/ or combined vision systems (CVS), as well as provisions to accommodate electronic flight bags (EFBs).[384]

G. *Annex 7: Aircraft Nationality and Registration*[385]

173. Annex 7, which is based on Articles 17–20 of the Convention, sets out standards and procedures for the use of letters, numbers and other graphic symbols to be used for the purposes of **nationality and registration marks of aircraft.** It also specifies where these will be located on different types of aircraft.[386]

174. All aircraft engaged in international air navigation, whether commercial, non-commercial or general aviation, must bear **nationality and registration marks in order to permit identification**.[387] The Annex sets out procedures for selection by ICAO contracting States of nationality marks from the nationality symbols used in the radio call signs allocated by the International Telecommunication Union (ITU).[388]

175. Article 77 of the Convention permits **joint operating organizations** or **international operating agencies**. The Annex, therefore, defines the terms 'common mark', 'common mark registering authority' and 'international operating

Time Operations (EDTO); *see also* Attachment C to Annex 6, Part I; Doc. 10085: *Extended Diversion Time Operations Manual (EDTOM)*; and ICAO *Airworthiness Manual*, Doc. 9760.

381. *See: Operation of New Larger Aeroplanes at Existing Aerodromes*, ICAO Circular 305 (2004).
382. *See* https://www.icao.tv/remotely-piloted-aircraft-systems-symposium-rpas/season:4/videos/icao-updates-annex-6-part-iv-developments.
383. Doc. AN 6, Part I, Ch. 6, ss 6.15–6.22.
384. *Ibid.*, ss 6.24–6.25.
385. Doc. AN 7, 6th ed. (2012), incorporating Amendments 1-6; Supplement (22/12/04).
386. Doc. AN 7, s. 3: Location of Nationality, Common and Registration Marks.
387. Article 20 of the Convention. Under Art. 19, the registration or transfer of registration of aircraft in any contracting State shall be made in accordance with its laws and regulations.
388. *See* ss 2, 4 and 5 of Annex 7; for the ITU, *see infra* Ch. 6, §2, II.

agency', in order to allow aircraft operated by such joint organizations or international agencies to be registered on other than a national basis. Each joint or international operating agency may be assigned a distinctive common mark selected from symbols allocated by the ITU.[389] In practice, these facilities have hardly been used, even in the few cases when multinational airlines were established.[390]

176. The Annex also sets forth a **model registration certificate** for use by contracting States.[391] Each aircraft must carry its hardcopy registration certificate on board at all times, along with its airworthiness certificate and a number of other documents.[392]

H. Annex 8: Airworthiness of Aircraft[393]

177. The Annex contains broad standards which define, for application by national airworthiness authorities, the minimum basis for the **mutual recognition of certificates of airworthiness** for the purpose of flight of aircraft of other States into and over their territories.[394]

178. The issuance of **certificates of airworthiness** itself is subject to national regulations and national codes of airworthiness, for which Annex 8 provides only a broad framework. Thus, for example, aircraft produced in the US are issued certificates in accordance with US Federal Aviation Regulations (FARs).[395]

---

389. Annex 7, *see* Definitions and ss 3.1, 3.2, 3.4 including the Note after 3.4.
390. Jennings stated as early as 1945: 'It is idle to suppose that a concept as powerful as nationality can be disposed of merely by demonstrating that the Convention could be more conveniently administered without it' and ' … the existing law provides no status whatever for any but national aircraft of a contracting state.' *See* Jennings, R.Y., 'International Civil Aviation Organization,' (1945) 22 *Brit. Y.B. Int'l L.* 207–08. The ICAO Council provided a clarification on Art. 77 in a Resolution dated 14 Dec. 1967 on nationality and registration of aircraft operated by international operating agencies, Doc. 8743-C/978, Action of Council, 62nd Session, 25–27 and 48–54. The now defunct airline *Société Aérienne Africaine Multinationale,* which operated from 1961 until 2001 *as* 'Air Afrique' headquartered at Abijan, Cote d'Ivoire, decided to register their aircraft on the national registries of its Member States. Similarly, the 'Scandinavian Airlines System' (SAS) established in did not make use of international registration but registers all its aircraft in one of its three Member States registries. The SAS is a consortium of three Scandinavian airlines of Denmark, Norway and Sweden whose aircraft are registered approximately at 3/7 in Sweden, 2/7 in Denmark and 2/7 in Norway. For information concerning the SAS, *see* ICAO Circular 30-AT/5-*Report of the Scandinavian Airlines System (SAS)*, 1953; Bahr, H., 'Scandinavian Airlines System (S.A.S.). Its Origin, Present Organization and Legal Aspects,' (1961) *Arkiv for luftrett* 202.
391. Annex 7, s. 7, Figure 1.
392. *See* Art. 29 (a)–(g) of the Convention.
393. *See* Doc. AN 8–*Airworthiness of Aircraft*, 12th ed. (2018), incorporating Amendments 1-106 (2018).
394. *See* Art. 33 of the Convention – *Recognition of Certificates and Licenses.*
395. U.S. Federal Aviation Regulations (CFR 14), Parts 21, 23, 25; for engines, *see* Parts 33–35; for noise standards, *see* Part 36.

179. Certificates of airworthiness are based on the **type certificate**, which attests to the conformity of the aircraft type with all applicable requirements of the respective national safety code regarding aircraft design.[396] While the type certificate is not mentioned in the Convention, and was for many years regulated only nationally, a major revision of Annex 8 in 2001 included the type certificate for the first time[397] as an internationally recognized and regulated document.

180. The **technical standards** dealing with the **certification of aircraft** include minimum requirements related to performance, flying qualities, structural design and construction, engine design and installation, instrument and equipment design and installation, and operating limitations. They require the availability of an aircraft manual setting out the design and performance characteristics, maintenance requirements, and operating limitations of the aircraft, and containing instructions and warnings for the aircraft operator.

I. Annex 9: Facilitation[398]

181. This Annex is discussed in Chapter 3 §3, IV below since it relates to air transport.

J. Annex 10: Aeronautical Telecommunications[399]

182. The Annex provides **standards for telecommunications equipment, systems and radio frequencies** including Radio Navigation Aids (Vol. I), Communications Procedures including those with PANS status (Vol. II), Communications Systems (Vol. III), Surveillance and Collision Avoidance Systems (Vol. IV), and Aeronautical Frequency Spectrum Utilization (Vol. V).

183. As regards telecommunications, the Annex distinguishes between **aeronautical fixed services (AFS)** between points on the ground, and **aeronautical mobile services (AMS)** between aircraft in flight and points on the ground. AFS-type communications are in part handled through the Aeronautical Fixed Telecommunications Network (AFTN),[400] which is a dedicated worldwide network linking all significant ground points, including airports, ATC centres, airline operations centres, and meteorological offices.

---

396. *See* Annex 8, *ibid.* (n. 381), Ch. 1, Standard 1.4.
397. Amendment 99 to Annex 8, adopted by the ICAO Council on 2 Mar. 2001; *see* on this matter L. Weber & H. Holderbach, 'Type Certification of Commercial Aircraft Calls for Enhanced International Rules', 56 *ICAO Journal* No. 2 (2001), 4 et seq.
398. Doc. AN 9, *Facilitation*, 15th ed. (2017), incorporating Amendments 1–27.
399. Doc. AN 10-1 (Vol. I), 7th ed. (2018); AN 10-2 (Vol. II), 7 th ed.(2016); AN 10-3 (Vol. III), 2st ed.(2007); AN 10-4 (Vol. IV), 5th. ed. (2014); AN 10-5 (Vol. V), 3rd ed. (2013), incorporating Amendments 1-89.
400. *See* Doc. 9705, *Manual of Technical Provisions for the Aeronautical Telecommunication Network* (ATN), 3rd ed., 2002.

184. Aeronautical communications systems involve **voice information exchange by radio**, but they also involve increasingly **data transmission systems,**[401] e.g., for aircraft identification, altitude and positioning information. Furthermore, the introduction of CNS/ATM satellite technology involved increasingly the use of satellite transmission systems, including for communications and navigation, combined with ground-based augmentation systems.[402] The Organization's work in this area has focused on the development of required SARPs for the (Global Navigation Satellite System (GNSS)), including specifications for approach with vertical guidance (APV), and other related system components.

K. Annex 11: Air Traffic Services[403]

185. The Annex sets out the **types of services to be provided to VFR flights and IFR flights**, respectively. It specifies the ATC services, consisting of clearances and ATC information, to achieve vertical, longitudinal and lateral separation between aircraft. It also specifies the contents of clearances, the coordination of clearances between ATC units, and the coordination of transfer of control responsibility from one ATC unit to another.[404]

186. For cases of dense traffic saturating or exceeding the capacity of a particular airport or adjacent airspace or air routes, the Annex provides for ATC units to impose restrictions on the traffic flow, as required, and the parameters therefore.[405] Increasing **airspace congestion** in some parts of the world and affecting certain air routes, and the resulting need to rationalize traffic flows in these areas have given rise to the development of **air traffic management (ATM).** ATM seeks to optimize air traffic flows in defined geographical areas by continuous flow management supported by advanced surveillance technology, reduced separation minima, and flow management techniques developed in the 1990s.[406] More recently, the Global ATM concept has been developed and set out in the Global Air Navigation Plan (GANP).[407]

187. The Annex also contains **procedures for alerting services**, setting in motion all appropriate rescue and emergency organizations and services, as well as

401. *See* Annex 10, Vol. III, Part I: Digital Data Communication Systems, Doc. AN 10-3.
402. ICAO Circular 267: *Guidelines for the Introduction and Operational Use of the Global Navigation Satellite System (GNSS)*; Doc. 9750: *Global Air Navigation Plan for CNS/ATM Systems.*
403. Doc. AN 11 – *Air Traffic Services*, 14th ed., Amendments 1-50B (11 /07 /16). In practice, air traffic services have become a part of 'Air Traffic Management' (ATM), which is the notion increasingly used to denote the operational concept of managing all aspects of air traffic in a given airspace.
404. Doc. AN-11, 15th ed. (2018); Doc. 9426, *Air Traffic Services Planning Manual.*
405. This concept involves strategic airspace management (airspace infrastructure planning, and ATM requirements for communications, navigation and surveillance) as well as tactical airspace management (dynamic use of airspace, civil/military coordination). *See* Doc. AN 11 and Doc. 9426.
406. The latter involve air traffic flow management systems, air traffic flow management procedures, and air traffic management flow integration, *See* AN-11; *Procedures for Air Navigations Services – Air Traffic Management (PANS – ATM)*, Doc. 4444.
407. *See* above, Chapter para.2: Air Navigation, II: GASP and GANP, and *ibid.* (n. 331).

ATS requirements for AFS and AMS communications, including recording requirements, identification of air traffic services routes, and requirements for designation for significant waypoints, whether marked by radio aids or unmarked.[408] The SARPs set out in Annex 11 are supplemented by PANS.[409]

L. Annex 12: Search and Rescue[410]

188. The Annex provides for **standards and procedures for the establishment, maintenance and operation of search and rescue services (SAR)** by contracting States in their territories and in FIRs assigned to them.[411] It details the organization and cooperation requirements necessary to support SAR services, the preparatory measures and facilities required, and the operating procedures of SAR services in emergency situations. These situations are subdivided into three phases,[412] namely the 'uncertainty phase', during which the Rescue Coordination Centre (RCC) is activated, the 'alert phase' involving the alert of the appropriate SAR services units, and the 'distress phase', involving both RCC and SAR services units, as well other relevant parties. The latter phase involves searching and identifying the location of the aircraft and providing assistance, as required, as well as triggering an accident investigation and other related measures. A challenge to the present work of the organization in this field is the more cost-effective organization of SAR services by facilitating their organization on a cooperative, regional basic and their harmonization with maritime SAR services.[413]

M. Annex 13: Aircraft Accident Investigation[414]

189. The Annex serves to establish **authority, responsibilities, and procedure in the investigation of aircraft accidents**. Its main objective is not to identify parties responsible for the accident or lay blame but to contribute to the prevention of future accidents and incidents.[415]

190. It covers the protection of evidence as one of the **responsibilities of the State of occurrence** for instituting an investigation. This includes the taking of custody of the aircraft and the accident site, as well as the removal of the aircraft. The

408. On Search and Rescue aspects, *see* AN 11, Ch. 5, Doc. 9731 and Circular 185; on ATS requirements, *see* AN 11, Ch. 6 and Doc. 9426.
409. PANS-ATM, Doc. 4444. *See also* the related *Air Traffic Services Planning Manual*, Doc. 9426 and the *Manual of Air Traffic Services Data Link Applications*, Doc. 9694.
410. Doc. AN 12 – *Search and Rescue*, 8th ed. (2004), incorporating Amendments 1-18 (22/11/2007).
411. *Ibid.* (n. 404), Chs 1–5; *International Aeronautical and Maritime Search and Rescue (IAMSAR) Manual,* Vols I – III, Doc. 9731; *Satellite-Aided Search and Rescue, the COSPAS-SARSAT System*, ICAO Circular 185.
412. Doc. 9731, Vol. I: Organization and Management.
413. Doc. 9731, Vol. II: Mission coordination.
414. Doc. AN 13 – *Aircraft Accident and Incident Investigation,* 12th ed. (2020), Amendments 1-18.
415. *Manual of Aircraft Accident and Incident Investigation*, Doc. 9756, Vol. I, Ch. I, 1.1).

State of occurrence is also responsible for handling requests for participation in the investigation by the State of registry, the State of the operator and the State of manufacture of the aircraft.[416] If the accident occurs outside of the territory of any Contracting State, it is the State of registry of the aircraft which has the primary responsibility for the accident investigation.

191. In accordance with the provisions of Chapter 6 of Annex 13, the Organization has developed a database called **'ADREP'**, which promotes the exchange of accident investigation information contained in accident reports, namely Preliminary Reports and Accident/Incident Data Reports.[417] The ADREP system is updated from time to time to enhanced standards, and integrated with certain regional aviation incident reporting systems.

192. The Annex is supplemented by the ICAO Manual of Aircraft Accident and Incident Investigation, the ICAO Accident Prevention Manual, and the ICAO Aircraft Accident Digest.[418]

N. Annex 14: Aerodromes[419]

193. The Annex sets out **standards, recommended practices and procedures for the planning, design, operation and facilities/equipment of airports** of all types and sizes. The specifications for essential components of an airport, i.e., the runways, taxiways, aprons, terminal, gate facilities, emergency and rescue facilities, and other essential facilities are provided.[420] Similarly, specifications for the marking and lighting of essential ground facilities are spelt out. Specifications are also provided for the airspace requirements in the vicinity of the airport, in particular for take-off, landing and hold operations of aircraft.[421]

194. Up-to-date information on the condition of facilities at airports is vital today for the safety of civil aviation. Therefore, the Annex specifies the type of

416. Doc. AN 13, Ch. 3. ss 3.2–3.4.

417. *Accident/Incident Reporting (ADREP) Manual*, Doc. 9156, 2nd ed., 1987; *see also* AN 13, Ch. 6.

418. *Manual of Aircraft Accident and Incident Investigation*, Doc. 9756, Volumes I – IV, 3rd ed. – 2020; Manual on Accident and Incident Investigation Policies and Procedures (Doc. 9962); – Manual on Regional Accident and Incident Investigation Organization (Doc. 9946); – Human Factors Training Manual (Doc. 9683); – Manual of Civil Aviation Medicine (Doc. 8984); – Hazards at Aircraft Accident Sites (Circular 315); – Training Guidelines for Aircraft Accident Investigators (Circular 298); Human Factors Digest No. 7 – Investigation of Human Factors in Accidents and Incidents (Circular 240); *Accident Prevention Manual*, Doc. 9422, 1st ed. 1984.

419. ICAO Doc. AN 14 – *Aerodromes*, Vol. I, 18th ed. (2018), incorporating Amendments 1-15; Vol. II, 5th ed. (2020), incorporating Amendments 1-9; Doc. AN 14-2/E/05.

420. ICAO Doc. AN 14, Vol. I (Aerodrome Design and Operations); *Aerodrome Design Manual*, Doc. 9157, Part 1 (Runways), Part 2 (Taxiways, Aprons and Holding Bays), Part 3 (Pavements), Part 5 (Electrical Systems); *Airport Planning Manual*, Doc. 9184; *Airport Services Manual*, Doc. 9137 Part 1 (Rescue and Fire Fighting); Part 7 (Airport Emergency Planning).

421. ICAO Doc. AN 14, Vol I; *Airport Services Manual*, Doc. 9137, Parts 6 and 8.

information to be available (e.g., strength of pavements, condition of runway surfaces, construction sites at the airport, etc.), how it is to be reported and to whom. In Volume II, specifications for heliports are provided. Annex 14 is supplemented by the **ICAO Airport Services Manual**.[422]

O. Annex 15: Aeronautical Information Services[423]

195. The Annex, which has its origins in the NOTAM ('Notices to Airmen') system developed in the early years of civil aviation,[424] provides **specifications and procedures** under which contracting States' authorities issue **information to airlines, aircraft operators and other parties** involved in aircraft operations.

196. The three main types of Aeronautical Information Services (AIS) are the **Aeronautical Information Publication (AIP),**[425] the **NOTAMS,** and the aeronautical information circulars **('Circular')**. While the AIP publishes information of fundamental nature, e.g., changes to primary legislation affecting the responsibilities of aeronautical authorities, the NOTAMS provide official information affecting aircraft operations more directly and the timely knowledge of which is essential to personnel involved in flight operations. Such information may update users on the status of aeronautical facilities, services, procedures or hazards. Circulars provide other current information regarding facilities or services of supplementary nature not directly linked to the primary safety objectives of NOTAMS. Annex 15 sets out standards on how the information should be collected, how its adequacy and authenticity should be checked and how it should be exchanged and disseminated through predetermined channels.[426]

P. Annex 16: Environmental Protection[427]

197. The Annex deals with the **protection of the environment from the effects of aircraft noise and aircraft engine emissions.**[428] It does so by providing SARPs which set a combination of specifications, limitations and conditions in order to

422. *Ibid.* n. 409; *see also Aerodrome Design Manual*, Doc. 9157; *Airport Planning Manual*, Doc. 9184. *Heliport Manual* Doc. 9261; and *SMGCS Manual*, Doc. 9476.
423. Doc. AN 15 16th ed. (2018), incorporating Amendments 1-41; Supplemented by the *Aeronautical Information Services Manual*, Doc. 8126.
424. *See* Groenewege, *Compendium of International Civil Aviation* (Montreal, IADC, 3rd ed. 2003), p. 722; Doc. AN 15 *ibid.* (n. 411); Doc. 8126 and Annexes 10, 11 and PANS/RAC; PANS-ABC.
425. Doc. AN 15, Ch. 4; *Aeronautical Information Services Manual*, Doc. 8126; *Aeronautical Information Services Provided by States*, Doc. 7383.
426. Doc. AN 15 *ibid.* (n. 411); Doc. 8126.
427. Doc. AN 16, Vol. I – *Aircraft Noise,* 7th ed. (2014), incorporating Amendments 1-11A; Vol. II– *Aircraft Engine Emissions*, 3rd ed. (2011), incorporating Amendments 1-8.
428. *See*: *Environmental Technical Manual on the Use of Procedures in the Noise Certification of Aircraft*, 3d ed. 2004, with a revision of February 2004, ICAO Doc. 9501.

achieve a gradual reduction in the overall effects of aircraft noise and aircraft emissions on the environment.[429] While aircraft noise reduction through Annex 16 dates back to 1981, the comprehensive CORSIA scheme for reduction of greenhouse gases was added in 2018. Annex 16 comprises four volumes, namely Volume I – Aircraft Noise; Volume II – Aircraft Engine Emissions; Volume III – Aeroplane CO_2 Emissions, and Volume IV – Carbon Offsetting and Reduction Scheme for International Aviation (CORSIA). The CORSIA scheme is the civil aviation sector's contribution to the global efforts led by UNFFFC to reduce greenhouse emissions and it applies market-based measures.

198. Volume I deals with **aircraft noise abatement** (reduction) and uses **noise certification of aircraft** as the main methodology. For each classified aircraft type, a standardized noise evaluation measure is used.[430] At specified measurement points, maximum noise levels at lateral points, approach points and flyover points on the ground are designated for different types of aircraft along with flight test procedures.[431] They result in noise 'foot-prints' for each aircraft type which may then be used for the purposes of noise abatement measures.

199. Noise certification is granted by the State of registry of an aircraft, based on satisfactory evidence of compliance with national requirements based on the standards set out in Annex 16 Volume I.

200. Over time, noise standards have become more stringent by increments, from Volume I Chapter 2 to Chapter 3 and from there to Chapter 4.[432] Chapter 2 compliant aircraft have been gradually phased out over a period of seven years as of 2004. While Chapter 3 aircraft continue to operate, aircraft manufacturers are presently building aircraft compliant with Chapter 4.[433]

201. As an overall policy on the issue of aircraft noise reduction at airports, a **'balanced approach'**[434] was agreed upon at the 33rd Session of the Assembly in 2001. This approach uses a basket of measures involving the phase-out measures described in the preceding paragraph, reduction of noise at source, principles of

---

429. Doc. AN 16, Vol I; *Guidance on the Balanced Approach to Aircraft Noise Management*. Doc. 9829; *Environmental Technical Manual on the Use of Procedures in the Noise Certification of Aircraft*, Doc. 9501; AN 16, Vol II; ICAO Assembly Resolution A39-1 Appendices C – G; previously A38-17 Appendices C-F; A35-5, Appendix H.

430. *See Environmental Technical Manual, ibid.* (ICAO Doc. 9501). Vol. I (2nd. Ed. 2015), Vol. II (2nd. Ed. 2014).

431. *Environmental Technical Manual, ibid.* (Doc. 9501).

432. AN 16, Vol. I – *Aircraft Noise*, Chs 2, 3 and 4; examples of aircraft designed before 1977 and covered by Ch. 2 are B-727 and McDonnell-Douglas DC-9. Aircraft designed to meet Ch. 3 are B 737-300/400, B 767 and A 319. Chapters 5 and 6 of Vol. I apply a similar methodology to propeller-driven aircraft.

433. Assembly Resolution A35-5, Appendix D; *see* now Assembly Resolution A40-17: *Consolidated statement of continuing ICAO policies and practices related to environmental protection – General provisions, noise and local air quality*; previously A39-1.

434. *Guidance on the Balanced Approach to Aircraft Noise Management*. Doc. 9829; *see also* Ch. 3, §3. IX. C. below for further reference.

land-use planning and management, noise abatement operational procedures, operating restrictions, and other measures. The 'balanced approach' has since served as a valuable working tool in dealing with the competing interests of the various stakeholders. In recent years, work has focused in ICAO on ensuring that the technical data serving as the basis for the ICAO standards, guidance and policies associated with reducing aircraft noise are current and up to date. This has included investigations into emerging subsonic **aircraft noise reduction technologies**, studies into the status of aircraft and helicopter noise reduction technology and the continuing development of SARPs for future supersonic aircraft. ICAO has also focused on the environmental aspects of airport land-use planning and airport community engagement best practices.

202. As regards **aircraft emissions**, Annex 16 Vol. II provides standards which limit the engine emissions of hydrocarbons (HC), carbon monoxide (CO), carbon dioxide (CO_2), and nitrogen oxides (NOx) from turbojet and turbofan engines intended for subsonic propulsion.[435]

203. From 2013 onwards, the work of the organization in this field has focussed on rendering the limitations for emissions more stringent, in particular for NOx emissions[436] and greenhouse gases. At the 39th Assembly in 2016, an agreement was reached on the **Carbon Offsetting and Reduction Scheme for International Aviation (CORSIA)**. Market-based measures have been chosen as the preferred mechanism in the absence of consensus on prescriptive standards for emissions reduction.[437] Subsequent to its adoption, the required SARPs for its implementation have been developed and set out in Vol. IV of Annex 16, adopted in October 2018.[438] Under CORSIA, international operators are entitled to a limited amount of emission units. If they exceed the limit, they need to purchase either unused units from other operators who do not need them, or offset units by making financial contributions to carbon-offsetting activities. Emission entitlements, use of emissions, purchase of unused units and contributions to offsetting activities are monitored, reported, and verified through the MRV process.[439] The CORSIA scheme is discussed in more detail below, Chapter 3, §3 IX H, paragraphs 265–271.

435. Doc. AN 16, Ch. II; on aircraft emission reduction policy, *see* Assembly Resolutions A40-18 and A40-19, superseding A39-1, A39-2 and A39-3; *see also* A36-22 and A35-5, Appendix J.
436. *See*: *ICAO Council Adopts New Standards for Aircraft Emissions*, ICAO News Release PIO 03/05, dated 2 Mar. 2005.
437. *See* the Appendix J; *see also ICAO Engine Exhaust Emissions Data Bank*, ICAO Doc. 9646.
438. Assembly Resolution A40-18: *Consolidated statement of continuing ICAO policies and practices related to environmental protection – Climate change*; previously A39-2, A38-18, A37-19, A-36-22 and A35-5, Appendix J.
439. Doc. AN 16 Vol. IV – *Carbon Offsetting and Reduction Scheme for International Aviation (CORSIA); see also* Doc. 9501 (ETM), Vol. IV (CORSIA) (2d ed.); and the 14 CORSIA Implementation Elements referenced in Annex 16 Vol. IV.

Q. Annex 17: Security[440]

204. The Annex, which is not primarily an air navigation matter, is discussed in Chapter 3, §7 Part III below.

R. Annex 18: The Safe Transport of Dangerous Goods by Air[441]

205. The Annex provides SARPs to enable **dangerous goods (explosive, corrosive, flammable, toxic and radioactive materials)** to be carried safely by air.[442] The Annex itself contains nine hazard classes, which correspond to those determined by the UN and used for all modes of transport.[443] Further, it contains only broad, stable framework procedures regarding handling, packing, labelling, etc., while detailed rules, procedures and instructions are set out in the 'Technical Instructions for the Safe Transport of Dangerous Goods by Air'.[444] The Technical Instructions are frequently updated in accordance with developments in the air cargo, chemical, manufacturing or packaging industries.

S. Annex 19: Safety Management

206. This Annex, first adopted in February 2013, provides SARPs for the **Safety Management System (SMS)** and related safety management matters. A Safety Management System (SMS) is defined in the Annex as 'a systematic approach to managing safety, including the necessary organizational structures, accountabilities, policies and procedures'. The SARPs are intended to assist States in managing aviation safety risks. Given the increasing complexity of the global air transportation system and its interrelated aviation activities required to assure the safe operation of aircraft, the Annex supports the continued evolution of a proactive and inclusive strategy to improve safety performance, based on the implementation of a State Safety Plan (SSP) that systematically addresses safety risks at the level of the State, in particular effective safety oversight over all operators and providers of services. An effective SSP is the cornerstone of Safety Management at the State level, and its implementation is a gradual process requiring frequent feedback and update.[445]

---

440. Doc. AN 17, 11th ed. (2020) incorporating Amendments 1-17; Annex 17 is supplemented by the *Security Manual for Safeguarding Civil Aviation Against Acts of Unlawful Interference*, Doc. 8973 (Restricted).
441. Doc. AN 18, 4th ed. (2011), incorporating Amendments 1-12; the Annex is supplemented by the *Technical Instructions for the Safe Transport of Dangerous Goods by Air*, Doc. 9284.
442. *Ibid.*, n. 429.
443. *See* Doc. AN 18 and Doc. 9284.
444. Doc. 9284. *See also* the *Supplement to the Technical Instructions*, Doc. 9284 SU, and the *Dangerous Goods Training Programme*, Doc. 9375.
445. ICAO Doc. AN19: Annex 19 – *Safety Management*, 2nd ed. July 2016 (Amendment 1), Foreword; Doc. C-WP/13935, Appendix A; *see also* A38-WP/82.

207. Annex 19 consolidated material from previously existing Annexes regarding SSP and SSMs, as well as related elements including the collection and use of safety data and State safety oversight activities. The benefit of drawing together this material into a single Annex is to focus the States' attention on the importance of integrating their safety management activities. It also facilitates the evolution of safety management provisions.[446]

IV. Procedures for Air Navigation Services

208. On the basis of Articles 37 and 38 of the Convention under which the Organization shall adopt and amend from time to time SARPs and procedures, ICAO has adopted and issued **Procedures for Air Navigation Services (PANS)** which contain regulatory material not suited for inclusion in an Annex.[447]

209. PANS are essentially operating procedures applicable worldwide which have not yet attained 'a sufficient degree of maturity for adoption as International Standards and Recommended Practices, as well as material of a more prominent character which is considered too detailed for incorporation in an Annex, or is susceptible to frequent amendment, for which the processes of the Convention would be too cumbersome'.[448]

210. The following PANS have been adopted:

- ICAO Abbreviations and Codes (PANS-ABC: Doc. 8400).
- Air Traffic Management (Procedures for Air Navigation Services – ATM (PANS-ATM): Doc. 4444).
- Aircraft Operations (PANS-OPS: Doc. 8168).
- Aerodromes Aeronautical Information Management (PANS-AIM: Doc. 10066).
- Aerodromes (PANS-Aerodromes: Doc. 9981).
- Training (PANS-TRG: Doc. 9868).

---

446. *See* AN-WP/8715 and Doc. C-WP/13935, Appendix A.

447. *See* A39-22: *Formulation and implementation of Standards and Recommended Practices (SARPs) and Procedures for Air Navigation Services (PANS) and notification of differences*, Doc. 10022; T. Buergenthal, *Law-making in the International Civil Aviation Organization* 114–115 (New York, Syracuse U. Press 1969).

448. *Rules of Procedure for the Conduct of Air Navigation Meetings and Directives to Divisional-type Air Navigation Meetings*, Part II, Rule 2.2.1, ICAO Doc. 8143. It should be noted however that Assembly Resolution A39-22: *Formulation and implementation of Standards and Recommended Practices (SARPs) and Procedures for Air Navigation Services (PANS) and notification of differences* treats Annexes and PANS largely on an even footing. *See also* previously A38-11, Appendices A: *Formulation of Standards and Recommended Practices (SARPs) and Procedures for Air Navigation Services (PANS))* and D: *Implementation of Standards and Recommended Practices (SARPs) and Procedures for Air Navigation Services (PANS)* of Resolution A35-14 '*Consolidated Statement for continuing ICAO polices and associated practices related specifically to air navigation' See*: A35-14 in ICAO Doc. 9848.

The PANS-ATM and PANS-OPS are of particular importance as they supplement Annexes 6 and 11 and serve as supporting tools for rule-making to enable **Global Navigation Satellite System (GNSS)** use.[449] Recent amendments support, in particular, reduced vertical separation minimum (RVSM) and GNSS navigation, including **GNSS area navigation (RNAV)** departure and approach procedures, as well as **satellite based augmentation system (GBAS)** procedures.[450] The PANS-AIM and PANS-Aerodromes have been added since 2018 in order to support the transition from product-based AIS to data-centric information management and set out procedures for initial aerodrome certification as well as continuing aerodrome safety oversight. The PANS-TRG specify, in greater detail than in the SARPs, the actual procedures to be applied by training organizations when providing training for aeronautical personnel and global training needs.

V. Other Activities

A. Aeronautical Use of Radio Frequency Spectrum

211. The Organization has been closely involved in the **ITU World Radio Communications Conferences (WRC)**, which allocate spectrum frequencies to specific use and meet every two to three years.[451] Certain bandwidths of the spectrum are allocated for aeronautical use. However, rapidly increasing use of mobile phone systems around the world has rendered available frequency bandwidths scarce, and it has therefore proved more difficult to obtain allocations for new aeronautical communication systems and to protect existing aeronautical radio frequencies. ICAO continues to coordinate and represent the positions of the aeronautical community in this regard.[452]

---

449. *See* the *Global Air Navigation Plan for CNS/ATM Systems*, Doc. 9750; and the *Guidelines for the Introduction and Operational Use of the Global Navigation Satellite System (GNSS)*, ICAO Circular 267.
450. PANS-ATM, Doc. 4444, 16th ed., Amendment 9 (2018); Global Air Navigation Plan 2020-2022, 6th ed. 2019, Doc. 9750; PANS-OPS, Doc. 8168, Vol. I–*Flight Procedures*, 5th ed., Amendment 4; Vol II – *Construction of Visual and Instrument Flight Procedures*, 7th ed., Amendment 9 (2020), with a Note on Software; Vol. III – Aircraft Operating Procedures, 1st ed. 2018.
451. ITU Final Acts – WRC – 2019, Geneva 2019, Doc. 190-19; ITU Rules of Procedure (2017 7th update); *See also*: ICAO Position for the ITU WRC – 2019 (Position Paper, unnumbered); *Handbook on Radio Frequency Spectrum Requirements for Civil Aviation*, including Statement of Approved ICAO Policies, Doc. 9718.
452. Assembly Resolution A38-6: *Support of the ICAO policy on radio frequency spectrum matters*; Annex 10, Volume V – *Aeronautical Radio Frequency Spectrum Utilization*, 3rd ed. 2013; ICAO Position paper, *ibid.* (n. 439); *Handbook on Radio Frequency Spectrum Requirements for Civil Aviation* (Doc. 9718): Volume I – *Handbook on Radio Frequency Spectrum Requirements for Civil Aviation*, 2nd Ed. (2018); Volume II – *Frequency assignment criteria for aeronautical radio communication and navigation system,* 1st ed. Amendment No.1 (2017).

B. Flight Safety and Human Factors

212. For a number of years, the work of the Organization has emphasized the **importance of human factors for flight safety**, including in particular fatigue, with the objective of further reducing the overall aircraft accident rate.[453] Reference is made to the GASP. The Organization is issuing a Human Factors Digest and has developed guidance material in the form of Manuals for the monitoring of safety during normal air traffic services operations.[454] A special Working Group on Human Factors has assisted in this matter.

C. Runway Safety

213. Increasing attention has been given to **runway incursions** in recent years, which are mainly the result of steadily increasing traffic at aerodromes.[455] The Organization has carried out a worldwide awareness and education campaign, has developed a tool-kit on runway safety, and has included a revised definition for runway incursion in the PANS-ATM. A Manual on runway safety was also developed.[456]

D. Global Planning and CNS/ATM Implementation

214. The implementation of the Communications, Navigation and Surveillance/ Air Traffic Management System **(CNS/ATM)** continues as part of Global Planning although with a more regional and institutional focus.[457] ICAO essentially coordinates the implementation activities of contracting States in this regard. Implementation takes place in accordance with SARPs, PANS and guidance material developed by the Organization, and coordinated through and assisted by regional implementation groups (PIRGs).[458]

---

453. Human factors were first highlighted by Assembly Resolution A26-9: *Flight Safety and Human Factors*; *see* now ICAO Global Aviation Safety Plan, updated version 2020 –2022, Doc. 10004; Resolution A39-12 Appendix A, Doc. 10022; A38-2, operating clause 6.
454. *See* the Human Factors Manuals, ICAO Docs. 9683, 9758, 9803, 9806, 9808 and 9824; Doc. 10151 – *Human Performance (HP) Manual for Regulators*; and the Human Factors Digests, ICAO Circulars 234, Circular 300 – *Human Factors in Cabin Safety*, and Circular 302 – *Cross-Cultural Factors in Aviation Safety*. *See also* Doc. 9826 – Supplement, p. 4.
455. *See,* e.g., the revised definition for 'runway incursion', effective as of 2004, in the PANS-ATM, Doc. 4444 14th ed. Amendment 3; a procedure requiring pilots and ATC to submit an air traffic incident report after a runway incursion was also adopted. *See* now the updated provisions in the PANS-ATM, Doc. 4444 16th. ed. 2016.
456. *See Manual on the Prevention of Runway Incursions*, Doc. 9870 AN463 (2007). Revised definition of Runway incursion: *Any occurrence at an aerodrome involving the incorrect presence of an aircraft, vehicle or person on the protected area of a surface designated for the landing and take-off of aircraft,* in: PANS-ATM, Doc. 4444 14th ed. Amendment 3, Part 1: definitions.
457. Assembly Resolution A39-11 Appendix F, Doc. 10022; previously A35-15: *Consolidated Statement of continuing ICAO policies and practices related communications, navigation and surveillance/air traffic management (CNS/ATM) systems,* ICAO Doc. 9848.
458. Regional Planning and Implementation Groups exist for all major regions. *See* the synopsis of their work in Doc. 9826 – Suppl., Table VIII-1; Global Aviation Safety Plan, Doc. 10004.

E. Performance Based Navigation (PBN)

215. Limited airspace capacity, the need to achieve measurable efficiencies in aircraft operations, and other related factors led to the development and implementation as of 2012 of performance-based navigation (PBN). PBN is a cornerstone for **air traffic management (ATM) optimization** programmes, as it moves away from fixed point-to-point guidance of aircraft operation to the approval of any desired flight path within coverage of station-referenced navigation aids, or within the limits of self-contained aids, or a combination of both. It offers significant advantages over the traditional principles for airspace design, ATS routes, instrument flight procedures and obstacle clearance criteria. ICAO provides essential support to Member States through its PBN Manuals, the PBN iKit, PBN training, and other PBN products and services.

F. Remotely Piloted Aircraft Systems

216. The Chicago Convention of 1944 already saw a need to regulate 'pilotless aircraft' in its Article 14. Today, the term 'drone' is used for small aircraft, generally below 25 kg, and 'Remotely Piloted Aircraft System' (RPAS) above that limit. They are part of the category of 'Unmanned Aircraft System' (UAS), also comprising meteorological balloons that fly freely. With the advent of a rapidly developing market of RPAS of all sizes for private, commercial or industrial use, the need to provide a regulatory framework for remotely piloted aircraft has become global. As of 2007, ICAO studied this matter and published the first edition of the **Manual on Remotely Piloted Aircraft Systems** (Doc. 10019) in 2015. Through its RPAS Panel, it is also developing SARPs for RPAS operations, with the objective to ensure global interoperability and safe, secure and efficient integration of RPAs into non-segregated airspace and aerodromes. It is anticipated that all nineteen Annexes to the Convention, except Annex 5 – Units of Measurement, will require an amendment to accommodate RPAS. In addition, ICAO has developed an online Toolkit for UAS operation and is developing a concept for UAS Traffic Management (UTM) for areas with high-density UAS operations including package delivery, infrastructure inspections, public safety surveillance, etc.

G. Global Aviation Safety Oversight System

217. The implementation of the Universal Safety Oversight Audit Programme (USOAP)[459] has highlighted the importance of effective and efficient State safety oversight capabilities. In States with a less developed aviation system and scarce

459. Assembly Resolution A32-11: *Establishment of an ICAO universal safety oversight audit programme*; *see also* A29-13: *Improvement of safety oversight*; A33-8: *Continuation and expansion of the ICAO Universal Safety Oversight Audit Programme*, ICAO Doc. 9790; *see also* A37-5: *The Universal Safety Oversight Audit Programme (USOAP) continuous monitoring approach*, in: Resolutions of the 37th Assembly (Provisional edition), November 2010.

resources, it has proven beneficial to pool capabilities and resources with neighbouring States by forming regional aviation oversight bodies, and many States have done so. These regional bodies need to act fully in line with the ICAO principles, methodologies and SARPs on safety oversight. In order to ensure that they do so, **the Global Aviation Safety Oversight System (GASOS)** has been set up as a voluntary ICAO assessment programme for safety oversight organizations (SOOs) and Accident Investigation Organizations (AIOs). The qualifications and capability of an SOO/AIO to provide specific functions or activities are assessed against a set of objective criteria. If the assessment is satisfactory, ICAO issues official recognition to the SOO or AIO, and will publish its name in an ICAO directory of recognized SOOs/AIOs and the functions and activities they are able to provide.

H. Conflict Zones

218. Military or other types of conflict zones have in the past posed significant risks to civil aviation operations over or near these zones. Under the Chicago Convention, Member States shall promptly communicate such risks arising in their respective airspace and such information is mostly disseminated through Notices to Airmen (NOTAMs), aeronautical information circulars (AIC), and AIP supplements. Commercial airlines operating over or near conflict zones will also usually conduct their own risk assessments sometimes using security monitoring data of third parties. After the shoot down of Malaysian Airlines Flight MH17 over eastern Ukraine in July 2014, ICAO initially set up a central repository of information on conflict zone risks on the ICAO website for access by all Member States. As of 2017, the repository has transited into a library of links on the ICAO public website to States' own aeronautical information. In parallel, ICAO has developed guidance material to assist States, operators and ANSPs regarding conflict zone risks in Doc. 10084, Risk Assessment Manual for Civil Aircraft Operations Over or Near Conflict Zones.

I. 'No Country Left Behind' Initiative

219. In 2015, at the initiative of the Council, ICAO launched the **'No Country Left Behind' initiative** in order to assist States with the implementation of SARPs. This includes assistance with removing deficiencies in line with action plans following ICAO USOAP audits. The overall objective of the initiative is to enable States, including in particular developing States, to fully benefit from the synergistic potential of a safe and reliable aviation system, including expanded tourism and trade and the macro-economic benefits of improved connectivity. With the support and collaboration of partners and donors, ICAO promotes the benefits of aviation, facilitates the mobilization of resources, partners with other international organizations, and assists States in suitable fields including aviation training and human resource development.

J. ICAO Partnership Programme

220. Along the lines of a similar UN programme, the **ICAO Partnership Programme** aims to provide a platform for collaboration with and support from the private sector and civil society on projects of joint interest. It seeks to strengthen ICAO's capacity to engage corporations, foundations and individuals in ICAO-generated projects and outreach efforts. It also fosters innovative strategies for engaging non-State actors with ICAO.

§3. AIR TRANSPORT

221. The activities of the Organization in the air transport field principally cover the following items:

- economic regulation;
- statistics;
- forecasting and economic planning;
- facilitation;
- taxation;
- airports and air navigation services;
- air carrier economics;
- air mail;
- environmental protection.

222. The **Consolidated Statement of continuing ICAO policies in the air transport field**, an Assembly resolution which is periodically updated at every Assembly, summarizes the ICAO policies in these areas.[460]

223. Policies and practices relating to environmental protection in civil aviation are set out separately in a **'Consolidated Statement of continuing ICAO policies and practices related to environmental protection'**.[461]

460. Assembly Resolution A41-27: *Consolidated statement of continuing ICAO policies in the air transport field*, in: Doc. 10184 *Assembly Resolutions in Force* (as of 7 Oct. 2022) which superseded Assembly Resolutions A39-15, A38-14 and A37-20, ICAO Doc. 10022.

461. Since 2010, the practice has been to issue the Consolidated Statement on environmental protection in two or more separate Assembly Resolutions; as from the 40th Assembly, this was done in three resolutions: *see* now A41-20 – *Consolidated statement of continuing ICAO policies and practices related to environmental protection – General provisions, noise and local air quality*, A41-21 – *Consolidated statement of continuing ICAO policies and practices related to environmental protection – Climate change*, and A41-22 – *Consolidated statement of continuing ICAO policies and practices related to environmental protection – Carbon Offsetting and Reduction Scheme for International Aviation (CORSIA)*, in: Resolutions in Force (as of 7 Oct. 2022, Doc. 10184; previously A39-1 and A39-2, A38-18, 37-18, A36-22, Doc. 9902, and A35-5, Doc. 10022, Assembly Resolutions in force (as of 4 Oct. 2013).

I. Economic Regulation

224. The activities of the Organization in this field have centred largely on **air transport liberalization** and, in recent years, on contracting States' policies and practices regarding air carrier ownership and control. The Organization convened six Worldwide Air Transport Conferences over the years, which have contributed to an evolution of policies and practices, including those relating to the conclusion of bilateral air transport agreements between contracting States and the exchange of commercial rights.

225. The 5th Worldwide Air Transport Conference held in 2003 adopted an important **Declaration on Global Principles for the Liberalization of International Air Transport** as well as conclusions and recommendations.[462]
They dealt in particular with the difficult issue of liberalization of air carrier ownership and control and with the future role of ICAO in air transport matters including its relations with the World Trade Organization (WTO-OMC).

226. Subsequently, the Organization embarked on two studies, one on the essential air services concept carried out in cooperation with the World Tourism Organization (WTO/OMT),[463] and the other on the safety and security implications of liberalization.[464]

227. The **Sixth Worldwide Air Transport Conference** in 2013 developed these subjects further and had extensive coverage under two main agenda items: Item 1 – Global overview of trends and developments; and Item 2 – Examination of key issues and related regulatory framework. The Conference examined in particular industry and regulatory developments, market access, air carrier ownership and control, consumer protection, fair competition, safeguards in the liberalization of international air transport, taxation and other levies, the economics of airports and air navigation services, and implementation of ICAO policies.[465]

228. On the basis of further study, the Organization was mandated with the examination of an international agreement by which States could liberalize market access; the development of an international agreement to liberalize air carrier ownership and control; and the development of a specific international agreement to facilitate further liberalization of air cargo services.[466] Taking into account the outcome of the work of the Air Transport Regulation Panel (ATRP), the Organization reported to the 40th Assembly in 2019 that the future development of a modern and

---

462. *See Consolidated conclusions, model clauses, recommendations and declaration of the 5th Worldwide Air Transport Conference,* (2003) Doc. 9810; Doc. AT Conf/5, Revised, 10/7/03.
463. Doc. 9826 – Supplement (July. 2004), p. 9.
464. *Ibid.* (n. 451).
465. *See*: *Outcome of the Sixth Worldwide Air Transport Conference*, Doc. A38-WP/56 (31/07/2013). Report of AT Conf/6, Doc. 10009; *see also* Docs. A39-WP/4, A39-WP/5 and A39-WP/66 (05/07/2016).
466. Progress Report on the Development of International Agreements on the Liberalization of Market Access, Air Cargo and Air Carrier Ownership and Control, A40-WP/16, EC/1 (21/6/19).

more ambitious multilateral agreement on the liberalization of market access will need a flexible and pragmatic approach which allows for reservations, so as to secure a high number of States acceding to the agreement. Building upon the progress made on the development of a **draft Convention on Foreign Investment in Airlines,** work should continue to address the remaining issues of concern on 'free riders' and regulatory oversight with a view to finalizing this draft Convention.[467]

229. The Organization is cooperating with regional and sub-regional bodies as well as groups of States as regards measures of liberalization including liberalized agreements and arrangements and the results of these measures, to explore the acceptability of such measures. It was mandated with the subject of core principles for consumer protection, has carried out studies on the subject, and developed a text for such non-binding principles as guidance material for contracting States.[468] It has also further updated a comprehensive Policy and Guidance Material on the Economic Regulation of International Air Transport as overall guidance for contracting States in the air transport field.[469]

II. Statistics

230. The collection of statistical air transport data by the Organization is foreseen in Articles 54(i), 55 and 67 of the Convention. On this basis, ICAO has developed an **integrated statistical database** providing an efficient online system for the validation, storage and retrieval of statistical data for States and other users. Such data are essential for planning purposes of civil aviation administrations, airlines, air navigation service providers and other civil aviation entities. Statistical information received from Member States on Air Transport Reporting Forms is made available in accordance with Articles 54(i) and 67 of the Convention.

231. Statistical data collected and processed by the organization, previously published in hardcopy (Digest of Statistics), are now available online. Some are available free of charge to staff of the national civil aviation administrations of Member States, who may share them with stakeholders.[470] In particular, **ICAO DATA+** is a tool that presents in a dynamic and graphical environment the air transport statistical data collected from its 193 Member States. ICAO DATA+ enables users to visualize trends, differences and similarities between air transport data selection and makes competitive analyses (benchmarking) accessible. Up to seven Data+ modules are accessible free of charge to the designated focal point of an ICAO Member State, other modules require a subscription.

467. *Ibid.* (n. 454).
468. Doc. 10078 A39-EC, Report of the Economic Commission to the 39th Assembly, para. 39:27.
469. ICAO Doc. 9587 4th ed. 2017; *see also* the *Manual on the Regulation of International Air Transport*, Doc. 9626; and the *Database on the World's Air Services Agreements*, Doc. 9511.
470. A large number of different types of statistics are available online: *see* the ICAO Products & Services Catalogue 2020 – Publications – Databases – Digital Products – Training Courses, pp. 99 et seq.

III. Forecasting and Economic Planning

232. In line with its mandate, the Organization prepares and maintains, as necessary, long-term and medium-term **forecasts of future trends and developments in civil aviation**. These may be of general or specified kind and may include regional as well as global data,[471] e.g., traffic forecasts for specific regions or globally. The Organization makes these available to contracting States, e.g., by publishing Circular 333 – Global Air Transport Outlook to 2030 and trends to 2040. It also keeps under development methodologies and procedures for the preparation of forecasts, analyses of cost-benefit or cost-effectiveness,[472] and the development of business cases to meet the needs of the regional air navigation planning groups and other bodies, including environmental planning groups, inside or outside of the Organization.[473]

IV. Facilitation

233. The work of the Organization includes the administration and updating of **Annex 9 – Facilitation**,[474] as well as other facilitation-related activities.

234. Annex 9 contains SARPs to facilitate the expeditious entry and departure of aircraft, passengers, baggage, cargo and other items at international airports. It aims at reducing and simplifying border formalities relating to customs, immigration, health, security and other related controls. The basic principle of Annex 9 is that 'clearance ... shall be applied and carried out in such a manner as to retain the advantage of speed inherent in air transport'.[475]

235. ICAO's work in this field is recognized as the first which succeeded in developing standards which are more than mere recommendations and with which contracting States comply. Other international organizations, such as the International Maritime Organization (IMO), the World Customs Organization (WCO) and the World Tourism Organization (WTO) have followed in ICAO's footsteps.[476]

236. Chapter 3 of Annex 9 deals with entry and departure of persons and their baggage. It establishes the principle that contracting States shall not require from visitors travelling by air any other document of identity than a valid passport.[477]

---

471. *See*, e.g., ICAO Circular 313: *Outlook for Air Transport to the Year 2025*; and ICAO Circular 327: *Regional Differences in International Airline Operating Economics: 2006 and 2007.*
472. *See*: *ICAO Manual on Air Traffic Forecasting*, Doc. 8991.
473. The Organization does forecasting work for certain outside bodies, e.g., the Universal Postal Union (UPU) and the IATA Prorate Agency.
474. Doc. AN 9, 15th ed. 2017 Amendments 1-27.
475. Annex 9, *ibid.* (n. 462), Ch. 1, s. 1.2.
476. The Convention on International Civil Aviation, Annexes 1 to 18, brochure ed. by ICAO (1991), p. 21.
477. Annex 9, Ch. 3, ss. B, 3.3 and 3.4.

237. This **'single document' principle** has been widely implemented among contracting States. In order to simplify processing, a machine-readable passport was designed at ICAO's initiative in the late 1980s permitting scanning by use of optical character reading (OCR). This type of passport, which contains enhanced security features and safeguards against alteration or counterfeiting of identity information, has been widely introduced among certain contracting States.[478] The specifications for **'Machine Readable Travel Documents' (MRTD)** were set out in detail in ICAO Manual Doc. 9303.[479]

238. As a result of 11 September 2001, a further generation of identity document control has been developed by ICAO, namely **identity confirmation with biometrics**. The concept developed by ICAO involves the selection of face as the primary biometric, fingerprint and iris as secondary biometrics, the use of integrated circuits (IC) as a storage medium, and a modified Public Key Infrastructure (PKI) as a safeguard against unauthorized alteration.[480] The system is designed as a worldwide, interoperable system of identity confirmation with MRTDs, in particular machine-readable passports.[481]

239. Chapter 4 of Annex 9 deals with the facilitation of cargo movements, including the use of electronic processing, electronic airway bills, and other computerized cargo handling procedures conducive to cargo facilitation.

240. Chapter 6 covers the facilities and services at international airports. It specifies the different categories of airport traffic flow arrangements and separates them. It also specifies facilities for the implementation of public health requirements and emergency medical relief provisions, so as to ensure rapid response to health and emergency issues.

241. More recent challenges in this field relate to the harmonization of the requirements of facilitation with those of aviation security and narcotic drug

---

478. In May 2004, 101 contracting States reported that they issue machine-readable passports (MRP's); *see* ICAO Doc. A35-WP/11. For more recent information, *see* the reports of TAG-MRTD, *infra* (n. 480).
479. ICAO Manual 9303, *Machine Readable Travel Documents* has been successively updated and developed. Part 1 of the Manual, *Machine Readable Passports,* (2 Vols.) 6th ed. (2006), which defines the specifications for passports in standardized formats presenting data in eye-readable and machine-readable form, contains enhanced security features. *See also* Part 2, 3rd ed. (2005) and Part 3 (2 Vols.), 3rd. ed. (2008), and Supplement, Release 13 (21 Oct. 2013).
480. *See* Technical Advisory Group on Machine Readable Travel Documents (TAG-MRTD), Fifteenth Meeting, Montreal 19–21 May 2004, Report; Nineteenth Meeting, 7–9 Dec. 2009, Report and 22nd Meeting, May 2014, Report; *see also* ICAO Doc. 9303 Part 1, Vol. 2 and Part 3 Vol. 2 (MRTD Specifications).
481. ICAO Doc. A35-WP/11. *See also*: *Machine-Readable Passports to be issued worldwide by 2010*, ICAO News Release PIO 07/05, dated 11 Jul. 2005; Assembly Resolution A37-17, Appendix C.

control,[482] access to aircraft by handicapped, elderly or incapacitated persons, inadequately documented passengers, and special facilities for courier and express cargo/mail shipments.

242. In view of the security implications of facilitation, the Organization is tasked to ensure that the provisions of Annex 9 – Facilitation and Annex 17 – Security are **fully compatible and complementary** to each other. SARPs are developed to address operational and security issues associated with persons found inadmissible by States[483] and further rules to provide for the facilitation of entry/departure requirements for aircraft accident victims and their families.

243. In 2013, a comprehensive strategy called TRIP was approved. At the centre of the **ICAO TRIP Strategy** is the notion that a coherent, coordinated approach to traveller identification management is essential, comprising the following elements:

(a) Evidence of identity – credible evidence of identity, involving the tracing, linkage and verification of identity against ‘breeder documents’ to ensure the authenticity of identity.
(b) Machine-readable travel documents (MRTDs) – the design and manufacture of standardized MRTDs, including ePassports, that comply with ICAO specifications.
(c) Document issuance and control – processes and protocols for document issuance by appropriate authorities to authorized holders, and controls to prevent theft, tampering and loss.
(d) Inspection systems and tools – inspection systems and tools for the efficient and secure reading and verification of MRTDs, including the use of the ICAO Public Key Directory system (PKD).
(e) Interoperable applications – globally interoperable applications and protocols that provide for timely, secure and reliable linkage of MRTDs and their holders to available and relevant data in the course of inspection operations.[484]

The overall objective of traveller identification management is that all Member States can uniquely identify individuals by their machine-readable travel documents with the highest degree of certainty, security and efficiency. It serves the entire transport sector as well as trade and tourism.

482. Assembly Resolution A37-17, Appendix C, para. 11(a); Doc. 9826–Supplement (*Supplementary Report on Activities of the Organization in the first half of 2004*), p. 11.
483. Doc. 9826 – Supplement (July. 2004), p. 11.
484. *See* Assembly Resolution A39-20*: Consolidated statement of continuing policies related to facilitation*, Doc. 10075. *See also* https://www.icao.int/Security/FAL/TRIP/Pages/default.aspx and ICAO Doc. 10022, A39-WP/40 and A38-WP/11.

V. Taxes and Charges

244. In many parts of the world, taxes and charges have increasingly been imposed in respect of international air transport by some contracting States, their territorial subdivisions, or their airports. Certain charges on or relating to air traffic, several of which resemble taxes on the sale or use of international air transport, have been proliferating.

The Organization has developed ***ICAO Policies on Taxation in the Field of International Air Transport,***[485] which seek to limit and circumscribe grounds for taxation of international air transport. It also provides useful rules and guidance on air transport charges as well as conditions and procedures. In the practice of the Organization, a charge is a '*levy that is designed and applied specifically to recover the costs of providing facilities and services for civil aviation*'.[486] A tax, on the other hand, is *a 'levy that is designed to raise national or local government revenues which are generally not applied to civil aviation in their entirety or on a cost-specific basis*'.[487]

245. On this basis, the Organization has developed and applied the longstanding **principle of non-taxation of aviation fuel, spare parts, lubricants**, etc., based on the principle of mutuality, and the principle that if **charges** are levied, **the proceeds should be applied entirely to civil aviation**.[488]

246. It is one of the important tasks of ICAO to ensure that the implementation of the ICAO Policies on taxation is monitored and remains transparent and that the Manual on ICAO Policies on Taxation in the Field of International Air Transport (Doc. 8632) is current and responsive to the needs of contracting States.[489]

VI. Airports and Air Navigation Services

247. With the privatization of many airports and the corporatization of many air navigation service providers, it has become important to develop international guidance on the charges which airports and air navigation services may levy, based on consensus.

248. The Organization has developed **ICAO Policies on Charges for Airports and Air Navigation Providers,**[490] including a supplement containing information on States' implementation. Furthermore, supplementary guidance material was

485. Doc. 8632, 3rd ed. 2000, with addendum, supplements and corrigendum March 2017.
486. Assembly Resolution A38-14, Appendix D (Taxation), has refined the distinction between a tax and a charge; *see* Second Whereas Clause of Appendix D.
487. Definition set out in A38-14 Appendix D, Second Whereas Clause.
488. *See ibid.* (n. 474), Appendix D, and Doc. 8632, *ibid.* (n. 473).
489. Doc. 8632, *ibid.* (n. 473).
490. *ICAO's Policies on Charges for Airports and Air Navigation Services*, 9th ed. (2012). Doc. 9082/9.

developed, namely the Airport Economics Manual,[491] the Manual on Air Navigation Services, Economics[492] and Tariffs for Airports and Air Navigation Services.[493]

VII. Air Carrier Economics

249. There is a continuing interest among users, and aviation and trade organizations in information on the costs of operation, fares, rates and yields of international air carriers. Furthermore, the Organization uses air carrier revenue and cost data for environmental planning, statistical studies and other purposes. ICAO's studies on air transport revenues and costs have been widely used by contracting States and international organizations. The Organization has been tasked to issue periodically studies on regional differences in air carrier operating costs,[494] including an analysis of how differences in operations and input price may affect cost levels, and the impact of cost changes on fares and rates.[495]

VIII. Air Mail

250. Due to the increasing privatization or corporatization of postal services, special regulations and provisions regarding transportation of airmail are gradually rescinded. However, a number of important aspects continue to be regulated by the **Universal Postal Union (UPU)**[496] Therefore, the Organization ensures close cooperation with UPU, including representation at meetings and exchange of documents and information, in dealing with air transport aspects of air mail regulation.[497]

IX. Environmental Protection

251. Since the early 1980s, environmental protection has been an increasingly important element of the work of the Organization. Starting with efforts to limit and **reduce aircraft noise**, in particular in the vicinity of airports, the activities have gradually included efforts to limit and **reduce emissions from aircraft engines** including greenhouse gases, carbon monoxide and nitrogen oxides.[498]

---

491. Doc. 9526.
492. Doc. 9161/3.
493. *Tariffs for Airports and Air Navigation Services*, 2016 Edition, Doc. 7100.
494. Regional Differences in International Airline Operating Economics, 2006 and 2007, ICAO Circular 327; *see also* the previous Circular 306; Doc. 9826 – Supplement (July. 2004), p. 10.
495. The respective statistical data are now issued in online format only and made accessible to staff of national civil aviation administrations, *see* above, §3 s. II Statistics.
496. *See* L. Weber, *Universal Postal Union*', in: R. Bernhardt (ed.), *Encyclopedia supra* (Ch. 1, n. 9) Vol. IV (2000), pp. 1235 et seq., with further references; *see also infra* Ch. 6, §2, II.
497. *See*, e.g., Annual Report of the Council – 1997, Doc. 9700, Ch. III.3.
498. *See* Annex 16, Part II: Aircraft Engine Emissions; Assembly Resolution A41-21: *Consolidated statement of continuing ICAO policies and practices related to environmental protection – Climate change;* https://www.icao.int/environmental-protection/CORSIA/Documents/Resolution_A41-22_CORSIA.pdf; *see also* the ICAO Engine Exhaust Emission Data Bank, Doc. 9646.

A. Objectives

252. The continuing policy statement first enounced in Resolution A35-5 stated three broad objectives for ICAO's work on environmental protection:[499]

(1) to limit or reduce the number of people affected by aircraft noise;
(2) to limit or reduce the impact of aviation emissions on local air quality; and
(3) to limit or reduce the impact of aviation greenhouse gas emissions on the global climate.

These objectives continue to apply, however at the 41st Assembly in autumn 2022 the following additional broad objective was added:

(1) to ensure future resilience of air transport by adapting its infrastructure and operations to the consequences of climate change.[500]

B. Development of SARPs, Procedures and Guidance Material

253. A number of SARPs, procedures and guidance materials have been developed in order to achieve the above objectives, namely those in **Annex 16, Vol. I: Aircraft Noise**, including noise certification standards and regarding emissions in Annex 16, Vol. II: Aircraft Engine Emissions, as well as in other related materials.[501]

254. In addition, the Committee on Aviation Environmental Protection (CAEP) has worked over a number of years to assist in the further development of SARPs, procedures and guidance material, and to develop appropriate solutions based on consensus.[502]

C. 'Balanced Approach' to Aircraft Noise Management

255. This important element of ICAO's policy[503] was achieved in 2001 as a result of lengthy and protracted multilateral negotiations. Its main elements were set

499. A35-5: *Consolidated Statement of continuing ICAO policies and practices related to environmental protection*, Appendix A, Operating Clause 1, superseded by A41-20, A41-21 and A41-22 while maintaining the above three main objectives.

500. *See* Resolution A41-21: *Consolidated statement of continuing ICAO policies and practices related to environmental protection – Climate change;* and Resolution A41-20: *Consolidated statement of continuing ICAO policies and practices related to environmental protection – General provisions, noise and local air quality*, ICAO Doc. 10184.

501. *Airport Planning Manual,* Doc. 9184, Part 2: *Land use and environmental management*; CAEP/5, Report, Doc. 9777; CAEP/10, Report.

502. *See* CAEP/1 Report to CAEP/12 Report (February. 2022); A41-WP/368, WP/371, WP/93; ICAO Docs. 9720, 9777 and 9836.

503. *See* A41-20, Appendix C: *Policies and programmes based on a 'balanced approach' to aircraft noise management*; previously A38-17, Appendix C; *Guidance on the Balanced Approach to Aircraft Noise Management*, Doc. 9829, and A35-5.

out in Assembly Resolution A33-7, supplemented by Doc. 9829: **Guidance on the Balanced Approach to Aircraft Noise Management**.[504]

256. The **balanced approach** consists essentially of a transparent process when considering measures to alleviate aircraft noise, in particular at airports, including:[505]

- assessment of noise problems based on objective, measurable criteria;
- evaluation of the likely costs and benefits of measures available, and selection of measures so as to achieve maximum environmental benefit most cost-efficiently; and
- dissemination of evaluation results for consultations with stakeholders and dispute resolution.

257. Based on the above assessment, States are encouraged to:[506]

- promote research in technologies aiming to reduce noise at source or through other means;
- apply land-use planning and management policies to limit encroachment of new developments into noise-sensitive areas;
- apply noise abatement operational procedures; and
- apply operating restrictions only as a last resort and consistent with Appendix E of A38-17.

D. Phase-Out of Subsonic Jet Aircraft Which Exceed the Noise Levels in Volume I of Annex 16

258. These principles supplement the provisions of Annex 16 Vol. I, which do not specify any time-limits or phase-out for aircraft.

259. They stipulate essentially the following:

- the phase-out of Chapter 2 aircraft (i.e., those noisy aircraft which exceed the noise levels of Chapter 3) should only be envisaged as a measure of last resort, after normal attrition, non-addition rules and airport usage restrictions have been considered and other States concerned have been consulted;[507]
- any phase-out of Chapter 2 aircraft should give existing operators a time frame of at least seven years for gradual replacement or withdrawal, and during these

504. *See* A41-20, Appendix C, *ibid.*; Assembly Resolution A33-7, which was superseded by Assembly Resolutions A35-5, A36-22, A37-18, A38-17, A39-1, and A41-20, Appendix C, while developing further the substance of the 'balanced approach'.
505. A41-20 Appendix C, Operating Clause 2.b). *See also* Doc. 9829 and ICAO Circular 315.
506. A41-20 Appendix C; previously A35-5, Appendix C. Operating Clause 3.b–d). *See also* Doc. 9829.
507. Assembly Resolution A41-20, Appendix D: *Phase-out of subsonic jet aircraft which exceed the noise levels in Volume I of Annex 16*, Operating Clause 1.a)–d); *see* previously A40-17, A38-17, A37-18, A36-22 and A35-5, App. D.

seven years, should not apply to aircraft which are less than twenty-five years old and should not apply to wide-body jets during such seven years.[508]

E. Local Noise-Related Operating Restrictions at Airports

260. As indicated in para. 258 above, operating restrictions for aircraft at noise-sensitive airports should, under the balanced approach, only be applied as a measure of last resort. However, if they are applied, the following conditions shall be applied:[509]

- before operating restrictions are imposed on Chapter 3 aircraft, the phase-out of all Chapter 2 aircraft at the airport concerned should first be completed;
- other available measures under the balanced approach should first be fully assessed;
- restrictions on Chapter 3 aircraft should be purely performance-based;
- restrictions should be tailored to the airport noise problem;
- restrictions should be partial whenever possible;
- the impact of such restrictions on air transport services (e.g., night curfews for long-haul services) should be taken into account; and
- Chapter 4 aircraft should not be made subject to noise-related operating restrictions.

F. Land-Use Planning and Management

261. **Land-use planning and management** is one of the principal elements of the balanced approach, as indicated in paragraphs 257 and 258 above; under Resolution A41-20, Appendix F, it should be used in combination with the other elements of the balanced approach so as to:[510]

- avoid inappropriate land use or encroachment by new developments in the noise-sensitive vicinity of an airport;
- locate new airports away from noise-sensitive areas;
- define zones around airports associated with different noise levels; and
- enact legislation or establish guidance to achieve compliance;
- ensure reader-friendly information on aircraft operations and their environmental effects are available to communities near airports.

508. A41-20, Appendix D, Operating Clause 2. a)–d).
509. A41-20 Appendix E, Operating Clauses 2–4.
510. A41-20, Appendix F, Operating Clause 3 a)–e).

G. Environmental Impact of Civil Aviation on the Atmosphere

262. At ICAO's request, a special report on 'Aviation and the Global Atmosphere' was prepared by the Intergovernmental Panel on Climate Change (IPCC), in collaboration with the Scientific Assessment Panel to the Montreal Protocol on Substances that Deplete the Ozone Layer, and was published in 1999.[511] According to the report, aircraft are estimated to contribute about 3.5% of the total radiative forcing (a measure of change in climate) by all human activities and this percentage is projected to grow. The subsidiary body for scientific and technological advice of the **UN Framework Convention on Climate Change (UNFCCC)** sought the assistance of ICAO on issues related to the collection and reporting of greenhouse gas emissions at a national level.[512] The Kyoto Protocol adopted in 1997 called for limitation or reduction of greenhouse gas emissions including those from aviation, and for aviation-related emissions, the Contracting Parties decided to work through ICAO.[513] The Paris Agreement of 2015 put in place a more ambitious and legally binding long-term goal requiring all parties to pursue a limit in temperature increase of 1.5°C and to provide measurable national contributions. Similarly, the Glasgow Climate Pact of 2021 reaffirmed the temperature goals set in the Paris Agreement, to hold the increase in the global average temperature to well below 2°C above pre-industrial levels, and to pursue efforts to limit the temperature increase to 1.5°C above pre-industrial levels.

263. Accordingly, the Organization worked closely with the IPCC and other organizations, notably with the UNFCCC, and assisted its subsidiary body with Scientific and Technological Advice.[514] It studied policy options to limit or reduce the environmental impact of engine emissions through operational and market-based measures and intends to develop concrete proposals and provide advice as soon as possible to the Conference of Parties to the UNFCCC. Among the tools explored were, *inter alia*, ATM improvements and the use of operational measures as outlined in ICAO Circular 303.[515]

At the 37th Session of the Assembly in September/October 2010, a decision in principle on **global fuel efficiency improvement** as a contribution to greenhouse gas emissions reduction was achieved, under which the Assembly resolved that 'States and relevant organizations will work through ICAO to achieve a global annual average fuel efficiency improvement of 2% until 2020 and an aspirational global fuel efficiency improvement rate of 2% per annum from 2021 to 2050, calculated on the basis of the volume of fuel used per revenue tonne-kilometre performed; Further, that the goals mentioned in paragraph 4 above would not attribute specific obligations to individual States, and the different circumstances, respective

511. *See* A35-5, Appendix H: *Environmental impact of civil aviation on the atmosphere*, third whereas clause; on the impact of the report on ICAO policy *see ibid.*, Appendix H, fourth to ninth whereas clause.
512. A35-5, Appendix H, eight whereas clause.
513. *Ibid.* (n. 1), Operating Clause 2.a) and c).
514. ICAO has developed, *inter alia*, an *Engine Exhaust Emissions Data Bank*, ICAO Doc. 9646.
515. *Operational Opportunities to Minimize Fuel Use and Reduce Emissions*, Circular 303; A35-5, Appendix H, Operating Clause 2.d).

capabilities and contribution of developing and developed States to the concentration of aviation GHG emissions in the atmosphere will determine how each State may voluntarily contribute to achieving the global aspirational goals.'[516] This decision was confirmed at the 38th Session of the Assembly in 2013.[517]

264. After the 40th Session of the ICAO Assembly, a number of information-sharing conferences were organized by ICAO to consider the feasibility of a long-term global aspirational goal (LTAG) for international aviation in light of the temperature goals set by the Paris Agreement.[518]

265. A Report was published in March 2022 by CAEP on the '*Feasibility of a Long-Term Aspirational Goal for International Civil Aviation CO_2 Emission Reductions*' which assessed the technical feasibility of various aviation in-sector CO_2 emissions reduction scenarios.[519] The Report concluded that drop-in sustainable aviation fuels (SAF) are expected to have the largest impact on aviation CO_2 emissions reduction by 2050 and shall continue to have a large impact beyond 2050. It was further stated that the technological feasibility of SAF has been proven. For providing assistance to States to encourage deployment of SAF, in 2022 ICAO launched the '*ICAO Assistance, Capacity-building and Training for Sustainable Aviation Fuel (ACT-SAF) Programme*'.[520]

266. In furtherance of the above Report and conferences, the 41st Assembly reached an agreement on the collective LTAG for civil aviation of net-zero carbon emissions by 2050,[521] in support of the Paris Agreement, and encouraged States to collaborate to achieve this aspirational goal. While keeping in mind the varying capabilities of different States to contribute to the LTAG, no specific obligations were imposed on individual States and they were rather urged to contribute to the LTAG in accordance with their respective national circumstances.

---

516. Assembly Resolution A37-19: *Consolidated statement of continuing ICAO policies and practices related to environmental protection – Climate change*, paras 4–6; the same text is found in A38-18, paras 5–7.
517. *See* Assembly Resolution A38-18, paras 5–7.
518. Assembly Resolution A40-18, operative clause 9, had requested the ICAO Council to continue to explore the feasibility of a long-term global aspirational goal for international aviation CO2 emissions reductions (LTAG).The 2022 ICAO Global Aviation Dialogues on a Long-term Aspirational Goal (LTAG-GLADs) were organized with this objective in mind: https://www.icao.int/Meetings/2022-ICAO-LTAG-GLADS/Pages/default.aspx; Working Paper on 'The cost of achieving net-zero carbon in aviation' A41-WP/477 EX/225:https://www.icao.int/Meetings/a41/Documents/WP/wp_477_en.pdf. Likewise, the High-level Meeting on the feasibility of a long-term aspirational goal for international aviation CO2 emissions reductions had the same objective: https://www.icao.int/Meetings/HLM-LTAG/Pages/default.aspx.
519. *See* https://www.icao.int/environmentalprotection/LTAG/Documents/REPORT%20ON%20THE%20FEASIB ILITY%20OF%20A%20LONG-TERM%20ASPIRATIONAL%20GOAL_en.pdf.
520. *See* https://www.icao.int/Newsroom/Pages/Launch-of-ICAO-Assistance-Capacitybuilding-and-Training-for-Sustainable-Aviation-Fuels.aspx.
521. *See* Clause 7 of Resolution A41-21: *Consolidated statement of continuing ICAO policies and practices related to environmental protection – Climate change*:https://www.icao.int/environmental-protection/Documents/Assembly/Resolution_A41-21_Climate_change.pdf.

H. The CORSIA Scheme: Market-Based Measures to Reduce Aircraft Emissions

267. **Market-based measures to reduce greenhouse gas emissions** are one of the options foreseen in the Kyoto Protocol of 1997. Their application to domestically produced emissions is foreseen in other sectors than aviation.

Market-based measures consist of three types:[522]

(1) Voluntary measures.
(2) Emission-related levies.
(3) Emissions-trading.

268. While voluntary measures have been encouraged in the framework of ICAO's work, emission-related levies have not found a basis for sufficient consensus. For the introduction of an emission-trading system, two possible approaches were considered.[523] Under one approach, ICAO would develop a voluntary trading system if supported by interested States and international organizations.[524] Under the second approach, ICAO would provide guidance to include emissions from international aviation into contracting States' emissions trading systems consistent with the UNFCCC process.[525]

269. At the 37th Session of the Assembly, a number of principles for a **framework for market based measures (MBM)** were agreed under which MBMs should support sustainable development of the international aviation sector. Specifically, they should mitigate the GHG emissions from international aviation, contribute towards achieving global aspirational goals, should be transparent and administratively simple, and should be cost-effective. The ICAO Council was mandated to further develop the framework with the support of the Member States.[526]

270. At the 38th Session of the Assembly, this mandate was further developed and refined. The Assembly decided to develop a **'global MBM scheme for international aviation'** and mandated the Council to finalize the work on the technical aspects. It should identify the major issues and problems, including for Member States, and '*make a recommendation on a global MBM scheme that appropriately addresses them and key design elements, including a means to take into account special circumstances and respective capabilities …, and the mechanisms for the implementation of the scheme from 2020 as part of a basket of measures which also include technologies, operational improvements and sustainable alternative fuels to achieve ICAO's global aspirational goal*'.[527] On behalf of the Council, the CAEP and its subgroups carried out the mandate to develop this mechanism.

522. A35-5, Appendix J: *Market-based measures regarding aircraft engine emissions*, Operating Clause 2 a)–c).
523. A35-5, Appendix H, Operating Clause 2.c) 2).
524. A35-5, *ibid.* (n. 505); A36-22.
525. *Ibid.*
526. Assembly Resolution A37-19: *Consolidated statement of continuing ICAO policies and practices* related to environmental protection – Climate change, paras 13–20 and Annex.
527. Assembly Resolution A38-18, para. 19 a) and c).

271. At the 39th Session of the Assembly in 2016, a global MBM Scheme for international aviation referred to as **CORSIA (Carbon Offsetting and Reduction Scheme for International Aviation)** was adopted. Resolution A39-3: *Consolidated statement of continuing ICAO policies and practices related to environmental protection – Global Market-based Measures (MBM) Scheme*[528] established in detail the terms and conditions for CORSIA and represents a significant milestone and achievement for the Organization. It calls for international aviation to offset its emissions through the reduction of emissions outside of the international aviation sector. It is based on making use of allocated '*emissions units*' or purchasing unused emission '*allowances*', one emission unit represents one ton of CO_2. Offsetting can be done either through '*offset credits*' from recognized and validated crediting mechanisms (e.g., UNFCCC's Clean Development Mechanism), programmes (e.g., REDD+) or projects (e.g., substituting coal-fired generators with solar panel farms). Offsetting may also occur through 'allowances' from emissions trading schemes. The buying and selling of eligible emissions units will involve a carbon market, which is a commodity market trading with emissions units. Like any commodity market, it will be driven by the law of supply (eligible emissions units offered from different sources) and demand (eligible emissions units purchased by aircraft operators to offset their international aviation emissions under the CORSIA).[529]

272. CORSIA is intended to **supplement and support the COP21 Paris Agreement of 2015** as regards emissions from international aviation. In accordance with the outcome of the first CORSIA periodic review, at the 41st Assembly Session, the CORSIA baseline was revised for the phases of 2021–2023, and 2024–2035. It is introduced in 3 phases, namely a pilot phase from 2021–2023; a first operational phase from 2024–2026 involving States that have volunteered to participate in the scheme; and a second operational phase from 2027–2035, involving all States that have a share of international aviation activities above 0.5% of total RTKs (baseline 2018) or whose cumulative share of total RTKs exceeds a given threshold. Least Developed Countries (LDCs), Small Island Developing States (SIDS) and Landlocked Developing Countries (LLDCs) are exempted unless they volunteer to participate. States' implementation is based on a monitoring, reporting and verification (MRV) system involving emissions reporting by international operators and their registration in registries, including a consolidated central registry under the auspices of ICAO.[530]

528. ICAO Doc. 10075, pp. 25 et seq. Now superseded by Assembly Resolution A41-22, ICAO Doc. 10184.

529. Annex 16, Doc. AN 16 Vol. IV – *Carbon Offsetting and Reduction Scheme for International Aviation (CORSIA); see also* Doc. 9501 (ETM), Vol. IV (CORSIA) (2d ed.); and the 14 CORSIA Implementation Elements referenced in Annex 16 Vol. IV; Assembly Resolution A41-22: *Carbon Offsetting and Reduction Scheme for International Aviation (CORSIA)*, Doc. 10184.

530. Assembly Resolution A41-22, *ibid.* The sectoral and individual operators' growth factors for the calculation of offsetting requirements was also revised for the phases of 2021 – 2032, and 2033 – 2035. Further, it was provided that new entrants shall be exempted from the application of the CORSIA for three years or until the year in which their annual emissions exceed 0.1 percent of total emissions in 2019, whichever occurs earlier.

273. As of January 2023, 115 ICAO Member States representing more than 90% of international aviation activity had declared their intention to **participate on a voluntary basis in CORSIA** as of that date.[531] ICAO has supported the implementation of CORSIA by issuing SARPs as well as the necessary guidance material as of 2020.[532]

§4. Joint Financing

274. Under the terms of Chapter XV of the Convention (Airports and other Air Navigation Facilities), a **'Joint Support Policy'** was established by the Organization in Resolution A1-65 at the first Assembly in 1947, which continues to apply today.[533] The policy has the objective of rendering financial and technical aid, through ICAO, for the provision of air navigation facilities and services adequate for the safe, regular, efficient and economical operation of international air services in particular areas. These areas are territories of undetermined sovereignty, the high seas, and territories of States which are not providing the required facilities.[534]

The facilities and services for which provision may be made under the Joint Support Policy include:[535]

- Aerodromes and Ground Aids to Navigation.
- Air Traffic Control Service.
- Meteorological Service.
- Search and Rescue Service.
- Telecommunications and Radio Aids to Air Navigation.

275. In conformity with the principles of the Joint Support Policy, two Joint Financing Agreements were concluded in 1956, which provide for the financing of certain air navigation services over the North Atlantic route: the **Agreement on the**

---

531. https://www.icao.int/environmental-protection/CORSIA/Pages/default.aspx: *See also*: *Update on the Work on the Carbon Offsetting and Reduction Scheme for International Aviation (CORSIA)*, para. 1.3. As of August 2022, the number of States having reported 2019 CO2 emissions reports to ICAO through the CCR was 117, with 110 States having submitted their 2020 CO2 emissions. *See Carbon Offsetting and Reduction Scheme for International Aviation (CORSIA)*, A41-WP/370 EX/168, para. 1.5.
532. Standards and Recommended Practices (SARPs) in Annex 16 – *Environmental Protection*, Volume IV – *Carbon Offsetting and Reduction Scheme for International Aviation (CORSIA)*; guidance in Doc. 9501, *Environmental Technical Manual (ETM)*, Volume IV; and five CORSIA Implementation Elements. Also prepared were: *CORSIA Default Life Cycle Emissions Values for CORSIA Eligible Fuels and CORSIA Methodology for Calculating Actual Life Cycle Emissions Values* (C-WP/15158 refers); and *CORSIA Sustainability Criteria for CORSIA Eligible Fuels* (C-WP/15172 refers). At C222, the Council also considered an update of the ICAO document *CORSIA Eligible Emissions Units*, following recommendations from TAB (C-WP/15160 refers). *See also Implementation Issues Regarding the Scenarios for a Long-Term Aspirational Goal for International Aviation CO2 Emissions Reductions and their Interrelationship with CORSIA*, A41-WP/169 EX/76.
533. Assembly Resolution A1-65: *Joint Support Policy*, Doc. 9848, Part IV 1.
534. A1-65, Annex 1, s. 1. *See* Doc. 10140.
535. *See* ICAO Assembly Resolution A1-65, Annex 1, para. 1: *Objective of financial and technical aid*, ICAO Doc. 9790, IV-1.

Joint Financing of Certain Air Navigation Services in Iceland[536] and the **Agreement on the Joint Financing of Certain Air Navigation Services in Greenland and the Faroe Islands,**[537] concluded on the same date.[538] These agreements cover ATC, communications (COM) and meteorological (MET) facilities and services for North Atlantic flights provided by the Danish and Icelandic authorities in accordance with agreed conditions. Presently, 25 States are parties to the Iceland agreement and 24 States to the Danish Agreement. Yearly contributions to the separate budget under each Agreement are in proportion to the number of aircraft movements of each respective State. Expenditures under each budget, administered by ICAO on behalf of the 'Contributing States', serve to finance the full cost of the operation, maintenance of facilities and rendering of services by the two administrations, Denmark and Iceland.

276. Even though not all States whose air carriers operate services on the North Atlantic have joined the Agreements,[539] they have proven successful in supporting the administrations of the two relatively small States in providing large-scale services and facilities. The Agreements were amended twice, in 1982 and 2008.[540]

277. A separate **Arrangement on the Joint Financing of a North Atlantic Height Monitoring System** was concluded among six Contracting States in 1995, which serves mainly for purposes of equipment calibration. Its budget is also administered by ICAO.[541]

278. Similarly, the Organization provides administrative services to the parties to the **Agreement on the Sharing of Costs of the Satellite Distribution System for Information Relating to Air Navigation (SADIS).**[542] This Agreement, which provides satellite support for the supply of forecasts of en-route meteorological conditions, includes cost-recovery for SADIS support services. The Organization supports the administration of the cost-recovery mechanism through the SADIS Cost Recovery Administrative Group.[543]

536. ICAO Doc. 9586.
537. *Agreement on the Joint Financing of Certain Air Navigation Services in Greenland and the Faroe Islands*, ICAO Doc. 9585; *UNTS* Vol. 334 (1959), p. 89. The Agreement was adopted and entered into force on the same date respectively as the Iceland Agreement, (n. 521). *See also supra*, Ch. 2, §3, IV.
538. On 25 Sep. 1956. Previously, a related technical *Agreement on North Atlantic Ocean Stations* had been concluded on 25 Feb. 1954, ICAO Doc. 7510 (JS/559), *UNTS* Vol. 215 (1955), p. 268.
539. Assembly Resolution A14-37, *Increased Participation by 'User States' in the Joint Financing Agreements,* urged States using the North Atlantic route to consider as soon as possible acceding to the Agreements. ICAO Doc. 9790, IV-4.
540. *See* Doc. 9585-JS/681 – and Doc. 9586-JS/682.
541. Arrangement signed on 31 Jul. 1995 at Montreal, ICAO Reg. No. 4004. It entered into force on 12 Dec. 1995.
542. *See SADIS User Guide*, 4th ed. (June. 2008), ed. by ICAO.
543. *Ibid.* (n. 531), Ch. 1.5; ICAO Doc. 9826 Supplement (July. 2004).

§5. Legal Matters

I. General

279. The main body dealing with legal matters in ICAO is the **Legal Committee**. Reference is made to paragraphs 82 8–84 and 116–118 above for its tasks, composition and mode of operation, including the procedure for approval of draft conventions on international air law.[544]

280. At the Assembly, legal matters are discussed in the **Legal Commission**, which is distinct from the Legal Committee, and which is a subsidiary body of the Assembly.[545] The Legal Commission prepares the decisions of the Assembly regarding legal matters, such as decisions regarding the legal work programme of the Organization, adoption of resolutions on legal issues, and providing views on matters of legal significance. In those cases where ICAO has adhered to international instruments to which international organizations may become parties, the decision whether to adhere was taken by the Assembly[546] in the form of a 'confirmation'.

II. Ratification of International Instruments

281. The Assembly has also taken an active role in promoting the **ratification of air law instruments** which were developed by the Organization. It has frequently called on contracting States which have not yet done so to ratify as soon as possible certain instruments, the entry into force of which was deemed important, or wide adherence to which was considered useful.[547] The President of the Council and the Secretary General were requested to follow up during visits to States. At the Assembly's request, administrative ratification packages were developed and issued for most international air law instruments, which provide States with detailed information and model documents about the various instruments.

282. Furthermore, the Assembly has actively promoted the teaching of air law.[548] In this context, in 1996 the Organization awarded its Edward Warner Medal, the highest distinction in civil aviation, to the Institute of Air and Space Law of McGill University, Montreal, in recognition of its teaching and research in air law.

---

544. Assembly Resolution A37-22, Appendix B.
545. *Standing Rules of Procedure of the Assembly of ICAO*, ICAO Doc. 7600/8, Rules 14 and 18. *See also supra,* Ch. 2. §2, I *supra.*
546. *See,* e.g., Assembly Resolution A33-5: *Confirmation of the 1986 Vienna Convention on the Law of Treaties between States and International Organizations or between International Organizations*, ICAO Doc. 9790, p. I-26.
547. *See* Assembly Resolution A40-28: *Consolidated Statement of Continuing ICAO Policies in the Legal Field*, Appendix C; previously A39-11 Appendix C; A37-22 Appendix C; and A36-26 Appendix C.
548. *Ibid.* (n. 530), Appendix D.

III. Depositary Functions for International Instruments

283. As of March 2023, the Organization is the depositary of thirty-five international air law instruments and performs related functions. In some cases, the **depositary functions** are assigned and exercised jointly with contracting States or other international organizations.[549] The Organization maintains a database called 'Treaty Collection', through which it keeps information current on signatures, ratifications, entry into force, declarations and reservations regarding all instruments for which it performs depositary functions.[550]

IV. Registration of Aeronautical Agreements and Arrangements

284. In accordance with Articles 83 and 83bis, the Organization maintains a registry of all **aeronautical agreements and arrangements** which contracting States, international organizations or other parties file for that purpose. The registry is maintained by the Legal Affairs and External Relations Bureau of the Organization and is publicly accessible.[551]

285. Under Article 83 of the Convention, contracting States shall register all aeronautical agreements and arrangements they conclude. Under Article 83bis, agreements and arrangements which provide for the transfer between States of safety oversight functions over aircraft involved in lease, charter or interchange require registration with ICAO in order to become effective *erga omnes* as regards the transfer.[552]

286. The registration of agreements and arrangements is subject to the **ICAO Rules for Registration of Aeronautical Agreements and Arrangements.**[553] The registry contains close to 6,000 agreements. Reference is made to paragraphs 119–121 above.

---

549. *See,* e.g., *the Protocol for the Suppression of Unlawful Acts of Violence at Airports Serving International Civil Aviation,* signed at Montreal on 24 Feb. 1988, for which the Russian Federation, the UK, the US and ICAO serve as depositaries; ICAO Doc. 9518.
550. The database is accessible at http://www.icao.int/Secretariat/Legal/Pages/TreatyCollection.aspx.
551. The registry is accessible at http://cfapp.icao.int/dagmar/main.cfm?UserLang=_e. ICAO has also created a Website of Aeronautical Agreements and Arrangements (WAGMAR) which is accessible at https://dna.icao.int/WAGMAR. ICAO is working on the transition from DAGMAR to WAGMAR. While presently not all of the registered aeronautical agreements and arrangements are yet available online, it is the objective to achieve this. *See also Database of the World's Air Services Agreements,* ICAO Doc. 9511.
552. *See*: *Guidelines on the Implementation of Article 83bis*, ICAO Circular 295; *Manual on the implementation of Article 83 bis of the Convention on International Civil Aviation*, Doc. 10059.
553. *Rules for Registration with ICAO of Aeronautical Agreements and Arrangements,* Approved and published by decision of the Council, Doc. 6685-C/767, 3rd ed. 2020.

V. Legal Advice to the Governing Bodies and the Secretary General

287. Whenever the governing bodies of the Organization (Council, Assembly) are in need of legal advice and such advice cannot await meetings of the Legal Committee or the Legal Commission, the **Legal Affairs and External Relations Bureau** of the Organization has the task to provide such legal advice. Due to the rapidly changing nature of today's environment, legal advice is frequently required from the Bureau without prior reference to the other legal bodies of the Organization.

VI. Dispute Settlement

288. As discussed in more detail in Chapter 2, paragraphs 122–127 above, the **Council of ICAO** has **dispute settlement** functions in accordance with Articles 84–88 of the Convention as regards disputes between contracting States relating to the interpretation or application of the Convention or its Annexes.[554]

289. It has similar functions relating to the interpretation or application of the International Air Services Transit Agreement, in accordance with Article 66 of the Convention and Article II Transit Agreement.[555]

290. From time to time, the Council is also called upon to settle disputes by means of less formal avenues, either under Article 54(n) or through informal mediation.[556] Reference is made to Chapter 2, paragraphs 128–129 above for further details on these quasi-judicial functions of the Council.

VII. Work Programme of the Legal Committee

291. Under its **Rules of Procedure**, the Legal Committee shall establish and maintain a work programme, subject to the approval of the Council. The Assembly also has direct input into **the work programme of the Legal Committee.**

---

554. *See* on this matter T. Buergenthal, *Law-making in the International Civil Aviation Organization* (New York, Syracuse Univ. Press, 1969), Part III, p. 123–198; B. Cheng, *The Law of International Air Transport* (London, Stevens 1962); pp. 100 et seq.; R. Mankiewicz, 'Organisation internationale de l'aviation civile', Vol. III *AFDI* (1957), pp. 383 et seq. *See* further Assembly Resolution A1-23: *Authorization to the Council to Act as an arbitral body*, Doc. 9790, p. I-19.
555. Article 66 of the Convention confers such disputes settlement functions expressly on the Organization; Art. II of the Transit Agreement provides that a contracting State which deems that action by another contracting State under this Agreement is causing injustice or hardship to it, may request the Council to examine the matter. *See* 84 *UNTS* 389 et seq.
556. While dispute settlement through Art. 54(n) will involve a hearing of the parties by the Council, informal mediation may involve the President of the Council, the Secretariat, or an informal group of the Council in accordance with verbal discussions with the parties.

292. As of March 2023, as a result of decisions of the 41st Assembly and of the Council, the work programme of the Legal Committee stood as follows:[557]

(1) Review of the ICAO Rules for the Settlement of Differences.
(2) International legal aspects of unmanned (pilotless) aircraft operations and integration into civil aviation.
(3) Processes and procedures for States to fulfil their obligations under Article 12 of the Chicago Convention.
(4) Acts or offences of concern to the international aviation community, including cyber threats, that may not be adequately covered by existing air law instruments.
(5) Promotion of the ratification of international air law instruments.
(6) Study of international legal issues relating to global satellite systems and services supporting international air navigation services.
(7) Consideration of guidance on conflicts of interest.
(8) Implementation of Article 21 of the Chicago Convention.

§6. Technical Cooperation

I. Overview

293. Technical Cooperation is an important field of activity within the Organization. The **Technical Cooperation Bureau (TCB)**, which is one of the five bureaux of the Organization, operates on a budget which is self-financing (AOSC budget) and therefore separate from the Regular Budget of the Organization.[558]

294. Its main objective is to provide advice and assistance to contracting States in the **development and implementation of projects** in all fields of civil aviation aimed at improving the safety, efficiency, regularity and security of international civil aviation, and with a view to achieving standardization as specified in ICAO's SARPs.[559]

II. Activities and Services

295. The services which the Organization provides include:

– projects providing civil aviation expertise;
– planning studies;

557. As decided by the 41st Session of the Assembly, *Work Programme of the Organization in the Legal Field*, Doc. A41-WP/53 LE/2, and by the Council, C-DEC 223/2.
558. For more detail *see infra*, Ch. 4. §4 and Regulation 9.5 of the ICAO *Financial Regulations*, Doc. 7515, 16th ed. 2017.
559. *See* Assembly Resolution A40-24: Consolidated statement of ICAO policies on technical cooperation and technical assistance; A33-21: *Update on the new policy on technical cooperation*; and A26-16: *Technical Assistance*, ICAO Doc. 9790, pp. VI-1 et seq.

- procurement of equipment;
- training in civil aviation fields, such as flight operations safety or CNS/ATM;
- enhancement of aviation and airport security.

In cases of expert assistance to contracting States, the ICAO experts work alongside national staff to transmit know-how and on-the-job training as may be required. Such projects may include a single expert or a team of experts to strengthen the civil aviation authority or unit.[560]

296. In cases of planning studies, ICAO composes a field planning team of experts selected for the particular study to be carried out in close coordination with the contracting State.

297. In cases of **procurement of equipment,**[561] ICAO prepares specifications in line with the requesting Contracting State's requirements, issues a call for public tender, selects the contractor, and procures the equipment for delivery and if required installation on site. ICAO also procures combinations of equipment and services through 'turnkey' contracts, where appropriate.

298. As regards **training assistance,**[562] ICAO's activities include training school planning, course development, instructor training, and equipment procurement. The Organization has helped to develop or establish a number of national training schools for aviation around the world. ICAO also provides various types of cooperation and support to training schools through the organization's TRAINAIR and TRAINAIR PLUS programmes.[563]

299. As regards **aviation and airport security** enhancement, ICAO's activities may include an assessment of aviation security facilities and operations, the drafting of security regulations for airports and aviation operations, the establishment of emergency plans for response, and the correction of shortcomings and deficiencies in national aviation security programmes, facilities and operations following a USAP audit or a voluntary security assessment.[564]

300. Furthermore, the organization assists in the drafting of national aviation legislation or regulations through its legal experts, and in the drawing up of air transport studies through its air transport experts.

560. *See* Resolution A21-16, Part C: Experts. *See also* Resolutions A36-17 and A39-16.
561. *See* Resolution A21-16, Part A, para. 9; Resolutions A36-17 and A39-16.
562. *See* Resolution A21-16 part A, paras 5–6; and Part B, para. 13; *see also* A39-16, A36-17 and Doc. 9790, p. VI-6.
563. *See* http://www.icao.int/safety/TrainairPlus; *infra*, Ch. 3. §2 V.: Other Activities.
564. *Report on the ICAO Universal Security Audit Programme*, A39-WP/20; *Security Audit Reference Manual,* Doc. 9807.

III. Contracting and Financing of Projects

301. ICAO's technical cooperation activities have traditionally involved the **United Nations Development Programme (UNDP)**.[565] While UNDP projects initially made up the lion's share of ICAO's TCB activities, the volume of UNDP-financed projects has now dropped to less than 1%, mainly due to the reduction in UNDP financing.[566]

302. **Trust Fund projects** are administered under the same rules as UNDP projects,[567] whereas the funds are provided by either the State commissioning the project, or by a third donor State or international body, such as a development bank.[568] ICAO's administrative service fees under a Trust Fund project agreement are the same as for UNDP projects. Trust funds must be deposited with ICAO at the time of signing the Agreement to cover a given period of project activities, normally one year.

303. **Management Service Agreements** are another method to finance projects. They have features similar to Trust Fund Agreements but allow for greater flexibility in the administrative and financial aspects of project implementation.[569]

304. **Civil Aviation Purchase (CAPS) Agreements** are used for the procurement of equipment and/or services.[570] In these cases, funds are deposited with ICAO to cover the project, or the first phase of the project in complex cases, at the time of signing the CAPS Agreement. Purchasing/procurement is then carried out in accordance with the ICAO Procurement Code.[571] Procuring the entire range of civil aviation equipment/services is possible under these Agreements.

---

565. *See* Assembly Resolution A27-18: *Funding for Technical Assistance Activities*, ICAO Doc. 9790, p. VI-5.
566. For a comprehensive summary of ICAO' TCB activities, *see* A40-24 Appendix B; A39-WP/47: Policy And Activities On Technical Cooperation during The Period 2013 – 2015; Activities and Policy on Technical Cooperation provided under the UNDP and through Trust Fund (TF) Arrangements during the Period 2001–2003, A35-WP/6, paras 1.1, 1.2.;A37-WP/40; A37-WP/357 P/31, Corr. No. 1.
567. Assembly Resolution A26-16: *Technical Assistance*, para. 15 (ICAO Doc. 9790, p. VI-3).
568. *Transition to a New Policy on Technical Cooperation*, A35-WP/5, in particular para. 5; A36-17; A-39-16; A40-28. The New Policy was first endorsed by the 31st Session of the Assembly in 1995.
569. *See* A39-16, Appendix A, clause 14.
570. *See* Assembly Resolution A26-16, *ibid.* (n. 550), at para. 19 which describes CAPS as '*a facility provided by ICAO to developing countries to purchase high value items of civil aviation equipment and to contract for technical services*'. *See also* A36-17.
571. *ICAO Procurement Code,* Doc. 9761 (2013). The Code is adopted under the authority of the Secretary General.

§7. AVIATION SECURITY

I. Early Developments

305. In the early 1960s, cases of hijacking of civil aircraft, taking of hostages on board, and other **acts of unlawful interference with civil aviation** proliferated, calling for international attention. Many of these acts were politically motivated, received large world press coverage, and perpetrators who expressed sympathy with the political regime of the destination of such hijackings were in many cases not prosecuted but celebrated.[572] Member States called on the Organization to take international action.

II. Aviation Security Conventions

306. Successively, the Organization developed three **international instruments** in order to better protect international civil aviation against acts of unlawful interference, namely:

- the *Convention on Offences and Certain Other Acts Committed on Board Aircraft* (Tokyo Convention, 1963);[573]
- the *Convention for the Suppression of Unlawful Seizure of Aircraft* (The Hague Convention, 1970);[574] and
- the *Convention for the Suppression of Unlawful Acts Against the Safety of Civil Aviation* (Montreal Convention, 1971).[575]

307. The main purpose of these conventions was to establish hijacking, taking of hostages and similar acts as international criminal offences, and render them punishable by severe penalties; to establish the principle of 'prosecution or extradition',[576] and to establish the legal authority of the aircraft commander and flight crew to take the necessary measures on board.

308. The principles of the Montreal Convention 1971, were later extended to apply to unlawful acts of violence at international airports by means of the Montreal Supplementary Protocol of 1988.[577]

572. *See* on this matter K. Hailbronner, 'Civil Aviation, Unlawful Interference with', in: R. Bernhardt (ed.) *Encyclopedia, supra* (Ch. 1, n. 9) Vol. I, (1992), 583 et seq., with further references.
573. *UNTS* Vol. 704 (1969), pp. 219 et seq.; ICAO Doc. 8364. This Convention was amended by the Protocol to Amend the Convention on Offences and Certain Other Acts Committed on Board Aircraft, signed on 4 Apr. 2014 (not in force), Doc. 10034, with regard to the problem of unruly/disruptive passengers.
574. *UNTS* Vol. 860 (1973), pp. 105 et seq.; ICAO Doc. 8920.
575. *UNTS* Vol. 974 (1975), pp. 177 et seq.; ICAO Doc. 8966.
576. Article 7 of the Hague Convention of 1970; Art. 7 of the Montreal Convention of 1971.
577. *Protocol for the Suppression of Unlawful Acts of Violence at Airports Serving International Civil Aviation Supplementary to the Convention for the Suppression of Unlawful Acts against the Safety of Civil Aviation* done at Montreal on 23 Sep. 1971, signed on 29 Feb. 1988, ICAO Doc. 9518.

309. In 1991, the Organization developed the Convention on the Marking of Plastic Explosives for the Purpose of Detection (MEX Convention, 1991),[578] which provides for the mandatory marking of all plastic explosives by chemical markers which are detectable by appropriate equipment.

310. In order to deal with **new and emerging threats** not adequately covered by the preceding instruments, the Organization developed in response to the events of 11 September 2001:

- the *Convention on the Suppression of Unlawful Acts Relating to International Civil Aviation, done in Beijing on 10 September 2010*;
- the *Protocol Supplementary to the Convention for the Suppression of Unlawful Seizure of Aircraft, done in Beijing on 10 September 2010.*[579]

They add the acts of organizing, directing and abetting crimes on board aircraft, as well as the use of aircraft as weapons, the use of bacteriological, chemical or nuclear materials (BCN) and other related acts, to the list of international crimes. Furthermore, in order to strengthen the protection provided in the Tokyo Convention of 1963 and adapt its provisions to present-day needs, the Organization developed:

- the *Protocol To Amend the Convention on Offences and Certain Other Acts Committed on Board Aircraft, done in Montreal on 4 April 2014.*[580]

311. The aviation security conventions and protocols have contributed to a gradual and significant reduction in the number of hijackings and other acts of unlawful interference. Their effect was enhanced by a significant improvement in the effectiveness of aviation security measures taken at national and international airports. For these measures, **Annex 17 – Security**[581] provides applicable SARPs which are continuously updated, *see* paragraphs 310–312 above.

III. Annex 17

312. Annex 17 sets out **standards and recommended practices** for measures **to safeguard civil aviation and its facilities against acts of unlawful interference.** It also provides the basis and structure for the ICAO-mandated programmes in this field, including the national civil aviation security programme.

578. Beijing Convention 2010, ICAO Doc. 9560. It entered into force on 1 Jul. 2018, and has thirty-three parties as of February 2021.
579. Beijing Protocol 2010, ICAO Doc. 9959. It entered into force on 1 Jan. 2018, and has thirty-four parties as of February 2021.
580. Montreal Protocol 2014, ICAO Doc. 10034. It entered into force on 1 Jan. 2020, and has 25 parties as of February 2021.
581. ICAO Doc. AN-17, 9th ed. July 2011, incorporating Amendment 14.

313. The Annex requires each contracting State *inter alia* to establish its own **national civil aviation security programme,** providing for inspection, screening and control measures to be taken at airports, and access control to restricted areas.[582] It also provides requirements for airline operators, airports and ground handling companies who shall develop and apply their own security programme compatible with the national programme.[583] Since 2011, additional measures, such as screening and control of cargo and mail, apply. Guidance for the implementation of Annex 17 by Member States is provided in the **ICAO Aviation Security Manual** (Doc. 8973).

314. In recent years, the work of the Organization in this field has focussed on further amendments to counter the new and emerging threats to civil aviation and on developing and implementing the ICAO **Universal Security Audit Programme (USAP)**.[584] This programme developed as part of the ICAO Aviation Security Plan of Action,[585] provides for the mandatory audit of all ICAO contracting States and their security system and airport facilities.[586] Details on this programme are provided in §10 of this Chapter, paragraphs 327–334 below.

IV. Global Aviation Security Plan

315. Since November 2017, a **Global Aviation Security Plan (GASeP)** has been developed and issued by the Organization in order to support and coordinate the planning of Member States in the field of aviation security.[587] The GASeP has received strong support from Member States since it was approved for implementation and strong efforts were made by States to implement the Plan. In accordance with the ICAO Global Risk Context Statement (Doc. 10108), technical aviation security measures such as MRTD,[588] use of information exchange mechanisms such as Advance Passenger Information (API) and Passenger Name Record (PNR) data are additional means to strengthen aviation security. In order to provide assistance to Member States, the ICAO Implementation Support and Development – Security

582. Doc. AN 17, Ch. 3, ss 3.1 et seq.
583. Doc. AN 17, Ch. 3, s. 3.3.
584. New and emerging threats include man-portable air defence systems (MANPADS), other surface-to-air missiles systems, chemical threats, attacks using Remotely Piloted Aircraft Systems (RPAS), abuse of the air cargo system for terrorist purposes, cyber-attacks, insider threat, concealed explosive devices, landside attacks, and other threats. On the USAP, *see infra*, Ch. 3. §10, for more detail.
585. High-level, Ministerial Conference on Aviation Security, 19–20 Feb. 2002, Report, Doc. 9800.
586. Assembly Resolution A39-18 Appendix E; A37-17 Appendix E; A36-20 and A35-9, Appendix E; *see infra*, Ch. 3, §10.
587. ICAO Global Aviation Security Plan, Doc. 10118; Assembly Resolution A40-11: *Consolidated statement on continuing ICAO policies related to aviation security*, Appendix A-General policy, 11th preambular clause.
588. *See* above, Ch. 3 §3 IV. paras 238–239.

Programme (ISD-SEC)[589] facilitates or coordinates short-term remedial assistance and long-term assistance to remedy deficiencies identified by USAP in their implementation of Annex 17 SARPs. ICAO's programme makes extensive use of USAP audit results for defining and targeting aviation security capacity-building activities for the benefit of Member States.

V. Cybersecurity

316. As regards cybersecurity issues, the Organization has increased its focus in recent years on the best possible synergy between specifications for safety and security.[590] The ICAO Aviation Security Plan of Action included a safety-related component (air navigation) which deals with various aspects of safety-security synergy. In the consideration of safety specifications contained in ICAO Annexes, security aspects are playing a more prominent role. In addressing cybersecurity, a **Cybersecurity Action Plan** based on a document developed in 2019 was approved by the ICAO Council during its 219th Session.[591] As part of the strategy, an **international aviation trust framework (IATF)** is under development to allow logistic isolation of aviation data communications from the public Internet. It also involves a Certificate Policy for digital identity management and development of an Internet Protocol version 6 (IPv6) address scheme.[592]

§8. Organization and Personnel

317. The framework for a general personnel policy of the Organization was adopted at the first session of the Assembly in Resolution A1-51.[593] On this basis,

589. This programme makes the expertise of the ICAO Secretariat and of associated AVSEC experts available to Member States for remedial assistance. *See* Assembly Resolution A40-11, *ibid.* (n. 586), Appendix E: The ICAO Implementation Support and Development – Security Programme (ISD-SEC).

590. *See* Assembly Resolution A41-19; previously A40-10. Specifically on cybersecurity strategy, *see*: *Aviation Cybersecurity Strategy,* October 2019, unnumbered, https://www.icao.int/cybersecurity/Pages/Cybersecurity-Strategy.aspx.

591. C-DEC 219/2 refers; *see* the Cybersecurity Strategy Paper, *ibid.* (n. 590), and Assembly Resolution A41-19: Addressing Cybersecurity in Civil Aviation, Doc. 10184. *See also* for a status report: *Cybersecurity in Civil Aviation*, A41-WP/22 EX 10. The Aviation Cybersecurity Strategy which was published by ICAO in 2019, identifies seven essential pillars for developing cybersecurity strategy, comprised of: 1. International cooperation, 2. Governance, 3. Effective legislation and regulations, 4. Cybersecurity Policy, 5. Information sharing, 6. Incident management and emergency planning, 7. Capacity building, training and cybersecurity culture. The Cybersecurity Action Plan lays out a roadmap consisting of various principles to be followed for achieving the objectives of the Aviation Cybersecurity Strategy's seven pillars. It lists 32 Priority Actions, which are further divided into 51 tasks to be followed by the Member States, industry, and various other stakeholders. Until January, 2022, two editions of the CyAP were released.

592. *See Cybersecurity in Civil Aviation*, A41-WP/22 EX 10. C-WP/15155*: Update on ICAO Cybersecurity Activities. See also* C-DEC 219/2, C-DEC 221/4, C-WP/14997, C-WP/14998, and C-WP/15104.

593. ICAO Doc. 9790, p. VIII-1. The general policy was later supplemented by Resolutions A4-31, A14-6, A24-20, A1-51 and A1-8.

the Council adopted the **ICAO Service Code**[594] consisting of Staff Regulations, later supplemented by an **Ethics Framework**. The Staff Regulations are supplemented by Staff Rules issued under the authority of the Secretary General. The Service Code and the Staff Rules are inspired by and based on equivalent rules and regulations of the UN and the UN 'Common System'.[595] As a UN Specialized Agency, the Organization follows the UN 'Common System' in all respects relating to human resources matters.

318. At its 14th Session, the Assembly established the principle of **'equitable geographic representation'** in posts of the ICAO Secretariat.[596] For appointments and promotions, this principle was given equal weight with all other relevant factors. Later, this principle was further upgraded,[597] to be taken into account in all decisions regarding appointments and promotions of staff in established posts, except in the categories of General and Language Services.[598] Furthermore, on the basis of Assembly Resolution A36-27 – Gender Equality and the UN 1995 Beijing Platform for Action, an ICAO **Gender Equality Programme** was established in 2016 by the Assembly at its 39th session.[599] Its objective is to promote gender equality within all levels of staff categories in the ICAO Secretariat.

319. Appointments and promotions of staff of the Organization in the Professional category for P-1 to P-5 posts and in the General Service category are made by the Secretary General upon advice and recommendation by the Appointment and Promotion Boards.[600] Their composition and procedure are laid down in the ICAO Service Code.[601]

320. Appointments of Senior staff (D-2 Directors) are made by the Secretary General, subject to advise from the Human Resource Committee of the Council and subject to the approval of the President of the Council.[602] For appointments of D-1 Deputy Directors and D-1 Regional Directors, the same rules apply except that advice from the Panel of Directors is required. Re-appointments follow the same

594. *ICAO Service Code, Doc. 7350, Loose-leaf.* The ICAO Service Code was adopted on the basis of Resolution A1-51.
595. *See* Art. XII of the *Agreement between the United Nations and ICAO* dated 13 May 1947, ICAO Doc. 7970; *see also* Resolutions A21-12 and A22-7.
596. Assembly Resolution A14-6: *Compliance with the principle if equitable geographical representation in posts of the ICAO Secretariat and regional offices*, ICAO Doc. 9790.
597. Assembly Resolution A24-20: *Compliance with and implementation of the principle of equitable geographical representation in the posts of the Secretariat of ICAO.*
598. *See* A14-6, Clause 2. The exception for the General and Language Services is to be explained by the factual difficulties of applying the EGR principle to these two categories of services.
599. A39-30: *ICAO Gender Equality Programme promoting the participation of women in the global aviation sector.*
600. ICAO Service Code *ibid.* (n. 594) Art. IV 4.11; *see also* Assembly Resolution A1-8: *Appointments and Promotions in ICAO*, ICAO Doc. 9790.
601. ICAO Service Code, Approved by the Council and published by its decision, Doc. 7350/9, 9th ed. 2011, Amendments 1-35 (2021).
602. ICAO Service Code, Art. IV, 4.10–4.18; Annex IV – Human Resource Committee; Assembly Resolution A1-8, Resolving Clause b).

rules.[603] Directors, Deputy Directors and Regional Directors are appointed for a term of four years, renewable only once.[604]

321. The **Secretary General** is appointed by the Council for a term of three years which is renewable only once. The **President of the Council** is elected by the Council for a term of three years which is also renewable only once.[605] The President of the Council is an international civil servant, but not a member of the Organization's staff.[606]

Reference is made to additional information in Chapter 2, §2, VII, paragraphs 95–98 above.

§9. Universal Aviation Safety Oversight Audit Programme

322. Article 33 of the Convention requires contracting States to recognize as valid certificates of airworthiness and personnel licenses issued by another contracting State, provided that the requirements under which such documents were issued are equal to or above the minimum standards established under the Convention.[607] Article 37 requires each contracting State to collaborate in securing the highest practicable degree of uniformity in regulations and practices in all matters in which such uniformity will facilitate and improve air navigation. Article 38 requires contracting States which find it impracticable to comply in all respects with such standards or procedures to give immediate notification to ICAO of the differences.

323. In practice, however, these provisions in particular Article 38 were not always followed by contracting States. Before 1998, in the absence of systematic filing of notification of differences under Article 38 by States, neither the Organization nor contracting States had any clear and objective information on the degree of implementation of SARPs set out in the Annexes to the Convention. This situation presented a major safety issue.[608]

324. For this reason, at its 32nd Session in 1998, the Assembly established the **Universal Aviation Safety Oversight Audit Programme (USOAP),**[609] for implementation starting 1 January 1999.

---

603. ICAO Service Code, Art. IV 4.10.
604. ICAO Service Code, Art. IV 4.15 and 4.20.
605. Assembly Resolution A38-21: *Term limits for the Offices of the Secretary General and the President of the Council*; *see also* Assembly Resolution A36-28.
606. Article 51, first sentence of the Convention. While under Arts 58–60, the President of the Council is mentioned in the Chapter entitled 'Personnel', it is recognized that he does not fall under the *Staff Rules* of the Organization.
607. *See* the wording of Art. 33 of the Convention. M.B. Jennison, *The Chicago Convention and Safety after 50 years*', XX *Ann ASL* Part I, pp. 283 et seq. (1995).
608. *See* the DGCA Conference Report (1997), Doc. 9707; Assembly Resolution A29-13: *Improvement of Safety Oversight,* ICAO Doc. 9790.
609. Assembly Resolution A32-11: *Establishment of an ICAO Universal Safety Oversight Audit Programme*; on this subject, *see* M. Milde, 'Aviation Safety Oversight Audits and the Law', XXVI *AnnASL* (2001), pp. 165 et seq.

325. The programme comprises the following elements:[610]

- regular, mandatory, systematic and harmonized safety audits, which shall be carried out by ICAO;
- applicable to all contracting States;
- greater transparency and increased disclosure in the release of audit results;
- systematic reporting and monitoring mechanisms in the implementation of safety-related SARPs.

326. The scope of the programme initially included audits relating only to Annex 1 – Personnel Licensing, Annex 6 – Operation of Aircraft, and Annex 8 – Airworthiness of Aircraft,[611] the scope was later widened in the third phase to comprise all safety-related Annexes. The audits are performed by audit teams of ICAO, composed of experts from the Secretariat and from contracting States, other than the audited State, in accordance with an administrative framework, including a standard Memorandum of Understanding (MOU) and the **ICAO Safety Oversight Manual**.[612]

327. In the first phase of audits, 1999–2001, nearly 180 States were visited and audited.[613] In the second phase, 2001–2004, the focus shifted to the issue of how to resolve deficiencies identified by the USOAP programme.[614] In the third phase, 2004–2010, steps were taken to increase transparency by making final audit reports available to all contracting States showing audit findings, recommendations, the audited States' action plan and comments[615] and giving access to the Audit Findings and Differences Database (AFDD), (FSIX) established by ICAO.[616]

328. From the fourth phase (from 2010 onwards), the **'Continuous Monitoring Approach' (CMA)** was taken, involving a continuous data exchange between the Member States and ICAO on the implementation of safety-related SARPs. This data-driven approach replaces on-site audits with online data to the largest degree possible[617] but maintains follow-up on-site visits to the extent required. The Organization, in line with the USOAP principle of transparency, makes the audit results

610. DGCA Conference Report (1997), Doc. 9707; *ICAO Safety Oversight Audit Manual,* ICAO Doc. 9735, AN/960.
611. The main purpose of limiting audits to these three Annexes was to provide a focused starting point. *See* DGCA Conference Report (1997) Doc. 9707; 2279th Report to Council by the President of the Air Navigation Commission, C-WP/10898 (16/06/98), p. 2.
612. ICAO Doc. 9734; on the Standard MOU, *see*: Sample Memorandum of Understanding between (State) and ICAO Regarding Safety Oversight Audit, in: *ICAO Safety Oversight Audit Manual*, ICAO Doc. 9735, AN/960.
613. *See* Annual Report of the Council for 2001, Doc. 9786; *Annual Report of the Council for 2002*, Doc. 9814; *Annual Report of the Council for 2003*, Doc. 9826, and Supplement.
614. Assembly Resolution A33-9, Clauses 1-9; the Assembly adopted at its 35th Session Resolution A35-7: *Unified strategy to resolve safety-related deficiencies*, supplementing A33-9.
615. *See* Assembly Resolution A35-6, Clause 7.
616. *Ibid.* (n. 598).
617. Assembly Resolution A37-5: *The Universal Safety Oversight Audit Programme (USOAP) continuous monitoring approach* in: Resolutions adopted at the 37th session of the Assembly, ICAO Doc. 9958.

available to all Member States through the **Interactive Safety Audit Results** database. The database presents the 'Effective Implementation' (EI) score for each Member State under ICAO's USOAP, and users may compare a country against the current global average in each category. Arguably, the USOAP/CMA has contributed to a significant improvement in global aviation safety in recent years. During the period from 2008 to 2020, the worldwide accident rate for scheduled commercial flights on aircraft above 5.7 t has been reduced from 4.74 to 0.86 per 1 million flights. Similarly, the number of accidents on such flights has been reduced from 139 in 2008 to 19 in 2020. The number of accident fatalities on these flights has been reduced from 523 in 2008 to 121 in 2020.[618]

§10. Universal Aviation Security Audit Programme

329. Following the events of 11 September 2001, the ICAO High-level, Ministerial Conference on Aviation Security held in February 2002 recommended adopting an **Aviation Security Plan of Action,**[619] including an Aviation Security Audit Programme. It called for a comprehensive programme of regular, mandatory, systematic and harmonized aviation security audits to be carried out by ICAO in all contracting States.[620]

330. The ICAO Aviation Security Plan of Action establishing the **ICAO Universal Aviation Security Audit Programme (USAP)**[621] was adopted by the Council in June and launched in November 2002.

331. The audit programme comprises the following elements:[622]

- regular, mandatory, systematic and harmonized aviation security audits of all ICAO contracting States;
- audits conducted at both national and airports levels;
- evaluation of States' aviation security oversight capabilities;
- evaluation of the actual security measures in place at selected key airports;
- audits to be carried out on the basis of a bilateral MOU signed between each contracting State and ICAO; and
- coordination with security-related audit programmes at regional and sub-regional levels.

618. ICAO Safety Accident Statistics, https://www.icao.int/safety/iStars/Pages/Accident-Statistics.aspx.
619. High-level, Ministerial Conference on Aviation Security, 19–20 Feb. 2002, Report. For the Declaration issued, *see* XXVI *Ann ASL* (2001), p. 441.
620. Assembly Resolution A35-9, Appendix E: *The ICAO Universal Security Audit Programme*, Operative Clause 1.
621. Council 166th Session (June. 2002). *See* A. Kotaite, *Aviation Safety and Security – Two Sides of the Same Coin*, Keynote Address to the Aviation Study Group at Linacre College, Oxford University, 27 Jun. 2003, pp. 2–3.
622. Assembly Resolution A35-9 Appendix E, Operative Clauses 1-4. *See* now A39-18 Appendix E; A37-17, Appendix E and previously A36-20, Appendix E.

332. The **methodology** for the USAP programme is similar to that used for the USOAP programme, including the audit visit, a preliminary report for comment by the audited State, a final report by ICAO, and an Action Plan by the audited State.[623] Access to audit results is restricted due to the need to keep this information from public view.[624]

333. During its first phase, the USAP was entirely financed from voluntary contributions received from States for that purpose[625] following the High-Level, Ministerial Conference of February 2002. Subsequently, the USAP was progressively integrated into the Regular Programme budget of ICAO.

334. The **ICAO Security Audit Reference Manual**[626] was issued in 2004, setting forth the elements, methodology and procedures for the conduct of the programme.

335. Two full audit cycles have been carried out under this programme. From 2002 to 2007, 181 Member States underwent a first audit and from 2008 to 2013, 178 Member States underwent follow-up audits. As of early 2015, the programme transitioned to the 'Continuous Monitoring Approach' (CMA). USAP CMA involves the continuous monitoring of Member States through online data exchange, a risk-based approach to auditing, the identification of 'serious security concerns' (SSecCs) and subjecting them to a formal procedure, training programmes, and limited transparency. In its report to the 36th Assembly, the Council noted that the USAP audit follow-up missions 'have validated a markedly increased level of implementation of ICAO security standards'.[627] This trend has continued, as confirmed more recently at the 39th and 40th sessions of the Assembly.

336. Similar in methodology to the USOAP database, ICAO has developed a **USAP database on audit findings** which greatly assists in addressing deficiencies but is not accessible publicly for security reasons. It has served the Organization in developing and drafting a **Global Aviation Security Plan (GASeP).**[628]

623. A. Kotaite, *ibid.* (n. 604), at pp. 2 et seq. It was considered not sufficient to audit only the security oversight arrangements in authorities of Member States, but also to audit directly installations and equipment *in situ*, namely at the major airports in each Member State. *See* L. Weber, *Convention on International Civil Aviation – 60 Years*, 53 ZLW 289–311, p. 307.

624. Confidentiality of information and restricted access was part of the USAP from the start in 2002, *see supra* n. 606; any public access would create a serious security risk for civil aviation.

625. *See* Assembly Resolution A35-10, sixth whereas clause, ICAO Doc. 9848.

626. ICAO Doc. 9807.

627. Assembly, 36th session, A36-WP/38 EX/9. For example, as regards national organization and administration, the follow-up audits found an increase in compliance of 24% of audited States.

628. Global Aviation Security Plan, Doc. 10118; *see* A40-11: *Consolidated statement on continuing ICAO policies related to aviation security*, Appendix D, *The ICAO Universal Security Audit Programme*, 7th preamble clause.

§11. OTHER ACTIVITIES

I. Aviation Medicine and the COVID-19 Pandemic

337. In the field of **aviation medicine,**[629] ICAO sets and updates related SARPs contained in Annex 1 – Personnel Licensing and Annex 6 – Operation of Aircraft. Recently, the Organization has done work to update the applicable SARPs on medical provisions, in particular those on board aircraft.[630] ICAO also has been participating since 2004 in a scientific research project called the 'Wright Project' on a possible link between air travel and deep vein thrombosis (DVT),[631] conducted under the auspices of WHO and ICAO with the cooperation of IATA.

338. In connection with the outbreak of SARS in 2003, ICAO worked with WHO successfully to put in place appropriate airport procedures to prevent the spread of SARS. This work resulted in 2006 in the establishment of the **Collaborative Arrangement for the Prevention and Management of Public Health Events in Civil Aviation (CAPSCA),**[632] in which other UN and aviation organizations are also participating. Its main objective is to ensure adherence to Article 14 of the Convention on International Civil Aviation,[633] ICAO Annexes and PANS-ATM, WHO IHR (2005) Regulations, and applicable guidelines. CAPSCA also promotes preparedness of States through national preparedness plans.

339. In the case **of COVID-19**, such measures were ultimately insufficient to prevent the spread of the pandemic in early 2020. CAPSCA recommended the implementation of a **'Public Health Corridor' (PHC)** concept using a risk-based approach, taking into account safety management principles. It envisaged continued flight operations with minimal restrictions whilst preventing the spread of infection of COVID-19 through protecting the health and safety of crew and passengers.[634]

---

629. R. L. de Hart/ J.R. Davis (eds), *Fundamentals of Aerospace Medicine*, 3rd ed., Williams and Wilkins, 1990.
630. This work is done with the assistance of the Medical Provisions Study Group (MPSG).
631. DVT has been the subject of litigation in a number of jurisdictions, including Australia, Germany and the UK. *See* on this matter, *inter alia* G. N. Thompkins, *DVT Litigation Update: September 2004*, 29 Air & Space L. 312 et seq. (2004).
632. Initially called '*Cooperative Arrangement for the Prevention of Spread of Communicable Disease through Air Travel*' and renamed in January 2013. On CAPSCA, *see* www.capsca.org and https://www.icao.int/safety/aviation-medicine/Pages/ CAPSCA.aspx.
633. Article 14, first sentence reads: '*Each contracting State agrees to take effective measures to prevent the spread by means of air navigation of cholera, typhus (epidemic), smallpox, yellow fever, plague, and such other communicable diseases as the contracting States shall from time to time decide to designate, and to that end contracting States will keep in close consultation with the agencies concerned with international regulations relating to sanitary measures applicable to aircraft.*' It thus imposes on contracting States the legal obligation to have in place at all times effective plans and measures to prevent outbreak of designated communicable diseases.
634. https://www.icao.int/safety/aviation-medicine/Pages/ CAPSCA.aspx.; *ICAO Safety Report 2020 edition*, p. 47.

The key elements of this strategy are 'clean' passengers and crew, and the use of 'clean' aircraft, cargo and airport facilities.[635]

340. In coordinating the response of Member States to the **COVID-19 pandemic**, ICAO developed guidance material for CAAs in its **Handbook for CAAs on the Management of Aviation Safety Risks related to COVID-19** (Doc. 10144). In addition, the Council established the ICAO **Council Aviation Recovery Task Force (CART)** to address the COVID challenges and to provide global guidance for a safe recovery of the aviation system. The CART, with participation from industry organizations, published three comprehensive reports (for Phases 1, 2 and 3) setting out principles, measures and recommendations for a restart and recovery.[636] The **CART Take-off guidance** included a section on public health risk mitigation measures and four modules with airport guidelines, aircraft guidelines, crew guidelines and cargo guidelines. ICAO recommended a phased approach to enable the safe return to high-volume air travel and a core set of measures to form a baseline aviation health safety protocol to protect air passengers and aviation workers from COVID-19.[637] It also recommended using the **ICAO Manual on Testing and Cross-border Risk Management Measures** (Doc 10152) for medical evaluation of passengers.

341. Further guidance has also been developed on COVID-19-related strategies for unmanned aircraft systems (UAS) and aerodrome operations.[638] Regarding UAS, their role involving transporting biological samples and medicines to isolated communities, delivery of essential goods and medicines to indigenous communities, or transporting supplies to food banks has been evaluated and ICAO has published **Humanitarian Aid and Emergency Response guidance** for UAS and has developed related UAS model regulations. ICAO is working on a cohesive UAS roadmap to assist States.[639] Regarding aerodrome operations, while many aerodromes were forced to close or operate with reduced capacity, the Organization published on its COVID-19 website guidance for States concerning issuance or renewal of aerodrome certificates, the need for stakeholder engagement before closing aerodromes, and a sample safety checklist for resuming aerodrome operations.[640]

342. At the 41st Session of the ICAO Assembly, a Resolution was adopted *inter alia* urging Member States to harmonize their respective national regulations and increase coordination to ensure smooth cross-border travel operations, and global

635. 'Clean' in this context refers to implementing measures to ensure as far as possible a 'COVID-19 free' status.
636. https://www.icao.int/covid/cart/Pages/default.aspx.
637. *ICAO Safety Report 2020 ed.*, p. 46. It also recommended States to update their respective COVID-19 Contingency Related Differences (CCRDs) in the Electronic Filing of Differences (EFOD) sub-system. In October 2021, certain recommendations pertaining to operational measures which may be undertaken for safe and efficient recovery of aviation from the COVID-19 crisis, were also made at the High-level Conference on COVID-19 (HLCC 2021), held in October 2021. *See* on this matter https://www.icao.int/Meetings/HLCC2021/Pages/default.aspx.
638. *Ibid.* (n. 620), pp. 50, 52.
639. https://www.icao.int/safety/UA/UAID/; RPAS@icao.int.
640. https://www.icao.int/safety/COVID-19OPS/Pages/aga.aspx.

interoperability in all passenger processing efforts.[641] On 4 November 2022, ICAO concluded a new **Memorandum of Understanding with the World Health Organization (WHO)** in which the Parties undertook to 'provide evidence-informed and risk-based advice to their member States and to industry stakeholders that have been reviewed and cleared under the Parties' respective legal and compliance processes including in the context of preparing for and responding to health emergencies'.[642]

343. In furtherance of providing support to Member States for developing their respective national strategies to deal with challenges posed by COVID-19, ICAO also endeavoured to develop **Implementation Packages (iPacks)**. These 'iPacks' are a bundle of standardized guidance material which aim to facilitate the implementation of ICAO provisions by various stakeholders engaged in civil aviation. This guidance material has been created in full alignment with the measures and recommendations contained in the CART Report. Through these iPacks, ICAO aims at assisting its Member States to recover from the impact of COVID-19 and to provide a roadmap for re-engaging with the civil aviation industry.[643]

II. Training

344. In the field of training, ICAO has widened its activities in the **TRAINAIR programme**. TRAINAIR provides for the accreditation of civil aviation training schools and centres in accordance with uniform criteria and procedures[644] TRAINAIR, supplemented by **TRAINAIR PLUS**, pursues the objective of enhancing the quality of aviation training school programmes worldwide and promotes the idea of harmonized training through Standardized Training Packages (STPs).[645] TRAINAIR has numerous civil aviation training centres in contracting States participating as members, many of them as public civil aviation academies or flying schools. Privately operated training centres are also able to join, subject to fulfilling certain conditions.

345. As of 2014, in a reversal of a longstanding policy, the Organization also decided to itself offer training courses to staff of its Member States and to the aviation community. It set up a Global Aviation Training (GAT) Office with headquarters in Montreal and developed a portfolio of **competency-based classroom training courses,** separate from STPs, for all essential fields of civil aviation. These

641. Assembly Resolution A41-11: *Declaration on air transport facilitation affirming global commitment to enable the safe and efficient recovery of aviation from the COVID-19 pandemic, and to make aviation more resilient in the future,* ICAO Doc. 10184.
642. *Memorandum of Understanding between ICAO and WHO*, signed on 6 Oct. and 4 Nov. 2022, Art. 1, https://www.icao.int/Newsroom/Documents/MoU WHO and ICAO_final_for publication.pdf.
643. *See* https://www.icao.int/secretariat/TechnicalCooperation/Pages/iPACK.aspx.
644. *ICAO TRAINAIR Operations Manual*, revised ed.;*TRAINAIR PLUS Operations Manual*, (TPOM), VO effective 1 Jan. 2022; https://www.icao.int/training/Documents/TPOM%20New%20Framework%20JAN%202022%20V0.1.pdf.
645. ICAO *Civil Aviation Training Policy* (25 May 2016), approved by the Council at its 208th Session, C-DEC 208/6.

were offered at ICAO headquarters, at the seven ICAO Regional Offices[646] and subsequently also for instruction at national civil aviation training centres. During the COVID-19 pandemic, many of these courses were also offered in virtual format, and they now form an important element in the overall training strategy of ICAO.[647]

---

646. *See* the *ICAO Training Catalogue*, at https://www.icao.int/training/Pages/Training-Catalogue.aspx; *see also* ICAO *Training Development Guide*, Doc. 9941.
647. A41-10: *Consolidated statement of continuing ICAO policies and associated practices related specifically to air navigation* APPENDIX D: *Qualified and Competent Aviation Personnel,* ICAO Doc.10184.

Chapter 4. Finance

§1. Relevant Provisions of the Convention

346. Financial matters are regulated in Chapter XII of the Convention (Articles 61–63), as well as in Article 49 paragraphs (e), (f) and Article 54 (f).

347. **Budgeting and apportionment of expenses** among Member States are regulated in Article 61. It provides that:

> *The Council shall submit to the Assembly annual budgets, annual statements of accounts and estimates of all receipts and expenditures. The Assembly shall vote the budgets whatever modification it sees fit to prescribe and, with the exception of assessments under Chapter XV to States consenting thereto, shall apportion the expenses of the Organization among the contracting States on the basis which it shall from time to time determine.*[648]

348. Under Article 62 of the Convention:

> *[t]he 'Assembly may suspend the voting power in the Assembly and in the Council of any contracting State that fails to discharge within a reasonable period its financial obligations to the Organization'.*[649]

The **late payment of annual contributions** by Member States[650] has been a longstanding challenge, negatively impacting the ability of the Organization to operate according to the programme budget.[651] In order to deal with this problem, the Organization took a three-pronged approach.

349. First, the Assembly adopted a **flexible system** in Resolution A21-10 (later superseded but not materially altered by Resolution A35-26) by which the Council invited contracting States whose annual contributions were in arrears to make settlement proposals to the Organization. The Council was authorized to conclude agreements with these contracting States for the settlement of their arrears. The arrears

648. This provision in its original version mentioned the word 'budget' in the singular only, since it was foreseen that each year an annual Assembly would take place which would vote on an annual budget. At the Eighth Assembly in 1954, it was decided that annual Assemblies would be replaced by triennial Assemblies, which would vote on the annual budgets for the three following years, and that Art. 61 would be amended accordingly. *See* Assembly Resolution A8-1, ICAO Doc. 9790, p. I-16; at the same time, it was decided to also change Arts 48 (a) and 49 (e) accordingly, *see* A8-1, Approval clause.

649. *See also* Ch. 2, §1. II *supra* (paras 45–47).

650. Notification of next year's contribution is sent in autumn of each year to all Member States, and contributions become due on 1st January of each year. However, contracting States may make payment at any time during the financial year, and payment becomes overdue only on 1st January of the following year. Article VI 6.5 a) and b) of the Financial Regulations.

651. *See* the official acknowledgement of this situation by the Assembly in Resolution A35-26, third clause.

could be paid *inter alia* in currencies other than those used officially by the Organization, subject to conditions, and could be spaced over several years.[652] However, this flexible system did not succeed in significantly improving the payment practices of Member States.

350. Therefore, the Assembly had to take a more coercive approach. Using the powers foreseen in Article 62 of the Convention, Assembly Resolution A31-26 (Arrangements to Settle Contributions in Arrears)[653] provided that with effect from 1 January 1998, the **voting power for those contracting States be suspended** that have failed to discharge their financial obligations to the Organization equivalent to the preceding three years or more, without having concluded a settlement agreement with the Council or having failed to comply with the terms of such agreement. Voting rights were to be restored upon payment in full of the outstanding arrears for at least three years or upon conclusion of an agreement with the Council to liquidate arrears in accordance with Resolution A21-10 or A35-26.[654]

351. In addition, at the following Assembly, the Organization also adopted an **incentive scheme for the settlement of long-outstanding arrears.** Resolution A32-27 provided that the distribution of cash surplus by the Organization at the time of the Assembly be withheld for any contracting States which have long-outstanding arrears.[655] Upon full payment of arrears, or in case of conclusion of agreements with the Council under Resolution A21-10 or A35-26 and compliance therewith, the contracting States concerned would receive a cash surplus distribution from the Organization which could be used to offset arrears in part[656] or wholly.[657]

352. Article 63 deals with the **expenses of delegations** and other representatives and stipulates that each contracting State shall bear the expenses of its own delegation to the Assembly and the remuneration, travel and other expenses of any

652. *See* Assembly Resolution A35-26, Operating Clause 5; for the payment period, *see* Operating Clause 4.b).

653. Resolution A31-26 was superseded by Resolution A36-36, which completed the action on the matter. Operating Clause 11 of Resolution A35-26 did not materially change the applicable provisions, but essentially refined them.A36-36 is now no longer in force.

654. Resolution A21-10 was superseded by Resolution A35-26, *see* Clause 11 of the latter Resolution; the provisions of 21-10 were not materially altered by A35-20, but were refined and rendered more flexible.

655. *See* Resolution A32-27. Long outstanding arrears was defined as those outstanding for more than 3 years. A32-27 was later superseded by Resolutions A33-27 and A35-27 (*see* Clause 5 of the latter Resolution).

656. Resolutions A21-10 and A31-26 were later merged into one Resolution, pursuant to Assembly Resolution A35-27, Operating Clause 2. Resolution A39-31 provides for the restoration of voting rights of contracting States having paid their arrears in full, or having entered into an agreement for settlement of their outstanding arrears, in Operating Clauses 8 and 9. Resolution A39-31 continues to be in force, ICAO Doc.10184.

657. Assembly Resolution A35-26 was superseded by A36-33, A37-32, A38-24 and A39-31: *Discharge by Contracting States of financial obligations to the Organization and action to be taken in case of their failure to do so,* which nevertheless retained the same main provisions. Resolution A39-31 continues to be in force, ICAO Doc. 10184.

representative whom it appoints to serve on the Council or on other bodies of the Organization. This provision serves mainly clarifying purposes.[658]

353. Article 49 paragraph (e) provides for the authority of the Assembly to 'vote annual budgets and determine the financial arrangements of the Organization, in accordance with the provisions of Chapter XII'.[659] Article 49 paragraph (f) gives the Assembly authority to 'review expenditures and approve the accounts of the Organization'.[660]

§2. Apportionment of Membership Contributions

354. The **apportionment of membership contributions** among the Member States of ICAO is a matter for the Assembly under Article 61 of the Convention. The Assembly determines the apportionment among States by way of assessments every three years by Resolution, taking into account new Member States, changes in the apportionment formula, if any, and other relevant factors.[661]

355. The principles to be applied in the determination of scales of assessment (apportionment formula) were first laid down in Assembly Resolution A12-30.[662] They provide a mixed formula based on:

- capacity to pay, measured by **national per capita income** (75% weight);
- interest and importance in civil aviation, measured **by capacity tonne–kilometres available on each State's scheduled air services** (25% weight);
- minimum contribution of 0.06% for any contracting State;
- maximum contribution of 25% for any contracting State.

356. For the national per capita income, the Organization utilizes the UN data as a matter of long-standing policy. For the capacity tonne-kilometres available on each State's scheduled air services, it largely relies on its own statistics.

357. Based on these two principles, the scales of assessment for each contracting State are calculated by the Secretariat for the purposes of the next triennial Assessment Resolution, which sets out the assessment of contracting States for the

658. This clarification is nevertheless useful in relation to a clear delimitation of financial responsibility as regards representatives of States including experts, on the one-hand, and the Organization's staff on the other hand.
659. The same change as to the wording of Art. 61 was made to Art. 49 (e) at the Eighth Assembly in 1954, i.e., replacement of 'budget' by 'budgets' in order to allow adoption of triennial budgets. *See* Assembly Resolution A8-1.
660. Since the 8th Session of the Assembly, it is the practice of the Organization that the Assembly reviews the expenditures and approves the financial statements for the preceding three financial years, *see*, e.g., A35-29.
661. Such other relevant factors may be e.g. changes in the maximum or minimum contributions for contracting States. *See* Resolutions A12-30 and A21-33.
662. ICAO Doc. 7998; later, Assembly Resolution A21-33 provided minor modifications, Doc. 9790.

three years following each Assembly. Assessments of individual Member States are expressed in per cent of the sum of all Member States' assessments.

358. For many years, the United States was assessed at the **maximum contribution** of 25%. This changed in 2013[663] and the United States is now (2023–2025) assessed at 21.7 %, while the assessment of the vast majority of contracting States is the **minimum contribution** of 0.06%, in line with the agreed apportionment formula.[664] By comparison, the assessment rates of other major Member States for 2023–2025 are China (13.71%), Japan (6.26 %), Germany (4.78%), the United Kingdom (3.37 %), France (3.43%), and India (0.99%).

359. On the basis of the scales of assessment, on the one hand, and the total authorized appropriations for the General Fund, on the other hand, each contracting State's **contribution to the General Fund** is calculated and notified.[665]

§3. The ICAO Financial Regulations

360. The ICAO Financial Regulations govern the financial administration of the Organization.[666]

361. The Regulations make an important distinction between the **Regular Programme Budget**, on the one hand, and the Technical Co-operation Programme Funds, in particular the **Administrative and Operational Services Cost Fund (AOSC),**[667] on the other hand. These are administered separately and they are subject to separate provisions.

I. Regular Programme (RP)

A. Budget

362. **Budgeting for the Regular Programme** is governed by Article IV of the Financial Regulations.[668] The Secretary General develops a draft Programme

663. *See* Assembly Resolution A38-26: Assessments to the General Fund for 2014, 2015 and 2016, Doc. 10022, and A38-WP/43-AD/13, providing for the first time for an assessment of the United States below 25%.
664. Assembly Resolution A41-29: *Assessment to the General Fund for 2023, 2024 and 2025;* in comparison, *see* ICAO Doc. A38-W/93 AD/13; and *A37-27 Assessment to the General Fund for 2011, 2012 and 2013.*
665. The Total Authorized Appropriations for the General Fund represent 100% of the total of all contracting States Assessments.
666. *The ICAO Financial Regulations*, 17th ed. (2023), ICAO Doc. 7515/17; the Financial Regulations were amended by the 41st session of the Assembly, *see* Resolution A41-31: *Amendment of the Financial Regulations.*
667. *See* Financial Regulations, Art. IX: *Technical Cooperation*, 9.4 and 9.5 of the Financial Regulations, *ibid.* (n. 666). Other TCB related funds are the subject of 9.1 to 9.3 of the Financial Regulations.
668. Financial Regulations, Article IV: *The Budget (Regular Programme).* It sets out the steps and requirements for the budgetary process of the Organization. The rules applicable to the AOSC are

Budget for each financial year in advance of each triennial Assembly for consideration by the Council. The draft Budget shall be divided into Strategic objectives, Supporting Strategies, and may include any other objective or strategy related to the results-based management structure of the business plan.[669]

363. After consideration by the Council, the draft budget is transmitted to all contracting States at least fifty days prior to the Assembly, accompanied by an explanatory message from the Council, comparative statements showing past, present and proposed budget figures, and a draft budget resolution for adoption at the Assembly.[670]

364. At the Assembly, the draft budget is then discussed by Strategic Objective, Supporting Strategy, and any other objective or strategy related to the results-based management structure of the business plan, and by Total Authorized Appropriation.[671] In the Organization's practice, **three annual budgets** for the three years following the Assembly are discussed and put up for adoption together.

B. Appropriations

365. The **Total Authorized Appropriation** is the total of the appropriations required for all Major Programmes for each financial year (the total approved budget for the Regular Programme for that year). It constitutes an authorization for the Secretary General to incur obligations and make payments or advances for the purposes stated in the programme budget, up to the amount approved.[672]

366. Due to the need to plan in advance for several years when drafting a triennial budget, and the fast pace of today's aviation environment, it has been necessary to introduce several **elements of flexibility** into the financial rules governing appropriations.[673] This was done *inter alia* by modifying Article V 5.2, under which the Council may approve appropriations in excess of the budget voted by the Assembly, as follows:

---

contained in Art. IX, 9.5, which provides for greater flexibility, in view of the fact that the '*Technical Cooperation Programme cannot be determined with a high degree of precision until such time as the Governments and recipient countries have decided on the relevant projects*' (*see* A41-31, Part C, second Whereas clause).

669. In accordance with the changes introduced by the 2022 amendments of the *ICAO Financial Regulations*, 17th ed. (2023), ICAO Doc. 7515/17 decided at the 41st Assembly.
670. Article IV 4.7 and 4.8 of the Financial Regulations.
671. Article IV 4.10 of the Financial Regulations as amended in 2022.
672. Article IV 4.7. c) and Art. V 5.1 of the Financial Regulations.
673. Article V 5.2, 5.9, Art. VII 7.3, 7.8, and Art. VIII 8.4 and other provisions were amended by the 37th Session of the Assembly in 2010, for effectiveness on 1 Jan. 2011. *See* Resolutions A37-29: *Amendment of the Financial Regulations.* Financial Regulations Article V 5.6 and VII 7.6 were amended by the 38th Session of the Assembly, *see* A38-28, effective immediately. Financial Regulations Art. V 5.9, VII 7.3 and XI 11.4 were further amended by the 39th Assembly in 2016, *see* A39-34, Resolving clause, and Financial Regulations IV to XIII were further amended by the 41st Assembly in 2022, *see* A41-31.

(a) up to 2% for the first year, up to 4% for the second year, and up to 2% for the third year of the triennial budget over and above that annual amount, for meeting unavoidable expenditures other than those in b) or c) below;
(b) up to 2% of the total annual appropriation for urgent new projects, in support of the Strategic Objectives, not included in the framework of the approved budget; and
(c) irrespective of a) and b) above, up to the amount by which, for one or more financial years not yet submitted to the Assembly, actual miscellaneous income exceeds the amount of income taken into account by the Assembly in approving the appropriations for that year or those years to finance expenditure on projects related to the efficient delivery of the Organization's Business Plan.[674]

Any such approval by the Council shall be reported to the next Assembly.[675]

367. Under amended Article V 5.9, the Secretary General also has the flexibility to effect **transfers between Strategic Objectives or Supporting Strategies** up to an amount of 20% of such programmes or strategies, and above that with the prior approval of the Council.[676] Any such transfers shall be reported to the next Assembly.

368. Under amended Article 5.6, the Secretary General may **carry over unspent amounts** of up to 10% of each Strategic Objective or Supporting Strategies to the next financial year, and above such amount with the prior approval of the Council. This rule, which was introduced in 1998, is particularly important in cases of large contribution payments at the end of the financial year, which runs from 1 January to 31 December. Previously, large contribution payments at the end of the calendar year, sometimes received in the last days of December, could usually neither be spent due to shortness of time nor be carried over; consequently, they had to be returned as cash surplus to contracting States, to the detriment of the Organization's own finances. The carry-over rule introduced in Article 5.6 permits avoiding most such return payments.[677] Any cash surplus at the time of the Assembly to the extent not required to meet obligations must be put to the disposal of the Assembly (Article VI 6.2);[678] they can be set off against any amounts outstanding from contracting States.[679] Under Article V 5.10, with the approval of the Council, the Secretary General may defer the implementation of specific activities planned for the third financial year of a triennium to the first financial year of the next triennium. That

674. Article V 5.2 of the Financial Regulations, as amended.
675. Article V 5.4 of the Financial Regulations; the report shall be made by the Council.
676. Assembly Resolution A32-29: *Amendment to the Financial Regulations*, ICAO Doc. 9790, effective since 25 Jun. 1998; the amount that can be transferred was raised from 10% to 20% at the 39th Assembly in 2016, Assembly Resolution A39-34, Doc. 10075.
677. Article V5.6, first sentence.
678. Article VI 6.2, third sentence: 'Any balance of cash surplus at the end of the year prior to the year in which the Assembly is held shall be disposed of in the manner to be decided by the Assembly … .'
679. Article VI 6.2 of the Financial Regulations, third sentence, last half sentence.

part of the appropriation shall then remain available to incur and discharge expenditures relating to the deferred activity.[680]

C. Provision of Funds

369. The **appropriations voted by the Assembly**, i.e., the expenditures foreseen in the triennial budget approved by the Assembly, are financed from the following sources, in accordance with Article VI 6.1:[681]

- contributions from contracting States in accordance with assessments;
- miscellaneous income;
- contributions from new contracting States having joined after the Assembly;
- cash surpluses; and
- advances from the Working Capital Fund.

370. Contributions from contracting States become **due and payable** thirty days from receipt of notification by them of the amount of their assessments, or on 1 January of each year whichever is later.[682] In practice, the notification is sent in the autumn of each year, so that contributions become due on 1 January of each year. However, contracting States may make payment at any time during the financial year, and payment becomes overdue only on 1 January of the following year.[683]

371. Miscellaneous income may arise from any revenue-generating activity of the Organization.[684]

372. Contributions from new contracting States are regulated in Article VI 6.9 of the Financial Regulations.

373. Any **deficits** arising during or at the end of a financial year shall be covered in the first instance by the **Working Capital Fund**. This Fund serves as a reserve fund to cover financial shortfalls primarily of the Regular Programme (General Fund), but may also be used to cover joint financing funds up to USD 100,000

680. Inserted in 2013. The approval of the Council is also required for incurring and discharging such expenditures, *see* Art. V 5.10 of the Financial Regulations.
681. Article VI 6.1 of the Financial Regulations. This Regulation should be interpreted as an exclusive list, i.e., no other sources shall be used to finance appropriations, except as expressly authorized by the Assembly. The borrowing authorization granted by the Assembly in Resolution A35-28, Clause 2d.) constitutes such an express exception.
682. Article VI 6.5 a) of the Financial Regulations.
683. Article VI 6.5 b) of the Financial Regulations.
684. Articles VI 6.1 b), 5.2 c), 7.2, 7.3 (as amended by A41-31, Doc. 10184), Art. VII 7.6 7.7 and Art. VIII 8.4 of the Financial Regulations. The Ancillary Revenue Generation Fund (ARGF) has been created for this purpose.

or special funds created by the decision of the Council.[685] The amount of the Working Capital Fund is determined by the Assembly.[686]

D. *Establishment and Administration of Funds*

374. Besides the General Fund and the Working Capital Fund, **other Funds, Reserves or special Accounts** may be set up either by the Assembly or the Council or by the Secretary General '*for the purpose of efficient financial administration*'.[687] This power of the Secretary General was previously limited to self-financing activities only, defined as those where costs are offset by revenues. In special accounts for self-financing activities, surpluses or deficits may be carried forward to the next financial year.

375. Under Article VII 7.2, deficits shall not be funded from the Regular Programme budget.[688]

376. In order to finance the Working Capital Fund, the Assembly may decide to levy special assessments on contracting States in the form of advances; the special assessments shall use the same scale of contributions as for the General Fund.[689]

II. AOSC Fund

377. For the purposes of the Technical Cooperation Programme, the Council has established the consolidated **Administrative and Operational Services Cost (AOSC) Fund**. This Fund is utilized to meet the needs and full cost of the administration, operation and support of TCB programmes.[690]

378. The draft budget for the Technical Cooperation Programme, also referred to as AOSC budget, is presented by the Council to the Assembly after review by the Technical Cooperation Committee and Finance Committee,[691] together with the Regular Budget.

379. The Assembly votes on the AOSC budget at the same time as on the Regular Budget and approves it usually in the same Resolution.[692]

685. Article VII 7.1, 7.3-7.6, Art. VI 6.3, 6.5 a) of the Financial Regulations. *See* in particular Regulation Art. VII 7.3 b) ii).
686. Article VII 7.4 a) of the Financial Regulations. *See* the discussion on increase of the level of the Working Capital Fund in paras 390–391 below.
687. Article VII 7.2 and 7.3 of the Financial Regulations, as amended by A41-31, Doc. 10184.
688. Article VII 7.2, last sentence, of the Financial Regulations.
689. Article VII 7.4 b) of the Financial Regulations.
690. Article IX 9.4 of the Financial Regulations.
691. Article IX 9.5 of the Financial Regulations.
692. *See*, e.g., Assembly Resolution A41-28 Parts B (Regular Programme) and C (Technical Cooperation).

380. Once approved, the Secretary General has the flexibility to make adjustments to the operational and administrative costs of up to 10% per year over the amount approved by the Assembly, and above that amount with the prior approval of the Council.

III. Internal and External Audit

381. The Secretary General shall provide and maintain a **system of internal control**, including an internal audit function, and shall provide for an effective current examination and *ex post* facto review of the operation of internal control.

382. Additionally, in line with the Financial Regulations, the Council appoints for every triennial budget cycle an **External Auditor**. The External Auditor, who shall be the Auditor General of a contracting State, is tasked with an independent audit of the funds, assets and accounts of the Organization. He reports to the Assembly, and it is the practice of the Assembly to confirm the appointment of the External Auditor.

383. The external audit is conducted in conformity with generally accepted common auditing standards and in accordance with the terms of reference set out in the Annex to the Financial Regulations. The **'common auditing standards'** refer to the standards recognized and used by the Auditors of the UN Common System. While in the 1950s and 1960s such audits included financial auditing activities only, they now include also operational and performance audits. Accordingly, the reports of the External Auditor will include evaluations not only of the financial statements but also of operational and performance aspects, including 'value for money' considerations.

§4. Overview of the ICAO Budget

384. The following brief overview is based on the most recent triennial budget, i.e., the **Programme Budget 2023–2024–2025,** adopted at the 41st Session of the Assembly in 2022 by Assembly Resolution A41-28. This Programme Budget was the first in the history of the Organization which used the Canadian Dollar (CAD) instead of the US Dollar (USD) as a unit of account for appropriations as well as Member State contributions.

I. Regular Programme

385. As regards the Regular Programme, the Assembly authorized appropriations of CAD 117,032,000 for 2023, CAD 117,704,000 for 2024, and CAD 122,824,000 for 2025, totalling CAD 357,560,000 for the three years.[693]

693. Assembly Resolution A41-28, Part B, Clause 1.

386. The budget is broken down into **Programmes** corresponding to the Strategic Objectives of the Organization, namely Safety, Air Navigation Capacity and Efficiency, Aviation Security and Facilitation, Economic Development of Air Transport, and Environmental Protection, as well as Transformational Objectives, Support to Strategic Objectives, and Management & Administration.

387. In terms of revenues, the authorized appropriations were to be financed from contracting States' contributions for 2023 in the amount of CAD 103,920,000; from AOSC Fund reimbursements of CAD 1,829,000; transfer from ARGF surplus of CAD 8,082,000; funds from Operational Reserve of CAD 2,364,000; funds from Incentive Scheme of CAD 57,000; and miscellaneous income in the amount of CAD 780,000.[694]

II. Technical Cooperation Programme (AOSC)

388. For the **AOSC budget,** Resolution A41-28 recognizes, as in previous triennia, the difficulty of determining it with precision until the Governments of donor and recipient countries have decided on the relevant projects. The Resolution, therefore, states the AOSC net budget figures for the years 2023–2025 as indicative budget estimates only.[695]

389. In case the AOSC operation produces a deficit in any given financial year, such deficit must first be met from the accumulated AOSC surplus; a call for support from the regular budget should only be the last resort.[696]

390. Due to the indicative nature of the AOSC budget figures, subsequent adjustments to the budget estimates shall be made in the framework of the annual AOSC Budget Estimates in accordance with Article IX 9.5 of the Financial Regulations.

§5. Special Problems

I. Delays in Payment of Current Year Contributions

391. In recent years, **delays in payment by contracting States** of their current year contributions have been a major problem for the implementation of the Organization's work programme, as they have created serious cash-flow problems.[697]

392. Although Article 6.5 of the **Financial Regulations** provides that contributions are due and payable as of 1 January of each year, few contracting States pay

694. Assembly Resolution A41-28, Part B, Clause 2.
695. *Ibid.* (n. 693), Part C. AOSC Budget figures for 2023-2025 are CAD 9 300 000, CAD 9 570 000 and CAD 9 780 000.
696. *See* Assembly Resolution A41-28, Part C., 6th Recognizing clause. Due to a number of factors and the pandemic, this situation arose in 2019 and 2020.
697. *See* the discussion above, paras 344–347.

on the due date or early in the year. Many contracting States have financial years which do not coincide with the financial year of the Organization. Their own budgetary approval process takes them often to the second half of the year, and in some cases to the end of the calendar year. Consequently, contributions are received at any time throughout the year, but not in a regular pattern. Since expenditures, on the other hand, arise every year basically in a regular pattern, serious cash-flow problems arise when payment of large amounts of contributions is delayed to the second half of the year or beyond.[698]

393. On average, by September of each year, the cumulative receipt of contributions was short of estimated disbursement by an average of 17.7%.[699] Based on past trends, the average annual cash-flow shortfall accumulated by the end of September could range between USD 15 million and USD 17 million.[700]

394. As a result, the **Working Capital Fund** has served as a reserve to make up for the shortfall. Accumulated cash surplus may also serve temporarily as a buffer. The 38th Assembly authorized the Council to increase the Working Capital Fund from USD 8 million to USD 10 million,[701] if the Council determines that it is warranted. This was endorsed by subsequent Assemblies. However, the Council has so far refrained from increasing the Fund[702] and the Assembly expressed its confirmation in Resolution A41-30.[703] Such increases are to be funded from special assessments on contracting States[704] and the Council is naturally reluctant in these circumstances. Furthermore, Assembly Resolutions A39-33, A40-31 and A41-30 also authorized the Secretary General to resort to external borrowing for up to USD 3 million to meet immediate obligations of the Organization if these cannot be financed from the General Fund and the Working Capital Fund.[705] This authorization is a special backup measure since the Assembly has always been reluctant to

698. This matter has been a long-standing problem for ICAO; *see* Assembly Resolutions A16-55, A18-28, A21-36. A22-33, A23-27, A24-28, A26-26, A27-27, A29-30, A31-25, A32-28, A33-28 (no longer in force); Resolution A35-28, clause 1. (g), spelled out the problem as follows: '[E]xperience has shown that payments are not made at the beginning of the year when contributions are due and that ICAO cannot rely on contributions being paid even by the end of the year to which they relate and that such unacceptable avoidance of their financial obligations under the Convention by some contracting States is leading to a grave financial crisis within the Organization that could impact all contracting States.' *See* now Resolution A41-30, para. 1.d) and previously A39-31 and A38-27, clause 1.d).

699. *See* Resolution A35-28: *Working Capital Fund*, clause 1.e), in: *Assembly Resolutions in force (as of 8 Oct. 2004)*, ICAO Doc. 9848.

700. The amounts for 2016 were slightly better: total contributions in arrears as at 15 Jun. 2016 were CAD 14.3 million of which CAD 11.4 million was for arrears in respect of 2014 and prior years and CAD 2.9 million was related to arrears for 2015. *See* A39-WP/61 EX/34, para. 2.2.1..

701. *See* Resolution A38-27, operating clause 3.a); *see* previously A35-WP/26, AD/8.

702. Resolution A38-27, operating clause 3.b) and c).

703. Resolution A41-30, Resolving clause 2.c).

704. Financial Regulations, Art. VII 7.4 b).

705. This borrowing authority granted to the Secretary General is subject to a number of conditions spelled out in clauses 2 c), d) and e) of Resolution A41-30. *See* previously A38-27, clause 3 d). *See also* previous Assembly Resolutions A35-28, A36-34, A37-28, A38-27.

authorize external borrowing.[706] However, it will not remove the underlying root problem, namely the continued delays in contributions of contracting States discussed in §3 I.B. above and §5 II. below.

II. Accumulation of Long-Outstanding Arrears

395. A significant number of ICAO Member States have fallen behind with the payment of their annual contributions for more than a year. When the arrears have reached three years or more, the term **'long-outstanding arrears'** is used.[707] The past measures of the Organization to deal with the problem of long-outstanding arrears (settlement agreements, incentive scheme for settlements, suspension of voting rights) have been discussed above, under Chapter 4, paragraphs 344–347.

396. The three-pronged approach mentioned in paragraphs 344–347 and in the preceding paragraph has been maintained in Resolution A39-31 which applies to this problem, but has been combined with the following further measures.

397. As regards **settlement agreements**, contracting States which have arrears of three years or more are expected to make a minimum payment of 5% of their arrears.[708] Within six months of such payment, they are expected to conclude an agreement with the Organization for the settlement of their arrears, which may extend to a maximum of twenty years.[709]

398. As regards **suspension of voting rights**,[710] the following additional measures are added for those States which do not make the payment or conclude an agreement:[711]

- lose eligibility to host meetings, conferences, workshops and seminars which are funded, in whole or in part, by the Regular Programme;

---

706. Under the ICAO Financial Regulations, Art. VI (Provision of Funds), external borrowing is not one of the five authorized methods of provision of funds to finance the Organization. Deficits are to be covered from special assessments, cash surplus, or the Working Capital Fund. The special authorization given to the Secretary General to resort to external borrowing in case the Working Capital Fund is depleted, up to USD 3 million, is therefore a narrow exception, *see* Resolution A41-30; A40-31, clause 2.d); A39-33, clause 2.d)); and previously Resolutions A38-27, A36-34, A35-28, clause 2.d, A33-28, 2.d) and A32-28.
707. This term was first used as defined in Assembly Resolution A32-27, which was superseded by Resolutions A33-27, A 35-27, A36-34, A38-25, A39-31. *See* Clause 3 of Resolution A35-27 for the definition of 'long-outstanding arrears'.
708. *See* Assembly Resolution A39-31, clause 4.a). *See* previously A38-24, A37-32, A36-33 and A35-26.
709. *See ibid.*, clause 4.b).
710. *See* on this matter Ch. 4, paras 344–347 above.
711. *See* Assembly Resolution A39-31, Clause 10. These additional measures were added at the 35th Session of the Assembly, since it was felt that the mere suspension of voting rights under Art. 62 of the Convention was not sufficient to improve the situation, A35-26.

- receive only the same free documentation as that provided to non-contracting States, including those available in electronic media, and any other documents that are essential for safety, regularity or efficiency of international air navigation;
- nationals or Representatives lose eligibility for nomination to elected offices;
- for purposes of recruitment to posts in the Secretariat, if all other circumstances are equal, candidates from States in arrears would be considered as having the status of candidates from a State that has already achieved the desired level of representation (under Equitable Geographical Representation (EGR) principles), even if it has not achieved that level;
- lose the right to participate in the ICAO Familiarization Course.

399. Furthermore, only those States that have no outstanding annual contributions except for the current year will be eligible for election to the Council, Committees and bodies.[712]

400. As regards the **incentive scheme for settlement of long-outstanding arrears**, Resolution A38-25 applies, which has superseded the previous Resolutions A35-27, A33-27 and A32-27.[713] Under the rules of Resolution A38-25, only that portion of a payment from a contracting State with long outstanding arrears that is in excess of the sum of the three preceding years' assessments, and all instalments paid which were due under agreements entered into with the Council, shall be retained in a separate account.[714] Furthermore, contracting States with arrears of three full years or more and which either have existing agreements with the Organization or enter into agreements for settlement of their arrears and which have complied with the terms of their agreements, shall have their share of cash surplus distributed even though they have not paid the assessments for the financial year for which the surplus had been determined.

712. Assembly Resolution A39-31 Clause 11. It is not clear from the wording, whether the terms 'Committees and bodies' means Committees and bodies of the Council or of the Organization. It is submitted that it refers to Committees of the Organization, e.g., the Legal Committee. Because of the significant practical implications of clause 10, this question will require clarification.

713. *See* Assembly Resolution A38-25. When compared with the mentioned previous Assembly Resolutions, A38-25 has enhanced the incentive scheme by adding the measures described in clauses 4 and 5; however it is doubtful whether the financial impact of this additional measure is strong enough to lead to a significant improvement in the settlement of long-outstanding arrears. *See also* Assembly Resolution A34-1: *Use of funds in the separate account established under Resolving Clause 3 of Assembly Resolution A33-27* and A37-32, clauses 7 and 8.

714. Under A38-25, clause 4, two actions are required from States which are three years or more in arrears: first, payment of a minimum amount of 5% of their arrears, and second, conclusion of an agreement with ICAO for the settlement of their arrears (usually providing for payment in instalments).

Chapter 5. Information and Publications

§1. General

401. Information and publications are important aspects of the work of ICAO, in particular in relation to its Member States. The Organization maintains a comprehensive **public website** with information on ICAO itself, its global priorities, events, information resources, careers, and other matters. It also maintains several **secure website portals** for access by Member States and international organizations involved in ICAO work. The websites and ICAO TV are available for the time being in English only. A second avenue for informing Member States is through **State Letters**. These are sent electronically and in hardcopy to Member States in all six official languages to inform them officially about the convening of important meetings or other important events, and to request them to nominate delegates and take other action in preparation. A third avenue to inform Member States is by sending **Electronic Bulletins**. These are also sent to Member States in all official languages on matters of a more technical nature or matters which require prompt action. Public relations matters and PR information are handled by the Communications Section (COM) of the Secretariat which is part of the Office of the Secretary General (OSG).

402. As regards the publication of documents, a **migration from hardcopy to online softcopy publication** is ongoing. The Organization continues to publish all of its constitutional and convention documents, the technical Annexes to the Convention and their Amendments, the PANS and SUPPs, the Manuals, Circulars and related documentation in hardcopy format. The international conventions and protocols, the Annexes to the Convention, and documents pertaining to the ICAO Doc. series including the Annual Reports of the Council are also available online in electronic format for purchase on the web.[715] Online subscription arrangements are available for International Conventions and Protocols, Annexes to the Convention and documents pertaining to ATM.[716] An online **E-Library** of aviation-related documents has been created for reference purposes and is available at elibrary.icao-.int.

403. The **Annexes to the Convention**, as well as a number **of ICAO Manuals** are also available on CD-ROM or DVD.[717] The Organization has produced a number of audiovisual training aids, designed to support the implementation of SARPs set out in the Annexes to the Convention,[718] which are available in online video and poster formats.

715. *See* the Organization's official website: http://www.icao.int. Free publications and documents may be downloaded; saleable publications may be purchased through the e-shop, or ordered by e-mail addressed to: sales@icao.int.

716. ICAO Products and Services Catalogue 2020, pp. 97; 115 et seq.

717. Catalogue, *ibid.* (n. 703), pp. 97 et seq. The Annexes to the Convention are available as a single copy (No.AN), or as single copy with amendment service (No. AN.YR).

718. These are available for Aerodromes (AGA), Air Traffic Management (ATM), Meteorology (MET) and Operations/Airworthiness (OPS/AIR).

404. As a bimonthly hardcopy periodical, the Organization publishes the **ICAO Journal,** which presents articles on topical issues and current information on important meetings and the Secretariat.[719] Other ICAO periodicals in hardcopy magazine format are the **TRIP Report Magazine,** the **Training Report**, and the **Technical Cooperation Review**. ICAO publishes online the **Air Transport Monthly** and **Yearly Monitor** that provides a snapshot and analysis of economic and aviation indicators. Since 2020, a web-based service called **ICAO TV** provides videos and video recordings on events, Skytalks, interviews, and topical subjects such as the Evolution of ATM, CORSIA, and the ICAO PKD. The **ICAO Newsletter** (ten items per year) and the **ICAO Events and Topics** (ten items per year) are available online for subscription. Finally, the online **ICAO Store** may be used to order publications, hardcopy or digital, as well as arrange subscriptions.

§2. Constitutional Documents; International Conventions

405. Under 'constitutional documents', the Organization publishes the **Convention on International Civil Aviation** and its Amending Protocols, as well as the **International Air Services Transit Agreement.**[720] Under 'International Conventions and Protocols', all international air law conventions and protocols for which the Organization is the depositary, and certain other instruments are published.[721] Furthermore, under 'Agreements and Arrangements', it publishes international and multinational agreements relating to civil aviation.

§3. Annexes

406. A particularly important publication from the viewpoint of the Member States of ICAO and that of the aviation industry are the technical **Annexes to the Convention**, as the SARPs are frequently updated. In order to keep current, Member States' authorities require the timely availability of amendments and updates, published in loose-leaf and electronic formats.[722]

407. The online version, a website-based publication (**ICAO e-shop**), and CD-ROM version in addition to the hardcopy format[723] are therefore important from a practical viewpoint. All amendments are published in the same series, e.g.,

---

719. *The Journal* is published six times annually in English only.
720. Convention, ICAO Doc. 7300/9; Transit Agreement, ICAO Doc. 7500; Amending Protocols to the Convention, ICAO Docs. 8970, 8971, 9123, 9208, 9217, 9318, 9436, 9544, 9561, 9663, 9664, 9721 and 9722. For publication and sales purposes, ICAO docs are classified under 'Groups' as shown in the *ICAO Catalogue of Publications*.
721. These are also available electronically through the ICAO e-shop, at a fee. For access to the e-shop through the ICAO website, *see* www.icao.int.
722. The Annexes to the Convention are published in the AN series (e.g., Annex 1 as Doc. AN 1) and through the ICAO e-shop, *ibid.*
723. The CD-ROM format of Annexes is available with a yearly amendment service, No. AN/YR.

Amendments 1 to 79 of Annex 10 – Aeronautical Telecommunications. The Supplement to each Annex contains the Notifications under Article 38 by Member States of differences relating to the Annex and is therefore likewise important for Member States.

408. The **Procedures for Air Navigation Services (PANS)** are published as hardcopy, including their Amendments.[724] The PANS/ATM are also available in CD-ROM format; in addition, a PANS/OPS software package is available in CD-ROM format.

§4. Air Navigation

409. Air Navigation documents published by the Organization cover a large number of mainly technical publications.

410. Apart from the ICAO Global Plans discussed in paragraphs 154–157 above, the **Regional Air Navigation Plans (ANPs)** are important as a planning tool for ICAO contracting States.[725] They each cover a specific ICAO region and are published both as hardcopy document and as electronic document. Of these certain plans are supplemented by a Facilities and Services Implementation Document (FASID). Related reports of Regional Air Navigation Meetings are also published.[726]

411. Reports of global air navigation meetings (so-called Divisional-type meetings) are likewise published as hardcopy and as electronic document.

412. A large number of **technical publications** are related to the safety of airports, including the Aerodrome Design Manual,[727] the Airport Planning Manual,[728] the Airport Services Manual,[729] the Heliport Manual, and the Manual on Certification of Aerodromes.[730] A related data bank called Airport Characteristics Data Bank (ACDB)[731] provides information on facilities at over one thousand of the world's main airports. It is available in hardcopy format (seven volumes) as well as in electronic format.

724. PANS/OPS Software, No. CD-101.

725. *See* Assembly Resolution A40-4: *Consolidated Statement of continuing policies and associated practices related specifically to air navigation,* Appendix E and F; *see also* previously Resolution A35-14, Appendix M, and Resolution A21-21, Appendix M: Implementation of Regional Plans, third whereas clause.

726. The ICAO Regional Air Navigation Plans are published as ICAO Docs. 7474, 9673, 7754, 9708, 8755, and 9634. The *FASID – North Atlantic Regions* is published as ICAO Doc. 9635. The reports are published as ICAO Docs 9702, 9748, 9477, 9639, and 9672.

727. ICAO Doc. 9184.

728. *Ibid.*

729. ICAO Doc. 9137.

730. ICAO Doc. 9774.

731. Available electronically as diskette (Order No. ACDB-D) or as hardcopy (Order No. 175016, 175022).

413. Other **publications, manuals and databanks** cover Accident Investigation and Prevention (AIG),[732] Aeronautical Information and Charts,[733] ATM[734] Communications, Navigation and Surveillance,[735] Aviation Medicine, Meteorology,[736] Operations/Airworthiness,[737] Personal Licensing and raining[738] and Safety Oversight Audit.[739]

§5. AIR TRANSPORT

414. Air transport publications of the Organization include circulars, manuals, studies and statistics in the economic, facilitation and environmental fields.

415. In the economic field, the circulars on ICAO's Policies on Charges for Airports and Air Navigation Services[740] and on Privatization in the Provision of Airports and Air Navigation Services,[741] are important publications. They provide information and guidance on charges and essential elements of privatization for airports and air navigation service providers. Other publications cover user charges, other aspects of the economics of airports and air navigation services, and air carrier economics.

416. The **ICAO Policies on Taxation in the Field of International Air Transport**[742] and the Policy and Guidance Material on the Economic Regulation of International Air Transport[743] provide essential guidance to Member States on taxation and economic regulation.

417. The *World of Civil Aviation,*[744] a hardcopy circular on background information and trends analysis in the air transport industry, is now replaced by the **World Civil Aviation Report (WCAR)**.[745] It appears annually and is primarily distributed in digital format.

---

732. *See,* e.g., the *Manual of Aircraft Accident Investigation.* Doc. 6920.
733. *See,* e.g., the *Aeronautical Information Services Provided by States*, Doc. 7383.
734. *See,* e.g., the *Air Traffic Services Planning Manual,* Doc. 9426.
735. *See,* e.g., the *Comprehensive Aeronautical Telecommunication Network (ATN) Manual,* Doc. 9739.
736. *See,* e.g., the *Manual of Aeronautical Meteorological Practice*, Doc. 8896.
737. *See,* e.g., the *Airworthiness Manual,* Doc. 9760.
738. *See,* e.g., the *Human Factors Manuals*, Docs 9806, 9808, 9683, 9758 and 9824.
739. *See,* e.g., the *Safety Oversight Audit Manual,* Doc. 9735.
740. ICAO Doc. 9082.
741. ICAO Circular 284.
742. ICAO Doc. 8632.
743. ICAO Doc. 9587.
744. Last published as Circular 307 (2004–2006). Previous versions Cir.299 (2002–2005); 291 (2001–2004); 287 (2000); 279 (1999–2002), 275 (1998–2001).
745. This annual publication reviews the state of the aviation industry through the lens of diverse global aviation experts analyzing how stakeholders are tackling today's most pressing civil aviation challenges.

418. Facilitation publications include guidance material on **Machine-Readable Travel Documents**,[746] Public Information Displays, international signs at airports and marine terminals, and access to air transport by persons with disabilities.

419. In support of air transport economics, the Organization also publishes the Airport Economics Manual,[747] the Manual on Air Traffic Forecasting,[748] the Manual on the Regulation of International Air Transport,[749] and the Manual on Air Navigation Services Economics.[750]

420. Furthermore, **Civil Aviation Statistics**[751] are available online. They publish statistical information received from contracting States in accordance with Articles 54 (i) and 67 of the Convention.

421. Reports on air transport meetings and conferences have been published as saleable publications.[752]

§6. Legal

422. Publications of the Organization in the legal field cover in particular the Minutes and Documents of the **Legal Committee**, and the Minutes and Documents of **Diplomatic Conferences on Air Law**[753] Such Minutes and Documents of the Legal Committee are available as saleable publications for meetings as of 2004, and for Diplomatic Conferences as of 1988. Minutes and Documents before these dates are out of print; the 2020 ICAO Catalogue of Publications does not indicate availability in digital format.

423. The former hardcopy digest of Aeronautical Agreements and Arrangements[754] covering the period 1946–2002 is discontinued. Aeronautical agreements and arrangements notified since 2002 are available on the public ICAO website.[755] It indicates that Agreements and Arrangements are migrating from ICAO's **Database of Aeronautical Agreements and Arrangements (DAGMAR)** to ICAO's **Website of Aeronautical Agreements and Arrangements (WAGMAR)** and not

746. ICAO Doc. 9302.
747. ICAO Doc. 9562.
748. ICAO Doc. 8991.
749. ICAO Doc. 9626.
750. ICAO Doc. 9161.
751. The *Civil Aviation Statistics* can be accessed online by purchasing an annual subscription, at http://icaodata.com.
752. E.g. *Report on the Fifth Air Transport Conference*, Doc. 9819; *Report on the Fourth Air Transport Conference*, Doc. 9644; *Report on the High-level, Ministerial Meeting on Aviation Security*, Doc. 9800.
753. ICAO Docs, 9773, 9775, 9783, 9801, and 9823 (Diplomatic Conferences) and Docs. 9832, 9907, 9926, 10014, 10061, and 10114 (Legal Committee, *Reports,* 32th–37th Sessions).
754. ICAO Doc. 9813.
755. https://cfapp.icao.int/dagmar/main.cfm?UserLang=_e.

all Agreements may be accessible for the time being.[756] The Organization also publishes legal guidance material, in particular on the implementation of Article 83bis, and on Legal Aspects of Unruly/Disruptive Passengers[757]

424. A Collection of ICAO Aviation Law Documents is available as an 'electronic bundle'. The Collection puts together ICAO aviation law documents of interest to States, the industry and the general public in a single edition. Included are the original texts of the Chicago and the Warsaw conventions with their related acts as well as other conventions, protocols, and international and multilateral agreements in three languages.[758]

§7. Other

425. In the field of aviation security, the Organization makes available **Aviation Security Training Packages (ASTPs)** and Courses,[759] which are available electronically. They are designed to assist aviation security professionals, managers and staff in developing a better understanding of ICAO SARPs in the field of aviation security, as well as transmitting specialized practical expertise in the implementation and monitoring of measures and provisions relating to aviation security programmes. These ASTPs are offered in ICAO's catalogue.[760]

426. In the environmental field, the Organization publishes a large number of manuals and materials as guidance material for Member States relating to greenhouse gas emission reduction, alternative fuels, Environmental Management System (EMS), noise reduction, and air quality at airports.[761] The ICAO 'Environmental Report', published triennially since 2007, reports on the environmental protection activities undertaken in the past three years. It also contains compendia of technical and scientific articles which inform the public about the work undertaken by ICAO, its Member States and stakeholders.

427. Furthermore, in the air navigation field, and to support the implementation of the ICAO SARPs found in the Annexes to the Convention, the Organization has published a large number **of audiovisual training aids**. They are available for

756. https://dna.icao.int/WAGMAR.
757. *See* Doc. 10059 – *Manual on the Implementation of Article 83 bis of the Convention on International Civil Aviation*; ICAO Circular 295 (*Guidance on the Implementation of Article 83 bis).* Doc. 10117 – *Manual on the Legal Aspects of Unruly and Disruptive Passengers*, and Circular 288 (*Guidance Material on Legal Aspects of Unruly/Disruptive Passengers*).
758. Available on a CD-ROM in English, French and Spanish, ICAO Products and Services Catalogue 2020, p. 93. The content of the Collection is reflected in the ICAO Products and Services Catalogue 2020, pp. 101–106.
759. *See* the ICAO Products and Services Catalogue 2022; material for STP's and AST's, No. STP 123 and ASTP 123, P3-P8.
760. Catalogue *ibid.* (n. 746), p. 89; *see also* https://www.icao.int/Security/isd/Training/packages/Pages /default.aspx or.
761. Catalogue *ibid.* (n. 746), pp. 77–81.

ATM,[762] Meteorology (MET),[763] Operations/Airworthiness (OPS/AIR)[764] and Aerodromes, Air Routes and Ground Aids (AGA).[765] A similar kit is available with information on ICAO generally.

428. The audiovisual training aids consist of a set of videos and posters.

762. For example, videos on Wake Turbulence (V544B), Ground Control (V658B) and Separation Between Aircraft (V679B) have been developed.
763. E.g., on MET Reports, Wind-Shear Factor and Volcanic Ash.
764. E.g., on Basics of Altimetry, and CFIT Awareness and Prevention.
765. E.g., on Alpha Simulation, Aerodromes Fire Safety, Emergency Preparedness, and Bird Strike.

Chapter 6. Network: Relations with Other International Organizations

§1. General

429. When ICAO was set up in December 1944, the UN did not yet exist; neither did any of the regional organizations which today supplement the work of ICAO at the regional level.

430. Nevertheless, it was foreseen that the new **Organization would become part of a network of international bodies** with an important role in the post-war period.[766] Article 64 of the Convention on International Civil Aviation provides: 'The Organization may, with respect to air matters within its competence directly affecting world security, by vote of the Assembly enter into appropriate arrangements with any general organization set up by the nations of the world to preserve peace'.[767] Furthermore, Article 65 of the Conventions reads: 'The Council, on behalf of the Organization, may enter into agreements with other international bodies for the maintenance of common services and for common arrangements concerning personnel and, with the approval of the Assembly, may enter into such arrangements as may facilitate the work of the Organization'. The Organization has made use of these provisions by concluding a number of agreements and arrangements with the UN and other international bodies.[768]

§2. United Nations and UN Specialized Agencies

I. United Nations and UN Programmes

431. The status of ICAO as a **Specialized Agency of the United Nations** is based on the Agreement between the UN and the ICAO[769] dated 13 May 1947, which makes the Organization part of the UN family. This status involves a number of formal obligations of the Organization and implies close working relations with

766. *See* Arts 64 and 65 of the *Convention on International Civil Aviation*, as well as Assembly Resolutions A1-10; A1-2; A2-24; A5-5; A27-17; A22-7 and A21-12.
767. This provision was implemented by concluding the *Agreement between the United Nations and the International Civil Aviation Organization*, dated 13 May 1947, ICAO Doc. 7970; 8 *UNTS*, 315 et seq., 343; it was approved by the ICAO Assembly in Assembly Resolution A1-2. The Protocol concerning the entry into force of the Agreement was signed on 10 Oct. 1947, while the Agreement came into force on 13 May 1947.
768. Agreements or arrangements exist with the UN, *ibid.* (n. 754), including a Supplementary Agreement (signed on 10 and 31 May 1948), Doc. 7970, a special *Agreement on Acceptance of the Competence of the UNAT* (399 *UNTS* 306 et seq.), as well as arrangements with the UPU, the IAEA, the WMO, the ITU, and the IMO. *See infra*, Ch. 6. §2 II para. 422.
769. ICAO Doc. 7970; 8 UNTS 315 et seq., 324 (1947); *see* ICAO Assembly Resolutions A1-2: *Approval of the Agreement with the United Nations*; and A2-24: *Relations with the United Nations*, ICAO Doc. 9796.

the UN and certain UN sister organizations.[770] It also involves being **part of the UN 'Common System'** as regards personnel and human resource matters, administered by the International Civil Service Commission (ICSC) of the UN,[771] and submission to the inspections of the UN Joint Inspection Unit (JIU).[772]

432. Under Article VII of the **Agreement between the UN and ICAO**, the Organization shall cooperate with the UN Economic and Social Council and shall furnish such information and render such assistance to the UN Security Council as that Council may request, including assistance in carrying out decisions of the Security Council for the maintenance and restoration of international peace and security.[773] Article XX of the Agreement provides for the possibility of further arrangements being concluded between the UN and ICAO with respect to aviation matters within the competence of the Organization directly affecting world security, as contemplated in the Convention on International Civil Aviation.[774]

433. The cooperation and assistance clause of Article VII of the Agreement has been applied in a number of cases, in particular where the UN Security Council has imposed **sanctions** on certain States affecting civil aviation directly or indirectly. Thus, the sanctions imposed by the UN Security Council on the Federal Republic of Yugoslavia, Libya, Afghanistan and Iraq involved a ban on civil aviation links to and from these States,[775] accompanied to varying degrees by a ban on financial transactions related to air transport links and other measures. In accordance with its obligations,[776] ICAO assisted the UN Security Council in applying these sanctions.

---

770. Assembly Resolution A2-24, *ibid.*, in particular clause 3; Resolution A2-25: *Supplementary Agreement Covering the Use of the United Nations Laissez-passer by ICAO Officials;* A22-7: *Statute of the Joint Inspection Unit;* and A21-12: *International Civil Service Commission,* ICAO Doc. 9848.
771. Assembly Resolution A21-12: International Civil Service Commission, Doc. 10140; *see also* above, Ch. 2 §2 VII, para. 95; Ch. 3 §8 para. 301; *Agreement between the United Nations and ICAO* dated 13 May 1947, Art. XII, ICAO Doc. 7970; ICAO Assembly Resolutions A21-12 and A22-7. On the International Civil Service Commission, *see* https://icsc.un.org/Home/Brief.
772. Assembly Resolution A22-7: Statute of the Joint Inspection Unit, in: Doc. 10140. However, under clause 2 of the Resolution, competence of the Unit extends only over the functions of the Secretariat, not over those of the Assembly, the Council and its subordinate bodies.
773. *Supra* n. 754, at Art. VII; *see also* Assembly Resolution A5-5: *Coordination of activities between the United Nations and ICAO relating to emergency action to assist in the maintenance of international peace and security,* ICAO Doc. 9796.
774. *See* Art. 64 of the Convention; *supra,* Ch. 6 §1, para. 430.
775. For the sanctions against Afghanistan, *see* UN Security Council Resolutions 1267 (15 Oct. 1999), 1333 (19 Dec. 2000), 1363 (30 Jul. 2001), 1388 (15 Jan. 2002), 1390 (16 Jan. 2002) and 1455 (17 Jan. 2003); for the sanctions against Libya, UN Security Council Resolutions 748 (31 Mar. 1992), 883 (11 Nov. 1993), 1192 (27 Aug. 1998) and 1506 (12 Sep. 2003); for the sanctions against Iraq, UN Security Council Resolutions 661 (6 Aug. 1990), 986 (14 Apr. 1995), 1051 (27 Mar. 1996), 1111 (4 Jun. 1997), 1137 (12 Nov. 1997) and 1284 (17 Dec. 1999). No fewer than fifteen sanction regimes were adopted by the UN Security Council during the decade from 1990 to 2000; however, not all of these had an aviation component.
776. Under the Agreement between the UN and ICAO, dated 13 May 1947, Art. VII, ICAO is under obligation to assist UN bodies, in particular the UN Security Council, with regard to decisions to maintain or restore international peace and security. *See supra* (n. 754).

In other cases, the Organization has assisted the UN Security Council with supply of information and with policy decisions in support of decisions or policies of the Security Council.[777]

434. At the level of the Secretary General, the Organization participates actively in the bi-annual meetings of the **UN 'Chief Executives Board'** (CEB, formerly called ACC), comprising the chief executive officers of all the UN organizations and chaired by the UN Secretary General. Similarly, it participates in the High-Level Committee on Management (HLCM), the High-level Committee on Programmes (HLCP), the meetings of the UN Chief Legal Advisors and other inter-agency meetings.[778]

435. The Organization also participates in meetings of UN bodies, such as the General Assembly and its Commissions, whenever subjects relevant to its work are discussed. Conversely, the UN receives invitations to major meetings of ICAO, including the Assembly.

436. ICAO cooperates actively with a number of **UN programmes**, such as the UNDP,[779] the United Nations Framework Convention on Climate Change (UNFCCC)[780] and other bodies.

II. UN Specialized Agencies

437. As regards the other UN Specialized Agencies, ICAO maintains active working relations with the following organizations:

- ***International Atomic Energy Agency (IAEA),*** headquartered in Vienna. ICAO and IAEA concluded an Agreement of Cooperation on 28 September 1959.[781]
- ***International Maritime Organization (IMO)***,[782] headquartered in London (UK). Long-standing working relations exist in the areas of air navigation, in particular

777. Such action was taken under Art. VII of the Agreement between the UN and ICAO, *supra* n. 754, and ICAO Assembly Resolution A5-5: *Coordination of activities between the United Nations and ICAO relating to emergency action to assist in the maintenance of international peace and security.*
778. *See,* e.g., *Supplementary Report on Activities of the Organization in the First Half of 2004,* ICAO Doc. 9826, Supplement (July. 2004).
779. In particular, the Technical Cooperation Programme of ICAO involves UNDP cost-sharing country projects, *see* Assembly Resolution A40-24 Appendix B, ICAO Doc. 10140; previous Resolutions A35-30; A33-31, ICAO Doc. 9848.
780. *See supra*, Ch. 3. §3, IX H.
781. For the contents of the Agreement of Cooperation, *see* C-WP/2990; for action of the Council in approving the Agreement, *see* ICAO Doc. 8042-C/921, 38th Session, p. 7.
782. Previously called *Inter-Governmental Maritime Consultative Organization (IMCO)*. The constitution of IMO is the *Convention on the International Maritime Organization,* UNTS Vol. 1276 I 4214 as last amended in 1993 (in force since 2002); for the Working Arrangement between ICAO and IMCO dated 24 Nov. 1959, *see* ICAO Doc. 8042 – C/921, action of Council, pp. 7–8.

SAR, AIS and Charts, as well as in the TRAINAIR programme. A Working Arrangement with IMCO (as it was called) was concluded on 24 November 1959.

- ***International Mobile Satellite Organization (IMSO)***,[783] headquartered in London (UK). ICAO and IMSO concluded an Agreement of Cooperation in 2000 in order to ensure that Inmarsat Inc., which is subject to supervision by IMSO, will continue to apply all relevant ICAO SARPs to its aeronautical satellite telecommunications activities and to provide for mutual information exchange.
- ***International Telecommunication Union (ITU)***,[784] headquartered in Geneva (Switzerland). ICAO is involved in the World Radio Conferences (WRC), which ITU organizes every five years with the objective of allocating radio frequencies to types of usage in accordance with globally changing requirements. Furthermore, ICAO bases itself on ITU-allocated radio call signs for the nationality marks used in Annex 7 – *Aircraft Nationality and Registration.*[785]
- ***Universal Postal Union (UPU),*** headquartered in Berne (Switzerland).[786] ICAO and UPU exchange information and cooperate on matters concerning airmail and related issues.
- ***World Customs Organization (WCO),***[787] formerly Customs Cooperation Council (CCC), headquartered in Brussels (Belgium). ICAO and WCO cooperate on matters regarding security and facilitation, in particular as regards air cargo and related customs procedures.
- ***World Health Organization (WHO)***,[788] headquartered in Geneva (Switzerland). ICAO and WHO cooperate on health issues affecting civil aviation. For example, during the outbreak of SARS in 2003, and more recently during the COVID-19 pandemic, the two organizations coordinated passenger screening procedures

---

783. Previously called INMARSAT. The operational section of INMARSAT was privatized in 1999, whereas the intergovernmental supervisory functions were vested in IMSO. *See* the *Amended Convention of the International Mobile Satellite Organization,* XXIV AnnASL 477 et seq. (1999). David Sagar, 'The privatisation of INMARSAT: Special problems', in: Harris, R. A. (ed.), *International Organisations and Space Law, Proceedings of the Third ECSL Colloquium, Perugia, Italy, 6–7 May 1999.* On IMSO, *see* https://imso.org/imso-today/.

784. *See* ITU, *Constitution and Convention of the International Telecommunication Union,* adopted by the 2018 Plenipotentiary Conference (Basic Texts, 2019).

785. A Memorandum of Cooperation between ICAO and ITU was concluded on 17 Dec. 2012 Providing a Framework for Enhanced Cooperation Regarding the Protection of the Global Navigation Satellite System from Harmful Interference with a potential Impact on Aviation Safety, https://www.itu.int/dms_pub/itu-r/oth/0a/0e/R0A0E0000A40001PDFE.pdf. A broad working arrangement with ITU had been concluded on 14 Dec. 1950, *see* ICAO Doc. 7188 – C/828, Proceedings of Council (Part II), 11th Session, p. 17–18. As regards Annex 7, *see supra* Ch. 3. §2, H.

786. A Joint Statement of ICAO and UPU was issued on 1 Sep. 2020 encouraging States to support their designated postal operators, air cargo carriers, and express mail operators through financial aid and operational flexibility. Relations with UPU are governed by Resolution A33-19 Appendix H, ICAO Doc. 9790; *see also* previously Assembly Resolutions A1-44, A4-21, A10-33, which were later declared inapplicable by Resolution A16-1. They were replaced by Resolution A16-26, and subsequently by Resolution A33-19 Appendix H, ICAO Doc. 9790.

787. WCO is governed by the *Convention establishing a Customs Co-operation Council* signed in Brussels on 15 Dec. 1950, 157 UNTS 129 et seq. The Organization has 183 Member States. Its name changed in 1994 to World Customs Organization.

788. *World Health Organization Constitution*, 14 UNTS 185 et seq. (22 Jul. 1946); *WHO, Basic Documents* (49th ed. 2020).

applied at affected international airports.[789] In the framework of the CAPSCA programme, they worked together to assist States with pandemic preparedness.[790] In December 2022, ICAO and WHO signed a MOU for the purpose of supporting the 'use of evidence-informed and risk-based approaches to international travel, both in the context of the COVID-19 pandemic and other potential public health emergencies.'[791]

- ***World Meteorological Organization (WMO),***[792] headquartered in Geneva (Switzerland). ICAO and WMO cooperate on a wide range of meteorological issues affecting civil aviation, including aeronautical meteorology, forecasting, emergency response activities, data representation and codes, tropical cyclones observation and other issues. Such cooperation is essential for keeping up to date with the provisions of Annex 3 – *Meteorological Services for International Air Navigation.*
- ***World Tourism Organization (UNWTO),***[793] headquartered in Madrid (Spain). ICAO and UNWTO cooperate on certain economic issues affecting air transport. In particular, a study proposed by the fifth ICAO World Air Transport Conference on the essential air services concept was carried out in collaboration between the two organizations. Furthermore, they exchange certain economic data and participate in meetings of mutual interest.

§3. REGIONAL ORGANIZATIONS

438. According to **Article 55(a) of the Convention on International Civil Aviation**, the Council of ICAO may 'create subordinate air transport commissions on a regional or other basis and define groups of States or airlines with or through which it may deal to facilitate the carrying out of the aims of this Convention'.[794] While a need was felt in the 1950s and 1960s to establish regional organizations of States in Europe, Africa and Latin America to cater for the regional needs in civil aviation matters, Article 55(a) was not used, mainly for political reasons.[795] Instead,

789. *ICAO Handbook for CAAs on the Management of Aviation Safety Risks related to COVID-19,* Doc. 10144, 1st ed., May 2020, Ch. 2.
790. *See supra*, Ch. 3, §11.I, paras 338–339, including the new MoU between ICAO and WHO signed 4 Nov. 2022.
791. https://www.icao.int/Newsroom/Pages/ICAO-and-WHO-heighten-their-public-health-emergency-partnership.aspx#:~:text=Montr%C3%A9al%2C%2013%20December%202022%20%E2%80%93%20A,other%20potential%20public%20health%20emergencies.
792. Its constitution is the *World Meteorological Convention*, 77 UNTS 143 et seq. *See also*: Basic Documents No. 1 (1999), WMO Publications No. 15. ICAO and WMO concluded a Working Arrangement on 21 May and 23 Oct. 1953, *see* Doc. 7475.
793. *Statutes of the World Tourism Organization* signed on 27 Sep. 1970; its name changed in 1974 from IUOTO to WTO (Lately, the acronym UNWTO is used to distinguish it from the World Trade Organization). UNWTO has 159 Member States, six associate members, and over 400 affiliate members representing regional and local promotion boards, tourism trade associations and private sector companies.
794. *See* L. Weber, 'Les éléments de la coopération dans le cadre de la Commission européenne de l'aviation civile (CEAC)', 31 *RFDA* (1977), 388 et seq., 408.
795. Assembly Resolution A10-5, ICAO Doc. 7707, pp. 22 et seq.; A10-WP/150, pp. 95 et seq.; *see also* Weber, *supra*. n. 794, at pp. 411–412.

four regional bodies were set up which were neither ICAO regional air transport commissions under Article 55(a) nor completely independent of ICAO, but which were given an 'intermediate' status.[796] This intermediate status involved the secretariat of each such organization being placed on the premises of the respective regional office of ICAO and the conclusion of an administrative arrangement with ICAO.[797] The arrangements provided for ICAO to take charge of indirect costs attributable to the secretariat of the regional body, while direct costs were borne by the regional body itself. The regional body established its own work programme, convened its own meetings and set its own agenda, but maintained close liaison with ICAO.[798]

439. These principles were initially built into Assembly Resolution A27-17: **Relationship between ICAO and regional civil aviation bodies.**[799] As of 2010, more individual arrangements were made, and Resolution A37-21: Cooperation with regional organizations and regional civil aviation bodies[800] currently governs the relationship with the regional organizations, in particular:

– ***African Civil Aviation Commission (AFCAC)***,[801] headquartered in Dakar (Senegal). AFCAC has fifty-four Member States[802] and is open to African States members of the African Union (AU). Its main objective is to coordinate matters of civil aviation in Africa and cooperate with ICAO, promote the development of the civil aviation industry in Africa, foster the application of ICAO SARPs, and examine any specific problems which may hinder the development and operation of the African civil aviation industry and where possible, take the necessary actions.[803] For many years, AFCAC has been active in the fields of air transport liberalization in Africa, aviation training and other matters. Under the so-called ICAO/AFCAC transitional arrangements, ICAO provided AFCAC with financial and administrative assistance until January 2007, when AFCAC became an organization autonomous from ICAO. In the same year, AFCAC also became the Executing Agency for the implementation of the Yamoussoukro Decision (YD)

796. *See* Assembly Resolutions A10-5; A18-21; A21-8; and A27-17. *See also* L. Weber, *European Civil Aviation Conference*, in R. Bernhardt (ed.), *Encyclopedia supra* (Ch. 1 n. 9), Vol. II (1995), pp. 137 et seq., 138.
797. For the policy on the administrative arrangements, *see* Assembly Resolution A10-5, superseded by Resolution A27-17; *see also* Resolutions A18-21 and A21-8, likewise superseded by Resolutions A27-17, ICAO Doc. 9848.
798. *See* Art. 3 of the *ECAC Constitution*, ECAC Doc. No. 20, 3rd ed.; ICAO Assembly Resolution A27-17; Weber, *supra* n. 66, at p. 138.
799. *See also* now A37-21: *Cooperation with regional organizations and regional civil aviation bodies*, as well as A1-10, which continues to be in force.
800. ICAO Doc. 10140.
801. AFCAC is governed by its 2009 Constitution: *Constitution of AFCAC*, Done at Dakar, Senegal on the 16th day of December 2009, https://afcac.org/en/images/Documentation/Constitution_eng.pdf.
802. *See* AFCAC Website, http://www.afcac.org/en/index.php?option=com_content&view. According to the official list of countries having signed or ratified the AFCAC Constitution of 2009, the African Union (AU), depositary of the instrument, indicates that as of early 2021 forty-six States had ratified or adhered to the instrument. *See* http://au.int/en/sites/default/files/afcac.pdf.
803. Article 6 of the Constitution of AFCAC, *supra* n. 801.

on air transport liberalization and it adopted a new Constitution on 16 December 2009, in force since May 2010.[804] It established partnerships with a number of other organizations and agencies.[805]

- ***European Civil Aviation Conference (ECAC),***[806] headquartered in Paris (France). ECAC has forty-four Member States and is open to any European State member of the Council of Europe. Its main objective is to promote the continued development of a safe, efficient and sustainable European air transport system.[807] ECAC has been active in the areas of air transport policy (scheduled and non-scheduled services), facilitation, liberalization of tariffs and capacity, aviation security and numerous other matters, and cooperates with Eurocontrol and the EU.[808] In December 2020, a revised version of the ECAC Constitution was issued which *inter alia* rendered ECAC autonomous from ICAO as regards financial and administrative matters while retaining its office on the same premises as the ICAO Regional Office.[809]
- ***Latin American Civil Aviation Commission (LACAC),***[810] headquartered in Lima (Peru). LACAC has twenty-two Member States and is open to any State in the American hemisphere. Its main objective is to promote orderly development and better utilization of air transport within the region. LACAC has been active in the field of air transport regulatory policy, safety and security oversight audits, aviation security, aviation environmental policy and many other matters.[811] ICAO provides continued administrative assistance to LACAC.[812]
- ***Arab Civil Aviation Commission (ACAC),***[813] headquartered in Rabat (Morocco). ACAC has fifteen Member States plus Palestine and is open to any Arab State

804. Constitution of AFCAC, *supra* n. 801.
805. *See* the AFCAC Website, Partnerships: https://www.afcac.org/legacy/en/index.php?option=com_content&view=category&layout=blog&id=38&Itemid=172.
806. *ECAC Constitution*, 9th ed., adopted at Paris, December 2020, ECAC Doc. No. 20, 9th ed. The first constitution had been adopted at Paris in 1955 at the first Session of ECAC as ECAC Resolution No. 1 (ECAC/1-Res. 1, 1955).
807. Article 1 of the ECAC Constitution, *supra* n. 798.
808. *ECAC/EU Dialogue with the Industry on European Air Transport competitiveness (2014), ECAC/EU Dialogue on Challenges and opportunities in financing aviation (2017), ECAC/ EU Dialogue with the air transport industry on Restart, reconnect, recover – rebuilding aviation in a changed world (2020): see* https://www.ecac-ceac.org/history.
809. ECAC Constitution, *ibid.* (n. 792).
810. *Statute of the Latin American Civil Aviation Commission (LACAC)*, adopted at Mexico City on 14 Dec. 1973, revised on 8 Nov. 1989, in: LACAC, *Statute and Rules of Procedure for Meetings of LACAC.*
811. In December 2020, the Latin American Civil Aviation Commission (LACAC) adopted and published its new multilateral agreement to liberalize air cargo services in the region, https://www.icao.int/Newsroom/Pages/New-ICAO-LACAC-air-cargo-liberalization-agreement-to-bolster-regional-vaccine-transport-long-term-recovery-.aspx.
812. *See* LACAC Statute, *supra* n. 810, at No. 2, Arts 27, 28, Rules of Procedure, *ibid.* (n. 796), No. 7, Rule 12; ICAO Assembly Resolution A 21-8; A27-17.
813. Initially called '*Civil Aviation Council of Arab States*'. Established on 7 Feb. 1996 when its founding Convention entered into force. It held its first General Assembly on 4–5 Jun. 1996, accepting the *Agreement on the Civil Aviation Council of Arab States* of 21 Mar. 1965, as amended on 3 Jul. 1975; Member States are Bahrain, Egypt, Iraqi, Jordan, Lebanon, Libyan Arab Jamahiriya, Morocco, Oman, Qatar, Saudi Arabia, Sudan, Syrian Arab Republic, Tunisia, United Arab Emirates and Yemen; Palestine is recognized as a member.

member of the League of Arab States. Its main objective is to provide the civil aviation authorities of Member States with a framework of joint action to develop general planning for civil aviation in the interest of safety, promote cooperation and coordination in the interest of uniformity, and ensure its growth and development for secure, safe and regular air transport.[814] ACAC has been active in the field of traffic and transit rights, air transport liberalization, aviation training, routes and airports, and harmonization of air law. No formal arrangements for administrative and financial assistance exist between ICAO and ACAC; however, working relations are maintained on an ad-hoc basis between the two organizations concerning invitations to meetings and the exchange of documentation and information of mutual interest.[815]

440. ICAO also maintains working relations with the following three other regional organizations which provide air navigation services on behalf of their Member States to airline operators within the airspace for which they have responsibility:

– ***Agency for the Safety of Aerial Navigation in Africa and Madagascar (ASECNA)***,[816] with headquarters in Dakar (Senegal). ASECNA has sixteen Member States and provides air navigation services as well as ATC at international airports of its Member States.
– ***Central American Corporation for Air Navigation Services (COCESNA)***,[817] with headquarters in Tegucigalpa (Honduras). COCESNA has six Members States and provides air navigation services as well as ATC at the international airports of its Member States.
– ***European Organisation for the Safety of Air Navigation (EUROCONTROL)***,[818] with its headquarters in Brussels (Belgium). EUROCONTROL has currently forty-one Member States and provides air navigation services in the upper air space of its Member States. It also provides services to certain other States which have associated themselves with EUROCONTROL or which have signed cooperation agreements. In particular, EUROCONTROL operates a harmonized route charges system, under which the organization sets, bills and collects route charges from aircraft operators for air navigation services rendered.[819] The EU has become a member of the organization, which plays an important role in the realization of the 'Single European Sky' concept. It has also done pioneering work for the development of an ATM concept for the partially saturated, and sometimes congested, European sky.

814. Article 5 of the Revised Agreement of ACAC, *ibid.* (n. 799).
815. *See,* e.g., ICAO – ACAC Civil Military Workshop, Algiers, Algeria 26–28 Mar. 2018.
816. *Convention Establishing ASECNA*, signed at St. Louis (Senegal) on 12 Dec. 1959; replaced by the Convention signed at Dakar (Senegal) on 25 Oct. 1974.
817. *Convention Establishing COCESNA*, signed at Tegucigalpa (Honduras) on 26 Feb. 1960.
818. *Revised Convention on EUROCONTROL*, signed on 27 Jun. 1997. On EUROCONTROL, *see* L. Weber, *European Organization for the Safety of Air Navigation (EUROCONTROL)*, in: R. Bernhardt (ed.), *Encyclopaedia* (*supra* n. 9), Vol. II (1995), pp. 270 et seq. with further references.
819. L. Weber, *The EUROCONTROL Route Charges Litigation before the Court of Justice of the European Communities*, III Annals of Air & Space L. 355–369 (1978).

441. In Europe, the **European Union (EU)** has been entrusted with progressively increasing responsibilities and tasks in the field of civil aviation.[820] The Member States of the EU have consented to a gradual, one-by-one transfer of responsibilities to the EU as part of the general integration process. The transferred responsibilities include regulatory, safety, security and environmental matters in the civil aviation field.[821]

442. Therefore, with respect to subject matters for which the EU is responsible, ICAO has established working relations with the EU institutions, in particular the European Commission. The Commission participates in numerous meetings at ICAO, and in 2005 established an observer delegation office of the Commission at the seat of the Organization in Montreal. The EU Commission Observer is invited to participate in meetings of the Assembly, Council, Council Committees and other bodies.

443. The EU established the **European Aviation Safety Agency (EASA)**[822] in 2003 with its headquarters in Cologne (Germany). This agency, which is a subsidiary of the European Commission, has been given important responsibilities for aviation safety matters, in particular personnel licensing, aircraft airworthiness certification, safety oversight including USOAP audits, and other subjects. Close working relations have been established between ICAO and EASA to ensure compatibility of measures and to avoid overlap and duplication.

§4. Non-governmental Organizations

444. The Organization maintains a close working relationship with a number of non-governmental organizations on the basis of Assembly Resolution A1-11.[823] The following should be mentioned:

- ***International Air Transport Association (IATA)***,[824] the trade association of more than 290 scheduled international airlines, headquartered in Montreal.

---

820. The Third Aviation Package in 1992, the creation of the Common Aviation Area, the Single European Sky Initiative, the ECJ decision in the 'Open Sky' cases (Cases C 466-469/98, C 471-472/98, C 475/98 and C 476/98), the EU Council decision on a negotiation mandate for aviation bilaterals, and the establishment of EASA have been important milestones in this process. *See* L. Weber, *Convention on International Civil Aviation – 60 Years*, 53 ZLW 289 et seq. (2004).
821. For a summary of the 'aquis communautaire', *see* Giemulla/Schmid/Mölls/v. Schyndel, European Air Law, Vols. 1-5 (incl. supp. 29), Vol. 1-2, part B: Measures adopted by the EEC; L. Weber, 'The European Union and the Chicago Convention of 1944', 19 Air Law 179 et seq. (1994). *See also* http://europa.eu/scadplus/leg/en/s13004.htm and http://ec.europa.eu/transport/air/index_en.htm.
822. *Regulation (EC) No. 1592/2002 of the European Parliament and the Council of 1 Jul. 2002 on common rules in the field of civil aviation and Establishing a European Aviation Safety Agency (EASA)*, OJ L 240, p. 1–21 (7 Sep. 2002); *see* U.-M. Stiehl, 'Die Europäische Agentur für Flugsicherheit (EASA)', 53 *ZLW* (2004), p. 312–333.
823. ICAO Doc. 10140, *Assembly Resolutions in force (as of 4 Oct. 2019).*
824. *See* A.D. Groenewege, *Compendium of International Civil Aviation* 219 et seq. (3d ed. 2003).

- ***Airports Council International (ACI)***,[825] the global trade representative of the world's airports, headquartered in Montreal.
- ***Civil Air Navigation Services Organisation (CANSO)***,[826] the global body of air navigation service providers (ANSPs) headquartered in Hoofdorp, the Netherlands.
- ***International Federation of Airline Pilot's Associations (IFALPA)***,[827] the world federation of national pilots' associations, headquartered in Chertsey (Surrey, UK) with an observer delegation office in Montreal.
- ***International Federation of Airline Traffic Controllers' Associations (IFATCA),***[828] the world federation of national air traffic controllers' associations, headquartered in Montreal.
- ***International Council of Aircraft Owner and Pilot Associations (IAOPA)***,[829] the world federation of national aircraft owner and pilot associations, headquartered near Washington, D.C.
- ***International Chamber of Commerce (ICC)***,[830] the world body of the national chambers of commerce, headquartered in Paris.
- ***International Business Aviation Council (IBAC)***,[831] the federation of national business aviation associations, headquartered in Montreal.

Many of these organizations participate in ICAO meetings as observers, receive relevant ICAO documentation and exchange information with ICAO. In some cases, such as IATA and IFALPA, they participate in ICAO's work on a day-to-day basis, in line with ICAO's policies in Assembly Resolution A1-11.

825. http://www.aci.aero/.
826. http://www.canso.org/cms/showpage.aspx.
827. Groenewege, *ibid.* (n. 810), pp. 324 et seq.
828. http://www.ifatca.org/.
829. http://www.iaopa.org/.
830. http://www.iccwbo.org/.
831. http://www.ibac.org/.

Appendices

Appendix A. Convention on International Civil Aviation

Signed at Chicago, on 7 December 1944

Preamble

WHEREAS the future development of international civil aviation can greatly help to create and preserve friendship and understanding among the nations and peoples of the world, its abuse can become a threat to the general security; and

WHEREAS it is desirable to avoid friction and to promote that cooperation between nations and peoples upon which the peace of the world depends;

THEREFORE, the undersigned governments having agreed on certain principles and arrangements in order that international civil aviation may be developed in a safe and orderly manner and that international air transport services may be established on the basis of equality of opportunity and operated soundly and economically;

Have accordingly concluded this Convention to that end.

Part I Air Navigation

Chapter I General Principles and Application of the Convention

Article 1 Sovereignty

The contracting States recognize that every State has complete and exclusive sovereignty over the airspace above its territory.

Article 2 Territory

For the purposes of this Convention, the territory of a State shall be deemed to be the land areas and territorial waters adjacent thereto under the sovereignty, suzerainty, protection or mandate of such State.

Article 3 Civil and state aircraft

a) This Convention shall be applicable only to civil aircraft, and shall not be applicable to state aircraft.

b) Aircraft used in military, customs and police services shall be deemed to be state aircraft.
c) No state aircraft of a contracting State shall fly over the territory of another State or land thereon without authorization by special agreement or otherwise, and in accordance with the terms thereof.
d) The contracting States undertake, when issuing regulations for their state aircraft, that they will have due regard for the safety of navigation of civil aircraft.

Article 3 bis[832]

a) The contracting States recognize that every State must refrain from resorting to the use of weapons against civil aircraft in flight and that, in case of interception, the lives of persons on board and the safety of aircraft must not be endangered. This provision shall not be interpreted as modifying in any way the rights and obligations of States set forth in the Charter of the United Nations.
b) The contracting States recognize that every State, in the exercise of its sovereignty, is entitled to require the landing at some designated airport of a civil aircraft flying above its territory without authority or if there are reasonable grounds to conclude that it is being used for any purpose inconsistent with the aims of this Convention; it may also give such aircraft any other instructions to put an end to such violations. For this purpose, the contracting States may resort to any appropriate means consistent with relevant rules of international law, including the relevant provisions of this Convention, specifically paragraph *a)* of this Article. Each contracting State agrees to publish its regulations in force regarding the interception of civil aircraft.
c) Every civil aircraft shall comply with an order given in conformity with paragraph *b)* of this Article. To this end, each contracting State shall establish all necessary provisions in its national laws or regulations to make such compliance mandatory for any civil aircraft registered in that State or operated by an operator who has his principal place of business or permanent residence in that State. Each contracting State shall make any violation of such applicable laws or regulations punishable by severe penalties and shall submit the case to its competent authorities in accordance with its laws or regulations.
d) Each contracting State shall take appropriate measures to prohibit the deliberate use of any civil aircraft registered in that State or operated by an operator who has his principal place of business or permanent residence in that State for any purpose inconsistent with the aims of this Convention. This provision shall not affect paragraph *a)* or derogate from paragraphs *b)* and *c)* of this Article.

832. On 10 May 1984 the Assembly amended the Convention by adopting the Protocol introducing Art. 3 *bis*. Under Art. 94 *a)* of the Convention, the amendment came into force on 1 Oct. 1998 in respect of States which have ratified it.

Article 4 Misuse of civil aviation

Each contracting State agrees not to use civil aviation for any purpose inconsistent with the aims of this Convention.

Chapter II Flight over Territory of contracting States

Article 5 Right of non-scheduled flight

Each contracting State agrees that all aircraft of the other contracting States, being aircraft not engaged in scheduled international air services shall have the right, subject to the observance of the terms of this Convention, to make flights into or in transit non-stop across its territory and to make stops for non-traffic purposes without the necessity of obtaining prior permission, and subject to the right of the State flown over to require landing. Each contracting State nevertheless reserves the right, for reasons of safety of flight, to require aircraft desiring to proceed over regions which are inaccessible or without adequate air navigation facilities to follow prescribed routes, or to obtain special permission for such flights.

Such aircraft, if engaged in the carriage of passengers, cargo, or mail for remuneration or hire on other than scheduled international air services, shall also, subject to the provisions of Article 7, have the privilege of taking on or discharging passengers, cargo, or mail, subject to the right of any State where such embarkation or discharge takes place to impose such regulations, conditions or limitations as it may consider desirable.

Article 6 Scheduled air services

No scheduled international air service may be operated over or into the territory of a contracting State, except with the special permission or other authorization of that State, and in accordance with the terms of such permission or authorization.

Article 7 Cabotage

Each contracting State shall have the right to refuse permission to the aircraft of other contracting States to take on in its territory passengers, mail and cargo carried for remuneration or hire and destined for another point within its territory. Each contracting State undertakes not to enter into any arrangements which specifically grant any such privilege on an exclusive basis to any other State or an airline of any other State, and not to obtain any such exclusive privilege from any other State.

Article 8 Pilotless aircraft

No aircraft capable of being flown without a pilot shall be flown without a pilot over the territory of a contracting State without special authorization by that State and in accordance with the terms of such authorization. Each contracting State undertakes to ensure that the flight of such aircraft without a pilot in regions open to civil aircraft shall be so controlled as to obviate danger to civil aircraft.

Appendix A. Convention on International Civil Aviation

Article 9 Prohibited areas

a) Each contracting State may, for reasons of military necessity or public safety, restrict or prohibit uniformly the aircraft of other States from flying over certain areas of its territory, provided that no distinction in this respect is made between the aircraft of the State whose territory is involved, engaged in international scheduled airline services, and the aircraft of the other contracting States likewise engaged. Such prohibited areas shall be of reasonable extent and location so as not to interfere unnecessarily with air navigation. Descriptions of such prohibited areas in the territory of a contracting State, as well as any subsequent alterations therein, shall be communicated as soon as possible to the other contracting States and to the International Civil Aviation Organization.
b) Each contracting State reserves also the right, in exceptional circumstances or during a period of emergency, or in the interest of public safety, and with immediate effect, temporarily to restrict or prohibit flying over the whole or any part of its territory, on condition that such restriction or prohibition shall be applicable without distinction of nationality to aircraft of all other States.
c) Each contracting State, under such regulations as it may prescribe, may require any aircraft entering the areas contemplated in subparagraphs *a)* or *b)* above to effect a landing as soon as practicable thereafter at some designated airport within its territory.

Article 10 Landing at customs airport

Except in a case where, under the terms of this Convention or a special authorization, aircraft are permitted to cross the territory of a contracting State without landing, every aircraft which enters the territory of a contracting State shall, if the regulations of that State so require, land at an airport designated by that State for the purpose of customs and other examination. On departure from the territory of a contracting State, such aircraft shall depart from a similarly designated customs airport. Particulars of all designated customs airports shall be published by the State and transmitted to the International Civil Aviation Organization established under Part II of this Convention for communication to all other contracting States.

Article 11 Applicability of air regulations

Subject to the provisions of this Convention, the laws and regulations of a contracting State relating to the admission to or departure from its territory of aircraft engaged in international air navigation, or to the operation and navigation of such aircraft while within its territory, shall be applied to the aircraft of all contracting States without distinction as to nationality, and shall be complied with by such aircraft upon entering or departing from or while within the territory of that State.

Article 12 Rules of the air

Each contracting State undertakes to adopt measures to ensure that every aircraft flying over or maneuvering within its territory and that every aircraft carrying its nationality mark, wherever such aircraft may be, shall comply with the rules and regulations relating to the flight and maneuver of aircraft there in force. Each contracting State undertakes to keep its own regulations in these respects uniform, to the greatest possible extent, with those established from time to time under this Convention. Over the high seas, the rules in force shall be those established under this Convention. Each contracting State undertakes to ensure the prosecution of all persons violating the regulations applicable.

Article 13 Entry and clearance regulations

The laws and regulations of a contracting State as to the admission to or departure from its territory of passengers, crew or cargo of aircraft, such as regulations relating to entry, clearance, immigration, passports, customs, and quarantine shall be complied with or on behalf of such passengers, crew or cargo upon entrance into or departure from, or while within the territory of that State.

Article 14 Prevention of spread of disease

Each contracting State agrees to take effective measures to prevent the spread by means of air navigation of cholera, typhus (epidemic), smallpox, yellow fever, plague, and such other communicable diseases as the contracting States shall from time to time decide to designate, and to that end contracting States will keep in close consultation with the agencies concerned with international regulations relating to sanitary measures applicable to aircraft. Such consultation shall be without prejudice to the application of any existing international convention on this subject to which the contracting States may be parties.

Article 15 Airport and similar charges

Every airport in a contracting State which is open to public use by its national aircraft shall likewise, subject to the provisions of Article 68, be open under uniform conditions to the aircraft of all the other contracting States. The like uniform conditions shall apply to the use, by aircraft of every contracting State, of all air navigation facilities, including radio and meteorological services, which may be provided for public use for the safety and expedition of air navigation.

Any charges that may be imposed or permitted to be imposed by a contracting State for the use of such airports and air navigation facilities by the aircraft of any other contracting State shall not be higher,

a) As to aircraft not engaged in scheduled international air services, than those that would be paid by its national aircraft of the same class engaged in similar operations, and
b) As to aircraft engaged in scheduled international air services, than those that would be paid by its national aircraft engaged in similar international air services.

All such charges shall be published and communicated to the International Civil Aviation Organization, provided that, upon representation by an interested contracting State, the charges imposed for the use of airports and other facilities shall be subject to review by the Council, which shall report and make recommendations thereon for the consideration of the State or States concerned. No fees, dues or other charges shall be imposed by any contracting State in respect solely of the right of transit over or entry into or exit from its territory of any aircraft of a contracting State or persons or property thereon.

Article 16 Search of aircraft

The appropriate authorities of each of the contracting States shall have the right, without unreasonable delay, to search the aircraft of the other contracting States on landing or departure, and to inspect the certificates and other documents prescribed by this Convention.

Chapter III Nationality of Aircraft

Article 17 Nationality of aircraft

Aircraft have the nationality of the State in which they are registered.

Article 18 Dual registration

An aircraft cannot be validly registered in more than one State, but its registration may be changed from one State to another.

Article 19 National laws governing registration

The registration or transfer of registration of aircraft in any contracting State shall be made in accordance with its laws and regulations.

Article 20 Display of marks

Every aircraft engaged in international air navigation shall bear its appropriate nationality and registration marks.

Article 21 Report of registrations

Each contracting State undertakes to supply to any other contracting State or to the International Civil Aviation Organization, on demand, information concerning the registration and ownership of any particular aircraft registered in that State. In addition, each contracting State shall furnish reports to the International Civil Aviation Organization, under such regulations as the latter may prescribe, giving such pertinent data as can be made available concerning the ownership and control of aircraft registered in that State and habitually engaged in international air navigation. The data thus obtained by the International Civil Aviation Organization shall be made available by it on request to the other contracting States.

Chapter IV Measures to Facilitate Air Navigation

Article 22 Facilitation of formalities

Each contracting State agrees to adopt all practicable measures, through the issuance of special regulations or otherwise, to facilitate and expedite navigation by aircraft between the territories of contracting States, and to prevent unnecessary delays to aircraft, crews, passengers and cargo, especially in the administration of the laws relating to immigration, quarantine, customs and clearance.

Article 23 Customs and immigration procedures

Each contracting State undertakes, so far as it may find practicable, to establish customs and immigration procedures affecting international air navigation in accordance with the practices which may be established or recommended from time to time, pursuant to this Convention. Nothing in this Convention shall be construed as preventing the establishment of customs-free airports.

Article 24 Customs duty

a) Aircraft on a flight to, from, or across the territory of another contracting State shall be admitted temporarily free of duty, subject to the customs regulations of the State. Fuel, lubricating oils, spare parts, regular equipment and aircraft stores on board an aircraft of a contracting State, on arrival in the territory of another contracting State and retained on board on leaving the territory of that State shall be exempt from customs duty, inspection fees or similar national or local duties and charges. This exemption shall not apply to any quantities or articles unloaded, except in accordance with the customs regulations of the State, which may require that they shall be kept under customs supervision.
b) Spare parts and equipment imported into the territory of a contracting State for incorporation in or use on an aircraft of another contracting State engaged in international air navigation shall be admitted free of customs duty, subject to compliance with the regulations of the State concerned, which may provide that the articles shall be kept under customs supervision and control.

Article 25 Aircraft in distress

Each contracting State undertakes to provide such measures of assistance to aircraft in distress in its territory as it may find practicable, and to permit, subject to control by its own authorities, the owners of the aircraft or authorities of the State in which the aircraft is registered to provide such measures of assistance as may be necessitated by the circumstances. Each contracting State, when undertaking a search for missing aircraft, will collaborate in coordinated measures which may be recommended from time to time pursuant to this Convention.

Article 26 Investigation of accidents

In the event of an accident to an aircraft of a contracting State occurring in the territory of another contracting State, and involving death or serious injury, or indicating serious technical defect in the aircraft or air navigation facilities, the State in which the accident occurs will institute an inquiry into the circumstances of the accident, in accordance, so far as its laws permit, with the procedure which may be recommended by the International Civil Aviation Organization. The State in which the aircraft is registered shall be given the opportunity to appoint observers to be present at the inquiry and the State holding the inquiry shall communicate the report and findings in the matter to that State.

Article 27 Exemption from seizure on patent claims

a) While engaged in international air navigation, any authorized entry of aircraft of a contracting State into the territory of another contracting State or authorized transit across the territory of such State with or without landings shall not entail any seizure or detention of the aircraft or any claim against the owner or operator thereof or any other interference therewith by or on behalf of such State or any person therein, on the ground that the construction, mechanism, parts, accessories or operation of the aircraft is an infringement of any patent, design, or model duly granted or registered in the State whose territory is entered by the aircraft, it being agreed that no deposit of security in connection with the foregoing exemption from seizure or detention of the aircraft shall, in any case, be required in the State entered by such aircraft.
b) The provisions of paragraph *a)* of this Article shall also be applicable to the storage of spare parts and spare equipment for the aircraft and the right to use and install the same in the repair of an aircraft of a contracting State in the territory of any other contracting State, provided that any patented part or equipment so stored shall not be sold or distributed internally in or exported commercially from the contracting State entered by the aircraft.
c) The benefits of this Article shall apply only to such States, parties to this Convention, as either 1) are parties to the International Convention for the Protection of Industrial Property and to any amendments thereof; or 2) have enacted patent laws which recognize and give adequate protection to inventions made by the nationals of the other States parties to this Convention.

Article 28 Air navigation facilities and standard systems

Each contracting State undertakes, so far as it may find practicable, to:

a) Provide, in its territory, airports, radio services, meteorological services and other air navigation facilities to facilitate international air navigation, in accordance with the standards and practices recommended or established from time to time, pursuant to this Convention;
b) Adopt and put into operation the appropriate standard systems of communications procedure, codes, markings, signals, lighting and other operational practices and rules which may be recommended or established from time to time, pursuant to this Convention;
c) Collaborate in international measures to secure the publication of aeronautical maps and charts in accordance with standards which may be recommended or established from time to time, pursuant to this Convention.

Chapter V Conditions to be Fulfilled with respect to Aircraft

Article 29 Documents carried in aircraft

Every aircraft of a contracting State, engaged in international navigation, shall carry the following documents in conformity with the conditions prescribed in this Convention:

a) Its certificate of registration;
b) Its certificate of airworthiness;
c) The appropriate licenses for each member of the crew;
d) Its journey log book;
e) If it is equipped with radio apparatus, the aircraft radio station license;
f) If it carries passengers, a list of their names and places of embarkation and destination;
g) If it carries cargo, a manifest and detailed declaration of the cargo.

Article 30 Aircraft radio equipment

a) Aircraft of each contracting State may, in or over the territory of other contracting States, carry radio transmitting apparatus only if a license to install and operate such apparatus has been issued by the appropriate authorities of the State in which the aircraft is registered. The use of radio transmitting apparatus in the territory of the contracting State whose territory is flown over shall be in accordance with the regulations prescribed by that State.
b) Radio transmitting apparatus may be used only by members of the flight crew who are provided with a special license for the purpose, issued by the appropriate authorities of the State in which the aircraft is registered.

Article 31 Certificates of airworthiness

Every aircraft engaged in international navigation shall be provided with a certificate of airworthiness issued or rendered valid by the State in which it is registered.

Article 32 Licenses of personnel

a) The pilot of every aircraft and the other members of the operating crew of every aircraft engaged in international navigation shall be provided with certificates of competency and licenses issued or rendered valid by the State in which the aircraft is registered.
b) Each contracting State reserves the right to refuse to recognize, for the purpose of flight above its own territory, certificates of competency and licenses granted to any of its nationals by another contracting State.

Article 33 Recognition of certificates and licenses

Certificates of airworthiness and certificates of competency and licenses issued or rendered valid by the contracting State in which the aircraft is registered, shall be recognized as valid by the other contracting States, provided that the requirements under which such certificates or licences were issued or rendered valid are equal to or above the minimum standards which may be established from time to time pursuant to this Convention.

Article 34 Journey log books

There shall be maintained in respect of every aircraft engaged in international navigation a journey log book in which shall be entered particulars of the aircraft, its crew and of each journey, in such form as may be prescribed from time to time pursuant to this Convention.

Article 35 Cargo restrictions

a) No munitions of war or implements of war may be carried in or above the territory of a State in aircraft engaged in international navigation, except by permission of such State. Each State shall determine by regulations what constitutes munitions of war or implements of war for the purposes of this Article, giving due consideration, for the purposes of uniformity, to such recommendations as the International Civil Aviation Organization may from time to time make.
b) Each contracting State reserves the right, for reasons of public order and safety, to regulate or prohibit the carriage in or above its territory of articles other than those enumerated in paragraph *a)*: provided that no distinction is made in this respect between its national aircraft engaged in international navigation and the aircraft of the other States so engaged, and provided further that no restriction shall be imposed which may interfere with the carriage and use on aircraft of apparatus necessary for the operation or navigation of the aircraft or the safety of the personnel or passengers.

Article 36 Photographic apparatus

Each contracting State may prohibit or regulate the use of photographic apparatus in aircraft over its territory.

Chapter VI International Standards and Recommended Practices

Article 37 Adoption of international standards and procedures

Each contracting State undertakes to collaborate in securing the highest practicable degree of uniformity in regulations, standards, procedures, and organization in relation to aircraft, personnel, airways and auxiliary services in all matters in which such uniformity will facilitate and improve air navigation.

To this end the International Civil Aviation Organization shall adopt and amend from time to time, as may be necessary, international standards and recommended practices and procedures dealing with:

a) Communications systems and air navigation aids, including ground marking;
b) Characteristics of airports and landing areas;
c) Rules of the air and air traffic control practices;
d) Licensing of operating and mechanical personnel;
e) Airworthiness of aircraft;
f) Registration and identification of aircraft;
g) Collection and exchange of meteorological information;
h) Log books;
i) Aeronautical maps and charts;
j) Customs and immigration procedures;
k) Aircraft in distress and investigation of accidents;

and such other matters concerned with the safety, regularity, and efficiency of air navigation as may from time to time appear appropriate.

Article 38 Departures from international standards and procedures

Any State which finds it impracticable to comply in all respects with any such international standard or procedure, or to bring its own regulations or practices into full accord with any international standard or procedure after amendment of the latter, or which deems it necessary to adopt regulations or practices differing in any particular respect from those established by an international standard, shall give immediate notification to the International Civil Aviation Organization of the differences between its own practice and that established by the international standard. In the case of amendments to international standards, any State which does not make the appropriate amendments to its own regulations or practices shall give notice to the Council within sixty days of the adoption of the amendment to the international standard or indicate the action which it proposes to take. In any such case, the Council shall make immediate notification to all other states of the difference which exists between one or more features of an international standard and the corresponding national practice of that State.

Article 39 Endorsement of certificates and licenses

a) Any aircraft or part thereof with respect to which there exists an international standard of airworthiness or performance, and which failed in any respect to satisfy that standard at the time of its certification, shall have endorsed on or attached to its airworthiness certificate a complete enumeration of the details in respect of which it so failed.
b) Any person holding a license who does not satisfy in full the conditions laid down in the international standard relating to the class of license or certificate which he holds shall have endorsed on or attached to his license a complete enumeration of the particulars in which he does not satisfy such conditions.

Article 40 Validity of endorsed certificates and licenses

No aircraft or personnel having certificates or licenses so endorsed shall participate in international navigation, except with the permission of the State or States whose territory is entered. The registration or use of any such aircraft, or of any certificated aircraft part, in any State other than that in which it was originally certificated shall be at the discretion of the State into which the aircraft or part is imported.

Article 41 Recognition of existing standards of airworthiness

The provisions of this Chapter shall not apply to aircraft and aircraft equipment of types of which the prototype is submitted to the appropriate national authorities for certification prior to a date three years after the date of adoption of an international standard of airworthiness for such equipment.

Article 42 Recognition of existing standards of competency of personnel

The provisions of this Chapter shall not apply to personnel whose licenses are originally issued prior to a date one year after the initial adoption of an international standard of qualification for such personnel, but they shall in any case apply to all personnel whose licenses remain valid five years after the date of adoption of such standard.

Part II The International Civil Aviation Organization

Chapter VII The Organization

Article 43 Name and composition

An organization to be named the International Civil Aviation Organization is formed by the Convention. It is made up of an Assembly, a Council, and such other bodies as may be necessary.

Article 44 Objectives

The aims and objectives of the Organization are to develop the principles and techniques of international air navigation and to foster the planning and development of international air transport so as to:

a) Ensure the safe and orderly growth of international civil aviation throughout the world;
b) Encourage the arts of aircraft design and operation for peaceful purposes;
c) Encourage the development of airways, airports, and air navigation facilities for international civil aviation;
d) Meet the needs of the peoples of the world for safe, regular, efficient and economical air transport;
e) Prevent economic waste caused by unreasonable competition;
f) Ensure that the rights of contracting States are fully respected and that every contracting State has a fair opportunity to operate international airlines;
g) Avoid discrimination between contracting States;
h) Promote safety of flight in international air navigation;

i) Promote generally the development of all aspects of international civil aeronautics.

Article 45[833] Permanent seat

The permanent seat of the Organization shall be at such place as shall be determined at the final meeting of the Interim Assembly of the Provisional International Civil Aviation Organization set up by the Interim Agreement on International Civil Aviation signed in Chicago on 7 December 1944. The seat may be temporarily transferred elsewhere by decision of the Council, and otherwise than temporarily by decision of the Assembly, such decision to be taken by the number of votes specified by the Assembly. The number of votes so specified will not be less than three-fifths of the total number of contracting States.

Article 46 First meeting of Assembly

The first meeting of the Assembly shall be summoned by the Interim Council of the above-mentioned Provisional Organization as soon as the Convention has come into force, to meet at a time and place to be decided by the Interim Council.

Article 47 Legal capacity

The Organization shall enjoy in the territory of each contracting State such legal capacity as may be necessary for the performance of its functions. Full juridical personality shall be granted wherever compatible with the constitution and laws of the State concerned.

Chapter VIII The Assembly

Article 48 Meetings of Assembly and voting

a) The Assembly shall meet not less than once in three years and shall be convened by the Council at a suitable time and place. An extraordinary meeting of the Assembly may be held at any time upon the call of the Council or at the request of not less than one-fifth of the total number of contracting States addressed to the Secretary General.[834] *

833. This is the text of the Article as amended by the Eighth Session of the Assembly on 14 Jun. 1954; it entered into force on 16 May 1958. Under Art. 94 a) of the Convention, the amended text is in force in respect of those States which have ratified the amendment. In respect of the States which have not ratified the amendment, the original text is still in force and, therefore, that text is reproduced below:

> The permanent seat of the Organization shall be at such place as shall be determined at the final meeting of the Interim Assembly of the Provisional International Civil Aviation Organization set up by the Interim Agreement on International Civil Aviation signed at Chicago on December 7, 1944. The seat may be temporarily transferred elsewhere by decision of the Council.

834. This is the text of the Article as amended by the 14th Session of the Assembly on 14 Sep. 1962; it entered into force on 11 Sep. 1975. Under Art. 94 *a)* of the Convention, the amended text is in

b) All contracting States shall have an equal right to be represented at the meetings of the Assembly and each contracting State shall be entitled to one vote. Delegates representing contracting States may be assisted by technical advisers who may participate in the meetings but shall have no vote.
c) A majority of the contracting States are required to constitute a quorum for the meetings of the Assembly. Unless otherwise provided in this Convention, decisions of the Assembly shall be taken by a majority of the votes cast.

Article 49 Powers and duties of Assembly

The powers and duties of the Assembly shall be to:

a) Elect at each meeting its President and other officers;
b) Elect the contracting States to be represented on the Council, in accordance with the provisions of Chapter IX;
c) Examine and take appropriate action on the reports of the Council and decide on any matter referred to it by the Council;
d) Determine its own rules of procedure and establish such subsidiary commissions as it may consider to be necessary or desirable;
e) Vote annual budgets and determine the financial arrangements of the Organization, in accordance with the provisions of Chapter XII;[835] *
f) Review expenditures and approve the accounts of the Organization;
g) Refer, at its discretion, to the Council, to subsidiary commissions, or to any other body any matter within its sphere of action;

---

force in respect of those States which have ratified the amendment. The previous text of this Article as amended by the 8th Session of the Assembly on 14 Jun. 1954 and which entered into force on 12 Dec. 1956 read as follows:

a) The Assembly shall meet not less than once in three years and shall be convened by the Council at a suitable time and place. Extraordinary meetings of the Assembly may be held at any time upon the call of the Council or at the request of any ten contracting States addressed to the Secretary General.

The original unamended text of the Convention read as follows:

a) The Assembly shall meet annually and shall be convened by the Council at a suitable time and place. Extraordinary meetings of the Assembly may be held at any time upon the call of the Council or at the request of any ten contracting States addressed to the Secretary General.

835. This is the text of the Article as amended by the Eighth Session of the Assembly on 14 Jun. 1954; it entered into force on 12 Dec. 1956. Under Art. 94 *a)* of the Convention, the amended text is in force in respect of those States which have ratified the amendment. In respect of the States which have not ratified the amendment, the original text is still in force and, therefore, that text is reproduced below:

e) Vote an annual budget and determine the financial arrangements of the Organization, in accordance with the provisions of Chapter XII.

h) Delegate to the Council the powers and authority necessary or desirable for the discharge of the duties of the Organization and revoke or modify the delegations of authority at any time;
i) Carry out the appropriate provisions of Chapter XIII;
j) Consider proposals for the modification or amendment of the provisions of this Convention and, if it approves of the proposals, recommend them to the contracting States in accordance with the provisions of Chapter XXI;
k) Deal with any matter within the sphere of action of the Organization not specifically assigned to the Council.

Chapter IX The Council

Article 50 Composition and election of Council:

a) The Council shall be a permanent body responsible to the Assembly. It shall be composed of thirty-three contracting States elected by the Assembly. An election shall be held at the first meeting of the Assembly and thereafter every three years and the members of the Council so elected shall hold office until the next following election.[836] *
b) In electing the members of the Council, the Assembly shall give adequate representation to 1) the States of chief importance in air transport; 2) the States not otherwise included which make the largest contribution to the provision of facilities for international civil air navigation; and 3) the States not otherwise included whose designation will ensure that all the major geographic areas of the world are represented on the Council. Any vacancy on the Council shall be filled by the Assembly as soon as possible; any contracting State so elected to the Council shall hold office for the unexpired portion of its predecessor's term of office.
c) No representative of a contracting State on the Council shall be actively associated with the operation of an international air service or financially interested in such a service.

Article 51 President of Council

The Council shall elect its President for a term of three years. He may be re-elected. He shall have no vote. The Council shall elect from among its members one or more Vice Presidents who shall retain their right to vote when serving as acting President. The President need not be selected from among the representatives of the

836. This is the text of the Article as amended by the 21st Session of the Assembly on 14 Oct. 1974; it entered into force on 15 Feb. 1980. The original text of the Convention provided for twenty-one Members of the Council. The text was subsequently amended at the 13th (Extraordinary) Session of the Assembly on 19 Jun. 1961; that amendment entered into force on 17 Jul. 1962 and provided for twenty-seven Members of the Council; a further amendment was approved by the 17th(A) (Extraordinary) Session of the Assembly on 12 Mar. 1971 providing for thirty Members of the Council; this amendment entered into force on 16 Jan. 1973.

members of the Council but, if a representative is elected, his seat shall be deemed vacant and it shall be filled by the State which he represented. The duties of the President shall be to:

a) Convene meetings of the Council, the Air Transport Committee, and the Air Navigation Commission;
b) Serve as representative of the Council; and
c) Carry out on behalf of the Council the functions which the Council assigns to him.

Article 52 Voting in Council

Decisions by the Council shall require approval by a majority of its members. The Council may delegate authority with respect to any particular matter to a committee of its members. Decisions of any committee of the Council may be appealed to the Council by any interested contracting State.

Article 53 Participation without a vote

Any contracting State may participate, without a vote, in the consideration by the Council and by its committees and commissions of any question which especially affects its interests. No member of the Council shall vote in the consideration by the Council of a dispute to which it is a party.

Article 54 Mandatory functions of Council

The Council shall:

a) Submit annual reports to the Assembly;
b) Carry out the directions of the Assembly and discharge the duties and obligations which are laid on it by this Convention;
c) Determine its organization and rules of procedure;
d) Appoint and define the duties of an Air Transport Committee, which shall be chosen from among the representatives of the members of the Council, and which shall be responsible to it;
e) Establish an Air Navigation Commission, in accordance with the provisions of Chapter X;
f) Administer the finances of the Organization in accordance with the provisions of Chapters XII and XV;
g) Determine the emoluments of the President of the Council;
h) Appoint a chief executive officer who shall be called the Secretary General, and make provision for the appointment of such other personnel as may be necessary, in accordance with the provisions of Chapter XI;
i) Request, collect, examine and publish information relating to the advancement of air navigation and the operation of international air services, including information about the costs of operation and particulars of subsidies paid to airlines from public funds;

j) Report to contracting States any infraction of this Convention, as well as any failure to carry out recommendations or determinations of the Council;
k) Report to the Assembly any infraction of this Convention where a contracting State has failed to take appropriate action within a reasonable time after notice of the infraction;
l) Adopt, in accordance with the provisions of Chapter VI of this Convention, international standards and recommended practices; for convenience, designate them as Annexes to this Convention; and notify all contracting States of the action taken;
m) Consider recommendations of the Air Navigation Commission for amendment of the Annexes and take action in accordance with the provisions of Chapter XX;
n) Consider any matter relating to the Convention which any contracting State refers to it.

Article 55 Permissive functions of Council

The Council may:

a) Where appropriate and as experience may show to be desirable, create subordinate air transport commissions on a regional or other basis and define groups of states or airlines with or through which it may deal to facilitate the carrying out of the aims of this Convention;
b) Delegate to the Air Navigation Commission duties additional to those set forth in the Convention and revoke or modify such delegations of authority at any time;
c) Conduct research into all aspects of air transport and air navigation which are of international importance, communicate the results of its research to the contracting States, and facilitate the exchange of information between contracting States on air transport and air navigation matters;
d) Study any matters affecting the organization and operation of international air transport, including the international ownership and operation of international air services on trunk routes, and submit to the Assembly plans in relation thereto;
e) Investigate, at the request of any contracting State, any situation which may appear to present avoidable obstacles to the development of international air navigation; and, after such investigation, issue such reports as may appear to it desirable.

Chapter X The Air Navigation Commission

Article 56 Nomination and appointment of Commission

The Air Navigation Commission shall be composed of fifteen members appointed by the Council from among persons nominated by contracting States. These persons shall have suitable qualifications and experience in the science and practice of aeronautics. The Council shall request all contracting States to submit nominations. The President of the Air Navigation Commission shall be appointed by the Council.[837] *

Article 57 Duties of Commission

The Air Navigation Commission shall:

a) Consider, and recommend to the Council for adoption, and modifications of the Annexes to this Convention;
b) Establish technical subcommissions on which any contracting State may be represented if it so desires;
c) Advise the Council concerning the collection and communication to the contracting States of all information which it considers necessary and useful for the advancement of air navigation.

Chapter XI Personnel

Article 58 Appointment of personnel

Subject to any rules laid down by the Assembly and to the provisions of this Convention, the Council shall determine the method of appointment and of termination of appointment, the training, and the salaries, allowances, and conditions of service of the Secretary General and other personnel of the Organization, and may employ or make use of the services of nationals of any contracting State.

Article 59 International character of personnel

The President of the Council, the Secretary General, and other personnel shall not seek or receive instructions in regard to the discharge of their responsibilities from any authority external to the Organization. Each contracting State undertakes fully to respect the international character of the responsibilities of the personnel and not to seek to influence any of its nationals in the discharge of their responsibilities.

Article 60 Immunities and privileges of personnel

Each contracting State undertakes, so far as possible under its constitutional procedure, to accord to the President of the Council, the Secretary General, and the other personnel of the Organization, the immunities and privileges which are accorded to corresponding personnel of other public international organizations. If a general international agreement on the immunities and privileges of international civil servants is arrived at, the immunities and privileges accorded to the President, the Secretary General, and the other personnel of the Organization shall be the immunities and privileges accorded under that general international agreement.

837. This is the text of the Article as amended at the 18th Session of the Assembly on 7 Jul. 1971; it entered into force on 19 Dec. 1974. The original text of the Convention provided for twelve members of the Air Navigation Commission.

Chapter XII Finance

Article 61[838] Budget and apportionment of expenses

The Council shall submit to the Assembly annual budgets, annual statements of accounts and estimates of all receipts and expenditures. The Assembly shall vote the budgets with whatever modification it sees fit to prescribe, and, with the exception of assessments under Chapter XV to States consenting thereto, shall apportion the expenses of the Organization among the contracting States on the basis which it shall from time to time determine.

Article 62 Suspension of voting power

The Assembly may suspend the voting power in the Assembly and in the Council of any contracting State that fails to discharge within a reasonable period its financial obligations to the Organization.

Article 63 Expenses of delegations and other representatives

Each contracting State shall bear the expenses of its own delegation to the Assembly and the remuneration, travel, and other expenses of any person whom it appoints to serve on the Council, and of its nominees or representatives on any subsidiary committees or commissions of the Organization.

Chapter XIII Other International Arrangements

Article 64 Security arrangements

The Organization may, with respect to air matters within its competence directly affecting world security, by vote of the Assembly enter into appropriate arrangements with any general organization set up by the nations of the world to preserve peace.

Article 65 Arrangements with other international bodies

The Council, on behalf of the Organization, may enter into agreements with other international bodies for the maintenance of common services and for common arrangements concerning personnel and, with the approval of the Assembly, may enter into such other arrangements as may facilitate the work of the Organization.

838. This is the text of the Article as amended by the Eighth Session of the Assembly on 14 Jun. 1954; it entered into force on 12 Dec. 1956. Under Art. 94 a) of the Convention, the amended text is in force in respect of those States which have ratified the amendment. In respect of the States which have not ratified the amendment, the original text is still in force and, therefore, that text is reproduced below:

> The Council shall submit to the Assembly an annual budget, annual statements of accounts and estimates of all receipts and expenditures. The Assembly shall vote the budget with whatever modification it sees fit to prescribe, and, with the exception of assessments under Chapter XV to States consenting thereto, shall apportion the expenses of the Organization among the contracting States on the basis which it shall from time to time determine.

Article 66 Functions relating to other agreements

a) The Organization shall also carry out the functions placed upon it by the International Air Services Transit Agreement and by the International Air Transport Agreement drawn up in Chicago on 7 December 1944, in accordance with the terms and conditions therein set forth.
b) Members of the Assembly and the Council who have not accepted the International Air Services Transit Agreement of the International Air Transport Agreement drawn up in Chicago on 7 December 1944, shall not have the right to vote on any questions referred to the Assembly or Council under the provisions of the relevant Agreement.

Part III International Air Transport

Chapter XIV Information and Reports

Article 67 File reports with Council

Each contracting State undertakes that its international airlines shall, in accordance with requirements laid down by the Council, file with the Council traffic reports, cost statistics and financial statements showing among other things all receipts and the sources thereof.

Chapter XV Airports and Other Air Navigation Facilities

Article 68 Designation of routes and airports

Each contracting State may, subject to the provisions of this Convention, designate the route to be followed within its territory by any international air service and the airports which any such service may use.

Article 69 Improvement of air navigation facilities

If the Council is of the opinion that the airports or other air navigation facilities, including radio and meteorological services, of a contracting State, are not reasonably adequate for the safe, regular, efficient, and economical operation of international air services, present or contemplated, the Council shall consult with the State directly concerned, and other States affected, with a view to finding means by which the situation may be remedied, and may make recommendations for that purpose. No contracting State shall be guilty of an infraction of this Convention if it fails to carry out these recommendations.

Article 70 Financing of air navigation facilities

A contracting State, in the circumstances arising under the provisions of Article 69, may conclude an arrangement with the Council for giving effect to such recommendations. The State may elect to bear all of the costs involved in any such arrangement. If the State does not so elect, the Council may agree, at the request of the State, to provide for all or a portion of the costs.

Article 71 Provision and maintenance of facilities by Council

If a contracting State so requests, the Council may agree to provide, man, maintain, and administer any or all of the airports and other air navigation facilities including radio and meteorological services, required in its territory for the safe, regular, efficient and economical operation of the international air services of the other contracting States, and may specify just and reasonable charges for the use of the facilities provided.

Article 72 Acquisition or use of land

Where land is needed for facilities financed in whole or in part by the Council at the request of a contracting State, that State shall either provide the land itself, retaining title if it wishes or facilitate the use of the land by the Council on just and reasonable terms and in accordance with the laws of the State concerned.

Article 73 Expenditure and assessment of funds

Within the limit of the funds which may be made available to it by the Assembly under Chapter XII, the Council may make current expenditures for the purposes of this Chapter from the general funds of the Organization. The Council shall assess the capital funds required for the purposes of this Chapter in previously agreed proportions over a reasonable period of time to the contracting States consenting thereto whose airlines use the facilities. The Council may also assess States that consent to any working funds that are required.

Article 74 Technical assistance and utilization of revenues

When the Council, at the request of a contracting State, advances funds or provides airports or other facilities in whole or in part, the arrangement may provide, with the consent of that State, for technical assistance in the supervision and operation of the airports and other facilities, and for the payment, from the revenues derived from the operation of the airports and other facilities, of the operating expenses of the airports and the other facilities, and of interest and amortization charges.

Article 75 Taking over of facilities from Council

A contracting State may at any time discharge any obligation into which it has entered under Article 70, and take over airports and other facilities which the Council has provided in its territory pursuant to the provisions of Articles 71 and 72, by paying to the Council an amount which in the opinion of the Council is reasonable in the circumstances. If the State considers that the amount fixed by the Council is unreasonable it may appeal to the Assembly against the decision of the Council and the Assembly may confirm or amend the decision of the Council.

Article 76 Return of funds

Funds obtained by the Council through reimbursement under Article 75 and from receipts of interest and amortization payments under Article 74 shall, in the case of advances originally financed by States under Article 73, be returned to the States which were originally assessed in the proportion of their assessments, as determined by the Council.

Appendix A. Convention on International Civil Aviation

Chapter XVI Joint Operating Organizations and Pooled Services

Article 77 Joint operating organizations permitted

Nothing in this Convention shall prevent two or more contracting States from constituting joint air transport operating organizations or international operating agencies and from pooling their air services on any route or in any regions but such organizations or agencies and such pooled services shall be subject to all the provisions of this Convention, including those relating to the registration of agreements with the Council. The Council shall determine in what manner the provisions of this Convention relating to the nationality of aircraft shall apply to aircraft operated by international operating agencies.

Article 78 Function of Council

The Council may suggest to contracting States concerned that they form joint organizations to operate air services on any route or in any region.

Article 79 Participation in operating organizations

A State may participate in joint operating organizations or in pooling arrangements, either through its government or through an airline company or companies designated by its government. The companies may, at the sole discretion of the State concerned, be state-owned or partly state-owned or privately owned.

Part IV Final Provisions

Chapter XVII Other Aeronautical Agreements and Arrangements

Article 80 Paris and Habana Conventions

Each contracting State undertakes, immediately upon the coming into force of this Convention, to give notice of denunciation of the Convention relating to the Regulation of Aerial Navigation signed in Paris on 13 October 1919, or the Convention on Commercial Aviation signed in Habana on 20 February 1928, if it is a party to either. As between contracting States, this Convention supersedes the Conventions of Paris and Habana previously referred to.

Article 81 Registration of existing agreements

All aeronautical agreements which are in existence on the coming into force of this Convention, and which are between a contracting State and any other State or between an airline of a contracting State and any other State or the airline of any other State, shall be forthwith registered with the Council.

Article 82 Abrogation of inconsistent arrangements

The contracting States accept this Convention as abrogating all obligations and understandings between them which are inconsistent with its terms and undertake not to enter into any such obligations and understandings. A contracting State which, before becoming a member of the Organization has undertaken any obligations toward a non-contracting State or a national of a contracting State or of a non-contracting State inconsistent with the terms of this Convention, shall take immediate steps to procure its release from the obligations. If an airline of any contracting State has entered into any such inconsistent obligations, the State of which it is a national shall use its best efforts to secure their termination forthwith and shall in any event cause them to be terminated as soon as such action can lawfully be taken after the coming into force of this Convention.

Article 83 Registration of new arrangements

Subject to the provisions of the preceding Article, any contracting State may make arrangements not inconsistent with the provisions of this Convention. Any such arrangement shall be forthwith registered with the Council, which shall make it public as soon as possible.

Article 83[839] bis Transfer of certain functions and duties

a) Notwithstanding the provisions of Articles 12, 30, 31 and 32 *a)*, when an aircraft registered in a contracting State is operated pursuant to an agreement for the lease, charter or interchange of the aircraft or any similar arrangement by an operator who has his principal place of business or, if he has no such place of business, his permanent residence in another contracting State, the State of registry may, by agreement with such other State, transfer to it all or part of its functions and duties as State of registry in respect of that aircraft under Articles 12, 30, 31 and 32 *a)*. The State of registry shall be relieved of responsibility in respect of the functions and duties transferred.
b) The transfer shall not have effect in respect of other contracting States before either the agreement between States in which it is embodied has been registered with the Council and made public pursuant to Article 83 or the existence and scope of the agreement have been directly communicated to the authorities of the other contracting State or States concerned by a State party to the agreement.
c) The provisions of paragraphs *a)* and *b)* above shall also be applicable to cases covered by Article 77.

Chapter XVIII Disputes and Default

Article 84 Settlement of disputes

If any disagreement between two or more contracting States relating to the interpretation or application of this Convention and its Annexes cannot be settled by negotiation, it shall, on the application of any State concerned in the disagreement,

839. On 6 Oct. 1980 the Assembly decided to amend the Chicago Convention by introducing Art. 83 bis. Under Art. 94 a) of the Convention the amendment came into force on 20 Jun. 1997 in respect of States which ratified it.

be decided by the Council. No member of the Council shall vote in the consideration by the Council of any dispute to which it is a party. Any contracting State may, subject to Article 85, appeal from the decision of the Council to an ad hoc arbitral tribunal agreed upon with the other parties to the dispute or to the Permanent Court of International Justice. Any such appeal shall be notified to the Council within sixty days of receipt of notification of the decision of the Council.

Article 85 Arbitration procedure

If any contracting State party to a dispute in which the decision of the Council is under appeal has not accepted the Statute of the Permanent Court of International Justice and the contracting States parties to the dispute cannot agree on the choice of the arbitral tribunal, each of the contracting States that are parties to the dispute shall name a single arbitrator who shall name an umpire. If either contracting State party to the dispute fails to name an arbitrator within a period of three months from the date of the appeal, an arbitrator shall be named on behalf of that State by the President of the Council from a list of qualified and available persons maintained by the Council. If, within thirty days, the arbitrators cannot agree on an umpire, the President of the Council shall designate an umpire from the list previously referred to. The arbitrators and the umpire shall then jointly constitute an arbitral tribunal. Any arbitral tribunal established under this or the preceding Article shall settle its own procedure and give its decisions by majority vote, provided that the Council may determine procedural questions in the event of any delay which in the opinion of the Council is excessive.

Article 86 Appeals

Unless the Council decides otherwise any decision by the Council on whether an international airline is operating in conformity with the provisions of this Convention shall remain in effect unless reversed on appeal. On any other matter, decisions of the Council shall, if appealed from, be suspended until the appeal is decided. The decisions of the Permanent Court of International Justice and of an arbitral tribunal shall be final and binding.

Article 87 Penalty for non-conformity of airline

Each contracting State undertakes not to allow the operation of an airline of a contracting State through the airspace above its territory if the Council has decided that the airline concerned is not conforming to a final decision rendered in accordance with the previous Article.

Article 88 Penalty for non-conformity by State

The Assembly shall suspend the voting power in the Assembly and in the Council of any contracting State that is found in default under the provisions of this Chapter.

Appendix A. Convention on International Civil Aviation

Chapter XIX War

Article 89 War and emergency conditions

In case of war, the provisions of this Convention shall not affect the freedom of action of any of the contracting States affected, whether as belligerents or as neutrals. The same principle shall apply in the case of any contracting State which declares a state of national emergency and notifies the fact to the Council.

Chapter XX Annexes

Article 90 Adoption and amendment of Annexes

a) The adoption by the Council of the Annexes described in Article 54, subparagraph *l)*, shall require the vote of two-thirds of the Council at a meeting called for that purpose and shall then be submitted by the Council to each contracting State. Any such Annex or any amendment of an Annex shall become effective within three months after its submission to the contracting States or at the end of a longer period of time as the Council may prescribe unless in the meantime a majority of the contracting States register their disapproval with the Council.
b) The Council shall immediately notify all contracting States of the coming into force of any Annex or amendment thereto.

Chapter XXI Ratifications, Adherences, Amendments, and Denunciations

Article 91 Ratification of Convention

a) This Convention shall be subject to ratification by the signatory States. The instruments of ratification shall be deposited in the archives of the Government of the United States of America, which shall give notice of the date of the deposit to each of the signatories and adhering States.
b) As soon as this Convention has been ratified or adhered to by twenty-six States it shall come into force between them on the thirtieth day after the deposit of the twenty-sixth instrument. It shall come into force for each State ratifying thereafter on the thirtieth day after the deposit of its instrument of ratification.
c) It shall be the duty of the Government of the United States of America to notify the government of each of the signatories and adhering States of the date on which this Convention comes into force.

Article 92 Adherence to Convention

a) This Convention shall be open for adherence by members of the United Nations, States associated with them, and States which remained neutral during the present world conflict.

b) Adherence shall be effected by a notification addressed to the Government of the United States of America and shall take effect from the thirtieth day from the receipt of the notification by the Government of the United States of America, which shall notify all the contracting States.

Article 93 Admission of other States

States other than those provided for in Articles 91 and 92 *a)* may, subject to approval by any general international organization set up by the nations of the world to preserve peace, be admitted to participation in this Convention by means of a four-fifths vote of the Assembly and on such conditions as the Assembly may prescribe: provided that in each case the assent of any State invaded or attacked during the present war by the State seeking admission shall be necessary.

Article 93 bis[840]

a) Notwithstanding the provisions of Articles 91, 92 and 93 above:
   1) A State whose government the General Assembly of the United Nations has recommended be debarred from membership in international agencies established by or brought into relationship with the United Nations shall automatically cease to be a member of the International Civil Aviation Organization;
   2) A State which has been expelled from membership in the United Nations shall automatically cease to be a member of the International Civil Aviation Organization unless the General Assembly of the United Nations attaches to its act of expulsion a recommendation to the contrary.
b) A State which ceases to be a member of the International Civil Aviation Organization as a result of the provisions of paragraph *a)* above may, after approval by the General Assembly of the United Nations, be readmitted to the International Civil Aviation Organization upon application and upon approval by a majority of the Council.
c) Members of the Organization who are suspended from the exercise of the rights and privileges of membership in the United Nations shall, upon the request of the latter, be suspended from the rights and privileges of membership in this Organization.

Article 94 Amendment of Convention

a) Any proposed amendment to this Convention must be approved by a two-thirds vote of the Assembly and shall then come into force in respect of States which have ratified such amendment when ratified by the number of contracting States

840. On 27 May 1947 the Assembly decided to amend the Chicago Convention by introducing Art. 93 *bis*. Under Art. 94 *a)* of the Convention the amendment came into force on 20 Mar. 1961 in respect of States which ratified it.

specified by the Assembly. The number so specified shall not be less than two-thirds of the total number of contracting States.

b) If in its opinion the amendment is of such a nature as to justify this course, the Assembly in its resolution recommending adoption may provide that any State which has not ratified within a specified period after the amendment has come into force shall thereupon cease to be a member of the Organization and a party to the Convention.

Article 95 Denunciation of Convention

a) Any contracting State may give notice of denunciation of this Convention three years after it's coming into effect by notification addressed to the Government of the United States of America, which shall at once inform each of the contracting States.
b) Denunciation shall take effect one year from the date of the receipt of the notification and shall operate only as regards the State effecting the denunciation.

Chapter XXII Definitions

Article 96

For the purpose of this Convention the expression:

a) 'Air service' means any scheduled air service performed by aircraft for the public transport of passengers, mail or cargo.
b) 'International air service' means an air service which passes through the air space over the territory of more than one State.
c) 'Airline' means any air transport enterprise offering or operating an international air service.
d) 'Stop for non-traffic purposes' means a landing for any purpose other than taking on or discharging passengers, cargo or mail.

SIGNATURE OF CONVENTION

IN WITNESS WHEREOF, the undersigned plenipotentiaries, having been duly authorized, sign this Convention on behalf of their respective governments on the dates appearing opposite their signatures.

DONE in Chicago on the seventh day of December 1944 in the English language. The texts of this Convention drawn up in the English, French, Russian and Spanish languages are of equal authenticity. These texts shall be deposited in the archives of the Government of the United States of America, and certified copies shall be transmitted by that Government to the Governments of all the States which may sign or adhere to this Convention. This Convention shall be open for signature at Washington, D.C.[841] *

Protocol[842]

on the Authentic Trilingual Text of the Convention on International Civil Aviation (Chicago, 1944)

Signed in Buenos Aires on 24 September 1968

The undersigned Governments

CONSIDERING that the last paragraph of the Convention on International Civil Aviation, hereinafter called 'the Convention', provides that a text of the Convention, drawn up in the English, French and Spanish languages, each of which shall be of equal authenticity, shall be open for signature;

CONSIDERING that the Convention was opened for signature, in Chicago, on the seventh day of December 1944, in a text in the English language;

CONSIDERING, accordingly, that it is appropriate to make the necessary provision for the text to exist in three languages as contemplated in the Convention;

CONSIDERING that in making such provision, it should be taken into account that there exist amendments to the Convention in the English, French and Spanish languages and that the text of the Convention in the French and Spanish languages should not incorporate those amendments because, in accordance with Article 94 *a)* of the Convention, each such amendment can come into force only in respect of any State which has ratified it;

HAVE AGREED as follows:

---

841. This is the text of the final paragraph as amended by the 22nd Session of the Assembly on 30 Sep. 1977; it entered into force on 17 Aug. 1999. Under Art. 94 *a)* of the Convention, the amended text is in force in respect of those States which have ratified the amendment. In respect of the States which have not ratified the amendment, the original text is still in force and, therefore, that text is reproduced below:

   DONE at Chicago the seventh day of December 1944, in the English language. A text drawn up in the English, French and Spanish languages, each of which shall be of equal authenticity, shall be open for signature at Washington, D.C. Both texts shall be deposited in the archives of the Government of the United States of America, and certified copies shall be transmitted by that Government to the governments of all the States which may sign or adhere to this Convention.

842. Came into force on 24 Oct. 1968.

Article I[843]

The text of the Convention in the French and Spanish languages annexed to this Protocol, together with the text of the Convention in the English language, constitutes the text equally authentic in the three languages as specifically referred to in the last paragraph of the Convention.

Article II

If a State party to this Protocol has ratified or in the future ratifies any amendment made to the Convention in accordance with Article 94 *a)* thereof, then the text of such amendment in the English, French and Spanish languages shall be deemed to refer to the text, equally authentic in the three languages, which results from this Protocol.

Article III

1) The States' members of the International Civil Aviation Organization may become parties to this Protocol either by:
   a) signature without reservation as to acceptance, or
   b) signature with reservation as to acceptance followed by acceptance, or
   c) acceptance.
2) This Protocol shall remain open for signature in Buenos Aires until the twenty-seventh day of September 1968 and thereafter in Washington, D.C.
3) Acceptance shall be effected by the deposit of an instrument of acceptance with the Government of the United States of America.
4) Adherence to or ratification or approval of this Protocol shall be deemed to be acceptance thereof.

Article IV

1) This Protocol shall come into force on the thirtieth day after twelve States shall, in accordance with the provisions of Article III, have signed it without reservation as to acceptance or accepted it.
2) As regards any State which shall subsequently become a party to this Protocol, in accordance with Article III, the Protocol shall come into force on the date of its signature without reservation as to acceptance or of its acceptance.

Article V

Any future adherence of a State to the Convention shall be deemed to be acceptance of this Protocol.

---

843. The text of the Convention in the French and Spanish languages mentioned in this Article will be found in the second and third columns at pages 1 to 44 of this document, subject to what is stated in the second paragraph of the Foreword at page (ii).

Article VI

As soon as this Protocol comes into force, it shall be registered with the United Nations and with the International Civil Aviation Organization by the Government of the United States of America.

Article VII

1) This Protocol shall remain in force so long as the Convention is in force.
2) This Protocol shall cease to be in force for a State only when that State ceases to be a party to the Convention.

Article VIII

The Government of the United States of America shall give notice to all States' members of the International Civil Aviation Organization and to the Organization itself:

a) of any signature of this Protocol and the date thereof, with an indication whether the signature is with or without reservation as to acceptance;
b) of the deposit of any instrument of acceptance and the date thereof;
c) of the date on which this Protocol comes into force in accordance with the provisions of Article IV, paragraph 1).

Article IX

This Protocol, drawn up in the English, French and Spanish languages, each text being equally authentic, shall be deposited in the archives of the Government of the United States of America, which shall transmit duly certified copies thereof to the Government of the States' members of the International Civil Aviation Organization.

IN WITNESS WHEREOF, the undersigned Plenipotentiaries, duly authorized, have signed this Protocol.

DONE in Buenos Aires this twenty-fourth day of September, one thousand nine hundred and sixty-eight.

Protocol[844] on the Authentic Quadrilingual Text of the Convention on International Civil Aviation (Chicago, 1944)

Signed in Montreal on 30 September 1977

The undersigned Governments

CONSIDERING that the 21st Session of the Assembly of the International Civil Aviation Organization requested the Council of this Organization 'to undertake the

844. Came into force on 16 Sep. 1999.

necessary measures for the preparation of the authentic text of the Convention on International Civil Aviation in the Russian language, with the aim of having it approved not later than the year 1977';

CONSIDERING that the English text of the Convention on International Civil Aviation was opened for signature in Chicago on 7 December 1944;

CONSIDERING that, pursuant to the Protocol signed in Buenos Aires on 24 September 1968 on the authentic trilingual text of the Convention on International Civil Aviation done in Chicago on 7 December 1944, the text of the Convention on International Civil Aviation (hereinafter called the Convention) was adopted in the French and Spanish languages and, together with the text of the Convention in the English language, constitutes the text equally authentic in the three languages as provided for in the final clause of the Convention;

CONSIDERING accordingly, that it is appropriate to make the necessary provision for the text of the Convention to exist in the Russian language;

CONSIDERING that in making such provision account must be taken of the existing amendments to the Convention in the English, French and Spanish languages, the texts of which are equally authentic and that, according to Article 94 *a)* of the Convention, any amendment can come into force only in respect of any State which has ratified it;

HAVE AGREED as follows:

Article I[845]

The text of the Convention and of the amendments thereto in the Russian language annexed to this Protocol, together with the text of the Convention and of the amendments thereto in the English, French and Spanish languages, constitutes the text equally authentic in the four languages.

Article II

If a State party to this Protocol has ratified or in the future ratifies any amendment made to the Convention in accordance with Article 94 *a)* thereof, then the text of such amendment in the Russian, English, French and Spanish languages shall be deemed to refer to the text equally authentic in the four languages, which results from this Protocol.

Article III

1) The States' members of the International Civil Aviation Organization may become parties to this Protocol either by:
   a) signature without reservation as to acceptance, or

845. The text of the Convention in the Russian language mentioned in this Article will be found in the fourth column at pp. 1 to 44 of this document, subject to what is stated in the second paragraph of the Foreword at p. (ii).

   b) signature with reservation as to acceptance followed by acceptance, or
   c) acceptance.
2) This Protocol shall remain open for signature in Montreal until 5 October 1977 and thereafter in Washington, D.C.
3) Acceptance shall be effected by the deposit of an instrument of acceptance with the Government of the United States of America.
4) Adherence to or ratification or approval of this Protocol shall be deemed to be acceptance thereof.

Article IV

1) This Protocol shall come into force on the thirtieth day after twelve States shall, in accordance with the provisions of Article III, have signed it without reservation as to acceptance or accepted it and after entry into force of the amendment to the final clause of the Convention, which provides that the text of the Convention in the Russian language is of equal authenticity.
2) As regards any State which shall subsequently become a party to this Protocol in accordance with Article III, the Protocol shall come into force on the date of its signature without reservation as to acceptance or of its acceptance.

Article V

Any adherence of a State to the Convention after this Protocol has entered into force shall be deemed to be acceptance of this Protocol.

Article VI

Acceptance by a State of this Protocol shall not be regarded as ratification by it of any amendment to the Convention.

Article VII

As soon as this Protocol comes into force, it shall be registered with the United Nations and with the International Civil Aviation Organization by the Government of the United States of America.

Article VIII

1) This Protocol shall remain in force so long as the Convention is in force.
2) This Protocol shall cease to be in force for a State only when that State ceases to be a party to the Convention.

Article IX

The Government of the United States of America shall give notice to all States' members of the International Civil Aviation Organization and to the Organization itself:

a) of any signature of this Protocol and the date thereof, with an indication whether the signature is with or without reservation as to acceptance;
b) of the deposit of any instrument of acceptance and the date thereof;
c) of the date on which this Protocol comes into force in accordance with the provisions of Article IV, paragraph 1.

Article X

This Protocol, drawn up in the English, French, Russian and Spanish languages, each text being equally authentic, shall be deposited in the archives of the Government of the United States of America, which shall transmit duly certified copies thereof to the Governments of the States' members of the International Civil Aviation Organization.

IN WITNESS WHEREOF, the undersigned Plenipotentiaries, duly authorized, have signed this Protocol.

DONE in Montreal this thirtieth day of September, one thousand nine hundred and seventy-seven.

Appendix A. Convention on International Civil Aviation

Appendix B. List of ICAO Member States

As of 1 November 2022

Total: 193 States

Afghanistan
Albania
Algeria
Andorra
Angola
Antigua and Barbuda
Argentina
Armenia
Australia
Austria
Azerbaijan
Bahamas
Bahrain
Bangladesh
Barbados
Belarus
Belgium
Belize
Benin
Bhutan
Bolivia (Plurinational State of)
Bosnia and Herzegovina
Botswana
Brazil
Brunei Darussalam
Bulgaria
Burkina Faso
Eritrea
Estonia
Eswatini
Jamaica
Japan
Jordan
Kazakhstan
Kenya
Kiribati
Kuwait
Kyrgyzstan
Lao People's Democratic Republic
Latvia
Lebanon
Lesotho
Liberia
Libya
Lithuania
Luxembourg
Madagascar
Malawi
Malaysia
Maldives
Mali
Malta
Marshall Islands
Mauritania
Mauritius
Mexico
Micronesia (Federated States of)
Monaco
Mongolia
Philippines
Poland
Portugal
Qatar
Republic of Korea
Republic of Moldova
Romania
Russian Federation
Rwanda
Saint Kitts and Nevis
Saint Lucia
Saint Vincent and the Grenadines
Samoa
San Marino
Sao Tome and Principe
Saudi Arabia
Senegal
Serbia
Seychelles
Sierra Leone
Singapore
Slovakia
Slovenia
Solomon Islands
Somalia
South Africa
South Sudan
Spain
Sri Lanka
Sudan

Appendix B. List of ICAO Member States

Ethiopia
Fiji
Finland
France
Gabon
Gambia
Georgia
Germany
Ghana
Greece
Grenada
Guatemala
Guinea
Guinea-Bissau
Guyana
Haiti
Honduras
Hungary
Iceland
India
Indonesia
Iran (Islamic Republic of)
Iraq
Ireland
Israel
Italy
Montenegro
Morocco
Mozambique
Myanmar
Namibia
Nauru
Nepal
Netherlands
New Zealand
Nicaragua
Niger
Nigeria
North Macedonia
Norway
Oman
Pakistan
Palau
Panama
Papua New Guinea
Paraguay
Peru
Suriname
Sweden
Switzerland
Syrian Arab Republic
Tajikistan
Thailand
Timor-Leste
Togo
Tonga
Trinidad and Tobago
Tunisia
Turkey
Turkmenistan
Tuvalu
Uganda
Ukraine
United Arab Emirates
United Kingdom
United Republic of Tanzania
United States
Uruguay
Uzbekistan
Vanuatu
Venezuela (Bolivarian Republic of)
Viet Nam
Yemen
Zambia
Zimbabwe

Appendix C. Vision and Mission; Strategic Objectives of ICAO

Vision and Mission of ICAO

Vision:

Achieve the sustainable growth of the global civil aviation system.

Mission:

To serve as the global forum of States for international civil aviation. ICAO develops policies and Standards, undertakes compliance audits, performs studies and analyses, provides assistance and builds aviation capacity through many other activities and the cooperation of its Member States and stakeholders.

Strategic Objectives of ICAO

In its ongoing mission to support and enable a global air transport network that meets or surpasses the social and economic development and broader connectivity needs of global businesses and passengers, and acknowledging the clear need to anticipate and manage the projected doubling of global air transport capacity by 2030 without unnecessary adverse impacts on system safety, efficiency, convenience or environmental performance, ICAO has established five comprehensive Strategic Objectives:

Safety:

Enhance global civil aviation safety. This Strategic Objective is focused primarily on the State's regulatory oversight capabilities. The Global Aviation Safety Plan (GASP) outlines the key activities for the triennium.

Air Navigation Capacity and Efficiency:

Increase the capacity and improve the efficiency of the global civil aviation system. Although functionally and organizationally interdependent with Safety, this Strategic Objective is focused primarily on upgrading the air navigation and aerodrome infrastructure and developing new procedures to optimize aviation system performance. The Global Air Navigation Capacity and Efficiency Plan (Global Plan) outlines the key activities for the triennium.

Security & Facilitation:

Enhance global civil aviation security and facilitation. This Strategic Objective reflects the need for ICAO's leadership in aviation security, facilitation and related border security matters.

Economic Development of Air Transport:

Foster the development of a sound and economically-viable civil aviation system. This Strategic Objective reflects the need for ICAO's leadership in harmonizing the air transport framework focused on economic policies and supporting activities.

Environmental Protection:

Minimize the adverse environmental effects of civil aviation activities. This Strategic Objective fosters ICAO's leadership in all aviation-related environmental activities and is consistent with the ICAO and UN system environmental protection policies and practices.

Appendix D. ICAO Business Plan 2023–2025

Message from the ICAO Secretary General

ICAO's strength as a United Nations specialized agency lies with its unique ability to provide a platform for its 193 Member States to develop safe, secure, sustainable and seamless air connectivity through partnership with each other and all stakeholders in the aviation ecosystem.

The 2023–2025 Business Plan presents the Secretariat's approach to supporting progress towards the Strategic Objectives of the Organization while helping to assure that air transport 'builds back better' from the impacts of the COVID-19 pandemic. The implementation of the recommendations of the High-Level Conference on COVID-19, on the basis of prioritized actions and available resources, is key to this vision.

Advocacy around interlinkages between ICAO's Strategic Objectives and the Sustainable Development Goals (SDGs) of the United Nations 2030 Agenda for Sustainable Development remains a critical component of ICAO's vision and commitment to both the Agenda and to aviation's ability to act as a catalyst for it achievement.

The timely development and update of Standards and Recommended Practices (SARPs) remains the cornerstone of ICAO's mandate, and the provision of assistance to Member States towards the implementation of SARPs, global plans and policies continues to be of paramount importance. High on the agenda within this context are the No Country Left Behind (NCLB) initiative, regional cooperation, reaching and exceeding the global target levels of effective implementation of safety and security oversight systems, cybersecurity, flight tracking, risks to civil aviation arising from conflict zones, safe integration of remotely piloted and other unmanned aircraft systems, and the management of public health events in the air transport system.

Furthermore, focused efforts will continue to support the aspirational goal of carbon neutral growth, including through the implementation of the Carbon Offsetting and Reduction Scheme for International Aviation (CORSIA), and by promoting ambitious goals for the decarbonisation of the aviation sector.

The resources allocated in our regular budget from Member States assessments will however alone not be sufficient for the Organization to completely fulfil its mandate. In recognition of this, efforts will continue to enhance the mobilization of voluntary contributions and expanding the revenue-generating activities, to identify new streams of sustainable and predicable revenue sources, and to foster strategic partnerships.

Various corporate innovative organizational reform initiatives within the ICAO Secretariat will be implemented to bring along a transformation in organizational culture, marked by enhancing the efficiencies and effectiveness of our internal operations, leveraging on technology and simplification of systems and procedures, and conduct of outreach to partners and donors. To implement the change management reforms will require focussed attention and dedicated resources; and as such a new corporate transformational objective is being introduced. Beyond efficiency, it also focuses on strengthened accountability, ethics principles and values, and increased transparency and communications.

Throughout the three years covered by this plan, ICAO must lead by example as we contribute to the recovery of international civil aviation and 'reconnect the world'. We must also find a way for our work to be more relevant to those we serve. Cooperation under the shared interest and responsibility of the Secretariat, ICAO Council, Member States, and aviation industry and stakeholders will be key to our success.

Juan Carlos Salazar
Secretary General

Appendix D. ICAO Business Plan 2023–2025

Table of Contents

Appendix D. ICAO Business Plan 2023–2025

1. Introduction

1.1. The ICAO Business Plan 2023–2025 comes at a time during which the world is enduring the unprecedented impacts of the COVID-19 pandemic, which inevitably has had devastating consequences for the aviation industry. With the advent of the COVID-19 global pandemic, aviation's raison d'être has been disrupted at its very core and the proliferation of public health measures restricting movement of passengers and goods by air has brought the industry back to 2003 traffic levels.

1.2. As the industry is starting to emerge from the crisis, its resilience has already been tested by the pandemic's evolving waves of variants. Overcoming the COVID-19 pandemic will require the aviation sector to face the many challenges that exist in re-establishing growth and delivering its socio-economic benefits in a sustainable and environmentally conscious manner while keeping the consumers' health, safety and benefits at the core of its endeavors. In doing so, the aviation sector will also be presented with opportunities to address long-standing and emerging concerns by incorporating innovative technologies and solutions.

1.3. To best support its Member States to recover from this unprecedented crisis, ICAO's Business Plan 2023–2025, revolves around transformation, innovation, efficiency and effectiveness in delivery and reporting on ambitious results, while taking into account lessons learned from the COVID-19 pandemic and building on the outcomes of the High level Conference on COVID-19 (HLCC 2021).

1.4. A new cross-cutting Transformational Objective will orient ICAO's work towards bringing the much needed changes to address a number of corporate change management and innovative initiatives within the Organization – resulting in an ICAO better fit-for-purpose to support its Member States. Those initiatives are necessary to bring along a transformation in organizational culture, marked by enhancing the efficiencies and effectiveness of internal operations, simplification of systems and procedures, and conduct of outreach to partners and donors during a period of unprecedented change in global aviation.

1.5. Innovation is mainstreamed throughout the Business Plan. Significant acceleration in the pace of innovations and the increase in the diversity of the innovators requires ICAO to evolve its approach, consistently with the provisions of the Chicago Convention. This will happen through the identification of initiatives and change in working methods that will promote more substantive interaction between ICAO and the industry as well the implementation of internal procedures within ICAO in order to drive innovation and disseminate an innovation culture.

1.6. The Business Plan 2023–2025 also illustrates the inter-connected nature of ICAO's work across all Bureaus and Regional Offices – underscoring the importance of working as 'one-ICAO'. Under the One-ICAO approach, by building on the mandates, strengths and expertise of each Bureau and

(Regional) Office and enabling a coordinated and collaborative response to the needs and expectations of Member States, the Organization aims to achieve more than the sum of its parts.

1.7. The Business Plan follows a results-based management approach, which has resulted in a leaner results framework. The Business Plan includes a strategic narrative, with descriptions illustrating the needs, challenges and opportunities, as well outputs of each of the five Strategic Objectives, the Supporting Strategies as well as the new Transformational Objective. The Business Plan is operationalized by a Triennial Operating Plan in which the Strategic Objectives are supported by tangible outputs and associated prioritized activities.

1.8. The Business Plan is a living adaptable document that may be updated to reflect emerging issues, new priorities and activities that may arise during the course of the triennium. Any new unplanned activities to be undertaken during the 2023–2025 triennium will be consistently added to the Triennial Operating Plan. Such changes will be reported annually to determine if activities can be accommodated within the level of resources available or require additional funding.

1.9. The achievement of the Strategic Objectives and their outputs are monitored through a comprehensive Performance Monitoring Framework, with Key Performance Indicators (KPIs) that will be tracked and reported to the Council on an annual basis in the winter session. The performance results will help ICAO to make the pertinent adjustments and implement corrective actions, where needed, to enhance the achievement of results. The performance results will be accompanied by a comprehensive performance analysis that explains the results to support decision-making. This will transform the Business Plan 2023–2025 into a tool that aims at enhancing accountability at ICAO.

1.10. The Triennial Operating Plan and the Performance Monitoring Framework are Appendices to the Business Plan (Annex I and Annex II respectively). The structure of the ICAO Secretariat can be found at https://www.icao.int/secretariat/Pages/default.aspx.

1.11. The Business Plan was prepared through an inclusive process that engaged colleagues from across the Secretariat at Headquarters as well the Regional Offices under the direction and leadership of the Secretary General and the Full Senior Management Group in consultation with the Council and its Committees.

2. Organizational Setting

2.1. ICAO Vision, Mission and Strategic Objectives

2.1.1. The ICAO strategic framework is defined by its Vision, Mission, and Strategic Objectives approved by the ICAO Council in 2012:

2.2. Vision

2.2.1. Achieve the sustainable growth of the global civil aviation system.

2.3. Mission

2.3.1. ICAO's Mission is to serve as the global forum of States for international civil aviation. ICAO develops international civil aviation Standards and policies, undertakes compliance audits, performs studies and analyses, provides assistance and builds aviation capacity through many other activities and the cooperation of its Member States and stakeholders.

2.3.2. ICAO works with the Chicago Convention's 193 Member States to reach consensus on international civil aviation Standards and Recommended Practices (SARPs) and policies in support of a safe, efficient, secure, economically sustainable, and environmentally responsible civil aviation sector. Industry groups with observer status to ICAO are consulted on the development of these SARPs and policies, which are used by ICAO Member States to ensure that their local civil aviation operations and regulations conform to global norms, which in turn permits more than 100, 000 daily flights (2019) in aviation's global network to operate safely and reliably in every region of the world.

2.4. Strategic Objectives

2.4.1. ICAO's Strategic Objectives (SOs) directly contribute to the betterment of civil aviation globally and form the foundation for all work undertaken by the Organization.

2.4.2. Recognizing the clear need to ensure that air traffic growth is managed safely, securely, and efficiently, with due respect for the aviation sector's environmental commitments, while fully capturing and realizing potential economic benefits to be generated from the increasing traffic, ICAO will continue to work under its five comprehensive Strategic Objectives. During the 2023–2025 triennium, there will be a heavy emphasis on activities relating to the recovery of the aviation sector from the impact of the COVID-19 pandemic.

2.4.3. The ICAO Strategic Objectives for 2023–2025 are as follows:

a) **Safety:** Enhance global civil aviation safety. This Strategic Objective is focused primarily on the State's regulatory oversight capabilities following the strategy outlined in the ICAO Global Aviation Safety Plan (GASP). The GASP sets the goals and targets, and outlines key safety enhancement initiatives (SEIs);

b) **Air Navigation Capacity and Efficiency:** Increase the capacity and improve the efficiency of the global civil aviation system. Although functionally and organizationally interdependent with Safety, this Strategic

Objective is focused primarily on upgrading the air navigation and aerodrome infrastructure and developing new procedures to optimize aviation system performance. The Global Air Navigation Plan (GANP) outlines the performance ambitions;

c) **Security and Facilitation:** Enhance global civil aviation security and facilitation. This Strategic Objective reflects the need for ICAO's leadership in aviation security, facilitation, and related border security matters. The Global Aviation Security Plan (GASeP) outlines the Key Activities;
d) **Economic Development of Air Transport:** Foster the development of a sound and economically viable civil aviation system. This Strategic Objective reflects the need for ICAO's leadership in harmonizing the air transport framework focused on economic policies and supporting activities; and
e) **Environmental Protection:** Minimize the adverse environmental effects of civil aviation activities. This Strategic Objective fosters ICAO's leadership in all aviation related environmental activities and is consistent with the ICAO and UN system environmental protection policies and practices.

2.5. ICAO Secretariat Values

2.5.1. The ICAO values are a set of shared basic principles and beliefs that underpin the work of the Organization and help in creating a unified institutional culture that supports ICAO's vision. These values are also guiding actions, standards of conduct and behaviours of ICAO personnel in carrying out their functions and duties, and they are critical to establishing and maintaining a healthy and respectful working environment, as well as the recruitment and retention of staff. They also help ensure trust in the Organization.

2.5.2. Recently, the relationship between the United Nations organizations and their personnel has evolved. Most organizations have undergone significant reforms and moved away from rules-based to values and results-based systems with increased decentralization and greater responsibilities given to lower-level management. Those developments demanded the identification of clear values, principles, and standards of conduct applicable to relations among colleagues and more transparent accountability systems.

2.5.3. ICAO already started a journey in this direction and requires its personnel to abide at all times during their service with the Organization by the principles and values of integrity, loyalty, independence, impartiality, tolerance and understanding, non-discrimination, gender equality, accountability, and respect for human rights. ICAO also has incorporated in its own regulatory framework the Standards of Conduct for the International Civil Service.

2.5.4. The Secretariat has decided to dedicate particular attention to institutional values through the development of a Transformational Objective output, which would enhance the existing resources, regulations, procedures, and efforts to strengthen compliance by all ICAO personnel at all levels, regardless of contract type or duration, with the above-referenced values, principles, and standards of conduct. In doing so, ICAO is expected to consider the best practices of other organizations of the United Nations system.

2.6. Global Aviation Context and the COVID-19 Pandemic

2.6.1. The Preamble to the Convention on International Civil Aviation (Chicago Convention) recognizes that 'the future development of international civil aviation can greatly help to create and preserve friendship and understanding among the nations and people of the world'.

2.6.2. Throughout its history, aviation has always connected people and the world, traversed oceans and crossed borders creating economic growth, and contributing to sustainable development. It has provided freedom to travel, expanded local access to foreign supplies and markets, and created business opportunities.

2.6.3. In pre-pandemic times, i.e., 2019, air transport moved 4.5 billion passengers, 58 million tons of freight via 38 million scheduled flights. With the onset of the global COVID-19 crisis, air traffic levels started to drop significantly as of early 2020 and reached their lowest point in April 2020 with passenger traffic at times reduced to only 8 per cent of 2019 levels. Such tremendous downturn reflected on the 2020 annual result closing off with 60 per cent less global passenger traffic, or 2.7 billion passengers less as compared to 2019.

Figure 1 World Passenger Traffic Evolution (1945–2022)

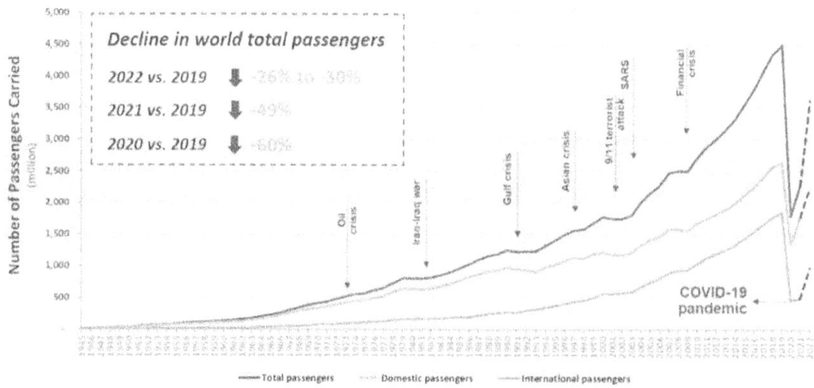

Source: ICAO Economic Impact Analysis of COVID-19 on Civil Aviation.

2.6.4. Entering 2021, virus resurgence and related shutdowns halted the air travel recovery globally. ICAO's near-term projection in October 2021[846] indicated that for the full year of 2021, the number of passengers would decline by 49 to 50 per cent, compared to 2019. The projected decline in traffic is estimated to translate into a potential loss for the airlines between USD 323 to 327 billion in gross passenger operating revenues.

2.6.5. Efficient movement of goods and people by air requires effective national organization and harmonized adoption of best practices and technologies to facilitate cross-border processes. ICAO's air transport facilitation activities involve provision of regulatory material and guidance to ensure that national structures, facilities and technical capabilities are appropriately established and maintained, for a more seamless and efficient passenger's journey.

2.6.6. The COVID-19 pandemic highlighted the disparities between the control measures and travel restrictions in place in the different regions and States that negatively affect the air transport facilitation of the passengers' journey. There is a need to develop a global and harmonized strategic approach in close coordination with the World Health Organization (WHO) to assure a safe and efficient staged return to normal air transport operations.

2.6.7. These impacts bring forth the truly international and global nature of the aviation industry. It is important, however, to remind ourselves that it remains by far the world's safest and most efficient mode of long-range mass transportation and that it has far-reaching impacts across industries and economies.

2.6.8. Aviation plays a considerable role in the modern global economy by enabling business and industries to generate wealth and employment through activities and supply chain. In 2019, aviation directly contributed to the creation of 10.2 million jobs and of around USD 704.4 billion in global Gross Domestic Product (GDP). Because of its cross-cutting nature and multiple links to other economic sectors, the total economic impact of aviation reached some 3.6 per cent of world GDP, equivalent to USD 2.7 trillion, with the creation of 65.5 million jobs. Returning to these pre-pandemic figures shall be the aspiration and the driver across the aviation industry in the upcoming years.

2.6.9. Recovering the connectivity brought about by air transport will also need to be at the core of ICAO's and all stakeholders' efforts and activities in the next triennium to support tourism. Aviation is at the heart of tourism development. Prior to the pandemic, over half of the 1.5 billion international tourists arrived at their destinations via air transport. Air connectivity is even more important for Small Island Developing States (SIDS) with international tourism facilitated by air transport reaching 80 per cent. As a result of the COVID-19 crisis, international tourism revenues in 2020 declined by USD 1.3 trillion compared to 2019 putting thousands of businesses and livelihoods at existential risk. Post-pandemic considerations and efforts shall aim to restore the air connectivity that is essential for the recovery and development of tourism worldwide.

846. https://www.icao.int/sustainability/Pages/Economic-Impacts-of-COVID-19.aspx.

2.6.10. Similarly, air transport is a driver of global trade and e-commerce. In pre-pandemic times, air freight constituted some 35 per cent of world trade by value, despite representing only 0.5 per cent by volume. The share of cross border business-to-consumer (B2C) e-commerce carried by air transport grew from 16 per cent in 2010 to around 90 per cent and was estimated to grow to 96 per cent by 2025. For Landlocked Developing Countries (LLDCs) and SIDS especially, aviation represents an essential lifeline, which in turn promotes tourism, trade and other vital business activities.

2.6.11. The recovery of air traffic needs to be managed safely, securely and efficiently with due respect for the aviation sector's concrete environmental commitments. Substantial investments are also required in the near-term to account for the need to rebuild a strong and robust system, and long-term considerations needs to account for the development and modernization of quality aviation infrastructure commensurate with the level of predicted traffic return and growth.

2.6.12. The sustainable and resilient recovery from the COVID-19 pandemic also requires that international aviation build back better. This green transition to a decarbonized future will be enabled through the development and implementation of CO_2 emissions reduction technologies, and innovations on a global scale.

2.6.13. Continuous improvement in global aviation safety and air transport facilitation as well as aviation security is the first and most obvious pre-condition to ensure that air transport continues to play a major role in driving sustainable economic and social development around the world. A safe, secure, efficient, economically viable and environmentally friendly air transport system is the ultimate goal of ICAO and its Member States.

2.6.14. Over the next three years, the Secretariat, ICAO Council, Member States, and the aviation industry and stakeholders have a shared responsibility and will work together to 'reconnect the world' through a more resilient and improved international civil aviation system.

2.7. Global Plans and Key Priorities

2.7.1. In order to support the recovery of international civil aviation and ensure its long-term sustainability and resilience, ICAO would need to focus on advancing its regulatory framework to meet evolving needs, particularly when taking into account lessons learned from the COVID-19 pandemic and building on the outcomes of the High-level Conference on COVID-19 (HLCC 2021), notably the safety and facilitation-related recommendations, and while advancing specifications and assistance to States to drive more seamless and contactless travel. In that context, ICAO and its Member States would need not only to implement the recommendations of the ICAO Council's Aviation Recovery Task Force and those of the HLCC 2021, but would also need to address the key priorities established in ICAO's Global Plans. The HLCC 2021 emphasized the need to strengthen crisis management capacity at the organizational level, leading to a better coordinated and integrated response, notwithstanding the nature of the crisis.

2.7.2. During the HLCC 2021, the Safety Stream highlighted the safety and operational measures applied during the COVID-19 pandemic, the importance of establishing contingency arrangements by States, lessons learnt, and how to plan for the mitigating effects of similar disruptions in the future. Proposals for the evolution of the Global Aviation Safety Plan (GASP) were widely supported, and the stream agreed on the need to take into consideration input from the conference, in preparation for endorsement of the GASP at the 41st Session of the ICAO Assembly. The safety stream also supported recommendations associated with the standardization of new oversight approaches, risk management and ground handling. The need for support to States and regional cooperation in accomplishing functions related to safety oversight, accident investigation and safety management were also addressed. In addition, other subjects included accident and incident investigation, the Universal Safety Oversight Audit Programme Continuous Monitoring Approach (USOAP CMA), the Global Air Navigation Plan (GANP), the Global Aeronautical Distress and Safety System (GADSS) as well as the impact of 5G to safety critical radio altimeter functions.

2.7.3. The HLCC 2021 Facilitation Stream reinforced the need for States to utilize best practices for the planning and implementation of facilitation-related operational mitigating measures dealing both with the immediate challenges imposed by the COVID-19 pandemic and future unforeseen wide scale disruptions. States should ensure effective implementation of Annex 9 provisions, and coordination amongst all relevant agencies, departments of the State, including public health authorities and relevant aviation stakeholders. These include the designation of an appropriate authority for the air transport facilitation, as States deem appropriate, and allocation of necessary resources.

Global Aviation Safety Plan (GASP)

2.7.4. During the preparatory work for the High-level Conference on COVID-19 (HLCC-2021), the Secretariat worked with the Global Aviation Safety Plan Study Group (GASP-SG) to review and update the GASP Goals and Targets, in preparation for the 2023–2025 edition of the plan. Several factors were considered when deciding specific actions for each target. The main factor for extending the deadline for targets was the impact of the COVID-19 pandemic on the aviation community, including the ability by ICAO, States, regional and international organizations, as well as industry to complete safety enhancement initiatives that support the achievement of the GASP goals.

2.7.5. The 41st Session of the ICAO Assembly will be invited to endorse the 2023 – 2025 edition of the GASP.

Global Air Navigation Plan (GANP)

2.7.6. New demands on the aviation system, emerging technologies, innovative ways of doing business and the shifting human role are bringing about not only challenges but also opportunities that call for an urgent transformation of the global air navigation system so that aviation can continue to boost social well-being worldwide. In aviation's fast and ever-changing landscape, achieving sustainable growth of international air transport strongly relies on a high-performing and seamless global air navigation system. The GANP is bringing the aviation community together to achieve an agile, safe, secure, sustainable, high-performing and interoperable global air navigation system. Developed in collaboration with, and for, the benefit of stakeholders, the GANP is a key contributor to the achievement of ICAO's Strategic Objectives and has an important role to play in supporting the United Nations 2030 Agenda for Sustainable Development.

2.7.7. The 40th Session of the ICAO Assembly endorsed the sixth edition of the GANP. This edition recognizes that a performance-driven, service-oriented and technologically advanced global air navigation system is critical to achieve the sustainability of the aviation sector worldwide. Furthermore, it recognizes safety as one of the fundamental principles of aviation performance, together with environment, security and facilitation as well as economic sustainability. In addition to these fundamental aviation principles, there are several performance requirements, in areas such as capacity and efficiency, that the air navigation system must meet to fulfil the expectations of the aviation community and society-at-large.

2.7.8. The 41st Session of the ICAO Assembly will be invited to endorse the seventh edition of the GANP.

Global Aviation Security Plan (GASeP)

2.7.9. The recovery, sustainability and resilience of international civil aviation is dependent on a robust global aviation security framework, based in particular on the five key priority outcomes of the GASeP: 1) enhance risk awareness and response; 2) develop security culture and human capability; 3) improve technological resources and innovation; 4) improve oversight and quality assurance; and 5) increase cooperation and support. Taking into account that the threats and risks faced by the civil aviation community continue to evolve, the GASeP roadmap remains a 'living' document and shall be periodically reviewed and adjusted as necessary, taking into account new and emerging aviation security threats and risks including those that arise as a result of the impacts of the COVID-19 pandemic. Alignment with the regional roadmaps shall also be maintained.

Appendix D. ICAO Business Plan 2023–2025

Carbon Offsetting and Reduction Scheme (CORSIA) and feasibility of a Long-Term Global Aspirational Goal (LTAG)

2.7.10. A major task is the periodic review of CORSIA due to take place at the 41st Session of the ICAO Assembly in 2022. This will involve the analysis of the impact of COVID-19 on CORSIA and recovery scenarios, ensuring a solid information base for the discussions at the forthcoming Assembly. Based on the results of the CORSIA review, work will continue on the implementation and operation of CORSIA in 2023 to 2025.

2.7.11. The work on exploring the feasibility of a Long-term Global Aspirational Goal (LTAG) for international aviation CO2 emissions reduction is supported by the technical work of the Committee on Aviation Environmental Protection (CAEP), the development of a set of ICAO innovation trackers on technology, operations, fuels and roadmaps, and the ICAO stocktaking process. The objective is to better understand the development and deployment of aviation in-sector CO2 emissions reduction opportunities toward the sector's decarbonization. The outcome of the work of the Assembly in 2022 will be crucial to the work of the Organization on climate change in 2023 to 2025.

Innovation

2.7.12. Assembly Resolution A40-27, Innovation in aviation established clear objectives for ICAO to enhance its interface with the aviation or non-aviation innovation community, as well as to support States integrate innovations in their international civil aviation system in a cost-effective manner. A high-level strategic dialogue between the Council and the industry was established in 2021 and will necessarily be intensified through to 2025, as understanding the nature and the impacts of future innovations on all aspects of international aviation operations, not only those for which the innovations were designed, will be critical to make the most appropriate and timely policy decisions.

2.7.13. The 2023–2025 triennium will provide the opportunity to accompany the transformational agenda of the aviation sector through the active engagement of ICAO with the aviation and non-aviation stakeholders in a coherent, coordinated and efficient manner. The intensification of the pace and the disruptive nature of innovations require ICAO to adopt a more inclusive and consistent approach towards all relevant stakeholders, with the view to facilitate their understanding of regulatory requirements, so that sustainable innovations can be deployed and their benefits delivered to States. Enhancing the interface between ICAO and the innovation community would also lead to increased understanding of the needs of the sector and ICAO's ability to adjust its response in an agile manner. An increased effort should be made towards ICAO Member States, in order to help them establish the most relevant partnerships for their specific circumstances, and identify and develop best practices aimed at better supporting Member States' implementation of ICAO SARPs within their regulatory frameworks.

2.8. No Country Left Behind (NCLB) Initiative

2.8.1. In line with Assembly Resolution A39-23, the primary objectives of the No Country Left Behind (NCLB) initiative for the 2023–2025 triennium will include: a) providing enhanced support for States in the effective implementation of ICAO's SARPs, plans and policies in a more coordinated, comprehensive and globally harmonized manner; b) support States in implementing a quick recovery of the air transport system and its resilient development; and c) promoting the resolution of significant safety concerns (SSCs) and significant security concerns (SSeCs).

2.8.2. The efforts of ICAO and its Member States will continue under the NCLB to support the recovery, sustainability and resilience of international civil aviation. Together, this work will allow States to adapt to changing circumstances over time and take advantage of new operational and technical innovations and developments, including green innovations for environmental sustainability and decarbonization of the aviation sector, while no country is left behind. This includes the provision of technical assistance and technical cooperation using multiple sources of funding including the regular budget, cost-recovery mechanisms, voluntary funds and/or in-kind assistance through ICAO.

2.8.3. ICAO implementation support is provided to Member States under a One-ICAO approach, with a focus on relevance, consistency, efficiency and effectiveness in managing the development and delivery. It contributes to the ICAO NCLB initiative and the United Nations Sustainable Development Goals. The new Policy on ICAO Implementation Support Provided to States is designed to strengthen the coordination and management of ICAO's implementation support activities to better meet the needs of Member States. The policy will ensure that the implementation support provided to States is consistent in content and delivery regardless of the source of assistance or the associated funding mechanism. This policy enhances ICAO's role in supporting States with their implementation of ICAO Policies, Plans, SARPs, PANS and guidance materials. It also expects to improve the performance and results of ICAO implementation support provided to States, with a more relevant, consistent, efficient and effective implementation support integrated within the ICAO Business Plan. This policy is designed with the following objectives:

a) increase State implementation of ICAO Policies, Plans, SARPs, Procedures for Air Navigation Services (PANS) and guidance material;
b) prioritize and enhance ICAO support provided to States for implementation of ICAO Policies, Plans, SARPs, PANS and guidance material;
c) increase the financial and human resources allocated to ICAO implementation support;

d) reinforce the State needs-based approach in ICAO implementation support in support of the NCLB initiative;
e) integrate ICAO implementation support within the ICAO Business Plan;
f) align the management of ICAO implementation support following a One-ICAO approach; and
g) improve the relevance, consistency, efficiency and effectiveness of the ICAO implementation support provided to States.

2.9. One-ICAO approach

2.9.1. The concept of functioning as One-ICAO stems from the United Nations General Assembly 2005 World Summit Outcome Document[847] and its follow-up reports[848], where the need for implementing a 'delivering as one' approach was identified with a view to ensuring a more effective, efficient, coherent, coordinated and better performing United Nations presence. These documents highlighted the need to overcome fragmentation and deliver as one through a stronger commitment to working together on the implementation of one strategy, in the pursuit of one set of goals.

2.9.2. If ICAO is to successfully lead the global aviation community in addressing its challenges, it must incorporate the principles outlined by the UN system at large and fully embrace the One-ICAO approach. This necessitates the ICAO Council and the Secretariat to work together by building on lessons learned from the Council Aviation Recovery Taskforce (CART) and the ICAO Secretariat COVID-19 Emergency Programme Group (SCEPG), and by expanding innovative implementation support and enhancing synergies among Headquarters Bureaus and Offices with the Regional Offices.

2.9.3. As defined in the new Policy on ICAO Implementation Support Provided to States, under the One-ICAO approach ICAO delivers implementation support to States as one organization. ICAO implementation support provided to States is managed in a well-coordinated and consistent manner. To manage complexity and deliver implementation support across all areas of civil aviation, the ICAO Secretariat will cooperate and collaborate efficiently and effectively, avoiding duplication and optimizing the allocation of resources.

2.9.4. Through strengthened internal coordination within the ICAO Secretariat, the Organization aims to ensure the provision of implementation support that is aligned and integrated with the process for developing policies, plans, SARPs, PANS and guidance material.

2.9.5. By securing the alignment with the ICAO Business Plan and focusing on relevance, consistency, efficiency, and effectiveness in managing the development and delivery of implementation support, this integrated approach will contribute to the achievement of the ICAO NCLB initiative and the United Nations Sustainable Development Goals.

---

847. https://undocs.org/en/A/RES/60/1.
848. https://undocs.org/en/A/61/583.

2.9.6. Moreover, the One-ICAO approach requires closer integration and alignment of Regional Offices who are at the forefront of ICAO's support to and coordination with Member States while reinforcing close coordination with the Headquarters Bureaus.

2.9.7. Enhancing the support structure, leveraging technology, streamlining processes, and ensuring financial transparency and accountability will be prioritized to facilitate the evolution of ICAO implementation support.

2.10. ICAO and United Nations 2030 Agenda for Sustainable Development

2.10.1. Adopted in September 2015, the United Nations Transforming our World: 2030 Agenda for Sustainable Development, with its 17 Sustainable Development Goals (SDGs) and the underlying 169 targets, defines global priorities and aspirations for 2030, provides a universal framework to strengthen collective action towards common goals. The 2030 Agenda includes ambitious visions and transformative steps that, once implemented, would 'shift the world onto a sustainable and resilient path'.

2.10.2. Sustainable aviation and transportation are essential to achieving the Sustainable Development Goals of the 2030 Agenda for Sustainable Development. Through its normative work, oversight and technical assistance and cooperation, ICAO serves the people of the world in facilitating international civil air transport that is safe, secure, efficient, economically viable and environmentally friendly. While there is no stand-alone SDG on sustainable transport, the sector is mainstreamed into many of the SDGs and tremendously contributes to all the three dimensions of sustainable development: economic growth, social development, and green goals. In the Triennium Operating Plan 2023–2025, each Output has been attributed to one or a number of the Sustainable Development Goals (SDGs) to demonstrate how the Output is supporting the achievement of SDGs. This will enable compliance with the requirements of Data Standards for United Nations System-Wide Reporting of Financial Data, based on which ICAO will be reporting on its expenditures as per the SDGs.

2.10.3. Through Assembly Resolution A40-21, Aviation contribution towards the United Nations 2030 Agenda for Sustainable Development, ICAO Member States emphasized the synergies between aviation and sustainable development and reaffirmed their commitment towards contributing to the attainment of the Sustainable Development Goals. With the COVID-19 pandemic around the world leaving a profound negative impact across all sectors, indeed a much deeper, faster, and more ambitious multi-stakeholder response is needed to unleash the social and economic transformation needed to achieve our 2030 goals.

2.10.4. Although the responsibility for implementing the 2030 Agenda lies primarily with States and their governments, ICAO has an important leadership role to play in maximizing its support in accelerating actions for the implementation of the SDGs. Driven by the urgency and ambition of the 'Decade of Action', and in light of the COVID-19 pandemic, as well as drawing upon the commitment that ICAO Member States expressed in Assembly Resolution A40-21, ICAO, more committed than ever, continues to highlight opportunities to leverage interlinkages between aviation and the SDGs, and to translate the ambition into collective action across the SDGs in line with its Strategic Objectives. To serve this purpose, a clear link is made in the Triennium Operating plan and the SDGs for each output in ICAO.

2.10.5. Multi-stakeholder partnerships and collaborations have become increasingly important in realizing the SDGs. Indeed, the global efforts to address the COVID-19 crisis have been a testimony to the importance of multi-stakeholder partnerships, unity, and solidarity so that the world could mobilize the required resources as well as the political will for advancing a comprehensive global response and recovery. In this light, ICAO continues to highlight the importance of partnerships as strong enablers that significantly assist the Organization to accelerate and scale up its efforts to enhance its efficiency, effectiveness, and impact.

3. Results-based Framework for the 2023–2025 Business Plan

3.1. During 2019, the Office of Internal Oversight (OIO) made an evaluation of results-based management (RBM) in ICAO. The purpose of the evaluation was to assess the application of RBM in the Organization, identify and learn lessons in implementing various aspects of RBM, including results-based planning, budgeting, monitoring, and reporting. The main recommendations include mainstreaming RBM in an integrated manner in every organizational programming process over the next 5–10 years, strengthening the strategic planning process of the Organization and individual Bureau/unit plans and reducing the number and improving the content of reports prepared on the Business Plan/work of the Organization by focusing on reporting on outcome level results. The 2023–2025 Business Plan and its Operating Plan present an opportunity to incorporate key recommendations from the evaluation report, Council Decisions and lessons learnt from the previous cycles into the new plans, as well as to reduce complexity.

3.2. According to the UN Development Group (UNDG), RBM is defined as 'a management strategy by which all actors [...] ensure that their processes, products, and services contribute to the achievement of desired results (outputs, outcomes and higher-level goals or impacts).'[849] RBM is based on a logic according to which resources will be used to implement activities which will in turn lead to outputs and higher-level results (outcomes and impacts). From an organizational perspective, the main purpose of RBM is to generate and use performance information for accountability and reporting to stakeholders and for decision-making. Managers within the organization also benefit from applying RBM by acquiring more control on the activities and outputs they are

849. UNDG RBM Handbook 2012.

responsible for, by becoming better equipped to take well-informed decisions and by learning from successes and failures.

3.3. In preparing the ICAO Business Plan 2023–2025 an organization-wide exercise was undertaken to review the outputs, activities and indicators under each Strategic Objective and Supporting Strategy. The responsibility for implementing an Output is taken on by a Headquarters Bureau or Office while the Regional Offices have one shared output per SO. The results framework follows a Results Based Management (RBM) approach which integrates outputs with activities, resources as well as performance measurement.

3.4. Figure 2, *ICAO results framework* for 2023–2025, consists of the Vision and Mission supported by its five Strategic Objectives, the Transformational Objective and the Supporting strategies outputs.

Appendix D. ICAO Business Plan 2023–2025

Vision: Achieve the sustainable growth of the global civil aviation system

Figure 2 ICAO Results Framework

Note – Output names in this figure are abbreviated.

4. Business Plan Funding Mechanisms

4.1. Funding mechanisms available in the Organization contribute to the achievement of the Business Plan objectives, strategies, related outputs, and associated activities. The funding in the Organization relies on two funding categories: Regular Budget and other resources that include the Ancillary Revenue Generation Fund (ARGF), cost-recovery mechanisms and the Administrative and Operational Service Cost (AOSC) Fund, voluntary funds, trust funds, in-kind contributions, and other funds.

Figure 3 Business Plan Funding Mechanism

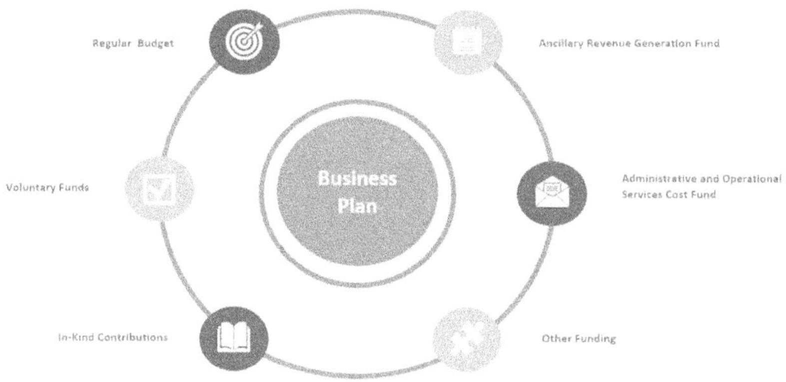

4.2. The Regular Budget and other resources are utilized to develop a complementary relationship and function as an integrated funding mechanism.

Appendix D. ICAO Business Plan 2023–2025

Figure 4 The Relationship Between the Regular Budget and the Business Plan

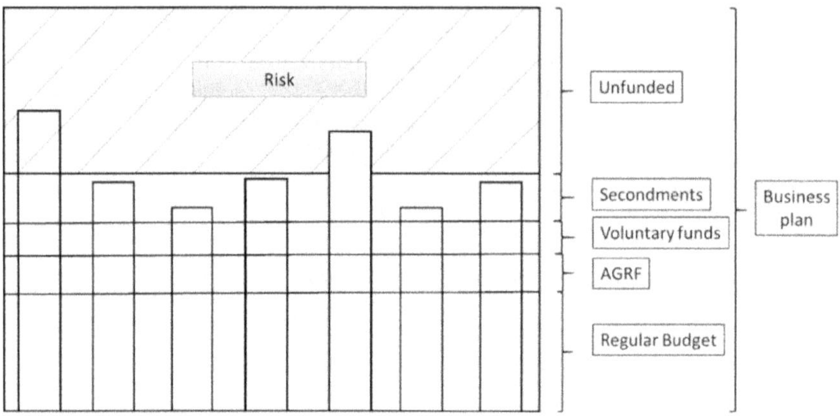

Regular Budget

4.3. The ICAO Secretariat is primarily funded by the Regular Budget, which is allocated over a triennial period and provides the required flexibility to the Organization to allocate funding to those areas where it is most needed to achieve the Business Plan objectives, strategies, related outputs, and prioritized activities.

4.4. The Regular Budget of ICAO for 2023–2025 is prepared in accordance with the guidance for the preparation of the Organization's Triennial Budget (C-DEC 210/1), forms an integral part of the Business Plan, and is financed by assessments of States, reimbursement from the Administrative and Operational Services Cost (AOSC) Fund, transfers from the ARGF surplus and other miscellaneous income.

Ancillary Revenue Generation Fund

4.5. The ARGF was established in 2006[850] to record all revenues and expenditures relating to self-financing activities. The ARGF activities explore and leverage ICAO's revenue-generating opportunities by developing and promoting products and services, including the ICAO global aviation training and TRAINAIR Plus programme, which facilitate the implementation of the Business Plan objectives and strategies within ICAO; and developing, promoting, and protecting the intellectual property of ICAO.

850. Established under the provision of Article VII of the ICAO Financial Regulations.

Administrative and Operational Services Cost (AOSC) Fund

4.6. The AOSC Fund was established[851] to administer the cost of administration and management of the ICAO technical cooperation programme, which earns income from technical cooperation projects it executes. The Fund is primarily financed from administrative overhead charges on technical cooperation projects.

Voluntary Funds

4.7. The Organization continues management and promotion of the thematic and multi-donor trust funds that are aligned with its Strategic Objectives. Voluntary contributions are received as earmarked or un-earmarked. Un-earmarked voluntary contributions provide the Organization with the flexibility to prioritize unfunded needs of activities in the Business Plan. The list of voluntary funds includes:

a) **Aviation Safety Fund (SAFE):** The purpose of the fund is to improve the safety of civil aviation by addressing serious safety deficiencies in countries which lack the financial means to do so.
b) **AFI Plan Fund (AFI PLAN):** The fund assists African States to improve their effective implementation of the critical elements in all safety-related areas, with priority given to resolving significant safety concerns.
c) **Aviation Security and Facilitation Fund (AVSEC/FAL):** The fund is used primarily for aviation security technical assistance and training activities coordinated by the Implementation Support and Development – Security Programme, and for the conduct of aviation security audits under the ICAO Universal Security Audit Programme Continuous Monitoring Approach. Such activities are undertaken in accordance with the Global Aviation Security Plan and the ICAO NCLB initiative.
d) **Environment Fund (ENV):** The fund targets to support the growing demands for environmental protection activities. The majority of the fund is received through the grant agreements and directed to support specific projects or initiatives.
e) **Human Resources Development Fund (HRDF):** The fund supports opportunities for capacity building in civil aviation in African States and to assist these States to better meet the human resources needs for operational efficiency and continuous implementation of ICAO Standards and Recommended Practices and other programme activities.

851. Established under the provisions of Article IX of the ICAO Financial Regulations.

f) **Voluntary Air Transport Fund (TRAF):** The fund serves to support ICAO's work in the air transport field in a consistent, transparent, efficient, and timely manner. The Secretariat continues to seek contributions on an on-going basis through promotion of the Fund on-line and during events, and through cooperation with other international organizations and UN agencies.
g) **ICAO Programme for Aviation Volunteers Fund (IPAV):** The fund provides a framework for the deployment of aviation professionals, working as volunteers, to respond to emergencies affecting the aviation system in a State; assist States in addressing shortcomings identified during ICAO safety and security audits; assist States in achieving high levels of effective implementation; develop capabilities in the implementation of ICAO Standards and Recommended Practices; and foster self-reliance and growth.
h) **Resource Mobilization Fund (RMF):** The fund is designed to manage the activities undertaken as per the Resource Mobilization Policy. The RMF accepts unearmarked voluntary contributions towards the NCLB initiative or earmarked to a specific programme from donors supporting the achievement of ICAO's mission and objectives at the global, regional, and State levels. Crucially, the RMF presents the only ICAO funding modality to donors to contribute funding in a cross-cutting fashion to the Organization's Strategic Objectives.
i) **Transformational Fund[852]:** This fund is created to enable change promoting organizational improvements, focused on progressing the transformational outputs included in the Business Plan under the Transformational Objective.

In-Kind Contributions

4.8. International and non-governmental organizations, as well as national civil services, or academic institutions often wish to contribute to work at the international level. In the area of civil aviation, ICAO is at the centre of multinational governance. Cognizant of the value of these contributions, ICAO's constituents have determined that it is in the interest of the Organization to use third party expertise in the form of secondees and gratis personnel from States and international organizations.

4.9. Aside from funds and personnel, ICAO receives in-kind contributions in the form of facilities, airline tickets, accommodations, commodities, and services from various contributors.

852. Approved by the Council (C-DEC 225/12).

Other Funds

4.10. ICAO makes use of other funds, which are subject specific and not voluntary; these trust funds are governed by special agreements including but not limited to, the Technical Cooperation Programme, Joint Financing, bilateral agreements, Junior Professional Officers, and associate experts.

Resource Mobilization

4.11. ICAO has established a dedicated Resource Mobilization (RM) capacity to mobilize voluntary resources towards supporting States for the improvement of global civil aviation, consistent with the achievement of the UN 2030 Development Agenda, UN SDGs as well as the ICAO NCLB Initiative. Mobilized resources are meant to supplement ICAO's work programmes not funded by the Regular Budget. The overall RM efforts of ICAO aim to also aid States in securing funding for their aviation development, enhance partnership and cooperation with global aviation stakeholders, including UN organizations, and assist in humanitarian operations and crisis management. It is the intent that for the 2023–2025 triennium, the RM capabilities will be strengthened by implementing a new organization-wide RM Strategy.

5. Enterprise Risk Management and Internal Controls

5.1. ICAO is committed to managing its risks efficiently and effectively, ensuring that risks are identified, assessed, mitigated, reported, monitored, and escalated in a way that enhances ICAO's capability to achieve its mission, Strategic Objectives and Outputs, as well as to implement projects/programmes and key activities outlined in the Business Plan. A risk is defined as the possibility that an event will occur and adversely affect ICAO, impacting, inter alia, its mission, Strategic Objectives, outputs, projects/programmes, key activities, reputation, and assets.

5.2. ICAO has an ERM Framework endorsed by Council in 2021 that sets out the roles and responsibilities for risk management and ensures that robust internal controls (Figure 5) are in place to support the efficient and effective management of risks in ICAO. In addition, a risk register process and assessment table to assess the likelihood and impact of a risk are integrated within ICAO's business processes and the outputs/activities in the Business Plan.

Figure 5 Risk and internal Control Process

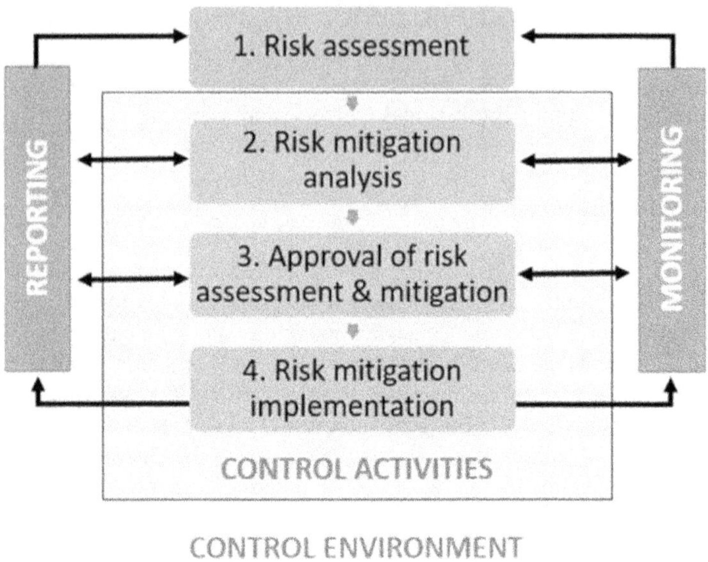

6. Strategic Objective Safety

6.1. Enhance global civil aviation safety

6.1.1. Managing and improving the safety of the global air transport system is ICAO's guiding and most fundamental Strategic Objective. The Organization works constantly to address and enhance global aviation safety through the following coordinated activities:
   a) policy and standardization;
   b) monitoring of key safety trends and indicators;
   c) safety analysis;
   d) specific programmes to address safety issues; and
   e) implementation support.

6.1.2. The ICAO Global Aviation Safety Plan (GASP) presents the strategy in support of the prioritization and continuous improvement of aviation safety. The GASP sets the goals, targets, and outlines key Safety Enhancement Initiatives (SEIs) aimed at improving safety at the global, regional, and national levels. In addition to the safety-related challenges and operational safety risks, the GASP supports the safe implementation of the Global Air Navigation Plan, which addresses the appropriate infrastructure to support the provision of the essential services.

6.2. Priorities

6.2.1. In support of the safety Strategic Objective, the Global Aviation Safety Plan (GASP) goals and targets, and the NCLB initiative, the ICAO key priorities are to:

a) continuously increase global civil aviation safety, while embracing and integrating the new and evolving public health safety measures, new airspace entrants, new technology and innovation, as well as trends in ownership, business, operating and oversight models;
b) modernize and improve the process for the development and maintenance of the robust global civil aviation regulatory framework, and the associated safety oversight audit programme, helping to underpin State and Industry actions for continued growth and development of a safe and resilient global air navigation system within Member States' economic and sustainability expectations;
c) continue to prioritize standardization and implementation efforts as agreed by States and Industry in the GASP; hold the trust and confidence of the global community to provide advice and lead the coordination, consultation and collaboration with all stakeholders in safety, focusing on timely standardization and harmonized, effective, scalable and affordable implementation for States and industry; enhance the regional cooperation; and narrow the gaps between States; and
d) ensure the organizational framework that will allow stakeholders to participate and contribute within the standard making process to enhance the capability of ICAO to deliver targeted solutions for the improvement of safety.

6.3. Challenges, emerging needs and opportunities

6.3.1. The main challenges being faced are related to the recovery of the aviation system from the pandemic. The NCLB initiative is more important than ever as the pandemic has served to further highlight the inequities between States. The SARPs development process has always been driven by Member States with the resources to support ICAO expert groups. However, our improved capability to hold virtual and hybrid meetings has the potential to increase participation and contribution. We have also seen that States with a State safety programme (SSP) have been able to adapt to address the new risks faced more easily than others, further emphasizing the importance of making progress in this important goal highlighted in the GASP to build resilience.

6.3.2. Opportunities exist to improve monitoring of States' performance by evolving USOAP CMA and to enhance the currency of information on States' performance. Regional cooperation is more important than ever as States are facing tremendous economic challenges during the recovery and harmonizing efforts at the regional level will support a stable operational environment for the industry.

6.3.3. Specific efforts to support the recovery will continue to take place as well as an opportunity to take the lessons learned to support a more resilient and flexible oversight of the aviation system. The development and delivery of implementation support is being recognized as an important element of ICAO's mandate. During the next triennium one of the challenges will be to establish mechanisms to prioritize and resource this work.

6.4. Safety outputs

SAF 1 Enhanced Standards and Recommended Practices (SARPs) and development process that continuously improve aviation safety

6.4.1. ICAO SARPs are constantly evolving. They are our primary regulatory risk control. The complexity of oversight continues to increase due to a number of new business models and cross-border operations, including short-term aircraft interchange operations. Due to resource challenges, ICAO must also find new ways to enhance the SARPs development process to ensure that it remains relevant, timely and effective at mitigating safety risks. During 2023–2025, the focus will be on the development of: 1) a cooperative oversight framework; 2) mechanisms to leverage available expertise; 3) a robust and inclusive coordination for processing amendment proposals to ensure that 'No Country is left behind'; and 4) performance based SARPs where practicable and cost effective. Information from Universal Safety Oversight Audit Programme (USOAP) activities will help to identify areas where ICAO SARPs are not well implemented, and the protocol questions will be reviewed and updated to remain relevant.

SAF 2 Enhanced capacity of the aviation community to proactively manage aviation safety

6.4.2. The global aviation system is in a period of intense change. The key to safely managing these changes is building upon proven strategies for improving safety, like the investigation of accidents and incidents and safety management. Advanced methodologies suitable for complex socio-technical systems are essential to address the introduction of new technologies, new business models, increasing automation and unpredictable disruptions like the COVID-19 pandemic. For 2023–2025, ICAO will focus on the evolution of ICAO SARPs, the development of complementary guidance material, the collection and sharing of practical examples, and tools to support a more proactive, predictive, and integrated approach to risk and resilience management. In recognition of the new competencies required across the aviation community, additional content for webinars, workshops, training, tools, and implementation packages (iPacks) will also be developed. Focus areas will include accident investigation, advanced risk assessment methodologies, change management, safety intelligence and human performance.

SAF 3 Increased regional harmonization and cooperation in regulatory oversight

6.4.3. Many States still struggle in properly implementing ICAO SARPs and ensuring adequate oversight of their service providers, due to insufficient resources and ever-growing industry and emergence of new technologies. As recognized by Assembly resolutions and HLCC 2021 recommendations, ICAO should support various forms of cooperation on safety issues on a regional level, in particular Regional Safety Oversight Organizations (RSOOs), Regional Accident and Incident Investigation Organizations (RAIOs) and Cooperative Development of Operational Safety and Continued Airworthiness Programme (COSCAPs). The experiences of the COVID-19 pandemic have proven the added value of regional organizations in assisting States, harmonizing regional measures, and creating a stable operational environment for the industry. For 2023–2025, ICAO will support regional organizations and other mechanisms through programmes and activities such as 1) GASOS Assessments, 2) RSOO and RAIO Cooperative Platforms and 3) input for technical assistance to States when regional organizations are available.

SAF 4 Improved ICAO monitoring function and enhanced information currency related to safety oversight and safety management implementation at the State and regional levels

6.4.4. Planning and prioritization efforts are better served with improved and up-to date information addressing safety oversight and safety management implementation at the State and regional levels. This information is critical for ICAO Standard-making and assistance functions. For States, it is also critical to have a baseline on the status of these responsibilities to implement corrective actions addressing deficiencies and/or progressing its safety responsibilities. The main strategy for change encompasses improving the monitoring function of ICAO by implementing the recommendations of the Group of Experts for a USOAP CMA Structured Review (GEUSR) and the USOAP CMA Advisory Group (USOAP-AG), as agreed by the Council, as well as the self-improvements introduced by its quality system. The conduct of USOAP CMA activities strives at continuously updating its data. The result of these actions will result in an enhanced USOAP CMA yielding improved information related to safety oversight and safety management implementation at the State and regional levels.

SAF 5 Continued support for post-COVID pandemic air transport recovery which includes improved ICAO provisions based on lessons learnt

6.4.5. From the onset of the COVID-19 pandemic crisis, the aviation system has faced a severe disruption to its operations and economic viability. ICAO has a leadership role in bringing the aviation community together to develop and promote harmonized and cooperative efforts for the aviation system recovery. This can be achieved through the implementation, monitoring and ongoing update of multi-layered risk mitigation strategies. For 2023–2025, the focus will be on identifying, amending, improving, and developing the content for initiatives to support ICAO Member States through the recovery process. In addition, a review of relevant ICAO SARPs and guidance material will be conducted to reflect the lessons learned from the COVID-19 pandemic in support of a more resilient aviation system. This will include developing a global common framework to assess and mitigate risks (including human performance risks) supported by appropriate mitigation measures in accordance with HLCC Safety stream recommendations. This will also include provisions related to the renewal and extension of medical assessments, licences and other certificates, guidance for mitigating the transmission of disease, granting, and lifting exemptions/alleviations and guidance for the conduct of remote oversight activities.

SAF 6 Increased access to aviation safety implementation support that addresses States' prioritised needs

6.4.6. Implementation support refers to the ICAO actions in managing the programmes, projects and activities which support and assist the implementation efforts of States through the provision of products and services. Implementation support packages content and material generated as part of other safety (SAF) outputs, finds funding for those activities, distributes responsibilities among actors and ensures the support is provided to the States in need. This output ensures that: 1) a needs-based approach is adopted in the development and deployment of implementation support; 2) that deployment is adequately prioritized; 3) that a common methodology is used throughout all implementation support; 4) that support is coordinated; and 5) that there is financial transparency and accountability among all actors.

SAF 7 Strengthened safety of civil aviation at the regional level

6.4.7. The evolution of air traffic and the challenges imposed by the COVID-19 pandemic restate the importance of increasing the safety compliance to global requirements and the sustainability of the measures taken by the States in ensuring their safety management framework. In this sense, the efforts adopted by the Regional Offices aim to enhance States' ability to implement

SARPs, provisions of Global Plans and directives of the Council and Secretariat in a sustainable and measurable manner.

6.4.8. The Regional Offices will continue to support States to enhance safety levels by increasing effective implementation of State oversight systems (validated through USOAP CMA) and by providing the necessary assistance for the implementation of Safety Management processes, through capacity building activities. Additionally, the Regional Offices will assist States in the identification of emerging safety challenges and the implementation of necessary safety improvements, as well as foster cooperation among stakeholders and measure progress on the implementation of the GASP and the regional priorities, through the RASGs.

SAF 8 Enhanced, accessible and guided ICAO training in safety to Member States to achieve and maintain competency of aviation personnel in compliance with the ICAO Civil Aviation Training Policy

6.4.9. As mandated by Resolution A40-25, ICAO will guide and support the training and learning opportunities offered to States to ensure quality, standardization, accessibility, effectiveness, and efficiency of the deliverables. It will do so by developing learning activities in safety that support the implementation of SARPs and ICAO programmes using competency-based training, an ISD approach, and by leveraging on latest technologies and innovative approaches. ICAO will also support the implementation of human performance and talent management strategies through the of expansion strategic partnerships for training in safety.

SAF 9 Enhanced, accessible and efficient implementation of civil aviation technical assistance and cooperation projects and activities in safety

6.4.10. ICAO will guide and support Member States in undertaking projects and activities to build and strengthen their institutional capacities in full compliance with ICAO SARPs. Assistance will be enhanced by developing new implementation products and services aimed at comprehensively addressing States' evolving needs. Increased harmonization, relevance, and consistency in outputs will be ensured across all projects and activities. Furthermore, improved effectiveness and efficiency in planning and implementation will be achieved by leveraging technology, standardizing, and streamlining processes, and enhancing due diligence and risk management. The optimal allocation of resources facilitated by strengthened collaboration with Bureaux and Regional Offices will lead to greater accessibility, affordability and added value in ICAO's support.

7. Strategic Objective Air Navigation Capacity and Efficiency

7.1. Increase the capacity and improve the efficiency of the global civil aviation system

7.1.1. The crisis caused by the COVID-19 pandemic in 2020 highlighted the importance of resilience of the aviation system, not only as a performance requirement but also as a fundamental principle, in terms of economic sustainability. ICAO serves as a global forum that brings together the aviation community to define a common strategy for the evolution of the global air navigation system to improve capacity and efficiency within the Global Air Navigation Plan (GANP).

7.1.2. To support the evolution of the global air navigation system, ICAO develops new and enhanced existing global provisions. ICAO ensures the timely availability of its provisions through its technical air navigation work programme. ICAO also provides tools and identifies which stakeholders need to be involved in the implementation of operational improvements. At the regional level, ICAO coordinates the review and update of the Regional Air Navigation Plans. ICAO also coordinates the activities of the PIRGs to ensure their alignment with the GANP. At the national level, ICAO facilitates access to resources and technical assistance and promotes capacity-building in different areas of expertise. During 2023–2025, ICAO will:

a) look for innovative ways to develop new or improve existing provisions;
b) provide a framework to promote an air navigation system that contributes to environmental protection;
c) integrate innovation and provide access to all users to the air navigation system;
d) protect ITU frequency spectrum required for aeronautical services;
e) develop a trust framework to enable the evolution of the air aviation system, and
f) improve mechanisms to support implementation and leverage available expertise.

7.2. Priorities

7.2.1. In support of the air navigation capacity and efficiency Strategic Objective, the GANP performance ambitions, and the NCLB initiative, the ICAO key priorities are to:

a) improve the efficiency of the global air navigation system performance, while embracing and integrating new airspace entrants and new technology and innovation;
b) develop and maintain the global civil aviation regulatory framework, helping to underpin State and industry actions for continued growth and development of a safe, efficient and resilient global air navigation system within Member States' economic and sustainability expectations;

c) continue to prioritize standardization and implementation efforts as agreed by States and industry in the GANP; hold the trust and confidence of the global community to provide advice and lead the coordination, consultation and collaboration with all stakeholders in air navigation capacity and efficiency, focusing on timely standardization and harmonized, effective, scalable and affordable implementation for States and industry; enhance the regional cooperation; and narrow the gaps between States; and
d) ensure the organizational framework that will allow stakeholders to participate and contribute within the Standard making process to enhance the capability of ICAO to deliver targeted solutions for the improvement of air navigation capacity and efficiency.

7.3. Challenges, emerging needs and opportunities

7.3.1. The aviation industry is facing a variety of challenges. Air traffic is expected to continue to grow in the long-term and the sustainability and resilience of the system should be ensured. At the same time, new demands on the aviation system, emerging technologies, innovative ways of doing business and the shifting human role are bringing not only challenges but also opportunities that call for an urgent transformation of the global air navigation system so that aviation can continue to boost social well-being worldwide. During 2023–2025, ICAO will address the following challenges and transform them into opportunities:

a) accommodation of increasing demand and new types of demand;
b) use of advanced technologies;
c) human capability and capacity;
d) emerging, new and adapted business models; and
e) expectations of the aviation community.

7.4. Air Navigation Capacity and Efficiency Outputs

CAP 1 Enhanced Standards and Recommended Practices (SARPs) and development process to increase air navigation systems operational efficiency, interoperability, and harmonisation

7.4.1. Many States struggle in effectively implementing ICAO SARPs. The reason being insufficient understanding, insufficient necessary expertise or reduced access to new technologies that sometimes come with high costs for deployment without a clear benefit that depends on the level of maturity and/or development of the State implementing them. ICAO should improve the SARPs development process to provide a scalable approach to allow an expedited deployment of new technologies and concept of operations in different operational scenarios. Closer regional coordination will help the deployment at regional and national levels. In 2023–2025 ICAO will support the development of performance-based standards that can be applied by States with different levels of maturity and density of traffic.

CAP 2 Enhanced gateway for receiving, reviewing, progressing, and integrating innovation initiatives including new entrants, technology, and processes

7.4.2. New entrants are evolving at a very rapid pace and the numbers of such aircraft requesting access to airspace increases steadily. States need to implement new regulations, provide oversight, and determine the type and extent of new services needed to safely manage this part of aviation. This activity is separate and additional to facilitating access by RPA to non-segregated airspace. To ensure that ICAO decision makers have information related to innovations well ahead of the need to act on them at a policy level, ICAO needs to keep abreast of all innovations that have been identified to the Organization. Under this part of the programme, innovations will be assessed at high level and information will be forwarded to the GANP or GASP Study Groups. This output is complementary to the existing mechanisms in the GASP and GANP to identify innovations related to their respective areas.

CAP 3 Improved guidance for the quantification of potential environmental benefits attainable through the implementation of new

ICAO provisions

7.4.3. Every single technology or concept of operations available for implementation affects different key performance areas, including environment. Considering the importance of the environment key performance area in the global discussions, in 2023–2025 ICAO will focus on means to leverage regulatory frameworks and improved guidance on how to derive the environment benefits of new technology or concepts of operations being developed and implemented.

CAP 4 Protected ITU frequency spectrum required for aeronautical services

7.4.4. Frequency spectrum is a valuable and limited commodity, managed by States' Spectrum Regulatory Authorities through the ITU World Radio communication Conferences (WRC) process. This process culminates in the WRCs held every four years. Aviation uses approximately 15 per cent of the most valuable spectrum for the provision of safety critical CNS functions and is only one of many spectrum users, all of which participate in the WRC process on an equal footing. ICAO represents aviation interests, providing a common coordinated voice and agenda. Currently preparations are underway for WRC-23 (Nov-Dec 2023), which will be followed by WRC-27 (2027). Each four-year WRC cycle consists of the following main activities:

a) ICAO Position developed and approved by Council for the upcoming WRC;
b) support of technical studies and preparations in ITU-R; and
c) advocacy for ICAO Position and aviation requirements in preparatory activities and during WRC, to ensure favourable outcome with no negative impact on aviation.

CAP 5 Advanced development of an international aviation trust framework for air navigation services and infrastructure

7.4.5. As the aviation industry moves towards more automation, digitalization and IP connectivity, there is a need to reduce the vulnerabilities to cyber-attacks brought by operations in cyber space. This reduction can be done through the operation in a more controlled environment where all stakeholders are identified, and the messages exchanged can be trusted. For this to happen, a framework must be in place to guarantee the confidentiality, integrity and availability of the information while stored or in transit and the deployment of an international aviation trust framework aims to provide that environment. In 2023–2025, ICAO will provide:

a) a concept of operations;
b) an information security framework including information security provisions, a dedicated block of IPv6 addresses for aviation, an integrated approach to information security and safety; and
c) a dedicated certificate policy for the aviation community.

CAP 6 Increased access to air navigation implementation support that addresses States' prioritized needs

7.4.6. Implementation support refers to the ICAO actions in managing the programmes, projects and activities which support and assist the implementation efforts of States through the provision of products and services. Implementation support packages content and material generated as part of other air navigation capacity and efficiency (CAP) outputs, finds funding for those activities, distributes responsibilities among actors and ensures the support is provided to the States in need. This output ensures that:

a) a needs-based approach is adopted in the development and deployment of implementation support;
b) that deployment is adequately prioritized;
c) that a common methodology is used throughout all implementation support;
d) that support is coordinated; and
e) that there is financial transparency and accountability among all actors.

CAP 7 Enhanced efficiency and increased capacity at the regional level

7.4.7. The development of a seamless airspace and interoperable air navigation communications and management frameworks stem from regional and inter-regional collaboration and coordination. The Regional Offices leading role in promoting the integration of the planning efforts, in line with the global provisions, is key to ensure the implementation of the air navigation plans in an orderly manner, supporting the proper planning, investment and capacity building by States.

7.4.8. The Regional Offices will support States to enhance their capabilities to access, develop, implement, and use technologies in air navigation systems to meet current and future demands and provide assistance for the implementation of ICAO policies and provisions. Additionally, the Regional Offices will continue to lead and coordinate response to airspace crises and contingencies. Through support to the PIRGs, the Regional Offices will continue to monitor and report the status of implementation by States of the required air navigation facilities, services, and procedures, as well as of the GANP and the regional priorities, for the continuous, interoperable, and harmonized improvement of air navigation systems.

CAP 8 Enhanced, accessible and guided ICAO training in air navigation to Member States to achieve and maintain competency of aviation personnel in compliance with the ICAO Civil Aviation Training Policy

7.4.9. As mandated by Resolution A40-25, ICAO will guide and support the training and learning opportunities offered to States by ICAO to ensure quality, standardization, accessibility, effectiveness, and efficiency of the deliverables. It will do so by developing learning activities in Air Navigation Capacity and Efficiency that support the implementation of Standards and Recommended Practices (SARPs) and ICAO programmes using competency-based training, an ISD approach, and by leveraging on latest technologies and innovative approaches. ICAO will also support the implementation of human performance and talent management strategies through the of expansion strategic partnerships for training in Air Navigation Capacity and Efficiency.

CAP 9 Enhanced, accessible and efficient implementation of civil aviation technical assistance and cooperation projects and activities in air navigation

7.4.10. ICAO will guide and support Member States in undertaking projects and activities to build and strengthen their institutional capacities in full compliance with ICAO SARPs. Assistance will be enhanced by developing new implementation products and services aimed at comprehensively addressing States' evolving needs. Increased harmonization, relevance, and consistency in outputs will be ensured across all projects and activities. Furthermore, improved effectiveness and efficiency in planning and implementation will be achieved by leveraging technology, standardizing, and streamlining processes, and enhancing due diligence and risk management. The optimal allocation of resources facilitated by strengthened collaboration with Bureaux and Regional Offices will lead to greater accessibility, affordability and added value in ICAO's support.

8. Strategic Objective Security and Facilitation

8.1. Enhance global civil aviation security and facilitation

8.1.1. Although the global civil aviation system is more secure than ever, vulnerabilities and threats to civil aviation security, cybersecurity and border integrity persist, affecting States across all regions. Such challenges must be addressed through constant and proactive preventive efforts, including systematic collaboration, coordination and communication amongst States, industry, and international organizations. It is important to ensure that the implementation of both security and facilitation requirements be improved, thereby enabling air passenger and cargo traffic to grow in a secure, seamless, resilient, and efficient manner.

8.1.2. The goal of this Strategic Objective is to enhance civil aviation security and air transport facilitation worldwide by advancing the regulatory framework to meet evolving needs and by taking into account lessons learned from the COVID-19 pandemic while building on the outcomes of the High-level Conference on COVID-19 (HLCC 2021). This objective is achieved by a) minimizing the risk of unlawful interference with civil aviation and ensuring appropriate responses when incidents occur; b) minimizing border integrity risks; and c) maximizing efficiency in border clearance operations to promote trade, tourism, and economic development.

8.1.3. The delivery of the results with respect to this Strategic Objective will contribute to reducing the level of global aviation security, cybersecurity, and border integrity risks, facilitating movement of people and movement of goods by air, and enhancing the efficiency of the global civil aviation system.

8.2. Priorities

8.2.1. The continuous risk of unlawful interference with civil aviation, whether by attacking it or using it as a means of transportation, requires ICAO to increase its efforts to raise the profile of aviation security, including border and cybersecurity in States, through the UN System and the counter-terrorism community. Conversely, the seamless and contactless crossing of borders through enhanced facilitation Standards, mechanisms and tools needs to be further supported and promoted. ICAO will prioritize work as follows:

a) improve the quality of the Standard setting process to better help States develop effective and applicable regulations;
b) develop and coordinate the management of implementation and assistance programmes and plans (Traveler Identification Programme (TRIP) Strategy, Global Aviation Security Plan (GASeP), Cybersecurity Action Plan (CyAP), Public Key Directory (PKD)); and
c) secure the resources and improve the processes for the continuous monitoring and oversight of States' implementation of security-related standards.

8.3. Challenges, emerging needs and opportunities

8.3.1. The COVID-19 pandemic highlighted the disparities between the control measures and travel restrictions in place in the different regions and States. There is a need to develop a global and harmonized strategic approach in close coordination with the World Health Organization (WHO) to assure a safe, efficient, and secure staged return to normal air transport operations. The continuous risk of unlawful interference with civil aviation, whether by attacking it or using it as a means of transportation, requires ICAO to increase its efforts to raise the profile of aviation security, including border and cybersecurity in States, through its active role in the UN's Global Counter-Terrorism Coordination Compact and multilateral counter-terrorism efforts. Conversely, the seamless and contactless crossing of borders through enhanced facilitation Standards, mechanisms and tools needs to be further supported and promoted. ICAO will prioritize support to States in implementing the recommendations of the High-level Conference on COVID-19 (HLCC 2021), as approved by the Council, to ensure a quick recovery of the air transport system and its resilient development.

8.4. Security and Facilitation outputs

SECF 1 Enhanced policies including but not limited to Standards and Recommended Practices (SARPs) and guidance material aimed at improving civil aviation security, border management and cybersecurity while monitoring innovation in these areas.

8.4.1. Various attacks against civil aviation infrastructure across the globe, along with the continuous intent and growing capability of terrorist groups to exploit vulnerabilities in the system, prove that international civil aviation remains a prime target for a variety of motives. Safeguarding civil aviation against acts of unlawful interference requires measures that are proactive, yet flexible, and must be able to respond rapidly to new and emerging threats. These measures must be sustained over time, providing an acceptable level of security regardless of the threat environment. This output aims to help ensure that:

a) ICAO and its Member States ensure the development and implementation of risk-based measures to reflect the evolving threat picture;
b) innovation in the areas of aviation security and cybersecurity is carefully monitored and duly considered in the development and update of policies, standards, recommended practices and guidance material;
c) there is continued capacity for ICAO to support its deliberative bodies and expert groups in identifying threats, addressing, and navigating risks and reducing vulnerabilities by making every effort to create a sustainable aviation security system; and
d) a coordinated and comprehensive approach continues to be implemented for all elements of the aviation sector i.e., safety, air navigation, facilitation, and counterterrorism to benefit from shared knowledge, strengthened efforts and improved aviation security.

SECF 2 Enhanced capabilities of States to facilitate the movement of people and goods by air, and uniquely identify individuals, including through implementation of innovations, leading to improved efficiency in border management operations and increased resilience to future challenges

8.4.2. Efficient movement of people and goods by air requires effective national organization and harmonized adoption of best practices and technologies to facilitate cross-border processes. ICAO's facilitation activities involve the provision of a) regulatory material and guidance to ensure that national structures, facilities, and capabilities are appropriately established and maintained; b) development of technical specifications and guidance to drive adoption of aligned capabilities to effect more seamless travel; and c) the offering of implementation and capacity building support to ensure comprehensive global capability development. Together, this work allows States to adapt to changing circumstances over time and take advantage of new operational and technical innovations and developments while ensuring no country is left behind. In the period from 2023–2025, ICAO will focus on advancing its regulatory framework to meet evolving needs, particularly taking into account lessons learned from the COVID-19 pandemic and building on the outcomes of the High-level Conference on COVID-19, while taking advantage of innovations and advancing specifications and assistance to States to drive more seamless and contactless travel.

Appendix D. ICAO Business Plan 2023–2025

SECF 3 Enhanced Member States' aviation security oversight capabilities and compliance with Annex 17 Standards and security-related Standards of Annex 9 through the conduct of USAP-CMA Activities

8.4.3. The ICAO USAP-CMA is the only global programme that measures States' aviation security performance, including the sustainability of such systems and an indicative compliance with Annex 17 Standards and security-related Standards of Annex 9. This output aims to help improve the sustainability and effectiveness of the global aviation security system by:

a) enabling States to implement corrective actions in a timely manner to address identified deficiencies;
b) enabling the targeting of assistance activities and the functioning of regional and global programmes, such as the AFI SECFAL and GASeP, which rely on USAP data; and
c) creating sound policy based on the first-hand experience of USAP-CMA auditors.

8.4.4. For the 2023–2025 triennium, the intent is to increase the number of USAP-CMA activities ICAO can undertake, while maintaining the quality of audit reports and continuing to improve the audit methodology.

SECF 4 Strengthened ICAO's leadership and mandate in aviation security, cybersecurity and facilitation globally, in partnership with other UN bodies and international organizations

8.4.5. Within the framework of the United Nations Global Counter-Terrorism Strategy and relevant Security Council resolutions on counter-terrorism, ICAO will continue to collaborate with the United Nations Offices, Directorates and Specialized Agencies (and other international organizations) to fulfil the commitments defined in the UN Global Counter-Terrorism Strategy to further strengthen and enhance cooperation and information-sharing relating to border management, aviation security, and counter-terrorism. ICAO will also work with other UN and international organizations to develop comprehensive multi-dimensional frameworks to handle future crises in aviation, such as those related to health. ICAO – UN collaboration will include implementation of joint activities and collaborative preparation of documents and tools, leveraging of expertise and optimization of resources to maximize the quality of deliverables to Member States. Such activities are related to aviation security and facilitation, notably in relation to identity, and border control management as described in UN Security Council resolutions 1373 (2001), 1624 (2005), 2178 (2014), 2309 (2016), 2341 (2017), 2395 (2017), 2396 (2017) and 2482 (2019).

SECF 5 Increased access to civil aviation security and facilitation implementation support that addresses States' prioritised needs

8.4.6. Although the civil aviation system is more secure than ever, vulnerabilities and threats to aviation security and border integrity persist, affecting States across all regions. It is important to ensure that the implementation of security and facilitation requirements be improved, enabling passenger and cargo traffic to grow securely and efficiently. Such challenges must be addressed through active preventive efforts, including systematic collaboration, coordination and communication amongst States and industry. This output aims to enhance aviation security and facilitation worldwide by a) minimizing the risk of acts of unlawful interference while ensuring appropriate responses when incidents occur, b) minimizing border integrity risks and, c) maximizing efficiency in border control operations to promote the movement of people and goods by air. This output will deliver results through:

a) assistance and capacity-building projects and programmes;
b) training programmes;
c) regional programmes and partner collaboration; and
d) GASeP and TRIP Strategy implementation support activities

SECF 6 Strengthened security and facilitation of civil aviation at the regional level

8.4.7. The expected aviation recovery from the COVID-19 pandemic and increased air connectivity in the next years harness the challenges to manage and mitigate the security risks, without affecting the intrinsic swiftness of civil aviation. In this sense, the implementation of the security and facilitation measures demand the Regional Offices to liaise with various international, regional, and national entities to champion the collaboration among the stakeholders to ensure sustained political commitment and technical capacity for the States to implement the global requirements.

8.4.8. The Regional Offices will continue to support States to improve the effective implementation of the aviation security SARPs (validated through USAP-CMA), in a sustainable manner, keeping a balanced approach based on risk management and considering the growth of air passenger and cargo traffic. The Regional Offices will foster cooperation among stakeholders and measure progress on the implementation of the GASeP and the regional priorities, through the Regional AVSEC/FAL Groups. Additionally, the Regional Offices will coordinate with ICAO HQ for the provision of capacity-building activities and support the ICAO ASTCs in the delivery of AVSEC/FAL trainings.

SECF 7 Enhanced, accessible and guided ICAO training in security and facilitation to Member States to achieve and maintain competency of aviation personnel in compliance with the ICAO Civil Aviation Training Policy

8.4.9. As mandated by Resolution A40-25, ICAO will guide and support the training and learning opportunities offered to States by ICAO to ensure quality, standardization, accessibility, effectiveness, and efficiency of the deliverables. It will do so by developing learning activities in Security and Facilitation that support the implementation of SARPs and ICAO programmes using competency-based training, an ISD approach, and by leveraging on latest technologies and innovative approaches. ICAO will also support the implementation of human performance and talent management strategies through the of expansion strategic partnerships for training in Security and Facilitation.

SECF 8 Enhanced, accessible and efficient implementation of civil aviation technical assistance and cooperation projects and activities in security and facilitation

8.4.10. ICAO will guide and support Member States in undertaking projects and activities to build and strengthen their institutional capacities in full compliance with ICAO SARPs. Assistance will be enhanced by developing new implementation products and services aimed at comprehensively addressing States' evolving needs. Increased harmonization, relevance, and consistency in outputs will be ensured across all projects and activities. Furthermore, improved effectiveness and efficiency in planning and implementation will be achieved by leveraging technology, standardizing, and streamlining processes, and enhancing due diligence and risk management. The optimal allocation of resources facilitated by strengthened collaboration with the Bureaux and Regional Offices will lead to greater accessibility, affordability and added value in ICAO's support.

9. Strategic Objective Economic Development

9.1. Foster the development of a sound and economically viable civil aviation system

9.1.1. A sound and economically viable civil aviation provides the freedom to travel affordably, a fair and equal opportunity for States and air transport users to benefit financially, a business environment where firms can operate profitably and a basis for sustainable economic development globally. A post-COVID-19 recovery of national and international economies will rely on the recovery of aviation. As such, maximizing aviation's contribution to economies, uniting efforts among States and the international communities will be required beyond the civil aviation sector.

9.1.2. Removing impediments to economic sustainability of air transport and overcoming the low priority given to aviation in financing are the ultimate goals of this Strategic Objective. States can use aviation as an effective development tool by pursuing liberalization efforts and placing aviation in the centre of the national/regional development framework and international financing for development flows, resulting in a) improving air connectivity; b) creating more competitive business opportunities in the marketplace; c) increasing consumer's benefits and choices; and at the same time d) reducing financial burden and costs in performing their regulatory oversight functions. These efforts shall be underpinned by quality data, analysis and forecasting for data-driven decision-making, operational improvement and, to the extent possible, the prediction of the various aspects of civil aviation development.

9.1.3. The delivery of the results with respect to this Strategic Objective will be essential for the aviation system's recovery from the COVID-19 crisis, for building its resilience beyond the recovery and for contributing to the growth of civil aviation activities and the efficiency of the air transport, and hence to the global economy, and the expansion of trade and tourism.

9.2. Priorities

9.2.1. The ever changing nature of civil aviation necessitates that ICAO be prepared for any significant shifts that may occur in the future. States' long-term policy agendas, including: a) improving air connectivity; b) creating more competitive business opportunities in the marketplace; c) increasing consumers' benefits and choices; d) promoting increased use of aviation as a development tool; and, e) removing impediments to sustainability of air transport, require continuous, holistic and coordinated efforts by States and the international communities.

9.2.2. ICAO will prioritize its work as follows:

a) Develop and update air transport policy and guidance related to economic regulatory frameworks;
b) finalize a draft multilateral convention on foreign investment in airlines;
c) evaluate economic contribution and benefits of aviation by using refined methodologies;
d) collect, analyze and disseminate aviation data/statistics under the Enterprise Data Management (EDM) framework.
e) update long-term traffic forecasts and harmonize databases in support of aviation development, air navigation planning and environmental economics work;
f) implement and manage aviation-related big data solutions and conduct joint projects related to ICAO's big data, including business intelligence dashboards;
g) facilitate States' air services negotiations and provide an exchange forum for States and aviation stakeholders to reduce regulatory costs; and
h) provide support to States in the recovery from the COVID-19 crisis, including following up and implementing CART recommendations and

the HLCC Declaration, as well as raising awareness of ICAO's air transport policies and guidance and developing State/Regional Action Plans.

9.3. Challenges, emerging needs and opportunities

9.3.1. The COVID-19 pandemic has had a devastating economic impact on the aviation industry worldwide, risking its viability and financial sustainability. The potential deterioration in future economic viability of the sector could affect the balance of the aviation ecosystem, the repercussion of which might have far-reaching impact on broader economy at all levels. It is therefore of urgency for aviation stakeholders to take bold and immediate steps to bolster their financial position and mitigate the impact from the massive revenue shortfall. It is also equally important that States take appropriate actions to stabilize and support the beleaguered aviation industry so that aviation can continue its pivotal role in providing connectivity, driving national economy, and supporting jobs, and as an enabler in the overall economic recovery. In the context of the current crisis, the following challenges, needs and opportunities have been identified under the Strategic Objective of Economic Development:

a) **Leading the post-COVID-19 economic recovery of aviation.** In the aftermath of the COVID-19 pandemic, re-establishing the economic viability of air transport will be vital to deliver its socio-economic benefits in a sustainably and environmentally conscious manner. This will be achieved through the Strategic Objective's regulatory and analytical agenda as well as through the follow-up and implementation of CART recommendations and the Ministerial Declaration of the High-Level Conference on COVID-19 (HLCC).
b) **Digital transformation of air cargo:** Implementation of a cross-sector, integrated approach to the digitalization of air cargo and the global supply chain to increase the sector's speed, safety, security, and efficiency and to promote global trade and commerce.
c) **Aviation infrastructure/system financing:** Promotion of diversified funding and financing sources, through the elevation of a role of the private sector and the effective use of domestic resources and international development funding, to develop and modernize quality aviation infrastructure/system commensurate with the level of predicted traffic growth and based on ICAO's Global Plans
d) **Big data analytics for aviation:** Leveraging and unlocking the potential value of big data to improve safety and operational efficiency of aviation, allow States and the industry to make more informed decisions and policymaking, and strengthen the customer relationship and commitments.

9.4. ECONOMIC DEVELOPMENT OUTPUTS

DEV 1 Enhanced capabilities of States to improve air connectivity, to create competitive business environment, and to perform economic regulatory oversight functions

9.4.1. Pursuing the continuous liberalization of international air transport benefits all stakeholders and the economy at large by providing for sustainable air connectivity, effectively supporting trade and tourism, and creating significant opportunities for local citizens, businesses, and producers to access foreign markets in addition to creating a competitive business environment, in which consumers benefit from more and improved choices and protection. In the context of the COVID-19 pandemic and recovery from it, emphasis will be on the need to strike an appropriate balance among the respective interests without prejudice to fair competition and market access or compromising safety, security and environmental commitments.

9.4.2. This output aims to reinforce ICAO's cornerstone role in this area by building better understanding of the benefits and challenges of liberalization, enhancing exchange of information and States' practices, developing, and updating air transport policy and guidance related to air transport, finalizing of a draft multilateral convention on foreign investment in airlines, developing new guidance on air cargo and e-commerce and leading the cooperation with the international community in this field.

DEV 2 Strengthened leadership of ICAO for addressing subjects related to the development of a sound and economically viable aviation system including addressing the economic and regulatory aspects of innovation in aviation

9.4.3. The dynamic nature of civil aviation necessitates that ICAO be prepared for any significant changes that may occur to effectively support States and the civil aviation system in the development of sustainable air transport, aligned with national and regional policy objectives and the NCLB initiative. The significant pace and uptake of various innovative technologies and processes, as well as the extended pool of conventional and unconventional innovators, across the aviation ecosystem requires ICAO to keep pace with the progress, monitor the developments and establish globally harmonized approaches where and if applicable.

9.4.4. Furthermore, the attainment of the UN SDGs relies on advances in sustainable air transport, which is a driver of sustainable development. Many of the SDGs are directly and indirectly connected to sustainable air transport. This output aims to support States in the strategic development of air transport at national, regional, and global levels to enable the sector's socio-economic potential by safely and efficiently accommodating the recovery and eventual increase in air traffic demand and taking full advantage of innovative ideas and solutions. In this regard, ICAO will continue to work closely with the other international organizations to deliver and promote results of economic analyses on emerging issues of global importance and various aspects of air transport.

DEV 3 Enhanced capabilities of States to use aviation as an effective means to achieve economic development, in particular, increase accessibility to funding and financing for aviation infrastructure development and improvement of air connectivity

9.4.5. To maximize the benefits of aviation in the economy, the priorities of the aviation sector should be integrated and reflected in State's economic and social development planning with an appropriately balanced development of transport modes, including multi-modal and urban planning initiatives. In addition, States should support sustainable funding and take pragmatic measures to build a transparent, stable, and predictable investment climate for aviation infrastructure development, which in turn contributes to the socio-economic development. This output aims to promote aviation's socio-economic benefits, its cross-cutting nature, and multiple links to other economic sectors and to support the desired level of funding and financing for quality aviation infrastructure development and modernization, including through enhancing adherence to ICAO policies and guidance, engaging multi-stakeholders, diversifying funding sources and elevating the role of the private sector.

DEV 4 Enhanced capabilities of states to maximize the utility of aviation data/ statistics and long-term traffic forecasts

9.4.6. Comprehensive and reliable aviation data, analysis and forecasts are the basis for States and the industry to make well-informed decisions and align the regulatory and financing regimes with the projected growth of air traffic demand. These enable States to act proactively to avoid inefficiencies and impediments, reduce risks and uncertainty, monitor progress and performance, evaluate the return on investments, and promote financing for air transport development. Under this output, ICAO will continue its extensive work on aviation data and statistics, analysis tools, long-term traffic forecasts and harmonizing databases in support of aviation development, air navigation planning and environmental economics work. In addition, ICAO will continue its efforts in the development of methodologies and data sources for establishing a global aviation competitiveness index.

DEV 5 Enhanced skills of States to implement and manage aviation-related big data solutions and take stock of innovations in support of data-driven policies

9.4.7. Aviation is at the cusp of data transformation with velocity and quantity of data growing and new technologies evolving to analyze such data. In tandem with the pace of the industry development, States need to improve capabilities and capacity to manage the trove of information and use advanced analytics to reap the tremendous value through developing data-driven strategies. This output aims to guide States in addressing and adopting emerging technologies and solutions for the development of data-driven policies and strategies. By providing advanced business analysis tools, implementing, and managing aviation-related big data solutions and conducting related projects, including advanced COVID-19 analyses, ICAO will reinforce its position to assist and contribute to States' efforts.

DEV 6 Increased access to economic development implementation support that addresses states' prioritised needs

9.4.8. ICAO's support to States in the implementation of its policies and guidance is vital for the economic development and improvement of the air transport industry, including enhanced crises response readiness. This support could be in the form of creating awareness, organizing workshops/seminars and granting of States' access to information on ICAO compendia, in particular on consumer protection, competition rules and emergency response planning.

9.4.9. ICAO continues to serve a pivotal role in the promotion of air transport bilateral, plurilateral and multilateral relations through the use of the ICAO Air Services Negotiation events (ICAN) as well as information provided on the World Air Services Agreements (WASA) database, even as it continues its efforts in developing multilateral agreements on liberalization of air transport in line with the ICAO Long-term vision on international air transport liberalization (ATConf/6 refers). In addition, ICAO will continue to provide tools to enhance good governance and transparency of the air transport regulatory framework, contribute to the development of relevant courses and training material and assist States and other stakeholders in addressing other economic regulatory issues. Under this output, ICAO will reinforce its outreach and awareness-raising efforts to promote and assist States in the implementation of existing ICAO's policies and guidance, while working with States to remove regulatory constraints on international air transport.

DEV 7 Enhanced economic viability and resilience of civil aviation at the regional level

9.4.10. The Regional Offices, in close coordination with ICAO HQ, will continue to support the sustainable development of an economically viable civil aviation system and the liberalization of air transport, through the promotion of ICAO policies and guidelines. Moreover, the Regional Office will enhance their capabilities in supporting the States for all ICAO Strategic Objectives with the provision of business intelligence, facilitated by ICAO HQ.

DEV 8 Enhanced, accessible and guided ICAO training in the economic development of air transport to Member States to achieve and maintain competency of aviation personnel in compliance with the ICAO Civil Aviation Training Policy

9.4.11. As mandated by Resolution A40-25, ICAO will guide and support the training and learning opportunities offered to States by ICAO to ensure quality, standardization, accessibility, effectiveness, and efficiency of the deliverables. It will do so by developing learning activities in Economic Development that support the implementation of SARPs and ICAO programmes using competency-based training, an ISD approach, and by leveraging on latest technologies and innovative approaches. ICAO will also support the implementation of human performance and talent management strategies through the of expansion strategic partnerships for training in Economic Development.

DEV 9 Enhanced, accessible and efficient implementation of civil aviation technical assistance and cooperation projects and activities in the economic development of air transport

9.4.12. ICAO will guide and support Member States in undertaking projects and activities to build and strengthen their institutional capacities in full compliance with ICAO SARPs. Assistance will be enhanced by developing new implementation products and services aimed at comprehensively addressing States' evolving needs. Increased harmonization, relevance, and consistency in outputs will be ensured across all projects and activities. Furthermore, improved effectiveness and efficiency in planning and implementation will be achieved by leveraging technology, standardizing, and streamlining processes, and enhancing due diligence and risk management. The optimal allocation of resources facilitated by strengthened collaboration with the Bureaux and Regional Offices will lead to greater accessibility, affordability and added value in ICAO's support.

10. Strategic Objective Environmental Protection

10.1. Minimize the adverse environmental effects of civil aviation activities

10.1.1. In light of the COVID-19 pandemic and the climate crisis, and particularly with the latest scientific evidence from the Intergovernmental Panel on Climate Change (IPCC), rapid action is required now from all sectors to reduce anthropogenic CO2 emissions. Defining and monitoring the achievement of ambitious goals for aviation to contribute to addressing climate change is a priority. Ambitious means and processes to do that need to be put in place. For aviation, all stakeholders must take significant action and ensure that no country is left behind and it is crucial that ICAO maintains its leadership to address the climate impacts of international aviation.

10.2. Priorities

10.2.1. All aviation stakeholders must take significant action and it is crucial that ICAO maintains its leadership in the development and implementation of globally harmonized policies and frameworks, SARPs and guidance to address the climate impacts of international aviation. Innovations will play a crucial part in building green transition pathways for a resilient international aviation sector, and progress will be closely monitored toward the achievement of global aspirational goals. ICAO will prioritize work as follows:

a) monitor environment-driven innovations and take stock of CO_2 emissions reduction;
b) develop and update the ICAO policies, legal frameworks, SARPs and guidance to facilitate the innovative solutions for aircraft technologies, operational improvements, sustainable fuels and clean energy sources, toward realization of collective aspirational goals by States;
c) ensure the continued implementation of the Carbon Offsetting and Reduction Scheme for International Aviation (CORSIA);
d) encourage and support States to develop, regularly update, and implement their State action plans and roadmaps on aviation CO2 emissions reduction, in light of new green innovations and ICAO global aspirational goals;
e) address other important and emerging areas, such as climate adaptation and infrastructure resilience, as well as recycling and circular economy; and
f) enhance leadership of ICAO for addressing all aviation environmental issues.

10.3. Challenges, emerging needs & opportunities

10.3.1. Environment is a fast-evolving subject in terms of new emerging areas and innovations (from noise to local air quality to climate change, and clean energy and climate adaptation), which provides challenges but also opportunities for ICAO, subject to available resources, to keep pace of progress and establish globally harmonized approaches. While the COVID-19 pandemic significantly impacted aviation, the pandemic also provided opportunities to consider the means for building back better for green transition, taking on board the latest environmental innovations (e.g., certification of new green technologies), developing pathways that guide the sector to a decarbonized future, and creating solid grounds for investments and facilitating access to green funding.

10.3.2. Further opportunity also exists to strengthen ICAO leadership, for example, by increasing States' voluntarily participation in CORSIA (88 States in 2021, and 107 States in 2022) and robust CORSIA implementation by all States, as well as enhancing State Action Plans to reduce aviation CO_2 emissions by facilitating States' access to green finance, feasibility studies and technology transfer. Various emerging and evolving areas are significant challenges, such as for the Long-term Aspirational Goal (LTAG), State Action Plans (SAP), ENV Tools, CORSIA Capacity Building, and Climate Adaptation.

10.4. Environmental protection outputs

ENV 1 Advanced ICAO policies, legal frameworks, SARPs and guidance for implementation of innovative solutions, toward realization of collective aspirational goals by States

10.4.1. To facilitate the realization of collective aspirational goals by States and subject to the outcomes of the 41st Session of the Assembly on environment-related policies, ICAO will undertake various activities, for example, studies and development of necessary ENV-related policies, SARPs and guidance, for new innovative green technologies, such as evolutionary and revolutionary aircraft technologies. As per the CAAF/2 outcome, the 2050 ICAO Vision for Sustainable Aviation Fuels (SAF) will be elaborated through the stocktaking process and convening of CAAF/3 Conference, with quantified 2050 goals and relevant ICAO policies and guidance to facilitate SAF development and deployment by States. ENV assistance projects in partnerships with external organizations will be established to facilitate financing for the implementation of specific aviation CO_2 reduction measures, in particular clean energy/SAF, as well as provide capacity-building activities and tools for States. It is also crucial to maintain and enhance ICAO tools, such as ICAO Carbon Emissions Calculator and other tools (e.g., IFSET, EBT, CERT) to respond to the needs of States and public, including enhancing transparency on environmental performance, and develop new tools, as necessary. ICAO will continue to update SARPs, and guidance related to Aircraft Noise, Local Air Quality and Aircraft CO_2 (Annex 16, Volumes I, II, III and Environmental Technical Manual, Volumes I, II, III, etc.).

ENV 2 Enhanced monitoring of environment-driven innovations and taking stock of CO_2 reduction information

10.4.2. It is important for ICAO to enhance the monitoring of the global progress on the achievement of climate aspirational goals, including through the development of integrated ICAO monitoring tools for environment-driven innovations on aviation technologies, operations, and fuels, as well as through annual ICAO stocktaking events to collect data on aviation CO_2 reduction information from environment-driven innovations and on the pace by which it is being implemented. Such monitoring activities will also be supported by the assessment on the contributions of submitted State Action Plans on aviation CO_2 reduction activities, as well as the following-up and review of scientific aspects of aviation's contribution to the global climate (e.g., IPCC). Developing and implementing relevant policies that incentivize and scale-up action for addressing CO_2 emissions from international aviation and facilitating a level playing field to access energy and green funding are crucial to achieve the climate objectives. The Secretariat will also provide support to the relevant technical work of CAEP, and regular updates to the Council and its standing bodies related to the assessment of ICAO global aspirational goals.

ENV 3 Active implementation of the Carbon Offsetting and Reduction Scheme for International Aviation (CORSIA)

10.4.3. Advancing the robust implementation of CORSIA, with active engagement of Member States, is crucial to maintain the continued leadership of ICAO on climate change, including the implementation of additional features of the CORSIA Monitoring, Reporting and Verification (MRV) requirements, as well as the support to encourage increasing the number of States that participate in CORSIA on a voluntary basis. ICAO will update SARPs, and guidance related to CORSIA (Annex 16, Volume IV and Environmental Technical Manual, Volume IV), and relevant CORSIA implementation elements such as the CORSIA CO_2 Estimation and Reporting Tool (CERT) and CORSIA eligible fuels, and CORSIA eligible emissions units, including support to CAEP and TAB. ICAO will also maintain and update the CORSIA Central Registry (CCR), and compile data submitted by States and publish necessary information. In addition, the Secretariat will continuously monitor the implementation and assess the economic impacts and environmental benefits of the Scheme, with a view to supporting any subsequent review of the Scheme, as necessary. Continued support to States will be provided for advancing the robust implementation of CORSIA such as for the reporting of additional information on CORSIA eligible fuels and emissions units, through ICAO ACT-CORSIA (Assistance, Capacity-building, and Training for CORSIA) programme, including buddy partnerships among States, training seminars, outreach materials, CORSIA website update.

ENV 4 Increased focus on other important and emerging environmental areas such as climate change adaptation and infrastructure resilience

10.4.4. To address emerging environment areas, such as climate change adaptation, ICAO will facilitate the exchange of best practices for aviation climate change adaptation measures implemented by States, such as seminars and workshops, in cooperation with other UN bodies and international organizations.

10.4.5. ICAO will develop necessary guidance for States for the development and implementation of climate change adaptation measures to aviation operations and infrastructure resilience, including support to CAEP work. ENV assistance projects in partnerships with external organizations will be established to facilitate capacity building and financing for the implementation of specific aviation climate adaptation measures by States. ICAO will also undertake studies and develop necessary guidance on other ENV-related emerging areas, such as circular economy, environment management practices, and carbon capture and storage (CCS).

ENV 5 Enhanced leadership of ICAO for addressing all aviation environmental issues

10.4.6. To enhance leadership of ICAO in addressing all aviation environmental issues, ICAO will actively develop and disseminate material on its activities and achievements on environment (e.g., environment reports, newsletters, symposia, and seminars) to Member States, aviation industry, civil society, and youth representatives. ICAO will also closely follow-up and provide input to the UNFCCC process, including statements, submissions, and side events, on issues relevant to international aviation (e.g., climate goals, CORSIA, State Action Plans, climate finance), as well as enhance cooperation with other relevant UN bodies and international organizations, including the provision of ICAO input to their conferences and events.

ICAO will also manage and coordinate its contribution to UN-wide environmental initiatives and groups (e.g., UN Climate Summits, UN Environment Management Group, UN Climate Neutral Initiative) including the use of ICAO Carbon Calculator and other tools.

ENV 6 Enhanced support to development, update and implementation of State Action Plans and roadmaps, in light of new green innovations and ICAO global aspirational goals

10.4.7. ICAO will provide enhanced support for the development, update, and implementation of State Action Plans (SAP), including the update of relevant ICAO guidance, tools, and website, as well as through seminars and exchange of best practices to support the SAP development and update to include new green innovations and roadmaps. ENV assistance projects in partnerships with external organizations will be established to facilitate financing for the implementation of specific aviation CO_2 reduction measures, as well as to provide capacity-building activities and tools for States. Assessment of the submitted State Action Plans on aviation CO_2 reduction activities, will also support the monitoring of environment-driven innovations and the achievement of ICAO's global aspirational goals.

ENV 7 Strengthened environmental sustainability of civil aviation at the regional level

10.4.8. The sustainable growth of the aviation system in the Regions is increasingly dependent on the adoption of environmentally sound measures by the States to meet global agreements and national commitments. The outcome of the 41st Assembly to meet the global needs will demand a coordinated and effective action by ICAO to engage the States in political and technical levels.

10.4.9. The Regional Offices, in close coordination with ICAO HQ, will identify States' needs for the implementation of ICAO provisions and policies related to Environment and facilitate the provision of required capacity-building activities, including for supporting States to voluntarily join CORSIA in its first Phases. In addition, the Regional Offices will support States to implement the CORSIA and other future requirements, as well as engage them in the process of development and update of their State Action Plans on CO_2 emissions reduction, and implementation of their selected mitigation measures.

ENV 8 Enhanced, accessible and guided ICAO training in environmental protection to Member States to achieve and maintain competency of aviation personnel in compliance with the ICAO Civil Aviation Training Policy

10.4.10. As mandated by Resolution A40-25, ICAO will guide and support the training and learning opportunities offered to States by ICAO to ensure quality, standardization, accessibility, effectiveness, and efficiency of the deliverables. It will do so by developing learning activities in Environmental Protection that support the implementation of SARPs and ICAO programmes using competency-based training, an ISD approach, and by leveraging on latest technologies and innovative approaches. ICAO will also support the implementation of human performance and talent management strategies through the of expansion strategic partnerships for training in Environmental Protection.

ENV 9 Enhanced, accessible and efficient implementation of civil aviation technical assistance and cooperation projects and activities in environmental protection

10.4.11. ICAO will guide and support Member States in undertaking projects and activities to build and strengthen their institutional capacities in full compliance with ICAO SARPs. Assistance will be enhanced by developing new implementation products and services aimed at comprehensively addressing States' evolving needs. Increased harmonization, relevance, and consistency in outputs will be ensured across all projects and activities. Furthermore, improved effectiveness and efficiency in planning and implementation will be achieved by leveraging technology, standardizing, and streamlining processes, and enhancing due diligence and risk management. The optimal allocation of resources facilitated by strengthened collaboration with the Bureaux and Regional Offices will lead to greater accessibility, affordability and added value in ICAO's support.

11. Supporting Strategies

11.1. Description

11.1.1. Developed alongside the Strategic Objectives and the transformational objectives, the supporting strategies reinforce the desired sequence to achieve the overall goals and programmes of the organization for the years 2023, 2024, and 2025.

11.1.2. The supporting strategies establish the specific contributions of the organizational enablers towards accelerating the progress of the high-level priorities of ICAO.

11.1.3. The supporting strategies are change-driven and highlight how the Organization will transform its business delivery and governance with a focus on operational responsiveness, transparency, accountability, versatility, efficiency, and resilience in varied settings.

11.1.4. Implementing the supporting strategies entails a robust results based framework, results based budgeting and risk management while keeping attuned to evolving threats, trends, and opportunities.

11.1.5. The supporting strategies afford the Organization better, more coordinated, and strengthened functioning of various operational components of the Organization, including efficiency and accountability of systems, internal policies, and procedures with a purpose to achieve innovation, and to make new or improved solutions possible.

11.1.6. The implementation of supporting strategies advocates increased alignment of programmes and resources with the best practices in the industry, and the United Nations System of Organizations. Building on the lessons learned and emerging needs, the supporting strategies foster inclusive, up-to-date, and positive changes in cross-cutting administrative areas of operation of the Organization including, human resources management, ICT and information security management, language and conference services, security and building management, etc.

11.1.7. With the engagement of all relevant stakeholders in implementing the activities established under each supporting strategy, the Organization is expected to be on track in achieving the desired outcomes and to the greater extent, the impacts of its high-level and programmatic priorities, accompanied by tangible results such as innovations, new business models, integrated systems, and refined and modern policies.

11.2. Challenges, emerging needs and opportunities

11.2.1. Several factors may negatively impact the implementation of the supporting strategies. Based on the ongoing COVID-19 situation, it is evident that the sudden occurrence of a global crisis can require drastic changes in priorities and business delivery. Additional investments may be required in addition to the resources that have been made available. Required skills may change which may entail the acquisition of new skills or diversifying existing knowledge and capabilities.

11.2.2. Regular assessment of internal policies, procedures, and systems will be crucial to ensure up-to-date applicability and alignment with emerging trends and needs.

11.2.3. It is also imperative for the Organization to continue to take stock of experiences, lessons learned and the emergence of potential opportunities brought by unforeseen crises and uncertainty. Work structure and priorities may need to be modified or further strengthened taking into account, among other things, staff turnover due to resignations and other reasons of separation from service, and building on emerging concepts and approaches, systems, and tools in business delivery. Through the supporting strategies, the Organization is reassured of continued resilience and to be fully equipped to address any crisis and uncertainty.

Appendix D. ICAO Business Plan 2023–2025

11.3. Supporting Strategies outputs

SS 1 Enhanced common legal framework, governance, and harmonious international relations on the basis of the rule of law

11.3.1. LEB is the vanguard of the legal work of the Organization, fostering the rule of law in international civil aviation and providing full-range legal advisory and legal resource services to ICAO's Governing Bodies, the President of the Council, the Secretary General, other Bureaus, and offices, as well as Member States. LEB also carries out ICAO treaty depositary functions and has been recently tasked with managing the appointment process for the external auditor. Additionally, LEB manages the processes for the system of internal administration of justice and performs external relations and protocol functions to maintain effective and harmonious relations with the Host Government and Member States. LEB is also responsible for providing comprehensive Secretariat services required for the administration of formal settlement of differences pursuant to Article 84 of the Chicago Convention, which when compared to historical data, are in increasingly greater demand. Focus areas in the next triennium are anticipated to include emerging technologies, interdisciplinary endeavors in the fields of cyber-security, data, automated mobility and space travel, and subject matter support for other ICAO policy priorities; settlement of disputes between Member States; and modernization of LEB's document management system.

11.3.2. However, the anticipated impact of inadequate staffing levels (officers, consultancy capacity, administrative support staff), not only to various emerging and evolving areas, but to LEB's core activities as well as its supporting activities across the Organization, is significant. The situation will further be exacerbated by increased demands with respect to the system of the internal administration of justice, which will remain seriously underfunded despite being a top priority item necessary for good governance. The foregoing situation may risk ICAO's work and reputation, and impact LEB's response and support to the Secretariat, Council and the Member States.

SS 2 Efficient, effective, transparent, and responsive administration services provided to the Secretariat, which facilitate the implementation of the Strategic Objectives

11.3.3. Areas of work under administration services are considered organizational enablers for the Organization from human resources, language services, ICT and information security, conference and general services, business continuity and security, revenue, and product management, to providing support and strategic advice on management issues to ICAO governing bodies as well as to the Secretary General. Administration services are also crucial in leading operational committees of the Organization. Successful delivery of well-defined administration services is key to the implementation of the Strategic Objectives.

SS 3 Efficient and effective management of Secretariat services provided to the ICAO governing bodies, including support to the presiding officer of the Council, which facilitate discussion and decisions relating to the implementation of the Strategic Objectives

11.3.4. The Assembly and Council Secretariat provides substantive, procedural and logistical support that is essential to the smooth functioning of the meetings of the governing bodies, including the Assembly and the Council. A robust performance in this area of work is vital since it contributes to meeting the expectations of the Member States in the expeditious preparation and dissemination of documentation for the sessions of the governing bodies, such as the summaries of decisions (C-DECs) and summary records of the meetings (C-MINs), as well as the Assembly Resolutions in Force.

SS 4 Improved staff recruitment results orientation, continuous learning, transparency, and accountability as well as gender equality and equitable geographical representation

11.3.5. This output is focused on Human Resources Management. It covers the development of a modern human resources strategy as well as implementation of innovative HR practices, in order to enable the Organization to attract and retain a competent and diverse workforce, with the highest level of integrity, which are required to implement ICAO Strategic Objectives. Human Resources Management encourages staff development and facilitates the acquisition of new skills and competencies, develops the necessary policies and tools to improve transparency, accountability and performance management, which contribute to building a results-oriented culture. Human Resources Management also supports the implementation of the Organization's strategy on gender equality and equitable geographical representation through better workforce planning.

SS 5 Efficient and timely provision of quality language and publication services in the six ICAO languages, as part of a comprehensive Multilingualism Strategy, which facilitates seamless international dialogue and communication on civil aviation matters, as well as the implementation of SARPs in all Member States

11.3.6. The efficient and timely provision of quality language and publication services in the six UN/ICAO languages, through the implementation of a comprehensive Multilingualism Strategy, is key to facilitate seamless international dialogue and communication on civil aviation matters, underpinning the provision of quality language services, effective communication in all six official languages, and mobilization and partnerships. Under the Language Services Management System (LSMS) Project, the use of UN best practices and innovative technologies (computer-assisted translation tools and artificial intelligence) will play a major role in this endeavour.

11.3.7. The Multilingualism Strategy will cover the areas listed below. In coordination with all stakeholders, the Secretariat will prepare an action plan for the implementation of the Strategy.

a) **Provision of language services:** This output ensures simultaneous interpretation for all approved meetings, as well as the timely delivery of quality documentation and publications in support of ICAO Strategic Objectives.
b) **Human resources:** Taking full advantage of and promoting the language skills of the Secretariat staff.
c) **Communication:** Enhancing communication between ICAO and the rest of the world in all official languages.
d) **Mobilization:** Promoting multilingualism as a universal value, including through partnerships.
e) **Organizational responsibility:** Through coordination between Secretariat, Council and Member States. Budget-wise, this would require action to streamline documentation, gain efficiencies and make language services less resource-intensive.

SS 6 Efficient and effective conference and general services solutions available which are leveraging on emerging tools, trends, and technologies, supporting security and safety, business continuity and inclusion and greater participation of the Member States and civil aviation community

11.3.8. Events and meetings are at the core of ICAO's mandate. Meetings are the key to bringing together ICAO stakeholders, from experts to government decision makers. The focus will be on conference and general services solutions that leverage trends and technologies that support security, business continuity, in particular the experience drawn from the COVID-19 pandemic.

SS 7 Improved use of oversight findings and recommendations for enhanced governance, organizational learning, programme improvement and accountability

11.3.9. In line with its mandate, OIO will continue providing independent and objective assurance, advice, insight, and foresight through performing internal audits, evaluations, and other oversight assignments to the Secretary General and the Council. In this regard, OIO will assess and contribute to the improvement of governance, risk management, and control processes;

and to the improvement of programme management and achievement of results, using a systematic and disciplined approach. In the triennium, OIO will conduct 18 audits and 6 evaluations. To ensure the quality and usefulness of its oversight reports, OIO will comply with IPPF and UNEG standards; use oversight manuals/ guidelines and implement External Quality Assessment (EQA) and Peer Review Recommendations. To improve the use of its oversight works, OIO will follow up the implementation of oversight recommendations, organize regular discussions with stakeholders and build the capacity of relevant staff and stakeholders, as necessary.

SS 8 Optimized management of the financial resources of the Organization through provision of financial and accounting services, transparent budgeting and enhanced financial reporting.

11.3.10. The Finance Branch plays a key role in the custody and oversight over the appropriate use of financial resources, and the strengthening of ongoing compliance with the International Public Sector Accounting Standards (IPSAS). It has a portfolio of focus areas including but not limited to budget and financial management, provision of accounting services, development of financial-related policies and guidelines, statutory and specialized financial reporting, processing and control of transactions and provision of advice, operational guidance, and support to other Bureaus/(Regional) Offices on key budget and financial management areas.

SS 9 Enhanced procurement services provided effectively and efficiently to all operations of the Organization in order to achieve best value for money in a fair and transparent manner.

11.3.11. The Organization will undertake activities that will reinforce efforts on strict adherence to the ICAO Procurement Code as well as with ICAO's Financial Rules and Regulations. Proactive collaboration with the allotment holders to implement the Individual Procurement Plan (IPP) for all the significant procurement will be carried out to bolster the discipline of early planning of procurement activities. ICAO's solicitation documents will be harmonized with the best practices in the United Nations System, specifically in sustainability aspects. ICAO will also advocate further collaboration with other UN organizations through the use of common long term Agreements and/or joint procurement, amongst others. This will strengthen ICAO's cooperation under the concept of 'Delivering as One' and other UN reform initiatives, which have accelerated efforts among UN entities to collaborate and cooperate on Supply Chain Management, including procurement. ICAO will also reinforce vendor performance monitoring to ensure ICAO suppliers always strive to provide the highest quality of services.

SS 10 Increased engagement with sector and global audiences

11.3.12. ICAO will continue to adopt and leverage new technologies and capacities to increase public knowledge and appreciation of ICAO's role, to diversify the content offerings, and to grow its social media and digital platform audiences continuously. It will also actively seek out partnerships among other UN agencies, industry groups, and local global civil society stakeholders whenever ICAO messaging priorities may benefit from their joint efforts and participation. The ICAO brand will continue to be effectively promoted and aligned among internal and external stakeholders and will be up for a ten-year review and update during this triennium. News products will promptly and professionally announce all applicable ICAO achievements, official statements, and updates, subject to the continuing authority of the Secretary General and Council President and supported by continuous media monitoring and effective media support and relations.

SS 11 Coordinated cross-organizational efforts to support governing bodies and OSG and advance innovation, gender equality, and aviation as an enabler of the SDGS, as well as facilitate contributions to UN and stakeholders' reports, documents, guidelines, policies and frameworks

11.3.13. Organization-wide coordination is inherent to Strategic Planning, Coordination and Partnerships (SPCP) Office's accountabilities as it directly supports the Office of the Secretary General on a variety of topics. The Office facilitates the organization and functioning of the Committee of Governance, the Council Small Group on Innovation as well the Small Group on Gender, which requires the management and oversight of different actions and appropriate cross-organizational contributions. This coordination is essential to support efficient Council procedures and decision-making. SPCP is also pro-active in organizing action and bringing cohesive, well-consulted inputs together into various products and tools to drive the Organization's accountabilities on innovation as well as gender equality which are of paramount importance. The Organization will also ensure that in line with the UN Gender Parity Strategy, a multi-pronged approach in reaching gender parity is applied, including in the areas of leadership and accountability, senior management, recruitment and retention, and creating an enabling environment. The multi-pronged approach will be geared towards a realistic gradual annual uptake in numbers. Furthermore, the Office coordinates ICAO-wide efforts to ideally position ICAO and aviation into discussions with the UN and stakeholders and related products and reports in support of the SDGs, and other UN-led global mechanisms, agendas, and frameworks.

SS 12 Optimised governance, management, and performance of the Secretariat to contribute to ICAO's Vision, Mission, and Strategic Objectives

11.3.14. The OSG is responsible for the efficient and effective management of the Secretariat. The OSG will safeguard and promote the good reputation of ICAO through the delivery of high-quality services and products in the interest of the international aviation community. The OSG will promote an organizational culture of transparency, integrity, and accountability. OSG shall promote a change management culture with the objective of modernizing the working methods of the Organization to keep pace with innovation. OSG is responsible for the general direction of the work of the Secretariat. OSG is responsible for developing and updating the Organization's Business Plan and preparing budget proposals, for implementing the work programme, and ensuring the efficient, transparent, and effective use of financial resources of the Organization. OSG will search for efficiencies within the Secretariat under the transformational objectives.

SS 13 Achieved revenue generation targets defined in annual ARGF budget and operating plan and protected the intellectual property of the Organization

11.3.15. The Revenue and Product Management Section manages the Ancillary Revenue Generation Fund (ARGF).The financial contribution of the ARGF to the Regular Budget is met by revenue-generating products and services that develop and promote intellectual property, support Strategic Objectives, and generate revenues. In addition, affordable and timely print services are provided to programme activities and aviation stakeholders.

SS 14 Enhanced promotion and improvement of ethics principles and values

11.3.16. In accordance with its independent mandate, the Ethics Office will be responsible for providing counsel and confidential advice on ethics related matters to senior leadership and staff. The Ethics Office will also assist the Secretary General and the Council in nurturing a culture of ethics and accountability by providing guidance to reflect ethical considerations in policies, practices, and processes as well as through the promotion and enhancement of ethical awareness and a 'speak up' culture through training and general outreach activities. This would assist in the prevention and early resolution of potential or actual conflicts among staff. At the same time, it will enable all ICAO personnel (regardless of contract type and duration) to be properly informed about the expected behaviour to abide by the highest standard of conduct, including with reference to conflicts of interest, and to come forward without fear of retaliation.

SS 15 Enhanced ICT services that are aligned with the industry and UN best practices

11.3.17. Information technology plays a vital role in all aspects of the Organization's work. To meet its organizational objectives, ICAO must undertake fundamental ICT operations and projects, with impacts ranging from increased productivity and efficiency to lower operating costs. ICT plans for the Triennium and beyond, that its services reflect digitalization initiatives and objectives for all identified business capabilities of the Organization. ICT has evolved continuously and is adapting its operations to accommodate the coming seismic shifts in ICT service delivery, technology, solution sourcing and the positioning of ICT as a partner for sustainable growth within the Organization.

12. Transformational Objective

12.1. Description

12.1.1. ICAO's Strategic Objectives continue to embody the main outcomes that address the priorities of the civil aviation system. However, to continue to deliver this mandate, there is a preeminent necessity for ICAO to drive a number of corporate change management and innovation initiatives to obtain efficiency gains in the Organization to manage its processes and resources.

12.1.2. It has become evident that to implement reforms and to make ICAO fit-for-purpose requires focused attention and dedicated resources. It is for this reason that a new corporate transformational objective is included in the Business Plan to support those reform activities and to account for the shifts needed to evolve towards efficient internal working methods, strengthened accountability, and increased transparency.

12.1.3. In this sense, the Transformational Objective forms a supplement to the Supporting Strategies that identifies a number of high priority items that are change enablers promoting the improvements in the Organization, focusing on its planning and management methods, providing transformation in organizational culture, the provision of reliable and secure technological systems, and the engagement and development of its human talent and outreach to partners and donors. The outputs for the Transformational Objective take into consideration the mandate of the Council to the Secretariat, audit recommendations, staff surveys and the risk registry, as well as the priorities identified by the Bureaux and Regional Offices of ICAO.

12.1.4. The Transformational Objective will demand organization-wide involvement that will only be successful with the proper allocation of resources and the engagement of all Bureaux and Regional Offices.

12.2. Priorities

12.2.1. The Transformational Objective includes the following priorities:

a) improved organizational culture and performance by implementing a results-oriented Human Resources Strategy including improved internal communications to support a culture of trust, teamwork and outstanding performance;
b) strengthened adherence and compliance by staff to ethics principles and values taking in due consideration of best practices of other organization of the United Nations system;
c) improved ICT Strategy and Services;
d) strengthened information security systems;
e) improved financial management mechanisms; and
f) good management implemented through robust RBM, strategic planning, ERM, a sound accountability framework, efficient and effective programme management, an adequate organizational structure, as well as enhanced partnerships and resource mobilization efforts.

12.3. Challenges, emerging needs and opportunities

12.3.1. The necessary involvement of the various Bureaux and Regional Offices in the implementation of the activities related to the Transformational Objective will be concurrent to the current demands placed on the human and financial resources available, which are focused on accomplishing the core activities set by the Strategic Objectives. The managerial and resource allocation challenges call for adaptation and training of human talent, improvement and enhancement of processes and activities, engagement in partnerships that can enhance the Organization's capacity, among other actions.

12.3.2. The emerging issues and new technologies will continue to affect the way the aviation system carries out its operations, the areas of expertise of the personnel involved, the investment priorities in its infrastructure and ultimately how the civil aviation authorities have to update their regulations and processes to timely address and respond to the evolving industry needs. In this regard, ICAO should establish means to support the States and respond to the sector's development, promoting an organization-wide transformation to expedite and improve the development of Standards and guidelines, and to provide assistance.

12.3.3. The main opportunities arise from the interactions and shared experiences of its Member States, industry partners and from other UN and international entities, as well as leveraging from the inputs provided by the various backgrounds and experience of the Organization's team members. In this sense, as the culture of any organization is the result of the interaction of its members, ICAO must ensure that diversity is one of its key strengths and not an element of dissention. This opportunity emerges as long as the Organization provides a healthy and safe work environment, where the individual and shared responsibilities are clear and a strong and reliable accountability and performance framework are in place.

12.4. Transformational Objective outputs

TO 1 A comprehensive Human Resources strategy implemented which improves organizational culture and performance

12.4.1. The ICAO People Strategy is multi-faceted and depends on the concerted effort of human resources, staff and managers to collaborate or lead on matters of performance management, building capacity and skills and workforce planning.

12.4.2. Through periodic staff engagement, the Secretariat can identify opportunities to enhance the efficiency and effectiveness of the Organization. Staff engagement can be measured through the Global Engagement Survey, with particular emphasis on the Key Factors for Engagement as a set of ten of the most important factors associated with engagement capturing staff perceptions of their commitment to the goals and values of the Organization and motivation to contribute to its success.

12.4.3. Building of capacity, skills and effective workforce planning should be complemented by career development support programmes that establish, maintain and update competency frameworks, as well as develop skills inventory and mapping to fill gaps and prepare staff for future opportunities and address evolving workforce needs.

12.4.4. Establishment of a periodic Global Staff Engagement Survey, as well as a career development support programme rely on the availability of additional funds and resources, as well as the acquisition of technological platforms to strengthen partnerships between Human Resources and key stake holders throughout the Organization.

12.4.5. An internal communication strategy and a roll-out programme to keep staff informed and engaged and to equip managers and personnel with skills and tools to build a culture of trust, teamwork and high performance will be developed.

TO 2 Strengthened adherence and compliance by staff to ethics principles and values taking in due consideration best practices of other organizations of the United Nations System

12.4.6. With an objective to address the need to strengthen and streamline the programme of activities of ICAO relating to ethics principles and values, this Transformational Objective output will accelerate the efforts of the Organization by initiating a set of changes and undertakings using existing and additional resources. The Organization will invest to improve coordination, strengthen the cooperation and harmonize the activities of all relevant actors in ICAO who play a key role in upholding ethics principles and values in ICAO. The Organization and its personnel will benefit considerably in a stronger informal conflict resolutions mechanisms in order to allow early solution of work-related dispute, including through access to different sources of support and guidance such as the Ombudsperson, the Ethics Office, designating Respectful Workplace Advisors/Ethical Ambassadors, and staff counselling services.

12.4.7. ICAO will also take stock on the progress of implementation of activities relating to handling of allegations of misconduct, including the efficiency of the services of the investigative entity to ICAO as well as the effectiveness of a revitalized procedural framework outlined in the Rules of Procedures for the Appeals Board.

12.4.8. This Transformational Objective is bolstered by a robust communication and training strategy to support the implementation of a plan of training and outreach activities to promote staff understanding and application of the necessary values, actions and personal characteristics to uphold the ethics principles and values of the Organization, including strict demonstration of ethical leadership at the senior management level.

TO 3 A comprehensive digital transformation achieved resulting in enhanced and modernized ICAO operations

12.4.9. Digital Transformation encompasses all aspects of the Organization's work, activities and operations. It includes a thorough assessment of the mission and future of the Organization, how it operates today, and which changes are necessary to move to the next level, not only in terms of efficiency or effectiveness of its processes, but in delivering lasting value to its stakeholder communities. It is imperative to start now as it is the first step in a series of actions necessary to improve transparency, modernize the Organization, and assure its continued relevance. With the backdrop of competing priorities and pressures on available resources, modernizing the Organization will facilitate its ability to leverage alternative opportunities while broadening its support to Member States at the same time. It will also enable the Organization to keep abreast of technological development, adopt emerging technologies and act as a catalyst for its stakeholder communities to understand and follow its path. The appetite and receptiveness of the Organization to rely on technology and collaboration tools for its work have changed significantly for the better due to the lessons learned from remote working during the pandemic. As a result, with the appropriate support, faster outcomes are achievable even with a reduced focus on change management. There is significant technology debt to overcome for many areas, but the initial mapping of the business capabilities has been completed. Several projects need to run concurrently with an adequately resourced Project Management Office. Key elements and projects include wider adoption of Cloud Technologies for ICT services, implementation of (To Be) business architecture as well as new enterprise tools and systems.

TO 4 Strengthened Information Security posture achieving the target level of 2.5 based on industry standard ISO 27001:2013 and the capability maturity model integration (CMMI) maturity model at the end of the implementation of the three-year information security roadmap

12.4.10. For the last three years, ICAO has worked on enhancing its security posture through a holistic risk-based and maturity-based information security strategy, covering both organizational security and operational security. To that end, the Organization's security posture must achieve the target level of 2.5 minimum based on the industry-standard ISO 27001 and the Capability Maturity Model Integration (CMMI) maturity model. ICAO is aiming to be ISO 27001 compliant in terms of its Information Security initiatives at the end of its three-year Information Security Roadmap implementation.

TO 5 Strengthened financial management by applying best practices in the areas of cost recovery

12.4.11. During the triennium 2023–2025, the Organization targets to seek efficiencies through applying best practices in the areas of cost recovery. In addition, the Organization endeavors to transform several areas, as outlined in various transformational objectives, that likely impact on the budget and/or financial management. To that affect, the Finance Branch plays an important role in supporting the Organization in achieving its transformative results.

TO 6 Good organization-wide management through implementation of innovations, strengthened RBM, strategic planning, ERM, a sound accountability framework, efficient and effective programme management, and an adequate organizational structure, as well as enhanced partnerships and resource mobilization efforts

12.4.12. This output addresses a number of issues to improve management in ICAO. An accountability framework will be developed to formalize the decision-making mechanisms pertaining to ICAO's management and programmes, and identify the relationship between the stakeholders involved, as well as their roles and responsibilities. Within the responsibilities of the Secretariat, it is key to implement a cohesive approach to the ICAO Secretariat strategic planning, monitoring, and reporting processes guided by Result Based Management practices, which will include an update to the corporate reporting and monitoring tool. To address unfunded areas of work in the Business Plan, the ICAO Resource Mobilization (RM) function will undergo a transformational change to render ICAO programmes fit for attracting voluntary contributions for donors. The transformation will revolve around the expansion of the ICAO portfolio of programmes linked to the Business Plan, UN SDGs and focusing on results, diversifying the donor base, and demonstrating that voluntary funds are managed in a transparent and efficient manner. Transformational partnerships will be increased through strategically planned advocacy, networking, and coordination with internal and with external stakeholders, especially with the UN system. This will include enhancement of the Partnerships framework Secretariat Guidelines and completion and management of the Partnerships Platform. As a support to the ICAO Business processes, Enterprise Risk Management and internal controls will need to be further matured and integrated into all ICAO processes. The ERM framework will need to be fully established to identify, assess, mitigate, report, monitor, and escalate risks including management commitment.

Annex I

ICAO SECRETARIAT PERFORMANCE MONITORING FRAMEWORK 2023–2025 (Under development)

Annex II

ICAO TRIENNIAL OPERATING PLAN 2023–2025 (Under development)

Appendix D. ICAO Business Plan 2023–2025

Appendix E.1. ICAO Secretariat

Secretary General

The Secretariat of the International Civil Aviation Organization (ICAO) is headed by the Secretary General.

The Secretariat consists of five bureaus: the Air Navigation Bureau, the Air Transport Bureau, the Technical Co-operation Bureau, the Legal Affairs and External Relations Bureau, and the Bureau of Administration and Services.

Reporting directly to the Secretary General are the five Bureau Directors as well as the senior officers in charge of Finance, Evaluation and Internal Audit, Communications, and ICAO's seven Regional Offices, i.e., Asia and Pacific Office in Bangkok, Thailand; Eastern and Southern African Office in Nairobi, Kenya; Western and Central African Office in Dakar, Senegal; Middle East Office in Cairo, Egypt; European and North Atlantic Office in Paris, France; South American Office in Lima, Peru; and North American, Central American and Caribbean Office in Mexico City, Mexico.

Appendix E.1. ICAO Secretariat

Appendix E.2. ICAO Secretariat Organigram

Appendix E.2. ICAO Secretariat Organigram

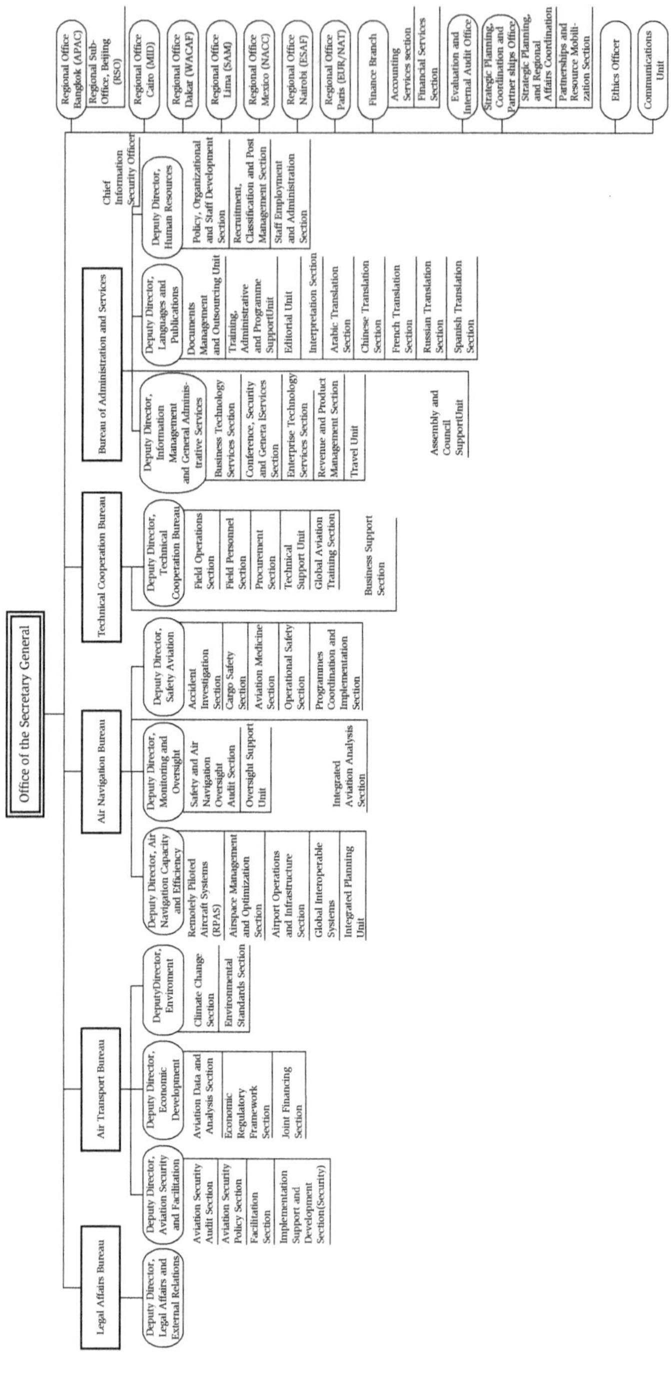

Selected Bibliography

Books and Articles

Abeyratne, R., *Convention on International Civil Aviation: A Commentary* (New York, Springer 2013).

Abeyratne, R., *Regulation of Air Transport* (New York, Springer 2014).

Abeyratne, R., *Aviation and International Cooperation* (New York, Springer 2015).

Antonini, D., Annex 17 Standards Will Be Primary Focus of Forthcoming Security System Audits, *ICAO Journal*, Vol. 57 No. 5 (2002), pp. 11 et seq.

Belai, H., Expanding Programme to Adopt Systems Approach to Future Audits, *ICAO Journal* Vol. 58 No. 9 (2003), pp. 4 et seq.

Bernhardt, R. (ed.), *Encyclopaedia of Public International Law*, (Amsterdam, London, New York, Tokyo, North Holland/Elsevier), Vol. I (1992), Vol. II (1995), Vol. III (1997), Vol. IV (2000).

Binaghi, W., The Role of ICAO, in E. McWhinney & M.A. Bradley (eds), *The Freedom of the Air* (Leiden/Dobbs Ferry, N.Y., Sijthoff/Oceana 1968), pp. 17 et seq.

Brandt, L., (ed.) *Beiträge zum Internationalen Luftrecht* (Festschrift zu Ehren von Alex Meyer (Düsseldorf, Droste Verlag 1954).

Buergenthal, T., *Law-Making in the International Civil Aviation Organization* (New York, Syracuse University Press 1969).

Cheng B., Beyond Bermuda, in N.M. Matte (ed.), *International Air Transport: Law, Organization and Policies for the Future* (Toronto, Paris, Carswell/Pedone 1976).

Cheng B., Crimes on Board Aircraft, *Current Legal Problems*, Vol. 12 (1959), pp. 177 et seq.

Cheng B., *The Law of International Air Transport* (London, Stevens and Sons 1962).

Chuang R.Y., *The International Air Transport Association* (Leiden, Sijthoff 1972).

Cooper J.C., 'Air Transport and World Organization, 55 *Yale Law Journal* (1946), pp. 1191 et seq.; reproduced in I.A. Vlasic (ed.), *Explorations in Aerospace Law* (Montreal, McGill 1968).

Cribbett G., The Influence of Bilateral Agreements, Tariffs and Subsidies in International Air Transport, *Journal of Aeronautical Science of India* Vol. 3 (1951), pp. 1 et seq.

de Hart, R.L. & Davis, J.R., *Fundamentals of Aerospace Medicine*, 3rd ed. (London, Lippencott, Williams and Wilkins 1999).

Erler J., *Rechtsfragen der ICAO: Die Internationale Zivilluftfahrtorganisation und ihre Mitgliedstaaten* (Berlin, Heymanns Verlag 1967).

Giemulla, E., Schmid, R. & v. Schyndel, H., *European Air Law*, Vols 1-4, Loose-leaf, (The Hague, Wolters/Kluwer, February 2005).

Giemulla, E. & Weber, L. (eds), *International and EU Aviation Law, Selected Issues* (Alphen aan den Rijn, Wolters Kluwer Law and Business Series, 2011).

Gillilland, M., Bilateral Agreements, in E. McWhinney & M.A. Bradley (eds), *The Freedom of the Air* (Leiden/Dobbs-Ferry, N.Y., Sijthoff/Oceana 1968), 159 et seq.

Groenewege A.D., *Compendium of International Civil Aviation*, (Montreal) IADC (International Aviation Development Corporation), 2nd ed. (1998/99); 3rd ed. (2003).

Guillaume G., *Les grandes crises internationales et le droit* (Paris, Editions Le Seuil 1994).

Hailbronner, K., Civil Aviation, Unlawful Interference With, in R. Bernhardt (ed.), *Encyclopedia of Public International Law* (Amsterdam, London, New York, Tokyo) North Holland/Elsevier, Vol. I (1992), pp. 583 et seq.

Hailbronner, K., *Der Schutz der Luftgrenzen im Frieden* (Köln/Bonn, Heymanns 1972).

Hailbronner, K., International Air Transport Association, in R. Bernhardt (ed.), *Encyclopedia of Public Int. Law* (Amsterdam, London, New York, Tokyo) North Holland/Elsevier, Vol. II (1995), pp. 1047 et seq.

Hailbronner, K., International Civil Aviation Organization, in R. Bernhardt (ed.), *Encyclopedia of Public International Law* (Amsterdam, London, New York, Tokyo) North Holland/Elsevier, Vol. II (1995) 1070 et seq.

Hailbronner, K., Jurisdiction of the ICAO Council Case, in R. Bernhardt (ed.), *Encyclopedia of Public International Law* (Amsterdam, London, New York, Tokyo) North Holland/Elsevier, Vol. III (1997), pp. 62 et seq.

Heuser, R., Taiwan, in R. Bernhardt (ed.), *Encyclopedia of Public International Law* (Amsterdam, London, New York, Tokyo) North Holland/Elsevier, Vol. IV (2000), pp. 753 et seq.

ICAO Secretariat, Historic Conference Agrees on Strategy for Strengthening Aviation Security, *ICAO Journal* Vol. 57 No. 2 (2002), pp. 5 et seq.

Jenks, C.W., *International Immunities* (London, Stevens and Sons 1961).

Joyner, D.D., *A Contemporary Concept of Piracy in International Law: The Status of Aerial Highjacking as an International Crime,* (Dobbs Ferry, N.Y./Leiden, Oceana/Sijthoff 1974).

Kelsen, H., *The Law of the United Nations* (London, Stevens and Sons 1950).

Kotaite, A., Civil Aviation Security Is an Integral Part of Our Global Security, *ICAO Journal* Vol. 57 (2002), pp. 4 et seq.

Kyriakopoulos, G.D., *La sécurité de l'aviation civile en droit international public* (Athènes/Bruxelles, A.N.Sakkoulas/Bruylant, 1999).

Lowenfeld, A.F., A New Takeoff for International Air Transport, *Foreign Affairs* Vol. 54 (1975), pp. 36 et seq.

Le Geoff, M., Les Annexes techniques à la Convention de Chicago, *Revue Générale de l'Air,* Vol. 19 (1956), pp. 146 et seq.

Mankiewicz, R., L'adoption des annexes à la Convention de Chicago par le Conseil de l'Organisation internationale de l'aviation civile, in L. Brandt (ed.), *Beiträge zum Internationalen Luftrecht*, Festschrift zu Ehren von Alex Meyer (Düsseldorf, Droste Verlag 1954), pp. 82 et seq.

Mankiewicz, R., Organisation internationale de l'aviation civile, III *Annuaire Français de droit international* (1957), pp. 383 et seq.
Matte, N.M., *Treatise on Air-Aeronautical Law* (Montreal, Toronto, McGill, Carswell 1981).
McKenzie, D., *ICAO: A History of the International Civil Aviation Organization* (Toronto, University of Toronto Press 2010).
McWhinney, E., *The Illegal Diversion of Aircraft and International Law* (Dordrecht, Boston, Lancaster, Martinus Nijhoff 1987).
Michaels D.D.B., *International Privileges and Immunities: A Case for a Universal Statute* (The Hague, Martinus Nijhoff 1971).
Milde, M., Aviation Safety Oversight Audits and the Law, XXVI *AnnASL* (2001), pp. 165 et seq.
Milde, M., Interception of Civil Aircraft vs. Misuse of Civil Aviation, XI *AnnASL* (1986), pp. 105 et seq.
Milde, M. *International Air Law and ICAO*, 2nd. ed. (Essential Air and Space Law Series, Vol. 10, The Hague 2).
Olson, D., Striving for Aviation Safety, in: ICAO & ISC (eds), *100 Years of Civil Aviation* (London and Montreal, International Systems and Communications Ltd. and ICAO 2003), pp. 114 et seq.
Park, K.G., *La protection de la souveraineté arienne* (Paris, Pedone 1991).
Rosenne, S., Conferences and Congresses, International, in R. Bernhardt, (ed.), *Encyclopaedia of Public International Law* (Amsterdam, London, New York, Tokyo), North Holland/Elsevier), Vol. I (1992), pp. 739 et seq.
Schwenk, W. & Giemulla E., *Handbuch des Luftverkehrsrechts*, 3rd ed. (Köln, Heymanns Verlag 2005).
Shawcross & Beaumont, *Air Law*, (McClean, J.D., General Editor, and Balfour, J. M., Gardiner, R.K., Goh, J. and Margo, R., eds), (London, LexisNexis Butterworth), Issues 99-101 (1997–2005).
Sohn, L.B., Expulsion or Forced Withdrawal from an International Organization, *Harvard Law Review* Vol. 77 (1963–1964), pp. 1381–1425.
Storm van's Gravesande, J.W.E & van der Veen Vronk, A. (eds), *Liber Amicorum Diederiks-Verschoor* (Deventer, Antwerp, London, Frankfurt, Boston, New York, Kluwer Law and Taxation Publishers 1985).
Thompkins, G.N., DVT Litigation Update: September 2004, *Air and Space Law* Vol. 29 (2004), pp. 312 et seq.
Thürer, D., Soft Law, in R. Bernhardt (ed.), *Encyclopaedia of Public International Law*, (Amsterdam, London, New York, Tokyo) North Holland/Elsevier, Vol. IV (2000), pp. 452 et seq.
Verhaegen, B., Air Law Instrument Facilitates Transfer of Safety Responsibilities Between States, *ICAO Journal*, Vol. 52, No. 8 (1997), pp. 15 et seq.
Weber L., The European Union and the Chicago Convention of 1944, *Air Law* Vol. 19 (1994), pp. 179 et seq.
Weber L., Universal Postal Union, in: R. Bernhardt (ed.), *Encyclopedia of Public International Law* (Amsterdam, London, New York, Tokyo), North Holland/ Elsevier, Vol. IV (2000), pp. 1235 et seq.
Weber, L. & Holderbach, H., Type Certification of Commercial Aircraft Calls for Enhanced International Rules, *ICAO Journal* Vol. 56, No. 2 (2001), pp. 4 et seq.

Weber, L., Convention on International Civil Aviation – 60 Years, *ZLW* Vol. 53 (2004), pp. 289 et seq.
Weber, L., European Civil Aviation Conference, in R. Bernhardt (ed.), *Encyclopaedia of Public International Law* (Amsterdam, London, New York, Tokyo) North Holland/Elsevier, Vol. II (1995), pp. 137 et seq.
Weber, L., European Organization for the Safety of Air Navigation (EUROCONTROL), in: R. Bernhardt (ed.), *Encyclopedia of Public International Law* (Amsterdam, London, New York, Tokyo) North Holland/Elsevier, Vol. II (1995), pp. 270 et seq.
Weber, L., Internationaler Luftverkehrsverband (International Air Transport Association/IATA), in U. Andersen & W. Woyke (eds), *Handwörterbuch Internationale Organisationen*, 2nd ed. (Opladen, Leske und Budrich 1995), 219 et seq.
Weber, L., International Civil Aviation Organization (ICAO), in S. Hobe, N. von Ruckteschell & D. Hefferman (eds), *Compendium on Air Law in Europe (*Cologne Compendium*)* (Heymanns Verlag Koeln 2013), pp. 28–54.
Weber, L., *International Civil Aviation Organization (ICAO)* (Alphen aan den Rijn, Wolters Kluwer Law & Business Series 2012).
Weber, L., Les éléments de la coopération dans le cadre de la Commission européenne de l'aviation civile (CEAC), *RFDA* Vol. 31 (1977), pp. 388 et seq.
Weber, L., The EUROCONTROL Route Charges Litigation before the Court of Justice of the European Communities, *Annals of Air and Space Law*, Vol. III (1978), pp. 355–369.
Weber, L. & Verhaegen B., Entrée en vigueur de l'Article 83 bis de la Convention de Chicago: un plus pour la sécurité aérienne, XLIII *Annuaire français de droit international* (1997), Paris 1998, 551 et seq.
Weiler, J.H.H., Korean Air Lines Incident, in R. Bernhardt (ed.), *Encyclopaedia of Public International Law* (Amsterdam, London New York, Tokyo) North Holland/Elsevier, Vol. III (1997), 93 et seq.
Zuleeg, M., International Organisations – Implied Powers, in R. Bernhardt (ed.), *Encyclopedia of Public International Law* (Amsterdam, London, New York, Tokyo), North Holland/Elsevier, Vol. II (1995), pp. 1312 et seq.

Documents

(Document numbers refer to those of ICAO, unless otherwise indicated)

Accident/Incident Reporting (ADREP) Manual, Doc. 9156, 2nd ed., 1987.
Aerodrome Design and Operations, Doc. AN 14, Vol. I.
Aerodrome Design Manual, Doc. 9157.
Aerodromes, Doc. AN 14, Vol. I 4th ed. (2004).
Aeronautical Chart Catalogue, Doc. 7101.
Aeronautical Chart Manual, Doc. 8697.
Aeronautical Information Services, Aeronautical Charts (AIS/MAP) Divisional Meeting (1998), Doc. 9733.
Aeronautical Information Services Manual, Doc. 8126.
Aeronautical Information Services Manual, Doc. 8126.
Aeronautical Information Services Provided by States, Doc. 7383.
Agreement between the UN and ICAO, Doc. 7970.

Agreement on the Joint Financing of Certain Air Navigation Services in Greenland and the Faroe Islands, (1956) as amended by the Montreal Protocol of 1982, Doc. 9585.
Agreement on the Joint Financing of Certain Air Navigation Services in Iceland (1956) as amended by the Montreal Protocol 1982, Doc. 9586.
Air Traffic Services Planning Manual, Doc. 9426.
Airport Planning Manual, Doc. 9184.
Airport Services Manual, Doc. 9137.
Airport Economics Manual, Doc. 9562, 3rd ed. 2013.
Airworthiness Manual, Doc. 9760, 3rd ed. 2014.
Annual Report of the Council – 1967, Doc. 8724 (1968).
Annual Report of the Council for 2001, Doc. 9786.
Annual Report of the Council for 2002, Doc. 9814.
Annual Report of the Council for 2003, Doc. 9826.
Assembly Resolutions in Force (as of 5 October 2001), Doc. 9790.
Assembly Resolutions in Force (as of 8 October 2004), Doc. 9848.
Authentic Six-language Text of the Convention, Doc. 9721.
Authentic Trilingual Text of the Convention on International Civil Aviation (Chicago, 1944), signed at Buenos Aires on 24 September 1968, Doc. 7300/8.
Civil Aviation Caretaker Authority in Somalia, Doc. 9732.
Comprehensive Aeronautical Telecommunication Network (ATN) Manual, Doc. 9739.
Convention on International Civil Aviation (Chicago, 1944), 9th ed., Doc. 7300/9.
Convention on International Interests in Mobile Equipment, Doc. 9793.
Convention on the Privileges and Immunities of the Specialized Agencies, adopted by the UN General Assembly on 21 November 1947, UNTS Vol. 33 (1948).
Database on the World's Air Services Agreements, Doc. 9511.
Directives for Panels of the Air Navigation Commission, Doc. 7984/4.
Directives for Panels of the Air Navigation Commission, Doc. 7984/4.
Directives to Divisional-type Air Navigation Meetings and Rules of Procedure for their Conduct, Doc. 8143.
Environmental Technical Manual on the Use of Procedures in the Noise Certification of Aircraft, 3rd ed. 2004, with a revision of February 2004, Doc. 9501.
Guidance on the Balanced Approach to Aircraft Noise Management, Doc. 9829.
Guidelines for the Introduction and Operational Use of the Global Navigation Satellite System (GNSS), Doc. 9750.
Handbook on Radio Frequency Spectrum Requirements for Civil Aviation, including Statement of Approved ICAO Policies, Doc. 9718, 3rd ed. (2003).
Heliport Manual, Doc. 9261.
Human Factors Manuals, Doc. 9806, 9808, 9683, 9758 and 9824.
Human Factors Training Manual, Doc. 9683.
ICAO Engine Exhaust Emissions Data Bank, ICAO Doc. 9646.
ICAO Financial Regulations, 15th ed. (2014), Doc. 7515/15.
ICAO Legal Committee, Rules of Procedure, Doc. 7669.
ICAO Manual on Air Traffic Forecasting, Doc. 8991.
ICAO Safety Oversight Audit Manual, Doc. 9735.
ICAO Safety Oversight Manual, Doc. 9734.

Selected Bibliography

ICAO Service Code, Doc. 7350.
International Aeronautical and Maritime Search and Rescue (IAMSAR) Manual, Vols I–III, Doc. 9731.
ITU, Constitution of the International Telecommunication Union and Convention of the International Telecommunication Union, Final Acts of the Plenipotentiary Conference, Nice 1989.
Machine Readable Travel Documents, ICAO Doc. 9303.
Manual for Safeguarding Civil Aviation Against Acts of Unlawful Interference, Doc. 8973.
Manual of Aeronautical Meteorological Practice, Doc. 8896.
Manual of Aeronautical Meteorological Practice, Doc. 8896.
Manual of Aircraft Accident Investigation, Doc. 6920.
Manual of Aircraft Accident Investigation, Doc. 6920, 4th ed. (1970).
Manual of Procedures for Establishment and Management of a State's Personnel Licensing System, Doc. 9379.
Manual of Technical Provisions for the Aeronautical Telecommunication Network (ATN), 3rd ed., (2002), Doc. 9705.
Manaual on Evidence-based Training (2013), Doc. 9995.
Manual on Surface Movement Guidance and Control Systems (SMGCS), Doc. 9476.
Manual on the Regulation of International Air Transport, Doc. 9626.
Meteorology (MET) Divisional Meeting (2002), Doc. 9812.
Mission Coordination – IAMSAR Manual Doc. 9731, Vol. II.
Procedures for Air Navigation Services – Air Traffic Management (PANS-ATM), Doc. 4444.
Procedures for Air Navigation Services – ICAO Abbreviations and Codes (PANS/ABC), Doc. 8400.
Protocol for the Suppression of Unlawful Acts of Violence at Airports Serving International Civil Aviation, Supplementary to the Convention for the Suppression of Unlawful Acts against the Safety of Civil Aviation, done at Montreal on 23 September 1971, signed on 29 February 1988, ICAO Doc. 9518.
Protocol for the Suppression of Unlawful Acts of Violence at Airports Serving International Civil Aviation, ICAO Doc. 9518.
Protocol on the Authentic Quadrilingual Text of the Convention on International Civil Aviation, (Chicago 1944), Doc. 9217.
Protocol on the Authentic Quinquelingual Text of the Convention on International Civil Aviation (Chicago 1944), Doc. 9663.
Protocol on the Authentic Six-Language Text of the Convention on International Civil Aviation (Chicago 1944), Doc. 9721.
Protocol relating to an Amendment to the Convention on International Civil Aviation, *(Article* 56) signed on 6 October 1989, which entered into force on 18 April 2005, Doc. 9544.
Repertory-Guide to the Convention on International Civil Aviation, 2nd ed. Doc. 8900/2.
Report of the 10th Air Navigation Conference, 5–20 September 1991, ICAO Doc. 9583.

Report of the Aeronautical Information Services Aeronautical Charts (AIS/MAP) Divisional Meeting (1998), Doc. 9733.
Report of the Council-1952, Doc. 7367(1953).
Report of the DGCA Conference on a Global Strategy for Safety Oversight, Doc. 9707.
Report of the ICAO fact-finding investigation into the shooting-down of Korean Airlines flight 007 by Soviet military aircraft on 1 September 1983 (unpublished).
Report of the ICAO fact-finding investigation regarding the shooting-down of two U.S.-registered private civil aircraft by Cuban military aircraft on 24 February 1996, Doc. C-WP/10412 (Restricted) and C-WP10441 (Restricted) (unpublished).
Report of the Meteorology (MET) Divisional Meeting (2002), Doc. 9812.
Report of the World-wide CNS/ATM Systems Implementation Conference, Doc. 9719.
Report on the Fifth Air Transport Conference, Doc. 9819.
Report on the High-level, Ministerial Meeting on Aviation Security, Doc. 9800.
Rules of Procedure for Standing Committees of the Council, Doc. 8146.
Rules of Procedure for Standing Committees of the Council, ICAO Doc. 7559/5.
Rules of Procedure for the Air Navigation Commission, Doc. 8229.
Rules of Procedure of the Assembly of the International Civil Aviation Organization, 8th ed. (2014), Doc. 7600/8.
Rules of Procedure for the Council, Doc. 7559/8.
Safety Oversight Audit Manual, Doc. 9735.
Satellite-Aided Search and Rescue, the COSPAS-SARSAT System, ICAO Circular 185.
Security Audit Reference Manual, Doc. 9807.
Standing Rules of Procedure of the Assembly of ICAO, Doc. 7600/8 (2014).
Supplementary Agreement between the International Civil Aviation Organization and the Government of Canada Regarding the Headquarters of the International Civil Aviation Organization, ICAO Doc. 9591 – Supplementary Agreement.
Supplementary Report on Activities of the Organization in the first half of 2004, Doc. 9826.
Technical Agreement on North Atlantic Ocean Stations signed on 25 February 1954, Doc. 7510 (JS/559), 215 UNTS 268 (1955).
Technical Instructions for the Safe Transport of Dangerous Goods by Air, Doc. 9284.
Training Manual, Doc. 7192.
Accident/Incident Reporting (ADREP) Manual, Doc. 9156, 2nd ed., 1987.
Aerodrome Design and Operations, Doc. AN 14, Vol. I.
Aerodrome Design Manual, Doc. 9157.
Aerodromes, Doc. AN 14, Vol. I 4th ed. (2004).
Aeronautical Chart Catalogue, Doc. 7101.
Aeronautical Chart Manual, Doc. 8697.
Aeronautical Information Services, Aeronautical Charts (AIS/MAP) Divisional Meeting (1998), Doc. 9733.
Aeronautical Information Services Manual, Doc. 8126.

Selected Bibliography

Aeronautical Information Services Manual, Doc. 8126.
Aeronautical Information Services Provided by States, Doc. 7383.
Agreement between the UN and ICAO, Doc. 7970.
Agreement on the Joint Financing of Certain Air Navigation Services in Greenland and the Faroe Islands, (1956) as amended by the Montreal Protocol of 1982, Doc. 9585.
Agreement on the Joint Financing of Certain Air Navigation Services in Iceland (1956) as amended by the Montreal Protocol 1982, Doc. 9586.
Air Traffic Services Planning Manual, Doc. 9426.
Airport Planning Manual, Doc. 9184.
Airport Services Manual, Doc. 9137.
Airport Economics Manual, Doc. 9562, 3rd ed. 2013.
Airworthiness Manual, Doc. 9760, 3rd ed. 2014.
Annual Report of the Council – 1967, Doc. 8724 (1968).
Annual Report of the Council for 2001, Doc. 9786.
Annual Report of the Council for 2002, Doc. 9814.
Annual Report of the Council for 2003, Doc. 9826.
Assembly Resolutions in Force (as of 5 October 2001), Doc. 9790.
Assembly Resolutions in Force (as of 8 October 2004), Doc. 9848.
Authentic Six-language Text of the Convention, Doc. 9721.
Authentic Trilingual Text of the Convention on International Civil Aviation (Chicago, 1944), signed at Buenos Aires on 24 September 1968, Doc. 7300/8.
Civil Aviation Caretaker Authority in Somalia, Doc. 9732.
Comprehensive Aeronautical Telecommunication Network (ATN) Manual, Doc. 9739.
Convention on International Civil Aviation (Chicago, 1944), 9th ed., Doc. 7300/9.
Convention on International Interests in Mobile Equipment, Doc. 9793.
Convention on the Privileges and Immunities of the Specialized Agencies, adopted by the UN General Assembly on 21 November 1947, UNTS Vol. 33 (1948).
Database on the World's Air Services Agreements, Doc. 9511.
Directives for Panels of the Air Navigation Commission, Doc. 7984/4.
Directives for Panels of the Air Navigation Commission, Doc. 7984/4.
Directives to Divisional-type Air Navigation Meetings and Rules of Procedure for their Conduct, Doc. 8143.
Environmental Technical Manual on the Use of Procedures in the Noise Certification of Aircraft, 3rd ed., 2004, with a revision of February 2004, Doc. 9501.
Guidance on the Balanced Approach to Aircraft Noise Management, Doc. 9829.
Guidelines for the Introduction and Operational Use of the Global Navigation Satellite System (GNSS), Doc. 9750.
Handbook on Radio Frequency Spectrum Requirements for Civil Aviation, including Statement of Approved ICAO Policies, Doc. 9718, 3rd ed. (2003).
Heliport Manual, Doc. 9261.
Human Factors Manuals, Doc. 9806, 9808, 9683, 9758 and 9824.
Human Factors Training Manual, Doc. 9683.
ICAO Engine Exhaust Emissions Data Bank, ICAO Doc. 9646.
ICAO Financial Regulations, 15th ed. (2014), Doc. 7515/15.
ICAO Legal Committee, Rules of Procedure, Doc. 7669.

ICAO Manual on Air Traffic Forecasting, Doc. 8991.
ICAO Safety Oversight Audit Manual, Doc. 9735.
ICAO Safety Oversight Manual, Doc. 9734.
ICAO Service Code, Doc. 7350.
International Aeronautical and Maritime Search and Rescue (IAMSAR) Manual, Vols I–III, Doc. 9731.
ITU, Constitution of the International Telecommunication Union and Convention of the International Telecommunication Union, Final Acts of the Plenipotentiary Conference, Nice 1989.
Machine Readable Travel Documents, ICAO Doc. 9303.
Manual for Safeguarding Civil Aviation Against Acts of Unlawful Interference, Doc. 8973.
Manual of Aeronautical Meteorological Practice, Doc. 8896.
Manual of Aeronautical Meteorological Practice, Doc. 8896.
Manual of Aircraft Accident Investigation, Doc. 6920.
Manual of Aircraft Accident Investigation, Doc. 6920, 4th ed. (1970).
Manual of Procedures for Establishment and Management of a State's Personnel Licensing System, Doc. 9379.
Manual of Technical Provisions for the Aeronautical Telecommunication Network (ATN), 3rd ed., (2002), Doc. 9705.
Manaual on Evidence-based Training (2013), Doc. 9995.
Manual on Surface Movement Guidance and Control Systems (SMGCS), Doc. 9476.
Manual on the Regulation of International Air Transport, Doc. 9626.
Meteorology (MET) Divisional Meeting (2002), Doc. 9812.
Mission Coordination – IAMSAR Manual Doc. 9731, Vol. II.
Procedures for Air Navigation Services – Air Traffic Management (PANS-ATM), Doc. 4444.
Procedures for Air Navigation Services – ICAO Abbreviations and Codes (PANS/ABC), Doc. 8400.
Protocol for the Suppression of Unlawful Acts of Violence at Airports Serving International Civil Aviation, Supplementary to the Convention for the Suppression of Unlawful Acts against the Safety of Civil Aviation, done at Montreal on 23 September 1971, signed on 29 February 1988, ICAO Doc. 9518.
Protocol for the Suppression of Unlawful Acts of Violence at Airports Serving International Civil Aviation, ICAO Doc. 9518.
Protocol on the Authentic Quadrilingual Text of the Convention on International Civil Aviation, (Chicago 1944), Doc. 9217.
Protocol on the Authentic Quinquelingual Text of the Convention on International Civil Aviation (Chicago 1944), Doc. 9663.
Protocol on the Authentic Six-Language Text of the Convention on International Civil Aviation (Chicago 1944), Doc. 9721.
Protocol relating to an Amendment to the Convention on International Civil Aviation, *(Article* 56) signed on 6 October 1989, which entered into force on 18 April 2005, Doc. 9544.
Repertory-Guide to the Convention on International Civil Aviation, 2nd ed. Doc. 8900/2.

Selected Bibliography

Report of the 10th Air Navigation Conference, 5–20 September 1991, ICAO Doc. 9583.

Report of the Aeronautical Information Services Aeronautical Charts (AIS/MAP) Divisional Meeting (1998), Doc. 9733.

Report of the Council-1952, Doc. 7367(1953).

Report of the DGCA Conference on a Global Strategy for Safety Oversight, Doc. 9707.

Report of the ICAO fact-finding investigation into the shooting-down of Korean Airlines flight 007 by Soviet military aircraft on 1 September 1983 (unpublished).

Report of the ICAO fact-finding investigation regarding the shooting-down of two U.S.-registered private civil aircraft by Cuban military aircraft on 24 February 1996, Doc. C-WP/10412 (Restricted) and C-WP10441 (Restricted) (unpublished).

Report of the Meteorology (MET) Divisional Meeting (2002), Doc. 9812.

Report of the World-wide CNS/ATM Systems Implementation Conference, Doc. 9719.

Report on the Fifth Air Transport Conference, Doc. 9819.

Report on the High-level, Ministerial Meeting on Aviation Security, Doc. 9800.

Rules of Procedure for Standing Committees of the Council, Doc. 8146.

Rules of Procedure for Standing Committees of the Council, ICAO Doc. 7559/5.

Rules of Procedure for the Air Navigation Commission, Doc. 8229.

Rules of Procedure of the Assembly of the International Civil Aviation Organization, 8th ed. (2014), Doc. 7600/8.

Rules of Procedure for the Council, Doc. 7559/8.

Safety Oversight Audit Manual, Doc. 9735.

Satellite-Aided Search and Rescue, the COSPAS-SARSAT System, ICAO Circular 185.

Security Audit Reference Manual, Doc. 9807.

Standing Rules of Procedure of the Assembly of ICAO, Doc. 7600/8 (2014).

Supplementary Agreement between the International Civil Aviation Organization and the Government of Canada Regarding the Headquarters of the International Civil Aviation Organization ICAO Doc. 9591 – Supplementary Agreement.

Supplementary Report on Activities of the Organization in the first half of 2004, Doc. 9826.

Technical Agreement on North Atlantic Ocean Stations signed on 25 February 1954, Doc. 7510 (JS/559), 215 UNTS 268 (1955).

Technical Instructions for the Safe Transport of Dangerous Goods by Air, Doc. 9284.

Training Manual, Doc. 7192.

Index

The numbers here refer to paragraph numbers.

Index

Index

www.ingramcontent.com/pod-product-compliance
Lightning Source LLC
Chambersburg PA
CBHW071432230926
51846CB00001B/194
* 9 7 8 9 4 0 3 5 1 5 2 7 4 *